Taking Sides: Clashing Views in
Drugs and Society, 12/e

Dennis K. Miller

http://create.mheducation.com

ISBN-10: 1259922790   ISBN-13: 9781259922794

2-LKV-20

Contents

Handwritten annotations:

First paper — Should we legalize (next to 1.1)

3rd (next to 2.1)
5th (next to 2.3)

4th — should just we legalize it. — Should Federal Govt move marijuana from schedule 1 to 2. (next to 2.3/2.4)

2nd (next to 3.6)

Extra Credit — Is there a racial disparity when it comes to drug and alcohol treatment
• numbers of access
• and quality
• are people of color getting quality of treatment

Detailed Table of Contents

UNIT 1: Drugs and Public Policy

The Drug Enforcement Administration (DEA) is charged with enforcing the controlled substances laws and regulations of the United States. In "Speaking out against Drug Legalization," the DEA argues that enforcement of drug laws is not the cause of violence; drug legalization will not reduce crime and increase government revenue; and prohibition actions can be successful at decreasing drug use. The report from the U.S. Department of Health and Human Services points out that a number of factors affect drug use by young people. One of the most important factors is perception of risk. If young people perceive that drugs are harmful, they are less likely to engage in drug use. Other relevant factors include the perception of drug use by peers, religious beliefs, and parental involvement. Legal sanctions are not noted as a deterrent to drug use.

The U.S. State Department maintains that more effort is needed to interdict drugs coming into the United States because the trafficking of drugs represents a direct threat to national security. Better cooperation with countries in Latin America, the Caribbean, Africa, and Asia, where drugs are grown and exported, is essential. Ethan Nadelmann, the executive director of the Drug Policy Alliance, contends that attempts to stem the flow of drugs are futile and that it is unrealistic to believe that the world can be made free of drugs. Nadelmann points out that global production is about the same as it was 10 years earlier and that cocaine and heroin are purer and cheaper because producers have become more efficient.

Agnes Shanley argues that the enormous cost of developing a new drug justifies attempts to protect its exclusive access to the market after the patent has expired. Arthur Caplan and Zachary Caplan are skeptical of the "staggering cost" claims, and argue that consumers should have access to the generic version of the drug as soon as possible.

The National Institute on Alcohol Abuse and Alcoholism (NIAAA) considers underage drinking to be a serious health problem in the United States. Drinking by young people has numerous health and safety risks including injuries, impaired judgment, increased risk of assault, and death. The NIAAA makes recommendations for steps to decrease alcohol use by young people and to treat drinking problems. Jeffrey Tucker argues that despite "draconian" laws against alcohol use in the United States, many teens and young adults still drink. A legal drinking age of 21 years is not realistic and accomplishes nothing to actually stop drinking, according to Tucker. Moreover, the age probation encourages risk drinking behaviors.

Issue: Are Energy Drinks with Alcohol Dangerous Enough to Ban?
Yes: Don Troop, from "Four Loko Does Its Job with Efficiency and Economy, Students Say," *The Chronicle of Higher Education* (2010)
No: Jacob Sullum, from "Loco Over Four Loko," *Reason Magazine* (2011)

The Chronicle of Higher Education journalist Don Troop argues that the combination of caffeine and alcohol is extremely dangerous and should not be sold or marketed to college students and young people. Journalist and editor of *Reason Magazine* Jacob Sullum disagrees and claims that alcoholic energy drinks should not have been targeted and banned since many other products are far more dangerous.

Issue: Should Smoking Be Banned from Public Places?
Yes: Sheelah A. Feinberg, from "No-Smoking, Please," *Huffington Post* (2013)
No: John Stossel, from "Control Freaks Still Targeting Tobacco," *Reason Magazine* (2014)

Environmental tobacco smoke (a.k.a., "secondhand smoke") is classified as a carcinogen and government agencies declared that there are no safe exposure levels. Many communities have banned smoking in public areas (e.g., bars, restaurants, and parks) to minimize secondhand smoke exposure, including New York. Sheelah A. Feinberg, director of New York's Coalition for a Smoke-Free City, reports that her city's ban on public smoking has improved health and quality of life. Journalist John Stossel disagrees with this position in his opinion piece in *Reason Magazine* and believes that bans on public smoking are indicative of increased government control over American's lives.

Issue: Should Health Care Plans Cover Naturopathic Remedies?
Yes: Mary Flynn, from "Naturopathic Doctors Fighting for Inclusion Under Health Reform Insurance Policies," *California Health Report* (2014)
No: Brian Palmer, from "Quacking All the Way to the Bank," *Slate* (2014)

Naturopathy, or naturopathic medicine, emphasizes prevention, treatment, and optimal health via methods that stimulate self-healing processes. Mary Flynn, a reporter for *California Health Report*, describes efforts in California to have visits to naturopathic doctors covered in her state's new insurance marketplace. Brian Palmer, who writes for *Slate*, is concerned that taxpayers are forced to support, through state and federal public medical plans, alternative approaches that have little efficacy.

Issue: Does China Have an Effective Approach to Combat Drug Addiction?
Yes: Sheldon X. Zhang and Ko-lin Chin, from "A People's War: China's Struggle to Contain Its Illicit Drug Problem," *Foreign Policy at Brookings* (2016)
No: Yingxi Bi, from "On the Death Penalty for Drug-related Crime in China," *Human Rights and Drugs* (2012)

Sheldon X. Zhang and Ko-lin Chin provide an overview of China's approaches and its successes and failures in combating illicit drugs, including the use of capital punishment for severe offenses. Yingxi Bi examines the factors that have led to a relatively large number of Chinese citizens and noncitizens being subject to the death penalty.

UNIT 2: Drugs and Social Policy

Issue: Are Opiates Overprescribed?
Yes: Graeme Wood, from "Drug Dealers Aren't to Blame for the Heroin Boom. Doctors Are," *The New Republic* (2014)
No: Carol M. Ostrom, from "New Pain-Management Rules Leave Patients Hurting," *The Seattle Times* (2011)

Graeme Wood, a contributing editor at *The New Republic*, draws on his personal experience using potent opiates after dental surgery to explain the prevalence of opiate addiction. He describes an American medical system that precipitates opiate abuse and dependence. Carol M. Ostrom, who writes for *The Seattle Times*, acknowledges that prescription opiate addiction and drug diversion are important concerns; however, these concerns could be inflated. As a consequence, those who need opiates are denied appropriate management of their pain.

A heroin addict stays a heroin addict to avoid the misery of withdrawal, a sickness where the addict is unable to function: This is the experience of young man in Michigan who is dependent on opiates. The article by Heath Lynn Peters describes how addiction to heroin and other opiates has torn apart a community. Theodore Dalrymple is the pen name of Anthony Daniels, a retired prison doctor and psychiatrist. He reports that opiate withdrawal is medically trivial and the withdrawal symptoms are overstated. Dalrymple states, "the great majority, though not quite all, of the suffering caused by withdrawal from opiates, insofar as it is real and not feigned, is psychological in origin and caused by the mythology surrounding it."

Political columnist Kevin Drum contends that medical marijuana is now legal in more than a dozen states without any major serious problems or increased usage. The research report from the National Institute on Drug Abuse identifies various deleterious effects associated with marijuana. For example, marijuana alters perception and time, impairs memory and learning, and compromises academic performance. This report also notes that long-term marijuana use can lead to addiction and negatively affect the fetuses of women who used marijuana while pregnant.

3,4-Methylenedioxy-methamphetamine (MDMA) is a synthetic drug that is similar to both stimulants and hallucinogens and is associated with the club scene where it is known as "Ecstasy" and "Molly". Kelley McMillan in "Is Ecstasy the Key to Treating Women with PTSD?" notes the potential clinical benefits of MDMA to help those with the anxiety disorder and post-traumatic stress disorder. Rachel Patel and Daniel Titheradge reviewed preclinical and clinical literature on MDMA and conclude that, "the pharmacology of MDMA offers a promising target as a rapid-onset agent"; however, they note neurotoxicity and safety concerns for MDMA. These limit its wide adoption to help manage the symptoms of psychological disorders.

UNIT 3: Drug Prevention and Treatment

Alan I. Leshner, director of the National Institute on Drug Abuse at the National Institutes of Health, believes that addiction to drugs and alcohol is not a behavioral condition but a treatable disease. Addition Theorist Steven Slate counters that addiction is not a true disease since there is no physical malfunction and the brains of addicts are normal.

Markus Heilig, Clinical Director of the National Institute on Alcohol Abuse and Alcoholism, argues that molecular changes in the brain result in positive reinforcement from alcohol. Heilig notes that alcoholism has a behavioral component, but certain genes may be responsible in individuals who abuse alcohol despite its adverse consequences. Research by Rajita Sinha indicates that alcohol use disorders are associated with dysfunction in emotion and stress responses and that these dysfunctional responses contribute to the motivation to drink. Stress levels and mechanisms to manage stress are key factors for the desire to use alcohol and relapse to alcoholism.

Issue: Can One Become Addicted to the Internet and Social Media?

Yes: Elias Aboujaoude, from "Problematic Internet Use: An Overview," *World Psychiatry* (2010)
No: Antonius J. Van Rooij and Nicole Prause, from "A Critical Review of "Internet Addiction" Criteria with Suggestions for the Future," *Journal of Behavioral Addictions* (2014)

Internet access provides opportunities to learn and connect to others; however, excessive Internet use can become almost compulsive with feelings of dysphoria when one is offline. Can someone be "addicted" to the Internet as they might be addicted to drugs? Elias Aboujaoude describes behavioral addictions and the clinical scales that are used to assess Internet addiction. Antonius J. Van Rooij and Nicole Prause critically review addiction models and the limited research on Internet addiction. Their assessment is that there is not yet sufficient evidence to support an Internet addiction disorder, similar to that observed with drugs.

Issue: Is Drug Addiction a Problem of Youth?

Yes: National Institute on Drug Abuse, from "Drugs, Brains, and Behavior: The Science of Addiction," *National Institute on Drug Abuse Research Report* (2014)
No: Olivera Bogunovic, from "Substance Abuse in Aging and Elderly Adults," *Psychiatric Times* (2012)

The National Institute on Drug Abuse (NIDA) is charged with bringing the power of science to bear on drug abuse and addiction. In its publication *Drugs, Brains, and Behavior: The Science of Addiction*, NIDA provides an overview—based on the scientific literature—of the drug addiction problem. A strong focus of this research has been in preventing drug addiction in young people. Psychiatrist and author Olivera Bogunovic indicates that drug addiction is a formidable problem for older adults. In her article "Substance Abuse in Aging and Elderly Adults," she describes the unique challenges faced by older people.

Issue: Is Advertising Responsible for Alcohol Use by Young People?

Yes: Timothy S. Naimi, et al., from "Amount of Televised Alcohol Advertising Exposure and the Quantity of Alcohol Consumed by Youth," *Journal of Studies on Alcohol and Drugs* (2016)
No: National Institute on Alcohol Abuse and Alcoholism, from "Parenting to Prevent Childhood Alcohol Use," *National Institute on Alcohol Abuse and Alcoholism Research Report* (2017)

Alcohol advertisements stabilize alcohol use to cultural norms and associate it with fun and success. Companies spend on marketing because advertisements increase the likelihood of purchase of specific brands. Dr. Timothy S. Naimi and colleagues examined the relationship between the amount of exposure to alcohol advertising and alcohol consumption in underage youth. Their findings revealed that advertising has an effect on drinking behavior. The National Institute on Alcohol Abuse and Alcoholism (NIAAA) notes that parenting style has an important impact on a child's alcohol use and attitudes toward drinking.

Issue: Does Drug Abuse Treatment Work?

Yes: National Institute on Drug Abuse, from "*Principles of Drug Addiction Treatment: A Research-based Guide*," (National Institute on Drug Abuse, 2009)
No: Sacha Z. Scoblic, from "The Dogma of AA Has Taken Over," *The New Republic* (2013)

The National Institute on Drug Abuse report acknowledges that drug addiction is difficult to overcome but that treatment can be effective and works best when individuals are committed to remain in treatment for an extended time. Sacha Z. Scoblic, a Carter fellow for mental health journalism, argues that anti-addiction programs, such as Alcoholics Anonymous, can be ineffective and are misused. Popular programs might not adhere to the vast body of research on addiction treatment.

Preface

Drug misuse, abuse, dependence, and addiction are controversial topics. These are debated on television news programs and websites on the political left, right, and center. Political candidates for local, state, and national office are challenged on their positions. Pharmaceuticals and abused drugs are important parts of our legal and illegal economies. Our popular culture—movies, music, and television programs—is influenced by drugs and drug culture. Reasoned and educated people can differ greatly in their perspectives and opinions on what our drug policies should be. Are our drug policies too restrictive? Are physicians and pharmacists contributing to drug addiction? Is drug addiction a "disease" or is it a moral weakness? What are the appropriate treatments for minimizing drug abuse, dependence, and addiction?

There are many ways these controversies can be resolved and questions can be answered. However, the resolutions and answers can have a tremendous impact on our culture, nation and community, and on individual lives. Increasing criminal penalties for drug possession or use could serve as an effective deterrent against initial experimentation with an illicit substance, like marijuana or methamphetamine. Diminished initial experiences could prevent subsequent high rates of drug dependence and addiction. However, strong penalties against simple drug possession could increase the chance someone interacts with the criminal justice system, which could have a negative long-term impact on their educational and professional opportunities. What are policies and laws that decrease drug addiction and their accompanying social problems, while respecting the rights of the individual?

Regardless of their community, personal ethics or lifestyle choices, no one's life is free from the impact of drugs. Almost every one of us has a relative, friend, or classmate who has struggles with drug abuse or dependence. Billions of tax dollars are allocated to the "war on drugs" and criminal justice system. Medical treatment for drug-related illness and injuries creates burdens on our already-extended health-care systems. Babies are born to mothers who used drugs while pregnant, and many children enter the educational system from homes where drug use is the central factor in home life. Some of us face the challenge of drug addiction in our own, personal lives.

When we consider and debate drug policies, we tend to focus on recreational and/or illegal drugs, like marijuana,

cocaine, or hallucinogens. We don't always consider the impact of legal drugs that might be easily available over-the-counter or by prescription from a physician. Legal drugs, such as the stimulants used for hyperactivity disorders, can have a profound impact on behavior in an educational environment. Prescription drugs, such as the opiates like Oxycontin, are diverted from pain management to produce euphoria or to minimize aversive opiate withdrawal symptoms. The issues considered and debated in the eleventh edition of *Taking Sides: Clashing Views in Drugs and Society* deal with both legal and illegal drugs. We may come to question the definitions of "legal" and "illegal" or "licit" and "illicit" drugs.

Many of the issues in *Taking Sides: Clashing Views in Drugs and Society* will have an impact on the life of a college student. For example, the issue *Should the Legal Drinking Age Stay at 21 to Decrease Underage Alcohol Use?* has an impact on anyone under or just- over the age of 21 who drinks alcohol or is on a college campus where alcohol is widely consumed. The issue *Should "Smart Drugs" Be Used to Enhance Cognitive Functioning?* could have an impact on students considering taking drugs used to manage the symptoms cognitive disorders to improve their performance on an upcoming exam. Many students start or end their day with one—or several—caffeinated beverages, and the issues *Is Caffeine a Health Risk?* and *Are Energy Drinks with Alcohol Dangerous Enough to Ban?* will provide a new perspective.

Issues related to diverse populations are considered in *Taking Sides: Clashing Views in Drugs and Society*. The issue *Is the War on Drugs Based in Racism?* questions whether efforts to combat drug addiction and trafficking have had a disproportionate negative impact on black communities in the United States. Many issues in the volume focus on the United States, but *Does China Have an Effective Approach to Combat Drug Addiction?* Provides a historical and cross-cultural perspective on drug addiction problems in China and its use of capital punishment to decrease trafficking and possession.

Taking Sides: Clashing Views in Drugs and Society is organized as a series of issues on a variety of topics within the field. Each issue has a set of learning objectives—important concepts that should be considered or learned from the material provided. A brief introduction provides some background information and sets the stage for the debate as it is argued in the YES and NO selections. The selections are articles from scientific and medical field (e.g., reports from the National Institutes of Health) or articles written by journalists and opinion-makers in popular websites, magazines, or newspapers (e.g., *Marie Claire, Huffington Post* and *Reason Magazine*). After the YES and NO selections a summary is provided with questions for debate and further consideration. Finally, suggested additional resources, including Internet sites, are provided to follow up or learn more on a topic.

The issues are tools to encourage critical thinking on important and controversial topics. In reading an issue, students should form their own opinion. Students should not feel confined to accept and adopt one position. For many of the issues, students might find both positions are equally compelling. This conflict is expected when controversial and thought-provoking questions are considered. Hopefully, students will construct new thoughts and ideas on the issues—incorporating the best of both perspectives.

Dennis K. Miller
University of Missouri

Editor of This Volume

DENNIS K. MILLER is an Associate Professor and Associate Chair for Curriculum, Instruction and Advising for the Department of Psychological Sciences at the University of Missouri. He earned his PhD in psychology from Texas A&M University and completed postdoctoral training in neuropharmacology at the University of Kentucky. He teaches classes in general psychology and behavioral pharmacology.

Editors/Academic Advisory Board Members

Members of the Academic Advisory Board are instrumental in the final selection of articles for each edition of TAKING SIDES. Their review of articles for content, level, and appropriateness provides critical direction to the editor and staff. We think that you will find their careful consideration well reflected in this volume.

Virgil Adams, III
Cypress College

Cynthia Albro
State University of New York, Oswego

Victor O. Anyanwu
American InterContinental University, Buckhead Campus

Russel A. Arnett, III
Mount San Jacinto Community College

Larry Ashley
Central Michigan University

Yasemin Besen-Cassino
Montclair State University

Elaine Bryan
Georgia Perimeter College

Esther Castillo
California State University, Fullerton

Maria Decker
North Shore Community College

Karen Dennis
Illinois State University

Margaret Dobbs
Northeastern State University

Stanley Eisen
Christian Brothers University

Thomas Farnsworth
University of Dayton

Eltorry Ficklin
Jackson State University

Sheila Foley
Bay Path College

Brandon Fryman
University of La Verne

Jolynn Gardner
University of St. Thomas

Amy Grau
Shawnee State University

Neil Gregory
Lake Superior State University

Debra Hanselman
Marygrove College

Kelly Helm
Valparaiso University

Karen Jennison
University of Northern Colorado

Helen Just
St. Edward's University

Kenneth Kovach
Notre Dame College

Andrea Krieg
Lewis University

Celia Lo
University of Alabama, Tuscaloosa

Tim Lubben
Kennesaw State University

Mary E. Lutz
City College of New York

William Malette
Lake Superior State University

Julie Merten
University of North Florida

James Metcalf
George Mason University

Jennifer Murphy
Penn State Berks

James Myers
Genesee Community College

Steven Namanny
Utah Valley University

Allison Nye
Cape Fear Community College

Sherry Obert
Allegany College of Maryland

Jean Oldham
St. Catharine College

Jane Petrillo
Kennesaw State University

Kimberly Pitts
Campbellsville University

Diana Quealy-Berge
Casper College

Barry Schecter
SUNY Cortland

Lori Simons
Widener University

Natalie Stickney
Georgia Perimeter College

Al Trego
McCann School

Elaine Whalen
McHenry County College

Joel Woods
Academy of Court Reporting

Mary Wright
Shenandoah University

Introduction

A candidate running for local, state, or national office will promise, "I will do something about the drug problem." On a cable news program, an opinionated host will declare, "the drug problem has been getting worse under the current political administration." A parent might fret, "I'm worried my child will get caught up in the big drug problem in their school." What worries these individuals? What is the "drug problem" that is so pervasive?

A drug is a nonfood substance that produces a biological effect on an animal. A therapeutic drug may be used to treat, cure, prevent or diagnose a disease, or it might enhance physical or mental well-being. Psychoactive drugs affect the activity of the nervous system and change consciousness, affect or perception. Recreational drugs are those that are not used for medical purposes but are used for their pleasurable effects. Some are habituating or addictive, where the effect of the drug is diminished with repeated administration and the user physically or psychologically needs more drug. Some drugs are classified as legal by the government, while others are deemed illegal.

Every person is touched in some way by drug use. According to the United States Department of Justice (National Drug Intelligence Center. *The Economic Impact of Illicit Drug Use on American Society*. Washington, DC: United States Department of Justice, 2011) cost Americans more than $700 billion a year in increased health-care costs, crime, and lost productivity. College students might use a stimulant, like methylphenidate (Ritalin) or amphetamine (Adderall), to stay up late and study for a final exam. After the exam, students might use a sedative, like alcohol, to rest and relax from the stresses of tests and grades. Some might combine sedatives and stimulants to achieve a relaxing evening, while not falling asleep. Across demographic groups, people use therapeutic psychoactive drugs to minimize the severity of the symptoms of depression, anxiety and hyperactivity disorders. Short- and long-term pain can be ameliorated through therapeutic drugs, like opiates (e.g., OxyContin or codeine), that are habituating and addictive. Psychoactive drugs that are legal might be diverted for illegal use to change mood or alleviate the painful withdrawal symptoms that accompany habituation.

It's not easy to get accurate information on overall patterns of drug use in a society. For example, many communities are negatively impacted by the potent psychostimulant methamphetamine. It has been called a "scourge," "plague," and "disease". However, what is the prevalence rate of methamphetamine use in a community? While the drug is available for legal use to manage hyperactivity disorders and extreme obesity, recording the number of prescriptions written by physicians or filled by pharmacists is not sufficient to get an accurate measure of the amount of drug available. This drug could be diverted from its government-approved uses to illicit uses. Illicit stimulants can be easily and effectively smuggled into the country across wide borders. Furthermore, methamphetamine can be synthesized in small batches by home chemists, referred to as "cooks," from ingredients readily available over-the-counter from any grocery or home-supply store. Political, law enforcement and public health agencies have no idea how much drug is actually on the streets of their community, and might have to rely on arrests for methamphetamine possession or distribution, overdoses reporting to medical clinics, and referrals to drug treatment programs.

Taking Sides: Clashing Views in Drugs and Society focuses primarily on psychoactive drugs, those that change communication in the nervous system and alter behavior. There are several categories of psychoactive drugs and they vary by their mechanisms of action in the brain and body, effects on behavior, therapeutic and recreational uses, and abuse and dependence liabilities.

- Alcohol is among the most commonly used drugs and has been used in varied forms by different cultures for almost 10,000 years. It alters the activity of most biological systems and produces both euphoria and sedation. Alcohol can impair learning and memory, blunt perception, and impair motor behavior. These pharmacological actions contribute to alcohol's problematic role in sexual assaults and in accidents. Alcohol's effects decline with repeated use, an effect referred to as tolerance, and consumption may increase to surmount tolerance. However, chronic consumption can lead to withdrawal symptoms, physiological changes that occur when drug use is stopped or the dosage is diminished. Tolerance and withdrawal are characteristic of alcoholism, and chronic drinking can have a negative impact on the liver and nervous system.
- Anxiolytics and Sedative Hypnotics are used to decrease anxiety and induce sleep. In the United States and many other countries, these

are typically classified as prescription, and not over-the-counter drugs. Prescription drugs must be prescribed by a medical professional because the drug has a high abuse potential, is new to the market, and/or is potentially dangerous. Examples of anxiolytics include the benzodiazepines (e.g., alprazolam [Xanax] and diazepam [Valium]) and "z-drugs" (e.g., zaleplon [Sonata] and zolpidem [Ambien]). Like alcohol, tolerance and withdrawal symptoms may develop to anxiolytics and sedative hypnotics. While they are therapeutic drugs, they are also used recreationally.

- Opiates are a class of drugs that produce analgesia, a loss of sensitivity to pain, and cause sleep. Opiate drugs mimic the activity of opiate-like substances prepared by the body, called endorphins. Examples of opiates include codeine, morphine, heroin, and oxycodone (Perocet and OxyContin). A significant problem for many communities is the diversion of prescription opiates from therapeutic to recreational use. Chronic opiate users may be motivated to continue using drugs to avoid withdrawal symptoms, but opiates may also cause overdose.

- Like alcohol, cannabis has been cultivated for thousands of years by different cultures and used for its effects on behavior. The effects of cannabis are varied by the preparation and can be individual to the user, and include euphoria, analgesia, a decrease in anxiety, and sedation. North Americans are most familiar with cannabis as marijuana, the dried leaves and flowers. The legal status of cannabis is controversial within the United States as the federal government currently considers it a drug with a high abuse potential and no medical benefits; however, some states and many communities approve of therapeutic (i.e., "medicinal") or recreational cannabis use without criminal penalty.

- Caffeine is consumed from a variety of commonly used sources, including energy drinks, soft drinks, coffee, tea, and cocoa. It causes excitation in the brain and body and increases attention, alertness, and arousal. While most individuals use some caffeine daily, the negative effects of caffeine on the body and behavior are controversial.

- Nicotine is a stimulant that is found in tobacco products. Smoking rates have generally declined in the United States since the 1960s, although they have remained steady or increased in poor and developing countries. The legal status of nicotine as a "drug" and its regulation is controversial in many countries and many communities have sought to restrict its use in public and private venues. Like caffeine, nicotine can increase

arousal, learning and memory performance, and fine motor skills; however, it tolerance and withdrawal symptoms and smoking tobacco causes heart disease, cancer and lung disease.

- Caffeine and nicotine are classified as psychomotor stimulants. Other psychomotor stimulants include cocaine, the amphetamines and methylphenidate (Ritalin). Cocaine is extracted from the leaf of the coca bush, which is found in South America. A variety of drugs are classified as amphetamines, including methamphetamine and d-amphetamine, based on their chemical structure. Stimulants are used to manage the symptoms of hyperactivity disorders (e.g., Attention Deficit Hyperactivity Disorder), narcolepsy, and obesity; however, they also can have a high abuse liability, as they induce a strong and intense euphoria, especially when smoked or injected. Like the anxiolytics and sedative-hypnotics, stimulants are available by prescription, but can be diverted to recreational use.

- A variety of drugs are used recreationally for their hallucinogenic or psychedelic properties, including lysergic acid diethylamide (LSD), psilocybin, and MDMA (ecstasy). These are also referred to as "club drugs" or "rave drugs" because they are associated with discothèques in the 1970s and dance clubs, parties, and raves in the 1980s to the 2000s. Many of these drugs have profound subjective and emotional effects, making the user feel in touch with others or enhancing the enjoyment of music and social situations. In the United States most of the drugs with strong hallucinogenic or psychedelic properties are illegal and strong penalties against their distribution are present.

Many of the drugs listed above and in the issues are classified as "controlled substances". What is a "controlled substance"? It is a drug or chemical whose manufacture, possession, or use is regulated under the Controlled Substances Act (CSA) in the United States. Other nations have similar acts and laws, but we will focus on the United States. The CSA was signed into law in 1970 and creates five schedules, or classifications, of drugs with varied qualifications to be included in each schedule. The qualifications to determine a drug's schedule are its abuse potential and its currently accepted medical use.

Schedule I drugs have a high abuse potential. They have no currently accepted medical use and there is a lack of accepted safety for the drug to be used under medical supervision. As such, a physician cannot write a prescription and a pharmacy cannot fill a prescription for a Schedule I drug. Examples of Schedule I drugs include marijuana, heroin, LSD, MDMA, and psilocybin. As mentioned the status of marijuana as a drug designated as having a high abuse potential and no accepted medical use is controversial.

Like Schedule I drugs, Schedule II drugs have a high abuse potential. Schedule II drugs have a currently accepted medical use, but there abuse may lead to severe physical or psychological dependence. Examples of Schedule II drugs include cocaine, methamphetamine, morphine, and oxycodone. It might seem strange to have cocaine and methamphetamine in a less-restrictive category than LSD and MDMA; however, cocaine can be used as a topical anesthetic and methamphetamine can be used for the treatment of obesity.

The potential for abuse decreases across Schedules III, IV, and V. Like Schedule II drugs, Schedule III, IV, and V drugs have a currently accepted medical use, but there abuse may lead to severe physical or psychological dependence.

The Drug Enforcement Agency (DEA) and Food and Drug Administration (FDA) determine which substances are included in each schedule, and the DEA has the responsibility to enforce the CSA.

Unit 1

UNIT

Drugs and Public Policy

*D*rugs impact a community and nation. Some drugs have a high abuse potential and their use may lead to physical and psychological dependence. Drug addiction can impact the family as individuals may become unable to fulfill family, work, and school responsibilities because of their drug use. Children with parents addicted to drugs might be deprived of opportunities for healthy physical and psychological growth. Drugs are frequently associated with and implicated in violent crimes. While we may recognize that there is a "drug problem" in our society, we are not clear on what we should do about this problem?

Over time societies change their attitudes about drugs in general or specific drugs. For example, through most of the twentieth century smoking in public was common. Only a few rows of seats on airplanes were designated as nonsmoking and there were no limitations on smoking in a public bar or restaurant. Now, in the early part of the twenty-first century, many communities have banned smoking in public as a matter of public health. The issues in this Unit, Drugs and Public Policy, address drug regulations. How do we view drugs when we develop new laws and enforce the laws?

Selected, Edited, and with Issue Framing Material by:
Dennis K. Miller, *University of Missouri*

ISSUE

Should Laws Against Drug Use Remain Restrictive?

YES: Drug Enforcement Administration, from "Speaking Out Against Drug Legalization" (2010)

NO: U.S. Department of Health and Human Services, from "Youth Prevention-Related Measures," *Results from the 2009 National Survey on Drug Use and Health: Volume 1*, U.S. Department of Health and Human Services (2010)

Learning Outcomes

After reading this issue, you will be able to:

- Define and understand the differences among legalization, decriminalization, medicalization, and harm reduction.
- Summarize the general principles that guide the creation of new laws and the enforcement of existing laws regarding recreational drugs.
- Describe the many relationships between drugs and the criminal justice system.
- Understand the relationship between drug laws and drug use rates, and the other variables that influence these associations.
- Identify factors that contribute to high and low rates of drug use in the United States.

ISSUE SUMMARY

YES: The Drug Enforcement Administration (DEA) is charged with enforcing the controlled substances laws and regulations of the United States. In "Speaking Out Against Drug Legalization" the DEA argues that enforcement of drug laws is not the cause of violence; drug legalization will not reduce crime and increase government revenue; and prohibition actions can be successful at decreasing drug use.

NO: The report from the U.S. Department of Health and Human Services points out that a number of factors affect drug use by young people. One of the most important factors is perception of risk. If young people perceive that drugs are harmful, they are less likely to engage in drug use. Other relevant factors include the perception of drug use by peers, religious beliefs, and parental involvement. Legal sanctions are not noted as a deterrent to drug use.

The federal government spent $15.5 billion in 2010 to control drug use and to enforce the laws designed to protect society from the problems created by drug use. According to the Office of National Drug Control Policy, these expenditures are minimal compared to the cost of $193 billion the United States lost in productivity, health care, and criminal justice costs in 2007. Some people believe that the expenditures and costs of the war on drugs could be decreased if governmental agencies and communities fought hard enough to stop drug use. They also hold that laws to halt drug use are too few and too lenient. We would not need to spend so much money on the criminal justice costs associated with drugs if we changed the laws. Others believe that the war against drugs is unnecessary. The war on drugs has already been lost. These individuals feel that the best way to remedy drug problems is to end the fight altogether by ending the current restrictive policies regarding drug use.

Some argue that we should legalize drug use, which is to make it legal or allow the government to authorize it. Others argue that drug use should be decriminalized, which is to eliminate the criminal penalties associated with drug use or remove its legal restrictions. Aren't *legalization* and *decriminalization* the same thing? There are some subtle, but important differences between the two. Decriminalization does not mean that someone can use drugs without legal consequences. Laws and regulations associated with drugs remain intact. Rather, it means that someone will not face severe penalties for small offenses. For example, someone will not receive a long prison sentence and criminal record for possessing a small amount of marijuana. Legalization means that there is no penalty at all. For example, in some states growing and selling marijuana is a legitimate occupation for which someone pays business taxes.

Supporters of drug legalization argue that laws create an illegal, underground market, which drives violence. Criminalization of drugs fuels organized crime and allows children to be pulled into the drug business. Legalization would eliminate the criminal marketplace for drugs. Legalization could take the profits out of drug sales on the street, thereby decreasing the value of and demand for drugs. Furthermore, if drugs could be bought and sold legally, they could be regulated. Reasonable restrictions—such as those with alcohol in the United States—could be put in place. These might include limiting children's access to drugs, ensuring drugs are manufactured safely, and controlling advertising and marketing. Drugs could be taxed, like any other product, raising revenue for government programs, including those to help people addicted to drugs. In the United States the legalization perspective is sometimes also referred to as "re-legalization." Before the start of the twentieth century almost all drugs were legal.

Some legalization advocates argue that the federal government's prohibition stance on drugs is an immoral and impossible objective. To achieve a "drug-free society" is self-defeating and a misnomer because drugs have always been a part of human culture. Furthermore, prohibition efforts disregard the private freedom of individuals— assuming that individuals are incapable of making their own choices. Drug proponents assert that their personal sovereignty should be respected over any government agenda.

Proponents of drug decriminalization argue that it is the strict enforcement of drug laws that damages society. People arrested for drug offenses overburden the court system, thus rendering it ineffective. A criminal record limits a person's opportunities (e.g., jobs and education) in society, and people completing treatment are productive members of society rather than convicted felons. Furthermore, individuals with drug abuse problems are much more likely to find help in a medical addiction center than in prison. Addiction treatment and rehabilitation is less expensive than incarceration. Finally, decriminalization removes some of the "rebellious or counterculture" essence of drug use.

The decriminalization approach can include a harm reduction model to manage drug abuse and dependence. A harm reduction model is a society-wide approach to drug abuse that focuses on reducing the negative outcomes experienced by the individual and society. Drug use is a part of our world, whether drugs are legal/criminal or not. People are going to use drugs and the best approach for our society is to minimize the harmful effects of drug use, rather than imposing broad punishments. Furthermore, strong legal penalties against drug use can make the factors that contribute to initial drug use (e.g., poverty, social isolation, and inequalities) worse. Under harm reduction, decriminalization should not minimize the harm and danger of drug abuse, but it should not increase the damage.

Supporters of drug legalization or decriminalization perspective generally believe society should focus on drug prevention. Drug prevention is an approach aimed at preventing and decreasing the health, social, and personal problems caused by drug addiction. A drug prevention program considers both the protective factors and the risk factors that contribute to someone using, or not using, a drug. Protective factors are those associated with preventing the potential for drug abuse, and include parental monitoring, anti-drug use polices, and adoption of conventional norms about drug use. Risk factors include lack of parental supervision, drug availability, and poverty. A drug prevention program seeks to increase protective factors and decrease risk factors.

Opponents of legalization and decriminalization maintain that less restrictive drug laws and relaxation of enforcement policies are not the solution to drug problems. In fact, these are very dangerous ideas. Less restrictive laws, they assert, will drastically increase drug use. This upsurge in drug use will come at an incredibly high price: society will be overrun with drug-related accidents, loss in worker productivity, and hospitals filled with drug-related emergencies. Drug treatment efforts would be futile because users would have no legal incentive to stop taking drugs. Also, users may prefer drugs to rehabilitation, and education programs may be ineffective in dissuading children from using drugs.

Advocates of legalization and decriminalization often maintain that drug abuse is a "victimless crime": The only person being hurt is the drug user. However, opponents argue that this notion is ludicrous and dangerous because drug use has dire repercussions for all of society. Regulations to control drug use have a legitimate social aim to protect society and its citizens from the harm of drugs. Individuals who favor restrictive laws maintain that such laws are not immoral or a violation of personal freedoms. Rather, they allow a standard of control to be established in order to preserve human character and society as a whole.

In the YES selection, the Drug Enforcement Administration argues that drugs should remain illegal and that criminalizing trafficking can be successful at decreasing drug use. In the NO selection, the report from the Department of Health and Human Services describes those factors that affect drug use and points out that restrictive drug laws did not serve as a deterrent.

YES ⤶

Drug Enforcement Administration

Speaking Out Against Drug Legalization

Increasingly the news is full of reports providing misleading or biased information about our nation's drug policies. Whether there are questions about the Drug Enforcement Administration's (DEA's) actions to enforce federal law, or challenges to the basic concept that drugs are dangerous, there is a growing discussion as to whether our current drug policies are effective and appropriate.

Speaking Out Against Drug Legalization is designed to cut through the current fog of misinformation with hard facts. It presents an accurate picture of America's experience with drug use, the nature of the drug problem, and the potential for damage if the United States adopts a more permissive policy on drug abuse. The information provides specific points in response to the most common myths and facts about drugs and drug abuse.

Drug abuse, and this nation's response to it, is one of the most important and complex challenges facing all Americans—especially our youth. The national drug policies presently in place were not dreamed up from an ivory tower of idealism, but instead were constructed from the cold realities of experience.

From a historical perspective, the unique freedoms offered by the United States have always depended on a well-informed public. Accordingly, the DEA hopes you will use the scrupulously researched facts presented here to help you educate your friends and family.

1 "The Enforcement of Drug Laws Contributes to Violence Along the Southwest Border."

Some have proposed legalizing drug consumption in the United States as a way to reduce border violence. This ignores scientific, legal, and social arguments that highlight what legalizing drugs would cost the United States, and that marijuana legalization would be a failed law enforcement strategy for both the United States and Mexico.

Criminals won't stop being criminals if we make drugs legal. Individuals who have chosen to pursue a life of crime and violence aren't likely to change course, get legitimate jobs, and become honest, tax-paying citizens just because we legalize drugs. The individuals and organizations that smuggle drugs don't do so because they enjoy the challenge of "making a sale." They sell drugs because that's what makes them the most money.

The violence in Mexico is a reflection of a larger battle as to whether Mexico will be governed under the rule of law, or the rule of the gun. We should take steps to reduce the killings by the drug cartels in Mexico and along our Southwest border, but suggesting that legalizing dope is going to make a difference in this effort makes no sense. The fight in Mexico is over money, and not just money generated by drugs, but for any illegal activity where profits can be made.

Drug-related violence in Mexico is not a fight over market access or distribution chains in the United States, but the result of major Mexican drug trafficking organizations vying for control of both the drug smuggling routes leading into and out of Mexico, and transportation corridors along the border.

Marijuana is only a part of the illegal drug traffic moving between Mexico and the United States. Changing the status of marijuana in the United States will not stop drug traffickers' motivations for moving drugs to U.S. markets. Remember, drug traffickers do what they do for money, not for altruistic reasons. Regardless of the legal status of marijuana, there will still be profits to be made in other drugs, guns, people, or other contraband. Just as organized crime didn't end when alcohol prohibition in the United States was lifted in 1933, drug trafficking and its associated violence isn't going to dissipate if the United States decides to legalize marijuana. . . .

A comprehensive strategy addressing drug use and trafficking from all angles can and does make a difference. DEA supports an effective, comprehensive national drug control strategy, and we are working with the Department of Justice and the Office of National Drug Control Policy as they develop this strategy.

U.S. Drug Enforcement Administration. "Speaking Out Against Drug Legalization," *www.dea.gov/pr/multimedia-library/publications/speaking_out*, 2010.

We need to be aware of the nature of addiction itself and support research in this key area. We should continue to be advocates for effective and proven prevention efforts that reduce drug abuse and addiction. We must provide treatment for those that need it, and we must enforce our nation's drug laws which fundamentally help protect our citizens and communities.

2 "Legalizing and Taxing Marijuana Will Help Local Economies by Reduceing Crime and Increasing Tax Revenue."

Marijuana is a dangerous, mind-altering drug. That's the conclusion the Food and Drug Administration (FDA) came to after reviewing all of the available information. The same can be said of alcohol and tobacco—both legal drugs (and currently outside of the FDA's jurisdiction). How could anyone argue that adding a third substance to that mix is going to be beneficial?

Alcohol and tobacco have proven harmful, addictive, and difficult to regulate. Alcohol is the third leading cause of death in the United States—each year over 100,000 Americans die of alcohol-related causes. The Surgeon General estimates that problems resulting from alcohol use and abuse cost society almost $200 billion every year, and that these costs are far higher than any revenue generated by alcohol taxes. (Marin Institute Fact Sheet, "The Costs of Alcohol," June 24, 2008.).

Tobacco, the other substance that often is suggested as a model for 'legal' marijuana, offers a picture of a similarly bleak future. The Center for Disease Control estimates that the total economic costs associated with cigarette smoking is approximately $7.18 per pack of cigarettes sold in the United States. The revenue generated to cover these costs? The federal excise tax is $1.01 per pack of cigarettes. The median state cigarette excise tax rate, as of January 1, 2007, is 80 cents (See: http://www.CDC.gov/tobacco). This hardly sounds like an "economic windfall" that cures our budget woes.

If we were to regulate marijuana, we would have to concede that it's acceptable for society to profit from a person's addiction. There were approximately 38,000 overdose deaths for illicit drugs and non-medical use of prescription drugs during 2006, according to the Center for Disease Control. (Heron, et al., "Deaths: Final Data for 2006," U.S. Dept of Health and Human Services, Centers for Disease Control and Prevention, National Vital Statistics Reports, Vol. 57, Number 14, April 2009, DHHS Pub No (PAS) 2009-1120 (Tables 21 and 22),

see: http://www.cdc.gov/nchs/data/nvsr/nvsr57/nvsr57_14.pdf). How much are those lives worth?

The cost of treatment and rehabilitation from addiction and usage associated illnesses far outweighs the cost of any revenue possibly be generated; a government estimate of the cost of drug use just for one year (2002) was more than $180 billion. Regulation hasn't kept prescription drugs, alcohol, or tobacco from being abused. The excise taxes that are collected from these activities only cover a portion of the costs of their misuse.

Studies demonstrate that when people perceive the use of drugs as harmless, drug use increases—if marijuana or other drugs were legalized, it is certain that the perceived harm would decrease, making the incidence of use rise, regardless of age-related regulations.

Suggesting that the only costs caused by the illegality of drugs are law enforcement costs ignores lives and livelihoods lost due to addiction and overdose. Lowering or eliminating the legal restrictions for drugs will result in increased availability, and greater use, with higher healthcare costs and increased criminal activity. We have seen these costs go up when other nations have gone down this path, and we should not make the same mistakes.

For example, when The Netherlands liberalized their drug laws allowing the public sale of marijuana, they saw marijuana use among 18–25 years olds double, and the heroin addiction levels triple. They have since reversed this trend, and have begun implementing tighter drug controls. Indeed, today over 70 percent of Dutch municipalities have local zero-tolerance laws (INTRAVAL Bureau for Research and Consistency, "Coffeeshops in the Netherlands 2004," Dutch Ministry of Justice, June 2005, http://www.intraval.nl/en/b/b45_html).

Similarly, when the United Kingdom relaxed their drug laws to allow physicians to prescribe heroin to certain classes of addicts, they saw an entirely new class of youthful users emerge. According to social scientist James Q. Wilson, the British Government's experiment with controlled heroin distribution resulted in a minimum of a 30-fold increase in the number of addicts in 10 years.

While the notion that each individual can make their own choices without affecting anyone is a nice theory, it is impractical in today's interconnected world. The health and social costs generated by addiction are borne not just by the drug user, but by everyone. The purpose of an effective drug policy should be to lessen the harm that illegal drugs do to our society. Lowering or eliminating the current legal and social restrictions that limit the availability and social acceptance of drug use would have the opposite result, both domestically and internationally.

Some have hypothesized that there has already been a loss of state tax revenue because of actions taken against marijuana traffickers who purport to be operating in furtherance of state marijuana legalization laws. In fact, this is a question that some jurisdictions in California have raised directly with the Department of Justice. In summary, the Department of Justice replied that income derived from the sale of marijuana, whether in California or not, represents proceeds of illegal drug trafficking, and as such is forfeitable under federal law. . . .

3 "Drug Laws Infringe on State's Rights."

The federal government does not focus its marijuana enforcement resources on individual patients with cancer or other serious illnesses, and the Attorney General has directed that this remain the case.

The Attorney General has determined that the Department of Justice will focus its investigation, enforcement, and prosecution efforts regarding the manufacture and distribution of marijuana on significant drug traffickers. Indicators of significant drug trafficking may include citizen complaints, use of firearms, violence, sales to minors, marketing, sales for profit, excessive amounts of cash, money laundering, excessive volumes of controlled substances, requests for federal assistance from local law enforcement, sale of other illegal drugs, or any other identified factor that would demonstrate that marijuana growers or distributors are trying to use state laws as a shield for illegal activity.

Any change to the legal status of marijuana should be done through the mechanisms established by the Controlled Substances Act (CSA), which requires action by the Food and Drug Administration (FDA) and the DEA, or by Congress.

The state's rights "argument" is most popular in discussions regarding "medical" marijuana ballot initiatives that have passed in 14 States. Marijuana remains a Schedule I controlled substance under the CSA (21 U.S.C. § 812(c), Schedule I(c)(10)). This is consistent with the fact that the drug has never been approved by the FDA for marketing in the United States because scientific studies have never established that marijuana can be used safely and effectively for the treatment of any disease or condition (See 66 Fed. Reg. 20038, 20050-52 (2001) (DEA denial of petition to remove marijuana from schedule I based on FDA scientific and medical evaluation), pet. for

review dismissed, Gettman v. DEA, 290 F.3d 430 (D.C. Cir. 2002)). Marijuana's placement in Schedule I of the CSA results in the following legal consequences: marijuana may not be dispensed for medical use in the United States; it is illegal to manufacture, distribute, or possess marijuana for any purpose (other than government-approved research); and there is no "medical necessity" defense to the CSA prohibitions relating to marijuana (U.S. v. Oakland Cannabis Buyers' Cooperative 532 U.S. 483, 491, 494 & n.7 (2001)).

The Supreme Court's decisions in *United States v. Oakland Cannabis Buyers' Cooperative* (OCBC 532 U.S. 483 (2001)) and *Gonzales v. Raich* (Gonzales v. Raich, 545 U.S. 1 (2005)) make clear that, regardless of whether one complies with the California marijuana legalization law, it remains illegal under the CSA for any person to cultivate, distribute, or possess marijuana for claimed "medical reasons."

The United States has also signed various international treaties to control illegal drug activity. The International Narcotics Control Board (INCB) of the United Nations is charged with monitoring compliance with the drug control treaties. The INCB pointed out that the state marijuana initiatives recently passed in the United States are contrary to United States federal law. The report called on the United States to "vigorously enforce its federal law" in the face of these initiatives. The report further stated: "The decision of whether a substance should be authorized for medical use has always been taken, and should continue to be taken, in all countries by the bodies designated to regulate and register medicines. Such decisions should have a sound medical and scientific basis and should not be made in accordance with referendums organized by interest groups." (U.N. International Narcotics Control Board, United Nations, "Report 1998" at par. 259, U.N. Sales No. E.99.XI.1, http://www.incb.org/incb/en /annual_report_1998.html.)

The authority of the DEA to investigate those growing, selling, or possessing marijuana, irrespective of state law, has been reaffirmed by recent rulings by the United States Supreme Court. . . .

The DEA is responsible for enforcing the CSA. Accordingly, DEA is obligated to take all appropriate law enforcement actions, use all of the tools at our disposal, and to investigate any organization, including marijuana distribution facilities (sometimes referred to by their operators as "cannabis clubs") that are engaged in the unlawful manufacture and distribution of controlled substances.

Portugal (Decriminalized)

Band wagon

Legacy with prohibition — Harry Enslinger was in charge

was in charge 30 years of drug laws

4 "Prohibition Didn't Work in the 20's and It Doesn't Work Now."

Claims that prohibition didn't work overlook the fact that most historians agree that national prohibition succeeded both in lowering consumption and in retaining political support until the great depression radically changed voters' priorities. Repeal resulted more from this contextual shift than from characteristics of prohibition itself.

One favorite argument of those who claim prohibition didn't work point to the growth of organized crime. Although organized crime flourished under its sway, historians trace the beginnings of organized crime in the United States to the mid to late-1800s. Organized crime existed before prohibition was enacted, and persists long after its repeal.

The laws and enforcement mechanisms created after 1919 by the 18th Amendment and the Volstead Act, which charged the Treasury Department with enforcement of the new restrictions, was far from all-embracing. The amendment prohibited the commercial manufacture and distribution of alcoholic beverages; it did not prohibit use, nor production for one's own consumption.

Alcohol consumption declined dramatically during prohibition. Cirrhosis death rates for men were 29.5 per 100,000 in 1911 and 10.7 in 1929. Admissions to State mental hospitals for alcoholic psychosis declined from 10.1 per 100,000 in 1919 to 4.7 in 1928.

Arrests for public drunkenness and disorderly conduct declined 50 percent between 1916 and 1922. For the population as a whole, the best estimates are that consumption of alcohol declined by 30 percent to 50 percent. Violent crime did not increase dramatically during prohibition. Homicide rates rose dramatically from 1900 to 1910 but remained roughly constant during prohibition's 14 year rule (Moore, Mark H., "Actually, Prohibition Was a Success," Harvard's Kennedy School of Government, October 16, 1989).Organized crime may have become more visible and lurid during prohibition, but it existed before and after.

Following the repeal of prohibition, alcohol consumption increased. Prohibition did not end alcohol use, but it did succeed in reducing, by one-third, the consumption of a product that had wide historical and popular sanction.

The parallel between alcohol prohibition in the 1920's and the current status of marijuana, heroin, and other dangerous drugs is tenuous. The 18th Amendment took a popular activity, alcohol sales, which was widely tolerated, and made it illegal. It did so after more than a century of growing concern over the effects of excessive alcohol consumption was having on society. In contrast, the use of marijuana, heroin, or other controlled drugs has never been a widely accepted activity.

In addition, the idealistic goals of prohibition went beyond what many initial supporters of prohibition thought they were supporting, and lacked flexibility that would allow policy adjustments to changes in the facts surrounding alcohol. In contrast, our nation's current drug laws are built upon the Controlled Substances Act, which contains a series of increasingly restrictive schedules that allow for the appropriate regulation of various drugs, as well as a mechanism to move substances from one regulatory status to another should new information about the use of a controlled substance be established.

Not only are the facts of prohibition misunderstood, but the lessons are misapplied to marijuana legalization. The real lesson of prohibition is that the society can, indeed, make a dent in consumption through laws. There is a price to be paid for such restrictions, of course. But for drugs such as heroin and cocaine, which are dangerous but currently largely unpopular, that price is small relative to the benefits.

5 "Through Drug Laws Congress Is Attempting to Legislate Morality."

John Adams, who helped draft the Constitution and later became our second president, declared, "Our Constitution was made only for a moral and religious people. It is wholly inadequate to govern of any other." This means that any and all just laws must be based on moral considerations. Our elected representatives are therefore bound to *legislate morality*.

Morality is about right and wrong, and that's what laws put into legal form. All laws legislate morality (even speed limits imply a moral moral judgement). Everyone in politics—conservatives, libertarians and liberals—is trying in some degree to legislate morality. The complaint then, is not whether or not Congress is attempting to legislate morality, but whose morality is Congress attempting to legislate?

The expectation that Congress will make these moral judgments comes from the Constitution, which decreed that a majority of the citizens, through the representatives elected to do our bidding, were given the right, the duty and responsibility, to make laws that would ensure domestic tranquility, defend our borders, and promote a safe and wholesome environment for us all. These are all moral judgments.

The Constitution also lays out the structure by which these moral judgments will be made. The principle of majority rule, the balance of power between the president, the judiciary, and the Congress, and even the bi-cameral structure of Congress all work to provide an effective mechanism to legislate morality that is consistent with the desires—and therefore we must assume the morals—of a majority of Americans.

The **Drug Enforcement Administration** (DEA) is part of the United States Department of Justice and is charged with enforcing controlled substances laws and regulations and bringing those involved in the growing, manufacture, or distribution of controlled substances to the criminal or civil justice systems. The DEA recommends and supports nonenforcement programs aimed at reducing the availability of illicit controlled substances.

U.S. Department of Health and Human Services

NO

Youth Prevention-Related Measures

The National Survey on Drug Use and Health (NSDUH) includes questions for youths aged 12 to 17 about a number of risk and protective factors that may affect the likelihood that they will engage in substance use. Risk factors are individual characteristics and environmental influences associated with an increased vulnerability to the initiation, continuation, or escalation of substance use. Protective factors include individual resilience and other circumstances that are associated with a reduction in the likelihood of substance use. Risk and protective factors include variables that operate at different stages of development and reflect different domains of influence, including the individual, family, peer, school, community, and societal levels (Hawkins, Catalano, & Miller, 1992; Robertson, David, & Rao, 2003). Interventions to prevent substance use generally are designed to ameliorate the influence of risk factors and enhance the effectiveness of protective factors.

This reading presents findings for youth prevention-related measures collected in the 2009 NSDUH and compares these with findings from previous years. Included are measures of perceived risk from substance use (cigarettes, alcohol, and illicit drugs), perceived availability of substances, being approached by someone selling drugs, perceived parental disapproval of youth substance use, feelings about peer substance use, involvement in fighting and delinquent behavior, participation in religious and other activities, exposure to substance use prevention messages and programs, and parental involvement.

In this reading, rates of substance use are compared for persons responding differently to questions reflecting risk or protective factors, such as the perceived risk of harm from using a substance. Because the NSDUH data for an individual are collected at only one point in time, it is not possible to determine causal connections from these data. However, a number of research studies of youths have shown that reducing risk factors and increasing protective factors can reduce rates of substance use (Botvin, Botvin, & Ruchlin, 1998). This report shows that marijuana, cigarette, and alcohol past month use among youths aged 12 to 17 decreased between 2002 and 2009, yet corresponding changes in individual risk and protective factors for the same period may or may not have occurred. There can be many reasons for this, such as the lack of or a weak causal connection, a lagged relationship between the occurrence of a risk factor and the change in drug use behavior, or that individual use is typically the result of multiple simultaneous risk factors rather than a single factor (Newcomb, Maddahian, & Bentler, 1986).

Perceptions of Risk

One factor that can influence whether youths will use tobacco, alcohol, or illicit drugs is the extent to which youths believe these substances might cause them harm. NSDUH respondents were asked how much they thought people risk harming themselves physically and in other ways when they use various substances in certain amounts or frequencies. Response choices for these items were "great risk," "moderate risk," "slight risk," or "no risk."

- The percentages of youths reporting binge alcohol use and use of cigarettes and marijuana in the past month were lower among those who perceived great risk in using these substances than among those who did not perceive great risk. For example, in 2009, 5.1 percent of youths aged 12 to 17 who perceived great risk from "having five or more drinks of an alcoholic beverage once or twice a week" reported binge drinking in the past month (consumption of five or more drinks of an alcoholic beverage on a single occasion on at least 1 day in the past 30 days); by contrast, past month binge drinking was reported by 11.4 percent of youths who saw moderate, slight, or no risk from having five or more drinks of an alcoholic beverage once or twice a week (Figure 1). Past month marijuana use was reported by 1.3 percent of youths who saw great risk in smoking marijuana once a month compared with 10.1 percent of youths who saw moderate, slight, or no risk.
- Decreases in the rate of current use of a substance often occur when there are increases in the level

Figure 1

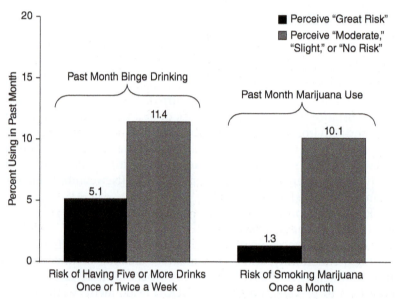

Figure 1

Past Month Binge Drinking and Marijuana Use Among Youths Aged 12 to 17, by Perceptions of Risk: 2009

of perceived risk of using that substance. Looking over the 8-year period, the proportion of youths aged 12 to 17 who reported perceiving great risk from smoking one or more packs of cigarettes per day increased from 63.1 percent in 2002 to 69.7 percent in 2008, but it declined between 2008 and 2009 (65.8 percent) (Figure 2). During the same period, the rate of past month cigarette smoking among youths aged 12 to 17 dropped from 13.0 percent in 2002 to 9.1 percent in 2008, but it remained statistically unchanged between 2008 and 2009 (8.9 percent).

- The percentage of youths aged 12 to 17 indicating great risk in having four or five drinks of an alcoholic beverage nearly every day increased from 62.2 percent in 2002 to 65.9 percent in 2008, but it decreased between 2008 and 2009 (64.3 percent) (Figure 2). The rate of past month heavy alcohol use among youths aged 12 to 17 decreased from 2.5 percent in 2002 to 2.0 percent in 2008, but it remained stable between 2008 and 2009 (2.1 percent).

- The percentage of youths aged 12 to 17 perceiving great risk in having five or more drinks of an alcoholic beverage once or twice a week increased from 38.2 percent in 2002 to 39.9 percent in 2009 (Figure 2). The rate of past month binge alcohol

use among youths decreased from 10.7 percent in 2002 to 8.8 percent in 2009.

- The percentage of youths aged 12 to 17 indicating great risk in smoking marijuana once a month increased from 32.4 percent in 2002 to 34.9 percent in 2003, remained unchanged between 2003 and 2008 (33.9 percent), then decreased to 30.7 percent in 2009 (Figure 3). The rate of youths aged 12 to 17 perceiving great risk in smoking marijuana once or twice a week also increased from 51.5 percent in 2002 to 55.0 percent in 2005, but the rate declined between 2005 and 2009 (49.3 percent). Coincident with trends in perceived great risk of marijuana use, the prevalence of past month marijuana use among youths aged 12 to 17 decreased between 2002 (8.2 percent) and 2005 (6.8 percent), remained level until 2008 (6.7 percent), then increased between 2008 and 2009 (7.3 percent).

- Between 2002 and 2009, the percentage of youths aged 12 to 17 perceiving great risk declined for the following substance use patterns: using heroin once or twice a week (from 82.5 to 81.0 percent), trying heroin once or twice (from 58.5 to 57.0 percent), using cocaine once or twice a week (from 79.8 to 78.5 percent), trying LSD once or twice (from 52.6 to 48.4 percent), and using LSD

Figure 2

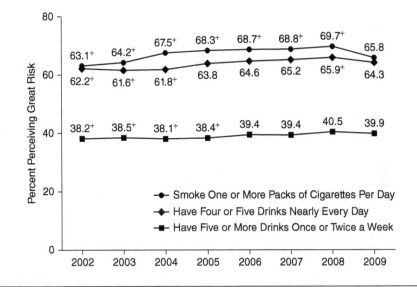

Perceived Great Risk of Cigarette and Alcohol Use Among Youths Aged 12 to 17: 2002–2009

+Difference between this estimate and the 2009 estimate is statistically significant at the .05 level.

Figure 3

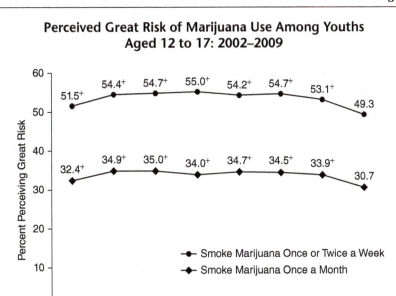

Perceived Great Risk of Marijuana Use Among Youths Aged 12 to 17: 2002–2009

+Difference between this estimate and the 2009 estimate is statistically significant at the .05 level.

Figure 4

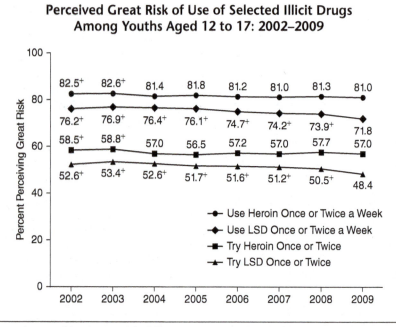

Perceived Great Risk of Use of Selected Illicit Drugs Among Youths Aged 12 to 17: 2002–2009

+Difference between this estimate and the 2009 estimate is statistically significant at the .05 level.

once or twice a week (from 76.2 to 71.8 percent) (Figure 4). However, over the same period there were no statistically significant changes in the percentages of youths aged 12 to 17 indicating great risk for using cocaine once a month (50.5 percent in 2002 and 49.5 percent in 2009). Moreover, percentages for the two heroin and the two cocaine perceptions of risk measures remained stable between 2008 and 2009, while the two LSD measures declined during this time period.

Perceived Availability

- In 2009, about half (49.9 percent) of the youths aged 12 to 17 reported that it would be "fairly easy" or "very easy" for them to obtain marijuana if they wanted some (Figure 5). One in eight (12.9 percent) indicated that heroin would be "fairly" or "very" easily available, and 13.5 percent reported so for LSD. Between 2002 and 2009, there were decreases in the perceived availability of marijuana (from 55.0 to 49.9 percent), cocaine (from 25.0 to 20.9 percent), crack (from 26.5 to 22.1 percent), LSD (from 19.4 to 13.5 percent), and heroin (from 15.8 to 12.9 percent). The perceived availability of cocaine declined from 22.1 percent in 2008 to 20.9 percent in 2009. However, the perceived availability of marijuana, crack, LSD,

and heroin did not change significantly during this 2-year period.
- The percentage of youths who reported that marijuana, cocaine, and LSD would be easy to obtain increased with age in 2009. For example, 19.8 percent of those aged 12 or 13 said it would be fairly or very easy to obtain marijuana compared with 52.9 percent of those aged 14 or 15 and 72.2 percent of those aged 16 or 17.
- In 2009, 14.3 percent of youths aged 12 to 17 indicated that they had been approached by someone selling drugs in the past month, which was down from the 16.7 percent reported in 2002 (Figure 6). The rate remained stable between 2008 (13.7 percent) and 2009.

Perceived Parental Disapproval of Substance Use

- Most youths aged 12 to 17 believed their parents would "strongly disapprove" of their using substances. In 2009, 90.5 percent of youths reported that their parents would strongly disapprove of their trying marijuana or hashish once or twice; this was similar to the 90.8 percent reported in 2008, but was higher than the 89.1 percent reported in 2002. Most (90.3 percent) reported that

Figure 5

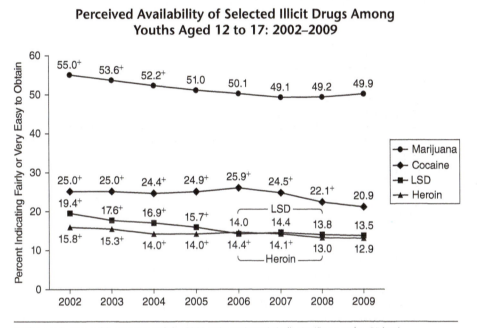

Perceived Availability of Selected Illicit Drugs Among Youths Aged 12 to 17: 2002–2009

+Difference between this estimate and the 2009 estimate is statistically significant at the .05 level.

Figure 6

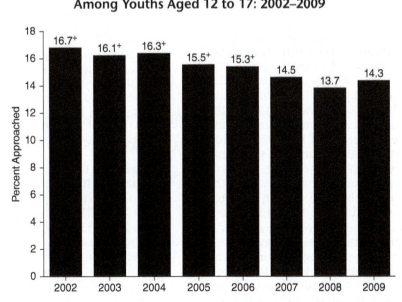

Approached in the Past Month by Someone Selling Drugs Among Youths Aged 12 to 17: 2002–2009

+Difference between this estimate and the 2009 estimate is statistically significant at the .05 level.

their parents would strongly disapprove of their having one or two drinks of an alcoholic beverage nearly every day, which was similar to the rate in 2008 (89.7 percent) and was higher than the rate in 2002 (89.0 percent). In 2009, 92.6 percent of youths reported that their parents would strongly disapprove of their smoking one or more packs of cigarettes per day, which was similar to the 92.4 percent reported in 2008, but was higher than the 89.5 percent reported in 2002.

- Youths aged 12 to 17 who believed their parents would strongly disapprove of their using substances were less likely to use that substance than were youths who believed their parents would somewhat disapprove or neither approve nor disapprove. For example, in 2009, past month cigarette use was reported by 6.5 percent of youths who perceived strong parental disapproval of their smoking one or more packs of cigarettes per day compared with 40.5 percent of youths who believed their parents would not strongly disapprove. Past month marijuana use also was much less prevalent among youths who perceived strong parental disapproval for trying marijuana or hashish once or twice than among those who did not (4.8 vs. 31.3 percent, respectively).

Feelings About Peer Substance Use

- A majority of youths aged 12 to 17 reported that they disapprove of their peers using substances. In 2009, 90.1 percent of youths "strongly" or "somewhat" disapproved of their peers smoking one or more packs of cigarettes per day, which was similar to the rate of 89.6 percent in 2008, but higher than the 87.1 percent in 2002. Also in 2009, 82.0 percent strongly or somewhat disapproved of peers using marijuana or hashish once a month or more, which was similar to the 82.7 percent reported in 2008, but was an increase from the 80.4 percent reported in 2002. In addition, 87.4 percent of youths strongly or somewhat disapproved of peers having one or two drinks of an alcoholic beverage nearly every day in 2009, which was similar to the 87.0 percent reported in 2008, but was higher than the 84.7 percent reported in 2002.

- In 2009, past month marijuana use was reported by 2.6 percent among youths aged 12 to 17 who strongly or somewhat disapproved of their peers using marijuana once a month or more, lower than the 28.7 percent among youths who reported that they neither approve nor disapprove of such behavior from their peers.

Fighting and Delinquent Behavior

- In 2009, 21.1 percent of youths aged 12 to 17 reported that, in the past year, they had gotten into a serious fight at school or at work; this was similar to the rates in 2008 (21.4 percent) and 2002 (20.6 percent). Approximately one in seven youths (14.4 percent) in 2009 had taken part in a group-against-group fight, which was similar to the rate in 2008 (14.5 percent) and lower than the rate in 2002 (15.9 percent). About 1 in 30 (3.2 percent) had carried a handgun at least once in 2009, which was the same as the rate in 2008 (3.2 percent) and was similar to the rate in 2002 (3.3 percent). An estimated 7.2 percent had, in at least one instance, attacked others with the intent to harm or seriously hurt them in 2009, which was the similar to the rate in 2008 (7.3 percent) and was similar to the 7.8 percent reported in 2002. An estimated 3.2 percent had sold illegal drugs in 2009, which was similar to the rate of 3.0 percent in 2008, but was lower than the 4.4 percent rate in 2002. In 2009, 4.4 percent had, at least once, stolen or tried to steal something worth more than $50; this was similar to the rate of 4.6 percent in 2008, but was lower than the rate of 4.9 percent in 2002.

- Youths aged 12 to 17 who had engaged in fighting or other delinquent behaviors were more likely than other youths to have used illicit drugs in the past month. For example, in 2009, past month illicit drug use was reported by 18.8 percent of youths who had gotten into a serious fight at school or work in the past year compared with 7.7 percent of those who had not engaged in fighting, and by 38.3 percent of those who had stolen or tried to steal something worth over $50 in the past year compared with 8.7 percent of those who had not attempted or engaged in such theft.

Religious Beliefs and Participation in Activities

- In 2009, 31.4 percent of youths aged 12 to 17 reported that they had attended religious services 25 or more times in the past year, which was similar to the rate in 2008 (31.7 percent), but was lower than the rate in 2002 (33.0 percent). Also, 74.7 percent agreed or strongly agreed with the statement that religious beliefs are a very important part of their lives, which was similar to the 75.0 percent reported in 2008, but was lower than the 78.2 percent reported in 2002. In 2009, 34.0 percent agreed or strongly agreed with the statement that it is important for their friends to share their religious beliefs, which was similar to the rate in 2008 (33.8 percent) and was lower than the rate in 2002 (35.8 percent).

- The rates of past month use of illicit drugs, cigarettes, and alcohol (including binge alcohol) were lower among youths aged 12 to 17 who agreed with these statements about religious beliefs than among those who disagreed. For example, in 2009, past month illicit drug use was reported by 7.4 percent of those who agreed that religious beliefs are a very important part of life compared with 17.6 percent of those who disagreed with that statement.

Exposure to Substance Use Prevention Messages and Programs

- In 2009, approximately one in eight youths aged 12 to 17 (12.0 percent) reported that they had participated in drug, tobacco, or alcohol prevention programs outside of school in the past year. This rate was higher than the 11.1 percent reported in 2008, but was similar to the rate reported in 2002 (12.7 percent) and lower than the rate reported in 2003 (13.9 percent). In 2009, the prevalence of past month use of illicit drugs, marijuana, or

cigarettes or past month binge alcohol use among those who participated in these prevention programs outside of school was not significantly different (10.5, 6.9, 8.9, or 8.1 percent, respectively) from the prevalence among those who did not (10.0, 7.4, 8.9, or 8.9 percent, respectively).

- In 2009, 77.0 percent of youths aged 12 to 17 reported having seen or heard drug or alcohol prevention messages in the past year from sources outside of school, which was similar to the 78.0 percent reported in 2008, but was lower than the 83.2 percent reported in 2002 (Figure 7). In 2009, the prevalence of past month use of illicit drugs was lower among those who reported having such exposure (9.7 percent) than among those who reported having no such exposure (11.3 percent).

- In 2009, 74.9 percent of youths aged 12 to 17 enrolled in school in the past year reported having seen or heard drug or alcohol prevention messages at school, which was similar to the 75.9 percent reported in 2008, but was lower than the 78.8 percent reported in 2002 (Figure 7). In 2009, the prevalence of past month use of illicit drugs or marijuana was lower among those who reported having such exposure (9.2 and 6.7 percent for illicit

Figure 7

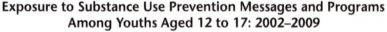

Exposure to Substance Use Prevention Messages and Programs Among Youths Aged 12 to 17: 2002–2009

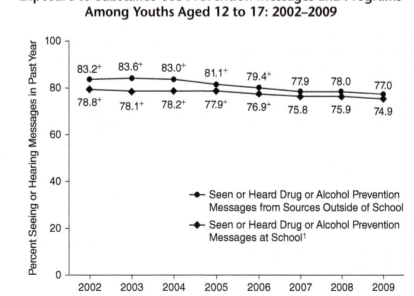

⁺Difference between this estimate and the 2009 estimate is statistically significant at the .05 level.
¹Estimates are from youths aged 12 to 17 who were enrolled in school in the past year.

drugs and marijuana, respectively) than among those who reported having no such exposure (12.7 and 9.7 percent, respectively).

- In 2009, 58.2 percent of youths aged 12 to 17 reported that in the past year they had talked at least once with at least one of their parents about the dangers of drug, tobacco, or alcohol use, which was similar to rates reported in 2008 (58.7 percent) and 2002 (58.1 percent). The prevalence of past month use of illicit drugs, marijuana, or cigarettes or past month binge alcohol use among those who reported having had such conversations with their parents (9.8, 7.3, 8.6, and 8.7 percent, respectively) was not significantly different from that among those who reported having no such conversations (10.4, 7.4, 9.4, and 9.1 percent, respectively).

Parental Involvement

- Youths aged 12 to 17 were asked a number of questions related to the extent of support, oversight, and control that they perceived their parents exercised over them in the year prior to the survey. In 2009, among youths aged 12 to 17 enrolled in school in the past year, 79.8 percent reported that in the past year their parents always or sometimes checked on whether or not they had completed their homework, and 70.6 percent reported that their parents limited the amount of time that they spent out with friends on school nights. Both of these rates reported in 2009 were similar to those reported in 2008 and remained statistically unchanged from the rates reported in 2002. However, in 2009, 79.9 percent reported that their parents always or sometimes provided help with their homework, which was similar to the rate in 2008 (80.0 percent), but was lower than the rate in 2002 (81.4 percent).

- In 2009, 87.4 percent of youths aged 12 to 17 reported that in the past year their parents made them always or sometimes do chores around the house, 85.7 percent reported that their parents always or sometimes let them know that they had done a good job, and 85.4 percent reported that their parents let them know they were proud of something they had done. All of these percentages in 2009 were similar to those reported in 2008 and remained statistically unchanged from the rates reported in 2002. In 2009, however, 40.1 percent of youths reported that their parents limited the amount of time that they watched television, which was similar to the rate in 2008 (39.9 percent), but was higher than the 36.9 percent reported in 2002.

- In 2009, past month use of illicit drugs, cigarettes, and alcohol (including binge alcohol) was lower among youths aged 12 to 17 who reported that their parents always or sometimes engaged in monitoring behaviors than among youths whose parents "seldom" or "never" engaged in such behaviors. For example, the rate of past month use of any illicit drug was 8.2 percent for youths whose parents always or sometimes helped with homework compared with 17.5 percent among youths who indicated that their parents seldom or never helped. Rates of current cigarette smoking and past month binge alcohol use were also lower among youths whose parents always or sometimes helped with homework (7.5 and 7.4 percent, respectively) than among youths whose parents did not (15.7 and 15.6 percent, respectively).

The mission of the **U.S. DEPARTMENT OF HEALTH & HUMAN SERVICES** is to enhance and protect the health and well-being of all Americans. It fulfills that mission by providing for effective health and human services and fostering advances in medicine, public health, and social services.

EXPLORING THE ISSUE

Should Laws Against Drug Use Remain Restrictive?

Critical Thinking and Reflection

1. Is it possible to create a "drug free society"?
2. What are the varied reasons why individuals use drugs? Which factors are more or less important? Which would be most critical to decrease rates of drug addiction?
3. What are the potential benefits and risks of legalization and/or decriminalization of specific drugs (e.g., marijuana and hallucinogens) that affect your community?
4. How does the legal status of tobacco and alcohol compare to the status of "harder" drugs, like marijuana, LSD, and cocaine? What is the impact of drug laws on their rates of use and perception by society?
5. What changes would you recommend at the federal, state, or local level to drug laws?

Is There Common Ground?

The decriminalization and legalization of marijuana is a rapidly-changing and controversial issue in the United States at the federal, state, and local level. The laws and enforcement of the laws are rapidly changing and there can be strong inconsistencies when traveling from one town to the next. There can be inconsistencies within a community when local versus national laws are applied. However, there are many drugs, such as cocaine, methamphetamine, and heroin, where there is little debate on decriminalization and legalization. How does the criminal justice system address these?

Many communities are adopting a drug court program, where the criminal justice system works closely with substance abuse treatment and social welfare programs. The overall goal is to divert individuals addicted to drugs into treatment and rehabilitation programs, rather than into jails and prisons. In a typical drug court program, the district attorney, the individual's attorney or public defender, the probation department, and an addiction health specialist collaborate. They determine if treatment is preferred over incarceration, and then what type of treatment is needed. Overall, those participating in drug court programs have lower rates of re-arrest than those in the traditional court system. In addition, drug court programs can save communities money, as they are more cost-effective than traditional incarceration in jails and prisons.

Additional Resources

Cheney-Rice, Z. (2015). 4/20 Is Over, and America's Weed Laws Are Still Racist as Hell. *Mic.* http://mic.com/articles/115932/420-is-over-weed-laws-are-still-racist-as-hell.

Author Zac Cheney-Rice describes marijuana laws in the United States and their disparate impact on minority groups.

Davis C.S., et al. (2014). Attitudes of North Carolina law enforcement officers toward syringe decriminalization. *Drug and Alcohol Dependence.* 144: 265-269.

North Carolina is disproportionately affected by HIV and hepatitis. This persistently high disease burden may be driven in part by laws that criminalize the possession and distribution of syringes for illicit drug use. Researchers from the University of North Carolina discuss how law enforcement officers view syringe control policies and disease.

Hartnett, E. (2005). Drug Legalization: Why It Wouldn't Work in the United States. The Police Chief: The Professional Voice of Law Enforcement. http://www.policechiefmagazine.org/magazine/index.cfm?fuseaction=display_arch&article_id=533&issue_id=32005.

Edmund Hartnett, Deputy Chief and Executive Officer, Narcotics Division, New York City Police Department, New York, argues against drug legalization in the United States from a law enforcement perspective.

Kilmer, P. (2014). Policy designs for cannabis legalization: Starting with the eight Ps. *American Journal of Drug and Alcohol Abuse.* 40(4): 259-261.

The author discusses the policy landscape for drug legalization and indicates any policy should address the eight Ps—production, profit motive, promotion, prevention, potency, purity, price, and permanency.

Ostrowski, J. (1989). Policy Analysis 121: Thinking about Drug Legalization. CATO Institute. http://www.cato.org/publications/policy-analysis/thinking-about-drug-legalization.

The author from the libertarian Cato Institute argues in favor of drug decriminalization as, "there can be little doubt that most, if not all, 'drug-related murders' are the result of drug prohibition."

Internet References . . .

The Drug Policy Alliance

http://www.drugpolicy.org/

National Alliance for Model State Drug Laws

http://www.namsdl.org/

Office of National Drug Control Policy

https://www.whitehouse.gov/ondcp/

United States Department of Health and Human Services

http://www.hhs.gov/

US Department of Justice—Drug Enforcement Administration

http://www.dea.gov

Selected, Edited, and with Issue Framing Material by:
Dennis K. Miller, *University of Missouri*

ISSUE

Should the United States Put More Emphasis on Stopping the Importation of Drugs?

YES: Bureau of International Narcotics and Law Enforcement Affairs, from "2009 INCSR: Policy and Program Developments," (U.S. Department of State, 2009)

NO: Ethan Nadelmann, from "The Global War on Drugs Can Be Won," *Foreign Policy* (2007)

Learning Outcomes
After reading this issue, you will be able to: • Describe the varied approaches used to smuggle drugs, such as cocaine, cannabis, and heroin, into the United States.   • Explain the different approaches taken by government agencies to limit drug trafficking into the United States.   • Critically evaluate the effectiveness of anti-trafficking policies.   • Describe the relationship, if any, between drug availability and rates of drug use.   • Evaluate the efficacy of the "war on drugs" and areas where it has been successful and unsuccessful.

ISSUE SUMMARY

YES: The U.S. State Department maintains that more effort is needed to interdict drugs coming into the United States because the trafficking of drugs represents a direct threat to national security. Better cooperation with countries in Latin America, the Caribbean, Africa, and Asia, where drugs are grown and exported, is essential.

NO: Ethan Nadelmann, the executive director of the Drug Policy Alliance, contends that attempts to stem the flow of drugs are futile and that it is unrealistic to believe that the world can be made free of drugs. Nadelmann points out that global production is about the same as it was 10 years earlier and that cocaine and heroin are purer and cheaper because producers have become more efficient

The Drug Enforcement Administration (DEA) is charged with enforcing the controlled substances laws and regulations of the United States, bringing those involved in the illegal growing, manufacture, or distribution of controlled substances to the criminal and civil justice system, and supporting nonenforcement programs aimed at reducing the availability of illicit controlled substances. In 2015 its annual budget was $2.88 billion and it employs over 9,200 men and women. Over the past five years the DEA has averaged over 30,000 domestic arrests annually and has seized tons of cocaine, heroin, marijuana, methamphetamine, and hallucinogens. The DEA is on the front line of the "war on drugs."

Interdiction efforts, such as those supported and enforced by the DEA, have not proven to be successful in slowing the flow of drugs into the United States. Drugs continue to cross borders at record levels. This may signal a need for stepped-up international efforts to stop the production and trafficking of drugs. It may also signal the inadequacy of the current strategy. Should the position of the government be to improve and strengthen current measures or to try an entirely new approach?

Some people contend that rather than attempting to limit illegal drugs from coming into the United States, more effort should be directed at reducing the demand for drugs and improving treatment for drug abusers. Foreign countries would not produce and transport drugs like heroin and cocaine into the United States if there was no market for them. Drug policies, some people maintain, should be aimed at the social and economic conditions underlying domestic drug problems, not at interfering with foreign governments.

Many U.S. government officials believe that other countries should assist in stopping the flow of drugs across their borders. Diminishing the supply of drugs by intercepting them before they reach the user is another way to eliminate or curtail drug use. Critical elements in the lucrative drug trade are multinational crime syndicates. One premise is that if the drug production, transportation, distribution, and processing functions as well as the money laundering operations of these criminal organizations can be interrupted and eventually crippled, then the drug problem would abate.

In South American countries, such as Peru, Colombia, and Boliva, where coca—from which cocaine is processed—is cultivated, economic aid has been made available to help the governments of these countries fight the cocaine kingpins. An alleged problem is that a number of government officials in these countries are corrupt or fearful of the cocaine cartel leaders. One proposed solution is to go directly to the farmers and offer them money to plant crops other than coca. This tactic, however, failed in the mid-1970s, when the U.S. government gave money to farmers in Turkey to stop growing opium poppy crops. After one year the program was discontinued due to the enormous expense, and opium poppy crops were once again planted.

There are many reasons why people are dissatisfied with the current state of the war on drugs. For example, in the war on drugs, the casual user is generally the primary focus of drug use deterrence. This is viewed by many people as a form of discrimination because a vast majority of drug users and sellers who are arrested and prosecuted are poor, members of minorities, homeless, unemployed, and/or disenfranchised. Also, international drug dealers who are arrested are usually not the drug bosses but lower-level people working for them. Finally, some argue that the war on drugs should be redirected away from interdiction and enforcement because they feel that the worst drug problems in society today are caused by legal drugs, primarily alcohol and tobacco.

The drug trade spawns violence: People die from using drugs or by dealing with people in the drug trade; families are ruined by the effects of drugs on family members; prisons are filled with tens of thousands of people who were and probably still are involved with illegal drugs; and drugs can devastate aspirations and careers. The adverse consequences of drugs can be seen everywhere in society. How should the government determine the best course of action to follow in remedying the negative effects of drugs? Would more people be helped by reducing the availability of drugs, or would more people benefit if they could be persuaded that drugs are harmful to them?

Two paths that are traditionally followed involve reducing either the supply of drugs or the demand for drugs. Four major agencies involved in the fight against drugs in the United States—the DEA, the Federal Bureau of Investigation (FBI), the U.S. Customs Service, and the U.S. Coast Guard—have seized thousands of pounds of marijuana, cocaine, and heroin during the past few years. Drug interdiction appears to be reducing the availability of drugs. But what effect does drug availability have on its use? If a particular drug is not available, would other drugs be used in its place? Would the cost of drugs increase if there were a shortage of drugs? If costs increase, would violence due to drugs go up as well?

This issue addresses whether or not the war on drugs should be fought on an international level. The U.S. Department of State takes the view that international cooperation is absolutely necessary if we are to stem the flow of drugs and reduce drug-related problems in the United States. Ethan Nadelmann argues that an international approach to dealing with drugs has been ineffective because the production of drugs has not been curtailed.

YES ↵

**Bureau of International Narcotics
and Law Enforcement Affairs**

2009 INCSR: Policy and Program Developments

Overview for 2008

International narcotics trafficking directly threatens the national security of the United States. Drugs sold on U.S. streets lead to overdose deaths and ruined lives, erode families, and foster criminality and violence. Trafficking organizations, looking to build their customer base, sometimes pay in drugs instead of cash, promoting drug abuse and its social consequences in source and transit countries in Latin America, the Caribbean, Africa, and Asia. Many of these same countries are besieged by narcotics criminals who corrupt and financially undermine legitimate law enforcement and government institutions. The environment is equally threatened, as drug producers hack down forests and dump toxic chemicals in fragile ecosystems.

The United States Government (USG) confronts the threat of international narcotics trafficking through a combination of law enforcement investigation, interdiction, diplomatic initiatives, targeted economic sanctions, financial programs and investigations, and institutional development initiatives focused on disrupting all segments of the illicit drug market, from the fields and clandestine laboratories where drugs are produced, through the transit zones, to our ports and borders. In 2008, U.S. federal law enforcement officials worked cooperatively with the police of partner nations to conduct international investigations that successfully apprehended, among others, Zhenli Ye Gon, Eduardo Arellano Felix, and Haji Juma Khan. Another international law enforcement operation involving the DEA, the Royal Thai Police, the Romanian Border Police, the Korps Politie Curacao of the Netherlands Antilles, and the Danish National Police Security Services led to the arrest of Victor Bout on charges of attempting to provide sophisticated weapons to the narco-terrorist organization the Fuerzas Armadas Revolucionarias de Colombia.[1]

The USG continued to provide partner nations with essential training assistance to strengthen their law enforcement and judicial systems and helped them improve their capacity to investigate, prosecute, and punish transnational criminal activity. Closer international cooperation among governments and financial institutions continues to close the loopholes that allow narcotrafficking organizations to legitimize their enormous profits through sophisticated money laundering schemes.

Much of our cooperation with partner nations occurred under bilateral arrangements for mutual legal assistance, extraditions, and training programs. Multilateral efforts also continued to be a key component of the overall U.S. counternarcotics strategy. Through multilateral organizations, the United States has the opportunity to encourage contributions from other donors so that we can undertake counternarcotics assistance programs, jointly sharing costs and expertise. U.S. participation in multilateral programs also supports indigenous capabilities in regions where the United States is unable to operate bilaterally for political or logistical reasons. Counternarcotics assistance through international organizations promotes awareness that drug producing and transit countries inevitably become consuming nations; today it is clearly understood that drugs are not a U.S. problem, but a global challenge.

One example of working with partner donors is the Good Performers Initiative (GPI) in Afghanistan, a U.S.-UK-funded initiative launched in 2006 to reward provinces for successful counternarcotics performance. Based on the results of the UN Office on Drugs and Crime's annual Afghanistan Opium Cultivation Survey, this incentive program provides funds for development projects to provinces that were poppy-free or reduced their poppy cultivation by more than 10 percent from the previous year. In 2008, 29 of Afghanistan's 34 provinces qualified for over $39 million in GPI development assistance projects. To date, the U.S. government has contributed over $69 million to GPI and its predecessor the Good Performer's Fund, while the UK has provided approximately

From *2009 INCSR Report: Policy and Program Developments*, 2009. Published by Bureau of International Narcotics and Law Enforcement Affairs, U.S. Department of State.

$12 million. In Nangarhar province, for example, four micro-hydro projects that generate electricity for rural villages have been completed with these funds and 20 more are scheduled to be built in 2009.

International treaties are another key tool in the fight against international narcotics trafficking. Three mutually reinforcing UN conventions are particularly important:

- The Single Convention on Narcotic Drugs—1961
- The Convention on Psychotropic Substances—1971, and
- The United Nations Convention against Illicit Traffic in Narcotic Drugs and Psychotropic Substances (the "1988 UN Drug Convention")

The 1988 UN Drug Convention is nearly universally accepted and serves as one of the bases for this report (For a full explanation, see the chapter titled "Legislative Basis for the INCSR"). A list of the countries that are parties to the 1988 UN Drug Convention is included in this report (source: UNODC). In 2008, there were no additional parties to the 1988 UN Drug Convention. Although the Convention does not contain a list of goals and objectives, it does set forth a number of obligations that the parties agree to undertake. Generally speaking, it requires the parties to take legal measures to outlaw and punish all forms of illicit drug production, trafficking, and drug money laundering; to control chemicals that can be used to process illicit drugs; and to cooperate in international efforts to these ends.

In addition to the UN conventions that are focused exclusively on drugs, newer international instruments, such as the United Nations Convention against Transnational Organized Crime and the United Nations Convention against Corruption, have helped in the fight against the international narcotics trade by making law enforcement cooperation, extraditions, border security, and tracking of illicit funds more efficient among the parties to the treaties.

While most countries are parties to the UN conventions, the ultimate success of international drug control efforts does not hinge completely on whether countries are parties to them. The vast majority of countries also have their own domestic laws and policies to support their obligations under the conventions. Success in international drug control depends on international political will to meet the commitments made when countries joined the UN conventions. Sustainable progress also requires sufficient capacities to enforce the rule of law and implementing the objectives of committed governments. To assist this process, the United States is committed to enhancing the capacity of partner governments to uphold their international commitments.

Controlling Supply

Cocaine, amphetamine-type stimulants (ATS), marijuana, and heroin are the internationally trafficked drugs that most threaten the United States and our international allies. The United States is a producer of two of these drugs, marijuana and ATS. The USG is committed to confronting the illicit cultivation and manufacture of these drugs. In 2007, the DEA-initiated Domestic Cannabis Eradication/Suppression Program was responsible for the eradication of 6,600,000 cultivated outdoor cannabis plants and 430,000 indoor plants. In 2008, California alone eradicated 5,250,000 plants. Pharmaceutical preparations containing ephedrine and pseudoephedrine are the primary chemicals necessary for methamphetamine production. The Combat Methamphetamine Epidemic Act (CMEA), passed in 2005, established regulations for the sale of such products in the United States and became effective at the national level for the first time in late 2006. In 2008, the Methamphetamine Production Prevention Act was passed allowing states to institute computerized log books of purchases of methamphetamine precursor preparations. According to the National Clandestine Laboratory Database, methamphetamine lab incidents reported by all law enforcement agencies nationwide declined from more than 17,000 in 2005 to 5,900 in 2007 (2007 is the last complete year for which there are statistics, preliminary 2008 statistics are discussed later in this chapter, but the number in 2008 is expected to remain well below 50% of the 2005 figure). This dramatic decline is due to increased enforcement, the controls authorized by the two recent methamphetamine acts, and public and private demand reduction efforts.

In addition to eradicating marijuana crops found within the United States as part of our drug control strategy, the USG has provided assistance to countries that have made a policy decision to eradicate illicit crops as part of their own comprehensive drug control strategies. Crops in the ground are one of the critical nodes of production. Coca and poppy crops require adequate growing conditions, ample land, and time to reach maturity, all of which make them vulnerable to detection and eradication.

Perhaps the most acute and crucial challenge of achieving sustainable development in territories where drug cultivation takes place is the need to integrate otherwise marginalized regions into the economic and political mainstream of their country. The term that is most often used for this by the United States, the United Nations, and other international actors is "alternative development." Alternative development goes far beyond crop substitution, the usual assumed meaning. In some situations, crop substitution is neither feasible nor desirable. In some areas, the same soil that supports illicit drug crop cultivation does not have adequate nutrients to support licit crops. Licit crops rarely produce the same income as drug crops, and in some cases, farmers will need inducement to pursue non-agricultural pursuits. Anecdotal evidence suggests that in 2008 economic and environmental inducements caused many farmers in Afghanistan to plant wheat instead of poppy. One factor that possibly influenced this shift was the rise in global food prices, making wheat a more viable economic alternative to poppy. Other powerful inducements could include access to credit, improved security, and the provision of government services such as the building of roads, schools, and health centers, and a reliable supplying of basic services like electricity and water, and the threat of losing an investment in illicit crops to eradication or asset forfeiture. These programs are vulnerable to disruption from crime, corruption and non-state actors, such as the FARC in Colombia or the Taliban in Afghanistan. Establishing them on the ground is a lengthy, sometimes frustrating process; however, if implemented correctly, alternative development is an effective policy. Without it, crop eradication alone will never amount to more than a temporary palliative, and will not achieve sustainable reduction of illicit narcotic crops. However, without security and government control of outlaw areas, neither program can succeed.

For synthetic drugs, such as ATS, physical eradication is impossible. Instead, the United States and our allies must create a legal regime of chemical controls and law enforcement efforts aimed at thwarting those who divert key chemicals, and destroying the laboratories needed to create ATS. As with our domestic enforcement efforts, our international programs focus on all the links in the supply-to-consumer chain: processing, distribution, and transportation, as well as the money trail left by this illegal trade.

Cocaine

The rate of U.S. cocaine consumption has generally declined over the past decade. From 2002 to 2007, rates of past-year use among youths aged 12 to 17 declined significantly for cocaine as well as for illicit drugs overall (Source: SAMHSA, Office of Applied Studies, National Survey on Drug Use and Health). Despite the declines, cocaine continues to be a major domestic concern. Internationally, cocaine continues to pose considerable risk to societies in

the Americas, and increasingly to fragile transit states in West Africa. The 2008 World Drug Report by the UN Office of Drugs and Crime noted, as it has in previous years, that the decline in cocaine consumption and demand in North America has been replaced by demand in Europe. The UN report is hopeful that demand in Europe is leveling off, but notes that, "the growth in markets which are either close to source (South America) or on emerging trafficking routes (Africa) indicate that further containment is still a challenge."

Since all cocaine originates in the Andean countries of Colombia, Peru, and Bolivia, the U.S. Government provides assistance to help these countries develop and implement comprehensive strategies to reduce the growing of coca, processing coca into cocaine, abuse of cocaine within their borders, and illegal transport of cocaine to other countries.

Coca Eradication/Alternative Development: The 2008 Interagency Assessment of Cocaine Movement (IACM) estimates that between 500 and 700 metric tons (MT) of cocaine departed South America toward the United States in 2007, slightly less than the previous year's estimate of 510 to 730 metric tons. We support efforts by these governments to eliminate illegal coca. Alternative development programs offer farmers opportunities to abandon illegal activities and join the legitimate economy, a key tool for countries seeking to free their agricultural sector from reliance on the drug trade. In the Andean countries, such programs play a vital role in providing funds and technical assistance to strengthen public and private institutions, expand rural infrastructure, improve natural resources management, introduce alternative legal crops, and develop local and international markets for these products.

In Colombia, USG alternative development (AD) initiatives supported the cultivation of over 238,000 hectares of legal crops and completed 1,212 social and productive infrastructure projects in the last seven years. More than 291,000 families in 18 departments have benefited from these programs, and the USG has worked with Colombia's private sector to create an additional 273,000 full-time equivalent jobs.

At the close of the sixth year of the Peru alternative development program, more than 756 communities have renounced coca cultivation and over 49,000 family farmers have received technical assistance on 61,000 hectares of licit crops (cacao, coffee, African palm oil, etc.). With many of these long-term crops now entering their most productive years, the alternative development program has expanded business development activities to link AD producers to local and world markets at optimum prices.

The direct link between AD and eradication is successfully reducing coca cultivation and is a model for further progress against illicit cultivation.

In 2008, the annual value of USAID-promoted exports reached almost $35 million in Bolivia, assistance to farm communities and businesses helped generate 5,459 new jobs, new sales of AD products of nearly $28 million, and approximately 717 kilometers of roads were improved and 16 bridges constructed. However, these cooperative efforts were overshadowed by the Government of Bolivia's (GOB) ousting of USAID from the Chapare region.

The government of Colombia dedicates significant resources to reduce coca growing and cocaine production; however, its large territory and ideal climate conditions make Colombia the source of roughly 60 percent of the cocaine produced in the region and around 90 percent of the cocaine destined for the United States, with Peru and Bolivia a distant second and third respectively.

In 2008, the Colombian National Police (CNP) Anti-Narcotics Directorate reported aerial spraying of over 130,000 hectares of coca and manually eradicating over 96,000 hectares despite entrenched armed resistance by the FARC, a drug-trafficking organization that is also a designated Foreign Terrorist Organization. If harvested and refined, this eradicated coca could have yielded hundreds of metric tons of cocaine worth billions of dollars on U.S. streets.

In 2008, Peru exceeded its eradication goals for the second year in a row by eradicating more than 10,000 hectares. This success was achieved despite the continued targeting of eradication teams by the Shining Path, a designated Foreign Terrorist Organization (FTO). The Shining Path, which is reliant on drug trafficking for its funding, was reportedly responsible for attacks on police and military personnel in the Upper Huallaga Valley (UHV) and the Apurimac and Ene River Valleys and threatened eradication workers and other government authorities and alternative development teams. Coca growers in the UHV engaged in violent acts to resist eradication.

Bolivian President Evo Morales continued to promote his policy of "zero cocaine but not zero coca" and to push for legitimization of coca. His administration continues to pursue policies that would increase government-allowed coca cultivation from 12,000 to 20,000 hectares—a change that would violate current Bolivian law and contravene the 1988 UN Drug Convention, to which Bolivia is a party. On September 11, 2008, President Morales expelled the U.S. Ambassador to Bolivia. During 2008, President Morales also expelled the Drug Enforcement Administration (DEA) from Bolivia and the U.S. Agency for International Development from the coca-growing Chapare region. Coupled with continued increases in coca cultivation, cocaine production, and the Government of Bolivia's (GOB) unwillingness to regulate "licit" coca markets, President Bush determined on September 15 that Bolivia had "failed demonstrably" in meeting its international counterdrug obligations. For greater detail see the memorandum of justification in this report.

Cocaine Seizures: Colombian authorities reported seizing over 223 metric tons of cocaine in 2008, an all-time record, and destroyed 301 cocaine HCl labs and 3,238 cocaine base labs. Peru reported seizing over 22 metric tons of cocaine. In Bolivia, USG-supported counternarcotics units reported seizing 26 metric tons of cocaine base and cocaine hydrochloride (HCl) and destroying 6,535 cocaine labs and maceration pits.

Collectively, the eradication of coca and seizures of cocaine within the Andean source countries prevented hundreds of metric tons of cocaine from reaching U.S. streets and deprived international drug syndicates of billions of dollars in profits.

Interdiction in the Cocaine Transit Zone: The cocaine transit zone drug flow is of double importance for the United States: it threatens our borders, and it leaves a trail of corruption and addiction in its wake that undermines the social framework of societies in Central America, Mexico and the Caribbean. Helping our neighbors police transit zones has required a well-coordinated effort among the governments of the transit zone countries and the USG. With high levels of post-seizure intelligence collection, and cooperation with allied nations, we now have more actionable intelligence within the transit zone.

The U.S. Joint Inter-Agency Task Force—South (JIATF-S), working closely with international partners from throughout the Caribbean Basin, has focused its and regional partners' intelligence gathering efforts to detect, monitor, and seize maritime drug shipments. The USG's bilateral agreements with Caribbean and Latin American countries have eased the burden on these countries by allowing the United States to conduct boardings and search for contraband on their behalf. They also allow the USG to gain jurisdiction over cases, removing the coercive pressure from large drug trafficking organizations on some foreign governments.

Mexican law enforcement reported seizing 19 metric tons (MT) of cocaine in 2008.

Venezuela reported seizures of over 54 metric tons of cocaine in 2008. However, the Government of Venezuela does not allow the USG to confirm its seizures, and these figures include seizures made by other countries in international waters that were subsequently returned to Venezuela, the country of origin. According to the U.S.

government's Consolidated Counterdrug Database, 239 non-commercial cocaine flights departed Venezuela in 2008, some bound for Caribbean islands in route to major markets.

Dominican authorities seized approximately 2.4 metric tons of cocaine. There was a fifteen percent increase in drug smuggling flights to Haiti in 2008. While Haitian law enforcement units worked to improve their response to air smuggling of cocaine, the seizure and arrest results were limited.

West Africa has become a hub for cocaine trafficking from South America to Europe. Although according the UNODC's 2008 *World Drug Report,* Africa accounts for less than 2 percent of global cocaine seizures, this number is expected to rise in future years. Seizures of cocaine in Africa reached 15 MT in 2006, but were below 1 MT between 1998 and 2002. Out of the total number of cocaine seizures made in Europe in 2007 (where the 'origin' had been identified), 22% were smuggled via Africa, up from 12% in 2006 and 5% in 2004. This onslaught is due to more effective interdiction along traditional trafficking routes, and the convenient location of West Africa between Andean cocaine suppliers and European consumers. It also reflects the vulnerability of West African countries to transnational organized crime.

Synthetic Drugs

Amphetamine-Type Stimulants (ATS): Abuse and trafficking in highly addictive amphetamine-type stimulants (ATS) remain among the more serious challenges in the drug-control arena. The 2008 edition of the UN Office of Drugs and Crime's World Drug Report notes that a stabilization in the ATS market over the past three years appears to have occurred in parallel with the implementation of precursor control programs and prevention programs. The report states that ATS abuse has decreased in the United States and increases in consumption have slowed in some other markets, such as Europe and Asia. Consumption, however, has increased in the Middle East and Africa.

Methamphetamine production and distribution are undergoing significant changes in the United States. The number of reported methamphetamine laboratory seizures in the United States decreased each year from 2004 through 2007; however, preliminary 2008 data and reporting indicate that domestic methamphetamine production, while still well below its peak, is increasing in some areas, and laboratory seizures for 2008 outpaced seizures in 2007. The pattern of decreased lab presence from 2004–2007 was probably due in part to increasingly effective domestic controls over the retail sale of licit

pharmaceutical preparations containing ephedrine and pseudoephedrine, the primary chemicals necessary for methamphetamine. Regulations for the sale of such products in the United States became effective at the national level for the first time in late 2006 under the Combat Methamphetamine Epidemic Act (CMEA). To capitalize on these gains and prevent production from merely shifting ground, the U.S. Government enhanced the scale and pace of its law enforcement cooperation with the Government of Mexico to target the production and trafficking of methamphetamine. For its part, according to the National Drug Intelligence Center's 2009 National Drug Threat Assessment, ephedrine and pseudoephedrine import restrictions in Mexico contributed to a decrease in methamphetamine production in Mexico and reduced the flow of the drug from Mexico to the United States in 2007 and 2008. Methamphetamine shortages were reported in some drug markets in the Pacific, Southwest, and West Central Regions during much of 2007. In some drug markets, methamphetamine shortages continued through early 2008. In 2008, however, small-scale domestic methamphetamine production increased in many areas, and some Mexican drug trafficking organizations shifted their production operations from Mexico to the United States, particularly to California.

The United States is keenly aware that drug traffickers are adaptable, well-informed, and flexible. New precursor chemical trans-shipment routes may be emerging in Southeast Asia and Africa, and there is also ample evidence that organized criminal groups ship currently uncontrolled chemical analogues of ephedrine and pseudoephedrine for use in manufacturing illicit methamphetamine-type drugs. Some methamphetamine produced in Canada is distributed in U.S. drug markets and Canada is a source country for MDMA to U.S. markets as well as a transit or diversion point for precursor chemicals used to produce illicit synthetic drugs (notably MDMA, or ecstasy), according to the NDIC 2009 National Drug Threat Assessment.

The Netherlands remains an important producer of ecstasy as well, although the amount of this drug reaching the United States seems to have declined substantially in recent years, following new enforcement measures by the Dutch government. Labs in Poland and elsewhere in Eastern Europe are major suppliers of amphetamines to the European market, with the United Kingdom and the Nordic countries among the heaviest European consumers of ATS.

Pharmaceutical Abuse and the Internet: According to the National Drug Intelligence Center's December 2008 *National Drug Threat Assessment,* the number of Internet sites offering sales of controlled prescription drugs decreased in 2008, for the first time after several years of increase. It is not known what percentage of this abuse involves international sources. In the United States, the Ryan Haight Online Pharmacy Consumer Protection Act of 2008 was enacted in October 2008. The new federal law amends the Controlled Substances Act and prohibits the delivery, distribution, or dispensing of controlled prescription drugs over the Internet without a prescription written by a doctor who has conducted at least one in-person examination of the patient.

Cannabis (Marijuana)

Cannabis production and marijuana consumption continue to appear in nearly every world region, including in the United States. Marijuana still remains the most widely used of all of the illicit drugs. According to the December 2008 "Monitoring the Future" study, marijuana use among 8th, 10th, and 12th graders was not statistically different from the year before. However, since the peak years of the mid-1990s, annual use has fallen by over 40 percent among 8th graders, 30 percent among 10th graders, and nearly 20 percent among 12th graders. The prevalence rates for marijuana use in the prior year now stand at 11 percent, 24 percent, and 32 percent for grades 8, 10, and 12, respectively.

Drug organizations in Mexico produced more than 15,000 metric tons of marijuana in 2008, much of which was marketed to the more than 20 million users in the United States. Overall, Canada supplies a small proportion of the overall amount of marijuana consumed in the United States; however, large-scale cultivation of high potency marijuana is a thriving illicit industry in Canada. Other source countries for marijuana include Colombia, Jamaica, and possibly Nigeria. Production of marijuana within the United States may exceed that of foreign sources.

According to the U.S. Drug Enforcement Administration (DEA), marijuana potency has increased sharply. Of great concern is the high potency, indoor-grown cannabis produced on a large scale in Canada and the United States in laboratory conditions using specialized timers, ventilation, moveable lights on tracks, nutrients sprayed on exposed roots and special fertilizer that maximize THC levels. The result is a particularly powerful and dangerous drug.

Opium and Heroin

Opium poppy, the source of heroin, is cultivated mainly in Afghanistan, Southeast Asia, and on a smaller scale in Colombia and Mexico. In contrast to coca, a perennial which takes at least a year to mature into usable leaf,

opium poppy is an easily planted annual crop. Opium gum can take less than 6 months from planting to harvest.

In Afghanistan, a combination of factors led to a reduction in the cultivation and production of opium for the first time in several years. Among these factors were: including Afghan government and international donor programs that rewarded entire provinces for decreasing or eliminating opium cultivation; increased prices for other commodities such as wheat; decreased prices for opium; and bad weather. Nangarhar province alone shifted from having the second highest area of poppy cultivation in 2007 to achieving poppy-free status in 2008. This was due in large part to the high-profile law enforcement and incentives campaign implemented by the provincial governor. Even with this limited progress, Afghanistan continues to be the source of more than 90% of the world's illicit opiates. This glut of narcotics has fueled increasing addiction rates in Afghanistan, Pakistan, and Iran. The narcotics trade thrives in the conditions created by insurgents and warlords, who exact a portion of the profits for protection of crops, labs, trucks, and drug markets. Exact figures for the black market economy are impossible to obtain, but the UN estimates that the Taliban and other anti-government forces have extorted $50 million to $70 million in protection payments from opium farmers and an additional $200 to $400 million of income in forced levies on the more-lucrative drug processing and trafficking in 2008.

Most of the heroin used in the United States comes from poppies grown in Colombia and Mexico, although both countries are minor producers in global terms. Mexico supplies most of the heroin found in the western United States while Colombia supplies most of the heroin east of the Mississippi. Long-standing joint eradication programs in both countries continue with our support. Colombian law enforcement reported eradicating 381 hectares of opium poppy in 2008. We estimate that poppy cultivation decreased 25 percent from 2006 to 2007 in directly comparable areas of Colombia. This led to a 27 percent drop in potential production of heroin and a 19 percent decrease in purity of Colombian heroin seized in the United States, according to the DEA. The Government of Mexico (GOM) reported eradicating 12,035 hectares of opium poppy.

Controlling Drug-Processing Chemicals

Cocaine and heroin are manufactured with certain critical chemicals, some of which also have licit uses but are diverted by criminals. The most commonly used chemicals in the manufacture of these illegal drugs are potassium permanganate (for cocaine) and acetic anhydride (for heroin). Government controls strive to differentiate between licit commercial use for these chemicals and illicit diversion to criminals. Governments must have efficient legal and regulatory regimes to control such chemicals, without placing undue burdens on legitimate commerce. Extensive international law enforcement cooperation is also required to prevent their diversion from licit commercial channels, and to investigate, arrest and dismantle the illegal networks engaged in their procurement. This topic is addressed in greater detail in the Chemical Control Chapter of this report.

Drugs and the Environment

Impact of Drug Cultivation and Processing: Illegal drug production usually takes place in remote areas far removed from the authority of central governments. Not surprisingly, drug criminals practice none of the environmental safeguards that are required for licit industry, and the toxic chemicals used to process raw organic materials into finished drugs are invariably dumped into sensitive ecosystems without regard for human health or the costs to the environment. Coca growers routinely slash and burn remote, virgin forestland in the Amazon to make way for their illegal crops; coca growers typically cut down up to 4 hectares of forest for every hectare of coca planted. Tropical rains quickly erode the thin topsoil of the fields, increasing soil runoff and depleting soil nutrients. By destroying timber and other resources, illicit coca cultivation decreases biological diversity in one of the most sensitive ecological areas in the world. In Colombia and elsewhere, traffickers also destroy jungle forests to build clandestine landing strips and laboratories for processing raw coca and poppy into cocaine and heroin.

Illicit coca growers use large quantities of highly toxic herbicides and fertilizers on their crops. These chemicals qualify under the U.S. Environmental Protection Agency's highest classification for toxicity (Category I) and are legally restricted for sale within Colombia and the United States. Production of the drugs requires large quantities of dangerous solvents and chemicals. One kilogram of cocaine base requires the use of three liters of concentrated sulfuric acid, 10 kilograms of lime, 60 to 80 liters of kerosene, 200 grams of potassium permanganate, and one liter of concentrated ammonia. These toxic pesticides, fertilizers, and processing chemicals are then dumped into the nearest waterway or on the ground. They saturate the soil and contaminate waterways and poison water systems upon which local human and animal populations rely. In the United States, marijuana-processing operations take place in national parks, especially in California and Texas

near the border with Mexico. These marijuana growing operations leave behind tons of garbage, biohazard refuse, and toxic waste. They also contribute to erosion as land is compacted and small streams and other water sources are diverted for irrigating the illegal marijuana fields.

Methamphetamine is also alarming in its environmental impact. For each pound of methamphetamine produced in clandestine methamphetamine laboratories, five to six pounds of toxic, hazardous waste are generated, posing immediate and long-term environmental health risks, not only to individual homes but to neighborhoods. Poisonous vapors produced during synthesis permeate the walls and carpets of houses and buildings, often making them uninhabitable. Cleaning up these sites in the United States and Mexico requires specialized training and costs thousands of dollars per site.

Impact of Spray Eradication: Colombia is currently the only country that conducts regular aerial spraying of coca, although countries throughout the world regularly spray other crops with herbicides. The only active ingredient in the herbicide used in the aerial eradication program is glyphosate, which has been thoroughly tested in the United States, Colombia, and elsewhere. The U.S. Environmental Protection Agency (EPA) approved glyphosate for general use in 1974 and re-registered it in September 1993. EPA has approved its use on food croplands, forests, residential areas, and around aquatic areas. It is one of the most widely used herbicides in the world. Colombia's spray program represents a small fraction of total glyphosate use in the country. Biannual verification missions continue to show that aerial eradication causes no significant damage to the environment or human health. The eradication program follows strict environmental safeguards, monitored permanently by several Colombian government agencies, and adheres to all laws and regulations, including the Colombian Environmental Management Plan. In addition to the biannual verification missions, soil and water samples are taken before and after spray for analysis. The residues in these samples have never reached a level outside the established regulatory norms. The OAS, which published a study in 2005 positively assessing the chemicals and methodologies used in the aerial spray program, is currently conducting further investigations expected to be completed in early 2009 regarding spray drift and other issues.

Attacking Trafficking Organizations

Law enforcement tactics have grown more sophisticated over the past two decades to counter the ever-evolving tactics used by trafficking networks to transport large volumes of drugs internationally. Rather than measuring progress purely by seizures and numbers of arrests, international law enforcement authorities have increasingly targeted resources against the highest levels of drug trafficking organizations. Increasingly, international law enforcement authorities are learning the art of conspiracy investigations, using mutual legal assistance mechanisms and other advanced investigative techniques to follow the evidence to higher and higher levels of leadership within the syndicates, and cooperating on extradition so that the kingpins have no place to hide. These sophisticated law enforcement and legal tools are endorsed as recommended practices within both the 1988 UN Drug Control Convention and the UN Convention against Transnational Organized Crime.

The drug trade depends upon reliable and efficient distribution systems to get its product to market. While most illicit distribution systems have short-term back-up channels to compensate for temporary law enforcement disruptions, a network under intense enforcement pressure cannot function for long. In cooperation with law enforcement officials in other nations, our goal is to disrupt and dismantle these organizations, to remove the leadership and the facilitators who launder money and provide the chemicals needed for the production of illicit drugs, and to destroy their networks. By capturing the leaders of trafficking organizations, we demonstrate both to the criminals and to the governments fighting them that even the most powerful drug syndicates are vulnerable to concerted action by international law enforcement authorities.

Mexican drug syndicates continue to oversee much of the drug trafficking into the United States, with a strong presence in most of the primary U.S. distribution centers. President Calderon's counternarcotics programs seek to address some of the most basic institutional issues that have traditionally confounded Mexico's success against the cartels. The Government of Mexico is using the military to reestablish sovereign authority and counter the cartels' firepower, moving to establish integrity within the ranks of the police, and giving law enforcement officials and judicial authorities the resources and the legal underpinning they need to succeed.

To help Mexico achieve these goals, the United States Congress appropriated $465 million in June 2008 to provide inspection equipment to interdict trafficked drugs, arms, cash and persons; secure communications systems for law enforcement agencies; and technical advice and training to strengthen judicial institutions. Similarly, Congress has provided support to Central American countries, including the continued implementation of the USG's anti-gang strategy, support for specialized vetted units and judicial reforms, and enhanced land and maritime drug interdiction.

This appropriation will complement existing and planned initiatives of U.S. domestic law enforcement agencies engaged with counterparts in each participating country. On December 3, 2008, a Letter of Agreement (LOA) was signed with the Government of Mexico obligating $197 million of the funding for counternarcotics programs. On December 19, the governments of the United States and Mexico met to coordinate the implementation of the Mérida Initiative through a cabinet-level High Level Group, which underscored the urgency and importance of the Initiative. A working level inter-agency implementation meeting was held February 3 in Mexico City with the aim of accelerating the rollout of the 39 projects for Mexico under the Initiative. In addition, LOAs were signed with Honduras on January 9, El Salvador on January 12, Guatemala on February 5 and Belize on February 9.

Extradition

There are few legal sanctions that international criminals fear as much as extradition to the United States, where they can no longer use bribes and intimidation to manipulate the local judicial process. Governments willing to risk domestic political repercussions to extradite drug kingpins to the United States are finding that public acceptance of this measure has steadily increased.

Mexican authorities extradited 95 persons to the United States in 2008. Colombia has an outstanding record of extradition of drug criminals to the United States, and the numbers have increased even more in recent years. The Government of Colombia extradited a record 208 defendants in 2008. Since President Uribe assumed office in 2002, 789 individuals have been extradited.

Institutional Reform

Fighting Corruption: Among all criminal enterprises, the drug trade is best positioned to spread corruption and undermine the integrity and effectiveness of legitimate governments. Drugs generate illegal revenues on a scale without historical precedent. No commodity is so widely available, so cheap to produce, and as easily renewable as illegal drugs. A kilogram of cocaine can be sold in the United States for more than 15 times its value in Colombia, a return that dwarfs regular commodities and distorts the licit economy.

No government is completely safe from the threat of drug-related corruption, but fragile democracies in post-conflict situations are particularly vulnerable. The weakening of government institutions through bribery and intimidation ultimately poses just as great a danger to democratic governments as the challenge of armed insurgents. Drug syndicates seek to subvert governments in order to guarantee themselves a secure operating environment. Unchecked, the drug cartels have the wherewithal to buy their way into power. By keeping a focus on fighting corruption, we can help avoid the threat of a drug lord–controlled state.

Improving Criminal Justice Systems: A pivotal element of USG international drug control policy is to help strengthen enforcement, judicial, and financial institutions worldwide. Strong institutions limit the opportunities for infiltration and corruption by the drug trade. Corruption within a criminal justice system has an enormously detrimental impact; law enforcement agencies in drug source and transit countries may arrest influential drug criminals only to see them released following a questionable or inexplicable decision by a single judge, or a prosecutor may obtain an arrest warrant but be unable to find police who will execute it. Efforts by governments to enact basic reforms involving transparency, efficiency, and better pay for police and judges helps to build societies based on the rule of law.

Strengthening Border Security: Drug trafficking organizations must move their products across international borders. A key element in stopping the flow of narcotics is to help countries strengthen their border controls. Through training and technical assistance we improve the capability of countries to control the movement of people and goods across their borders. Effective border security can disrupt narcotics smuggling operations, forcing traffickers to adjust their methods and making them vulnerable to further detection and law enforcement action.

Note

1. The focus of this report is on the international aspects of drug trafficking, but we want also to acknowledge the hard work of law enforcement, drug prevention, and drug treatment professionals within the United States who work every day to reduce the demand for illicit drugs and to reduce the misery they bring to our own citizens. Federal, state, local, and tribal law enforcement agencies within the United States dedicate significant resources to confronting drug criminals. The United States has substantial public and private sector programs focused on drug prevention and treatment and has invested in cutting-edge medical and social research on how to decrease demand. We are proud of the results and have worked with the Organization of American States, the United Nations, and countries all over the world to share programs such as drug courts, early intervention, school and work-place drug testing coupled with counseling and other interventions, and medically sound treatment options that help addicted persons reclaim their lives. For more information about domestic drug control efforts, please see the National Drug Control Strategy of the White House Office of National Drug Control Policy, available on [the U.S. State Department] website.

The **U.S. Department of State's** mission is to shape and sustain a peaceful, prosperous, just, and democratic world and foster conditions for stability and progress for the benefit of the American people and people everywhere.

Ethan Nadelmann

 **NO**

The Global War on Drugs Can Be Won

No, it can't. A "drug-free world," which the United Nations describes as a realistic goal, is no more attainable than an "alcohol-free world"—and no one has talked about that with a straight face since the repeal of Prohibition in the United States in 1933. Yet futile rhetoric about winning a "war on drugs" persists, despite mountains of evidence documenting its moral and ideological bankruptcy. When the U.N. General Assembly Special Session on drugs convened in 1998, it committed to "eliminating or significantly reducing the illicit cultivation of the coca bush, the cannabis plant and the opium poppy by the year 2008" and to "achieving significant and measurable results in the field of demand reduction." But today, global production and consumption of those drugs are roughly the same as they were a decade ago; meanwhile, many producers have become more efficient, and cocaine and heroin have become purer and cheaper.

It's always dangerous when rhetoric drives policy—and especially so when "war on drugs" rhetoric leads the public to accept collateral casualties that would never be permissible in civilian law enforcement, much less public health. Politicians still talk of eliminating drugs from the Earth as though their use is a plague on humanity. But drug control is not like disease control, for the simple reason that there's no popular demand for smallpox or polio. Cannabis and opium have been grown throughout much of the world for millennia. The same is true for coca in Latin America. Methamphetamine and other synthetic drugs can be produced anywhere. Demand for particular illicit drugs waxes and wanes, depending not just on availability but also fads, fashion, culture, and competition from alternative means of stimulation and distraction. The relative harshness of drug laws and the intensity of enforcement matter surprisingly little, except in totalitarian states. After all, rates of illegal drug use in the United States are the same as, or higher than, Europe, despite America's much more punitive policies.

We Can Reduce the Demand for Drugs

Good luck. Reducing the demand for illegal drugs seems to make sense. But the desire to alter one's state of consciousness, and to use psychoactive drugs to do so, is nearly universal—and mostly not a problem. There's virtually never been a drug-free society, and more drugs are discovered and devised every year. Demand-reduction efforts that rely on honest education and positive alternatives to drug use are helpful, but not when they devolve into unrealistic, "zero tolerance" policies.

As with sex, abstinence from drugs is the best way to avoid trouble, but one always needs a fallback strategy for those who can't or won't refrain. "Zero tolerance" policies deter some people, but they also dramatically increase the harms and costs for those who don't resist. Drugs become more potent, drug use becomes more hazardous, and people who use drugs are marginalized in ways that serve no one.

The better approach is not demand reduction but "harm reduction." Reducing drug use is fine, but it's not nearly as important as reducing the death, disease, crime, and suffering associated with both drug misuse and failed prohibitionist policies. With respect to legal drugs, such as alcohol and cigarettes, harm reduction means promoting responsible drinking and designated drivers, or persuading people to switch to nicotine patches, chewing gums, and smokeless tobacco. With respect to illegal drugs, it means reducing the transmission of infectious disease through syringe-exchange programs, reducing overdose fatalities by making antidotes readily available, and allowing people addicted to heroin and other illegal opiates to obtain methadone from doctors and even pharmaceutical heroin from clinics. Britain, Canada, Germany, the Netherlands, and Switzerland have already embraced this last option. There's no longer any question that these strategies decrease drug-related harms without increasing drug use. What blocks expansion of such programs is not cost; they

Nadelmann, Ethan. "The Global War on Drugs Can Be Won," *Foreign Policy*, September 2007. Copyright ©2007 by Foreign Policy/Slate. Used with permission.

typically save taxpayers' money that would otherwise go to criminal justice and healthcare. No, the roadblocks are abstinence-only ideologues and a cruel indifference to the lives and well-being of people who use drugs.

Reducing the Supply of Drugs Is the Answer

Not if history is any guide. Reducing supply makes as much sense as reducing demand; after all, if no one were planting cannabis, coca, and opium, there wouldn't be any heroin, cocaine, or marijuana to sell or consume. But the carrot and stick of crop eradication and substitution have been tried and failed, with rare exceptions, for half a century. These methods may succeed in targeted locales, but they usually simply shift production from one region to another: Opium production moves from Pakistan to Afghanistan; coca from Peru to Colombia; and cannabis from Mexico to the United States, while overall global production remains relatively constant or even increases.

The carrot, in the form of economic development and assistance in switching to legal crops, is typically both late and inadequate. The stick, often in the form of forced eradication, including aerial spraying, wipes out illegal and legal crops alike and can be hazardous to both people and local environments. The best thing to be said for emphasizing supply reduction is that it provides a rationale for wealthier nations to spend a little money on economic development in poorer countries. But, for the most part, crop eradication and substitution wreak havoc among impoverished farmers without diminishing overall global supply.

The global markets in cannabis, coca, and opium products operate essentially the same way that other global commodity markets do: If one source is compromised due to bad weather, rising production costs, or political difficulties, another emerges. If international drug control circles wanted to think strategically, the key question would no longer be how to reduce global supply, but rather: Where does illicit production cause the fewest problems (and the greatest benefits)? Think of it as a global vice control challenge. No one expects to eradicate vice, but it must be effectively zoned and regulated—even if it's illegal.

U.S. Drug Policy Is the World's Drug Policy

Sad, but true. Looking to the United States as a role model for drug control is like looking to apartheid-era South Africa for how to deal with race. The United States ranks first in the world in per capita incarceration—with less than 5 percent of the world's population, but almost 25 percent of the world's prisoners. The number of people locked up for U.S. drug-law violations has increased from roughly 50,000 in 1980 to almost 500,000 today; that's more than the number of people Western Europe locks up for everything. Even more deadly is U.S. resistance to syringe-exchange programs to reduce HIV/AIDS both at home and abroad. Who knows how many people might not have contracted HIV if the United States had implemented at home, and supported abroad, the sorts of syringe-exchange and other harm-reduction programs that have kept HIV/AIDS rates so low in Australia, Britain, the Netherlands, and elsewhere. Perhaps millions.

And yet, despite this dismal record, the United States has succeeded in constructing an international drug prohibition regime modeled after its own highly punitive and moralistic approach. It has dominated the drug control agencies of the United Nations and other international organizations, and its federal drug enforcement agency was the first national police organization to go global. Rarely has one nation so successfully promoted its own failed policies to the rest of the world.

But now, for the first time, U.S. hegemony in drug control is being challenged. The European Union is demanding rigorous assessment of drug control strategies. Exhausted by decades of service to the U.S.-led war on drugs, Latin Americans are far less inclined to collaborate closely with U.S. drug enforcement efforts. Finally waking up to the deadly threat of HIV/AIDS, China, Indonesia, Vietnam, and even Malaysia and Iran are increasingly accepting of syringe-exchange and other harm-reduction programs. In 2005, the ayatollah in charge of Iran's Ministry of Justice issued a *fatwa* declaring methadone maintenance and syringe-exchange programs compatible with *sharia* (Islamic) law. One only wishes his American counterpart were comparably enlightened.

Afghan Opium Production Must Be Curbed

Be careful what you wish for. It's easy to believe that eliminating record-high opium production in Afghanistan—which today accounts for roughly 90 percent of global supply, up from 50 percent 10 years ago—would solve everything from heroin abuse in Europe and Asia to the resurgence of the Taliban.

But assume for a moment that the United States, NATO, and Hamid Karzai's government were somehow able to cut opium production in Afghanistan. Who would benefit? Only the Taliban, warlords, and other black-market entrepreneurs whose stockpiles of opium would skyrocket in value. Hundreds of thousands of Afghan peasants would flock to cities, ill-prepared to find work. And many Afghans would return to their farms the following year to plant another illegal harvest, utilizing guerrilla farming methods to escape intensified eradication efforts. Except now, they'd soon be competing with poor farmers elsewhere in Central Asia, Latin America, or even Africa. This is, after all, a global commodities market.

And outside Afghanistan? Higher heroin prices typically translate into higher crime rates by addicts. They also invite cheaper but more dangerous means of consumption, such as switching from smoking to injecting heroin, which results in higher HIV and hepatitis C rates. All things considered, wiping out opium in Afghanistan would yield far fewer benefits than is commonly assumed.

So what's the solution? Some recommend buying up all the opium in Afghanistan, which would cost a lot less than is now being spent trying to eradicate it. But, given that farmers somewhere will produce opium so long as the demand for heroin persists, maybe the world is better off, all things considered, with 90 percent of it coming from just one country. And if that heresy becomes the new gospel, it opens up all sorts of possibilities for pursuing a new policy in Afghanistan that reconciles the interests of the United States, NATO, and millions of Afghan citizens.

Legalization Is the Best Approach

It might be. Global drug prohibition is clearly a costly disaster. The United Nations has estimated the value of the global market in illicit drugs at $400 billion, or 6 percent of global trade. The extraordinary profits available to those willing to assume the risks enrich criminals, terrorists, violent political insurgents, and corrupt politicians and governments. Many cities, states, and even countries in Latin America, the Caribbean, and Asia are reminiscent of Chicago under Al Capone—times 50. By bringing the market for drugs out into the open, legalization would radically change all that for the better.

More importantly, legalization would strip addiction down to what it really is: a health issue. Most people who use drugs are like the responsible alcohol consumer, causing no harm to themselves or anyone else. They would no longer be the state's business. But legalization would also benefit those who struggle with drugs by reducing the risks of overdose and disease associated with unregulated products, eliminating the need to obtain drugs from dangerous criminal markets, and allowing

addiction problems to be treated as medical rather than criminal problems.

No one knows how much governments spend collectively on failing drug war policies, but it's probably at least $100 billion a year, with federal, state, and local governments in the United States accounting for almost half the total. Add to that the tens of billions of dollars to be gained annually in tax revenues from the sale of legalized drugs. Now imagine if just a third of that total were committed to reducing drug-related disease and addiction. Virtually everyone, except those who profit or gain politically from the current system, would benefit.

Some say legalization is immoral. That's nonsense, unless one believes there is some principled basis for discriminating against people based solely on what they put into their bodies, absent harm to others. Others say legalization would open the floodgates to huge increases in drug abuse. They forget that we already live in a world in which psychoactive drugs of all sorts are readily available—and in which people too poor to buy drugs resort to sniffing gasoline, glue, and other industrial products, which can be more harmful than any drug. No, the greatest downside to legalization may well be the fact that the legal markets would fall into the hands of the powerful alcohol, tobacco, and pharmaceutical companies. Still, legalization is a far more pragmatic option than living with the corruption, violence, and organized crime of the current system.

Legalization Will Never Happen

Never say never. Wholesale legalization may be a long way off—but partial legalization is not. If any drug stands a chance of being legalized, it's cannabis. Hundreds of millions of people have used it, the vast majority without suffering any harm or going on to use "harder" drugs. In Switzerland, for example, cannabis legalization was twice approved by one chamber of its parliament, but narrowly rejected by the other.

Elsewhere in Europe, support for the criminalization of cannabis is waning. In the United States, where roughly 40 percent of the country's 1.8 million annual drug arrests are for cannabis possession, typically of tiny amounts, 40 percent of Americans say that the drug should be taxed, controlled, and regulated like alcohol. Encouraged by Bolivian President Evo Morales, support is also growing in Latin America and Europe for removing coca from international antidrug conventions, given the absence of any credible health reason for keeping it there. Traditional growers would benefit economically, and there's some possibility that such products might compete favorably with more problematic substances, including alcohol.

The global war on drugs persists in part because so many people fail to distinguish between the harms of drug abuse and the harms of prohibition. Legalization forces that distinction to the forefront. The opium problem in Afghanistan is primarily a prohibition problem, not a drug problem. The same is true of the narcoviolence and corruption that has afflicted Latin America and the Caribbean for almost three decades—and that now threatens Africa. Governments can arrest and kill drug lord after drug lord, but the ultimate solution is a structural one, not a prosecutorial one. Few people doubt any longer that the war on drugs is lost, but courage and vision are needed to transcend the ignorance, fear, and vested interests that sustain it.

ETHAN NADELMANN is the founder and executive director of the Drug Policy Alliance (website, http://www.drugpolicy .org/), the leading organization in the United States working to end the war on drugs. He has authored two books (*Cops Across Borders* and *Policing the Globe*) and his writings have appeared in most major media outlets as well as top academic journals.

EXPLORING THE ISSUE

Should the United States Put More Emphasis on Stopping the Importation of Drugs?

Critical Thinking and Reflection

1. How might we evaluate the success, if possible, of a "war on drugs"? Where has the war been successful and where has it failed?
2. Which approach is more successful to decrease drug use—decreasing availability or decreasing demand?
3. What is the impact of America's "war on drugs" on other nations?
4. What law enforcement and judicial policies in the United States and in the rest of the world should be changed to decrease drug use?
5. Is drug legalization an appropriate approach for our country's "drug problem"? What might the unintended consequences be of legalization of cocaine, heroin, or cannabis in your community?

Is There Common Ground?

Drug trafficking (i.e., distribution) laws penalize the selling, transportation, and illegal importation of illegal drugs (e.g., cocaine, heroin, and marijuana) into the United States. Drug trafficking is a felony and the penalties are much more severe than those for drug possession (i.e., willfully holding illegal controlled substances). Sentences for trafficking can generally range from 3–5 years to life in prison. The severity of the punishments can vary widely depending on several factors, such as the type and amount of drugs trafficked, the geographic area of distribution, and if children were targeted in the trafficking. Both federal and state laws come into play on drug trafficking cases.

The Drug Enforcement Administration is charged with enforcing federal trafficking laws and they are summarized on their website (http://www.dea.gov/druginfo/ftp3.shtml). For example, the penalties for cocaine vary on the form of the cocaine (i.e., cocaine or cocaine base), the quantity, and whether it is a first or multiple offenses. A first offense for trafficking less than 5 kilograms of cocaine has a penalty of not less than five years in prison, while a second offense for trafficking this quantity of cocaine has a penalty of not less than ten years in prison. Penalties for both are enhanced if death or serious injury was associated with the trafficking.

In addition to a prison sentence, those convicted of drug trafficking face other penalties. A conviction for a U.S. citizen can result in the loss of civil rights and government benefits. For a noncitizen, a conviction can be

subject to immediate deportation from the United States and make someone ineligible for citizenship or entry into the country. Citizen and noncitizen offenders are subject to forfeiture of assets—seizure of money and property associated with the trafficking conviction.

Generally the United States does not have the death penalty for drug trafficking; however, drug "kingpins" could be subject to the death penalty for trafficking very large quantities of illicit drugs, as these could be considered offenses against the state. Furthermore, the death penalty could be applied for other crimes, such as murder, associated with trafficking. Executions of drug smugglers are becoming more common in other countries, such as Indonesia and China.

Additional Resources

Clancy, T. (1989). *Clear and Present Danger*, New York: Putnam.

> In this techno-thriller novel, the protagonist, Jack Ryan, becomes Acting Deputy Director of the Central Intelligence Agency (CIA) and discovers that his colleagues are conducting a covert war against a drug cartel based in Colombia.

Clawson, P. L., & Lee III, R. W. (1998). *The Andean Cocaine Industry*, New York: St. Martin's Press.

> Clawson and Lee provide a thorough review of the basics of cocaine, how cocaine is trafficked into the United States, and the impact of the cocaine industry

on the Andes region. The authors also provide commentary on the effects of counter-narcotics efforts in Latin America on U.S. cocaine use.

Keefe, P. R. (2012). Cocaine Incorporated. *The New York Times Magazine.* http://www.nytimes.com/2012/06/17/magazine/how-a-mexican-drug-cartel-makes-its-billions.html?_r=0.

This feature article describes drug trafficking from Mexico into the United States and the impact of the "war on drugs" on Mexico.

Schwartz, M. (2014). A Mission Gone Wrong: Why Are We Still Fighting the Drug War? *The New Yorker.* http://www.newyorker.com/magazine/2014/01/06/a-mission-gone-wrong.

The author reports on the effect of America's "war on drugs" on Honduras. He provides background on the history of U.S. action in Central/South America from the 1970s to the present, with a focus on policy and policy implementation failures.

Internet References . . .

Drug Policy Alliance

http://www.drugpolicy.org/

National Institutes of Health, National Institute on Drug Abuse: Drug Facts: Cocaine

http://www.drugabuse.gov/publications/drugfacts/cocaine

United Nations Office on Drugs and Crime—Drug Trafficking

http://www.unodc.org/unodc/en/drug-trafficking/

United States Department of Homeland Security—Customs and Border Protection

http://www.cbp.gov/

United States Department of Justice—Drug Enforcement Administration

http://www.dea.gov/

Selected, Edited, and with Issue Framing Materials by:
Dennis K. Miller, *University of Missouri*

ISSUE

Should Big Pharma Be Permitted to Discourage Access to Generic Drugs?

YES: Agnes Shanley, from "Legitimate Concerns over Patent Protection, Profits and Shareholder Value Are Being Balanced by Ethics and Humanism," *Pharmaceutical Manufacturing* (2005)

NO: Arthur Caplan and Zachary Caplan, from "How Big Pharma Rips You Off," *CNN* (2013)

Learning Outcomes

After reading this issue, you will be able to:

- Decide if pharmaceutical manufactures should be able to limit access to generics. If so, under what conditions?
- Determine whether or not there is an antitrust problem in the practice of big pharmaceutical companies purchasing access to the generic release of drugs.
- Explain whether or not you believe there are issues of quality of drugs in this debate. Explain.
- Distinguish what "sets" of patients appear to be most at risk in this issue.

ISSUE SUMMARY

YES: Agnes Shanley argues that the enormous cost of developing a new drug justifies attempts to protect its exclusive access to the market after the patent has expired.

NO: Arthur Caplan and Zachary Caplan are skeptical of the "staggering cost" claims and argue that consumers should have access to the generic version of the drug as soon as possible.

U.S. pharmaceutical companies have the ability to produce popular drugs that often have long-term patents granting them exclusive rights to market and sell their drug for as long as 20 years. The pharmaceutical companies also have the ability to produce an unpopular and needed drug at a loss to the company. However, the current ethical problem is not a discussion of losses; it is a discussion of high profits and a strategy known as "pay-for-delay." When a prescription drug reaches a high-profitability margin, it could bring in profits in the billions of dollars with no competitors in the marketplace. It must be noted that research and development is expensive for the drug companies. The companies also argue that they must be allowed to make profits off products that were for years in development with extensive research by many

scientists. In some cases, this is very true. However, in other cases the drug companies partner with universities or the National Institutes of Health to develop the vital drugs that are highly profitable. Many critics argue that research and development costs are only a small part of the drug manufacturer's expenses. They also claim that pharmaceutical companies use monopoly power to push up drug prices and that pharmaceutical prices are much higher in the United States than elsewhere.

Some of the tactics that have been debated as unethical include "pay-for-delay" compromises. It could start with the major corporation suing the generic drug manufacturer for copyright infringement. However, before the case goes through a long, litigious battle, an out-of-court settlement could occur. This means the brand-named drug company will pay (for a determined number of years) the generic business a cash settlement to delay putting the generic form of the drug on the market.

The Federal Trade Commission (FTC) has argued this practice is a violation of antitrust law. Specifically, they find the brand-name drug company and the generic drug company to be exchanging cash over future profits of the drug, specifically to prolong the monopoly. The FTC's court brief states, "Nothing in patent law . . . validates a system in which brand-name companies could buy off their would-be competitors." It is a system that has the potential to harm cash-strapped patients but not the corporations. The FTC states there were close to two dozen agreements in 2012 alone, which cost drug patients $3.5 billion annually. The profits were shared by the brand-name and generic manufacturers.

The FTC has petitioned the courts that the pay-for-delay strategy ceases, with no success. Federal courts have concurred with the drug industry's position that the agreements between the brand and generic companies are just standard legal settlements. These are settlements that honor the patent arrangement and do not delay the introduction of generics beyond that period. However, in October 2012, the FTC received a favorable ruling from the Federal Third Circuit Court regarding a blood pressure medication. The court held that the agreements between the generic and brand drug companies were presumptively illegal unless proven otherwise. It was after this that the Supreme Court decided to hear the case as an antitrust violation. At the time of this writing, the outcome of the case is unknown.

YES ↵

Agnes Shanley

Legitimate Concerns over Patent Protection, Profits and Shareholder Value Are Being Balanced by Ethics and Humanism

Pharmaceutical manufacturers can't be blamed for doing all they can to extend the life cycles of the drugs they invent and produce. After all, each new drug requires, on average, 10 years and over $800 million to get to market, plus an incalculable amount of dedication, sacrifice, paperwork and frustration.

The growth of generic drug manufacturing operations has challenged the pharmaceutical industry, legally, technologically and ethically. Generics manufacturers have injected some healthy competition into the industry, but they also have drug inventors scrambling to protect their hard-won intellectual property.

In this issue's cover story, Contributing Editor Angelo De Palma examines the techniques that pharmaceutical innovators are using to cheat patent death and hold off the advances of generics. Some of these techniques are truly innovative—PEGylation, for example, which not only changes a drug's form, but can improve some of its properties. Other techniques are definitely crafty. And legal. But are they always ethical? Should an existing drug in a new form be considered truly novel?

Amendments to Hatch-Waxman have limited options for extending patent life, and cut down on frivolous lawsuits. Litigation, once an automatic response to generic competition, is now a last resort. Instead of focusing on the back end, more companies are working at the front end, and reducing time to market, to extend drug life cycle.

In addition, more drug companies appear to realize that there's a need to balance legitimate concerns for intellectual property, profits and shareholder value with ethics and humanism. Consider the industry's initial response four years ago, when generic versions of antiretroviral therapies for HIV were first announced. These generics cost less than $600 per year per patient, a fraction of the $13,000 per year that similar name brand therapies cost in the U.S., and were launched by countries that had no tradition of patent protection. Understandably, drug makers felt threatened.

Activists focused more attention on this issue, and the industry backed down. Now, pharmaceutical innovators are even supporting some of these efforts.

As a result, a tiny but growing generic antiretroviral HIV drug market is taking root in the developing world, where only a few hundred thousand of the millions of people affected with HIV actually receive adequate treatment. Thailand, for example, now makes a number of AIDS drugs thanks to the pioneering work of Dr. Krisana Kraisintu.

Originally, Bristol-Myers Squibb sued Kraisintu over antiretroviral drug patents, although she argued that the intellectual property came from the National Institutes of Health. Ultimately, BMS withdrew the suit, voicing its support for the people of Thailand.

Kraisintu is now embarking on a project that would produce cheap antiretrovirals in the continent most devastated by HIV and AIDS: Africa. Starting in Tanzania, she has applied for funding to upgrade a 40-year-old manufacturing facility and is also scoping out projects in the Democratic Republic of Congo and Eritrea. This is truly missionary work—inspirational and worthy of support. It's more significant than merely donating drugs; as the old adage goes, "Give a man a fish and he'll eat one meal; enable him to fish and he'll eat for a lifetime."

The same drug companies that fought to block generics overseas are now supporting efforts like these (and, as Managing Editor Paul Thomas notes in "The Relief Tsunami," several have also donated generously to regions devastated by December's tsunami).

Late last month, the FDA approved the first generic AIDS antiretroviral treatment, which will be manufactured by Aspen Pharmacare, South Africa's largest generic drug firm. The drug will cost less than a dollar a day per patient. BMS, Glaxo and Boehringer Ingelheim have all licensed their antiretroviral technologies voluntarily to the project. And the U.S. government requested over

$3 billion to fund antiretroviral drug procurement and distribution.

What about the generics manufacturers at home? Given the cost of medication and the number of uninsured people in the U.S., generics serve a vital function. Isn't there room enough for everyone, the innovators and those who turn yesterday's cutting edge into tomorrow's commodity?

As more companies realize, focusing on the "back end" to extend drug life cycles and shut out generics is, at best, short-sighted. As more companies embrace new IT, process analytical technologies, and concepts like Lean and Six Sigma, development and manufacturing teams are working more closely together, weeding out discoveries that only look good on paper, and streamlining costs and adding years to their products' saleable lives.

Closed industries that stifle competition are often changed from without. Consider telecommunications. Generics, both here and abroad, offer big pharma the opportunity to change from within, to become more agile, and to "do the right thing."

Agnes Shanley is editor in chief of *Pharmaceutical Manufacturing*. She earned her BA in liberal arts from Barnard College, Columbia University, and her BS in chemistry and life sciences from the City University of New York. She has published articles on the pharmaceutical, biotech, and chemical industries in *Chemical Engineering, Chemical Processing, Chemical Business, Chemical Marketing Reporter,* and the *Homeland Defense Journal.*

Arthur Caplan and
Zachary Caplan

➡ NO

How Big Pharma Rips You Off

Whether you are young or old, man or woman, very healthy or quite sick, it is almost a certainty that you are going to use a prescription drug in the next year or two. These medicines are crucial for preventing diseases and treating all sorts of ailments and problems.

They are also expensive—really expensive. For example, the best-selling drug of all time, Pfizer's cholesterol lowering drug Lipitor, went for $3.50 per pill and up before going generic in late 2011. But these days some retail chains are giving away generic Lipitor while the rest are charging barely 50 cents a pill.

Prescription drugs cost Americans far more than they do people living in many other parts of the world. This is because drug companies spend a fortune on direct-to-consumer sales and marketing (which they don't do in other countries) and because other nations negotiate better deals for drugs than private insurers do in the United States.

Is there anything that can be done to lower costs and increase the availability of more affordable and equally effective drugs? Yes.

Earlier this year, the U.S. Supreme Court heard arguments in a case that drew little attention in the media: *Federal Trade Commission v. Actavis.* The stakes are high.

When the court decides this case, probably in June, it will either reinforce Big Pharma shenanigans that have helped keep prices high and skyrocketing, or finally bring some relief to our pocketbook and escalating national health care bill for drugs.

The issue is whether companies that own patents for prescription drugs can pay other companies that want to make cheaper generic versions not to do so, a practice known as pay-for-delay.

One way to get lower prices on drugs is to get generic versions out to replace name-brand drugs. Generic drugs include the exact same active ingredients as the brand names. The difference is the name of the medication and the color or shape of the pill.

Prescription drug manufacturers, fearing the arrival of cheaper generics and knowing or worrying that their patents alone won't keep out competitors, try to buy off the competition instead.

In the case before the court, Solvay Pharmaceuticals is accused of paying off would-be generic manufacturers of their blockbuster drug AndroGel, a synthetic testosterone used by hundreds of thousands of AIDS patients, cancer patients, elderly men and others who suffer from low levels of testosterone. The generic companies were happy; they made money for doing nothing. Solvay continued to reap huge profits by keeping its monopoly in the market. The only losers were patients who have had to keep paying much higher prices for their name-brand-only drug.

Usually, buying off your competitors is clearly illegal. Pay-for-delay deals run counter to basic antitrust principles. Nonetheless, some lower courts, declining to evaluate the strength of a patent, have let Big Pharma get away with these deals.

Big Pharma views the settlements as a bargain. Instead of losing up to 90% of their market share because of the introduction of a generic, companies can simply pay generic manufacturers and make the competition go away.

A 1984 law, the Drug Price Competition and Patent Term Restoration Act, commonly known as the Hatch-Waxman Act, was intended to speed up lower-cost generic competition. Big Pharma has managed to completely undermine Hatch-Waxman's intent, which was to put in place mechanisms that encouraged generic drug makers to challenge the weak patents often used to protect brand-name drugs.

Unfortunately, the AndroGel case is not unique. In recent years, deals between Big Pharma and generic drug makers have delayed the introduction of a diverse range of cheaper generics including cancer drugs, AIDS treatments, blood pressure medications, antidepressants, allergy medications, sleep aids, ADD medications and more.

The Congressional Budget Office says pay-for-delay tactics cost consumers billions of dollars and the Federal Trade Commission estimates these pay-for-delay deals will cost Americans up to $35 billion over the next 10 years.

Rep. Henry Waxman, D-California, who co-wrote the Hatch-Waxman Act, has been very vocal in arguing that a law Congress intended to help reduce the cost of prescription medicines has been hijacked by the drug industry to do the opposite.

What we have now are the generic manufacturers and Big Pharma making a fortune by agreeing to delay competition that would bring lower priced drugs to market.

A few weeks ago, the Indian Supreme Court took a hard look at the way big drug companies were using patent extensions to keep out low price competition. They said forget it—that sort of tomfoolery will not be allowed.

The U.S. Supreme Court would be wise to concur, heed the Federal Trade Commission's complaint and bring pay-for-delay to an abrupt end.

The right prescription for making medicines cheaper and better is to encourage competition, not stifle it with backroom deals where everyone gets a great deal except for the patients.

ARTHUR CAPLAN is the Drs. William F. and Virginia Connolly Mitty Professor and director of the Division of Bioethics at New York University's Langone Medical Center. Prior to this, he was the Emmanuel and Robert Hart Professor of Bioethics and director of the Center for Bioethics at the University of Pennsylvania. He was the associate director of the Hastings Center from 1984 to 1987. He received his undergraduate degree at Brandeis University and his PhD in the history and philosophy of science at Columbia University. He is editor or author of more than 20 books in bioethics.

ZACHARY CAPLAN, son of Arthur Caplan, is an associate in the antitrust practice group at Berger & Montague, in Philadelphia. He practices in the area of antitrust litigation. As a law student at the University of Pennsylvania, he was a senior editor of the *University of Pennsylvania Journal of Business Law*. He also interned with Agnes Shanley, the editor-in-chief of *Pharmaceutical Manufacturing*.

EXPLORING THE ISSUE

Should Big Pharma Be Permitted to Discourage Access to Generic Drugs?

Critical Thinking and Reflection

1. What distinguishes a brand-name drug from a generic drug? Is the brand-name drug superior to the generic drug?
2. What impact does the delay of generic drug availability have on the average American consumer?
3. Explain a strategy that would allow the brand-name drug company to make profits for a time sufficient to cover their research and development costs without breaching antitrust laws.
4. If it is possible for inexpensive generic drugs to be available for those in need, is this a sufficient reason to make the duration of the brand-name patent shorter?
5. Justify why drug manufacturers can't keep a patent indefinitely given the intellectual strengths as well as other corporate expenses that go into developing, marketing, and selling the drugs.

Is There Common Ground?

A common practice when purchasing a drug from a pharmacy is to question if a generic version of a brand-name drug is being marketed. The generic version is guaranteed by the FDA to be generally the same drug as the original patented drug. However, the generic drug sells for much less. The producers of the two versions of the drug are often competing for profits and market share. Big pharmaceutical companies explain that it can cost $175 million to develop new drugs. They explain their drug patents shouldn't run out only to be copied by generic drug manufactures and sold for a small portion of the brand-name price to the consumer. Big pharmaceutical companies have recently bought the rights to the drug from generic drug companies to keep the generic drug off the market. Many consumer advocates complain this is unethical and should be seen as an antitrust violation. Consumer advocates explain that high profits have been made for as many as 10 years, and that the generic drug can now assist in lowering high health care costs. However, each of our authors on this issue explains why it is important to protect patents, yet it is also important to avoid antitrust and consumer issues. The issue has been debated for many years marked with a landmark law in 1984—The Hatch-Waxman Act, or the Drug Price Competition and Patent Term Restoration Act. Twenty years later the law was used to encourage generic drug producers to compete with the pricy brand-name drugs by challenging their patents. The Supreme Court heard arguments on the issue in March 2013.

Many individuals use generic drugs. Once the patent on the drug has expired, the high-demand drugs are produced and sold at a fraction of the original cost—often by as much as 80 or 90 percent. As was previously mentioned, the U.S. Congress has attempted to keep the generic option in place as far back as 1984 with the Hatch-Waxman Act, which accelerated the FDA approval process for generic drugs. Under this act, companies can sell generics before the expiration of the exclusive patent by successfully challenging the patents' validity. However, the introduction of a generic drug essentially ends the profitability for the brand-name manufacturer of the drug, while delivering important economic benefits to the consumer. The major pharmaceutical companies want to keep the generic products off the market for as long as possible.

Additional Resources

"High Court to Weigh Big-money Big Pharma Generic Deals," *CBS News* (March 25, 2013).

Sarah Kliff. "Money, Drugs and the Supreme Court: The Multi-billion Dollar Case You Haven't Heard of," *Washington Post* (March 28, 2013).

Nina Totenberg. "Supreme Court Hears 'Pay To Delay' Pharmaceutical Case," NPR.org (March 25, 2013).

Edward Wyat, "Justices to Look at Deals by Generic and Branded Drug Makers," *New York Times* (March 24, 2013).

Internet References . . .

Courtenay Brinkerhoff, "Supreme Court To Hear AndroGel Reverse Payment Case," Pharma Patents, January 10, 2013

www.pharmapatentsblog.com/2013/01/10/supreme -court-to-hear-androgel-reverse-payment-case

Kurt Karst, "The Big Day Approaches," FDA Law Blog.net, March 24, 2013

www.fdalawblog.net/fda_law_blog_hyman _phelps/2013/03/the-big-day-approaches-supreme -court-to-hear-oral-argument-in-androgel-drug -patent-settlement-agreem.html

"Profiting from SCOTUS and BIG Pharma," The Mottley Fool

http://www.fool.com/investing/general/2012/12/15 /profiting-from-scotus-and-big-pharma-part-2.aspx

Selected, Edited, and with Issue Framing Material by:
Dennis K. Miller, *University of Missouri*

ISSUE

Should the Legal Drinking Age Stay at 21 to Decrease Underage Alcohol Use?

YES: National Institute on Alcohol Abuse and Alcoholism, from "Underage Drinking," *National Institute on Alcohol Abuse and Alcoholism Research Report* (2017)

NO: Jeffrey A. Tucker, from "Lower the Drinking Age!," *Foundation for Economic Education* (2015)

Learning Outcomes

After reading this issue, you will be able to:

- Assess the prevalence of alcohol consumption and approaches to decrease alcohol use in young people.
- Describe the social and personal problems that are associated with alcohol use among young people.
- Evaluate the prohibitions against alcohol use by young people and their efficacy in decreasing use and promoting long-term health.
- Consider new approaches to promote responsible alcohol use by young people.

ISSUE SUMMARY

YES: The National Institute on Alcohol Abuse and Alcoholism (NIAAA) considers underage drinking to be a serious health problem in the United States. Drinking by young people has numerous health and safety risks including injuries, impaired judgment, increased risk of assault, and death. The NIAAA makes recommendations for steps to decrease alcohol use by young people and to treat drinking problems.

NO: Jeffrey Tucker argues that despite "draconian" laws against alcohol use in the United States, many teens and young adults still drink. A legal drinking age of 21 years is not realistic and accomplishes nothing to actually stop drinking, according to Tucker. Moreover, the age probation encourages risk drinking behaviors.

Monitoring the Future is an ongoing study of the behaviors, attitudes, and values of high school and college students in the United States. According to this comprehensive survey, in 2014 almost 40% of high school seniors report using alcohol in the last 30 days and almost 90% report that alcohol is easy to obtain.

There is little doubt that many high school and college students drink to excess and that many young people drink alcohol irresponsibly. Regardless of any messages that many underage drinkers receive about the joys of alcohol use from peers or the media, it is unhealthy, unlawful, and potentially dangerous for young people to drink alcohol, especially in excess. The key concern for public health revolves around the best way to reduce the

harms associated with alcohol use. The strongest mechanism used to reduce the harms is setting the drinking age in the United States at 21 years old.

The National Minimum Drinking Age Act (NMDAA) was passed by Congress and signed into law by President Ronald Reagan in 1984. It established a national drinking age of 21 by punishing every state that allowed persons below 21 years to purchase and publicly possess alcoholic beverages. The punishment is a reduction in annual federal highway apportionment by 10 percent. Before the NMDAA, states established their own drinking age and varied theirs between 18 and 21 years of age. Since 1984 the NMDAA has been periodically challenged on several grounds—state's rights, youth rights, and public safety. For the latter, it is the argument that a high drinking age of 21 makes alcohol consumption a "forbidden fruit" that prevents high school and college students from learning responsible drinking behaviors for their lifetime. In other words, the high drinking age makes the problems of alcohol use, misuse, and abuse in young people worse.

Will reducing the drinking age make it easier to teach young people to drink responsibly? Or, is reducing the drinking age simply capitulating to the realities that young people drink?

One important question is whether or not young people will respond to a message of responsible alcohol consumption if they are legally allowed to drink. Because it is a recognized fact that the vast majority of people under age 21 drink alcohol, simply telling young people to not drink does not stop the drinking behavior. However, does it make more sense to teach young people how to drink alcohol responsibly so they do not endanger themselves, their friends, or innocent bystanders? The current message that one should wait until age 21 to drink is not being heard by the majority of people under that age. On the other hand, will someone be more amenable to being responsible if they are allowed to drink? Will reducing the drinking age result in very young people driving while under the influence?

Another relevant question is whether drinking laws discriminate against people under the age of 21. For example, one does not need to be 21 to enter the military. Obviously, being in the military can result in putting one's life in danger. Sixteen-year-olds are allowed to drive a car if they pass certain requirements. Driving a car safely requires one to be very responsible. However, should one be allowed to consume alcohol at age 16 simply because one can drive a car at age 16? Many young people become parents before age 21. Marriage is permitted before age 21. Again, if one can marry and have children, then should one not have the right to drink alcohol?

Whether or not young people under age 21 will drink responsibly if they are allowed legally to drink remains unclear. If the law is changed and the drinking age was lowered, and if the drinking rates increased or other problems surfaced, then would it be easy to change the law back to 21? Perhaps, whether or not young people drink responsibly has nothing to do with the current drinking age? Some people are responsible regardless of the drinking age. There are many older people who drink irresponsibly. One might be able to argue that one should pass certain requirements, besides age, before being allowed to drink. Maybe, individuals with a history of substance abuse or some other type of unlawful or inappropriate behavior should not be allowed to drink.

In 2007, the US Surgeon General published a paper with suggestions to reduce underage drinking. In this paper, the Surgeon General outlined numerous goals. One goal focused on societal changes that would reduce underage drinking. Another goal attempted to get parents, caregivers, schools, communities, and all social systems to work together to address this problem. The Surgeon General recommended improving surveillance of underage drinking as well as additional research on adolescent alcohol use.

In the YES section, the National Institute on Alcohol Abuse and Alcoholism (NIAAA) describes the prevalence of underage drinking and the dangerous associated with it. According to the NIAAA underage drinking poses a range of risks and negative consequences including impaired judgement, increased risk of alcohol problems later in life, injury and assault, and death. In the NO section, Jeffrey Tucker notes that the current restrictions against legal drinking until age 21 are ineffective and can lead to risky drinking behavior (e.g., binge drinking). Tucker recommends supervision of alcohol consumption, but not a complete prohibition for those under 21 years old.

YES ⬅

National Institute on Alcohol Abuse and Alcoholism

Underage Drinking

Underage drinking is a serious public health problem in the United States. Alcohol is the most widely used substance of abuse among America's youth, and drinking by young people poses enormous health and safety risks.

The consequences of underage drinking can affect everyone—regardless of age or drinking status. We all feel the effects of the aggressive behavior, property damage, injuries, violence, and deaths that can result from underage drinking. This is not simply a problem for some families—it is a nationwide concern.

Underage Drinking Statistics

Many young people drink alcohol

- By age 15, about 33 percent of teens have had at least 1 drink.[1]
- By age 18, about 60 percent of teens have had at least 1 drink.[1]

- In 2015, 7.7 million young people ages 12–20 reported that they drank alcohol beyond "just a few sips" in the past month.[2]

Youth ages 12–20 often binge drink

People ages 12 through 20 drink 11 percent of all alcohol consumed in the United States.[3] Although youth drink less often than adults do, when they do drink, they drink more. That is because young people consume more than 90 percent of their alcohol by binge drinking. Binge drinking is consuming many drinks on an occasion (see Box 1). Drinking alcohol and binge drinking become more prevalent as young people get older.

- 5.1 million young people reported binge drinking (for males 5 or more drinks and for females 4 or more drinks on the same occasion within a few hours) at least once in the past month.[2]
- 1.3 million young people reported binge drinking on 5 or more days over the past month.[2]

Figure 1

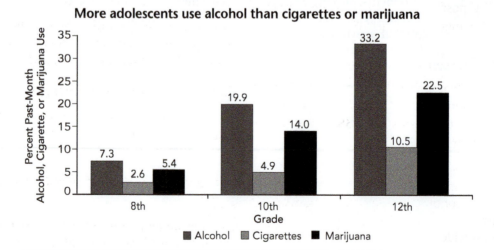

More adolescents use alcohol than cigarettes or marijuana

SOURCE: Johnston, L.D.; Miech, R.A.; O'Malley, P.M.; et al. *Monitoring the Future National Survey: Trends in 30-Day Prevalence of Use of Various Drugs in Grades 8, 10, and 12, 2015.* Ann Arbor, MI: Institute for Social Research, University of Michigan, 2016. Available at: http://monitoringthefuture.org/data/16data/16drtbl3.pdf. Accessed 1/10/17.

National Institute on Alcohol Abuse and Alcoholism. "Underage Drinking," National Institute on Alcohol Abuse and Alcoholism, February 2017.

Figure 2

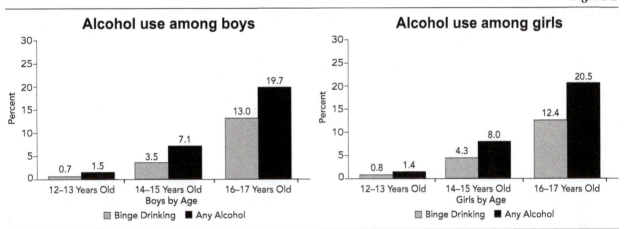

SOURCE: Center for Behavioral Health Statistics and Quality. *2015 National Survey on Drug Use and Health Public Use File Codebook.* Rockville, MD: Substance Abuse and Mental Health Services Administration, 2016.

NOTE. Binge Alcohol Use is defined as drinking 5 or more drinks on the same occasion for boys or 4 or more drinks on the same occasion for girls on at least one day in the past 30 days.

Drinking patterns vary by age and gender

As adolescents get older, they tend to drink more. Prevalence of drinking by boys and girls is similar, although among older adolescents, boys binge more than girls.

Underage Drinking Is Dangerous

Underage drinking poses a range of risks and negative consequences. It is dangerous because it:

Causes many deaths

Based on data from 2006 to 2010, the Centers for Disease Control and Prevention (CDC) estimates that, on average, alcohol is a factor in the deaths of 4,358 young people under age 21 each year.[4] This includes[4]:

- 1,580 deaths from motor vehicle crashes
- 1,269 from homicides
- 245 from alcohol poisoning, falls, burns, and drowning
- 492 from suicides

Causes many injuries

Drinking alcohol can cause kids to have accidents and get hurt. In 2011 alone, about 188,000 people under age 21 visited an emergency room for alcohol-related injuries.[5]

Impairs judgment

Drinking can lead to poor decisions about engaging in risky behavior, including drinking and driving, sexual activity (such as unprotected sex), and aggressive or violent behavior.

Increases the risk of physical and sexual assault

Underage youth who drink are more likely to carry out or be the victim of a physical or sexual assault after drinking than others their age who do not drink.

Can lead to other problems

Drinking may cause youth to have trouble in school or with the law. Drinking alcohol also is associated with the use of other drugs.

Increases the risk of alcohol problems later in life

Research shows that people who start drinking before the age of 15 are 4 times more likely to meet the criteria for alcohol dependence at some point in their lives.

Interferes with brain development

Research shows that young people's brains keep developing well into their 20s. Alcohol can alter this development, potentially affecting both brain structure and function. This may cause cognitive or learning problems and/or make the brain more prone to alcohol dependence. This is especially a risk when people start drinking young and drink heavily.

Why Do So Many Young People Drink?

As children mature, it is natural for them to assert their independence, seek new challenges, and try taking risks. Underage drinking is a risk that attracts many developing adolescents and teens. Many want to try alcohol, but often do not fully recognize its effects on their health and behavior. Other reasons young people drink alcohol include:

- Peer pressure
- Increased independence, or desire for it
- Stress

In addition, many youth may have easy access to alcohol. In 2015, among 12–14-year-olds who reported that they drank alcohol in the past month, 95.1 percent reported that they got it for free the last time they drank.[6] In many cases, adolescents have access to alcohol through family members, or find it at home.

WHAT IS "BINGE DRINKING?"

For adults, binge drinking means drinking so much within about 2 hours that blood alcohol concentration (BAC) levels reach 0.08 g/dL, the legal limit of intoxication.

For women, this typically occurs after 4 drinks, and for men, about 5. But, according to recent research estimates, children may reach these BAC levels after fewer drinks.

For boys:

- Ages 9–13:
  About 3 drinks
- Ages 14–15:
  About 4 drinks
- Ages 16–17:
  About 5 drinks

For girls:

- Ages 9–17:
  About 3 drinks

Preventing Underage Drinking

Preventing underage drinking is a complex challenge. Any successful approach must consider many factors, including:

- Genetics
- Personality
- Rate of maturation and development
- Level of risk
- Social factors
- Environmental factors

Several key approaches have been found to be successful. They are[7]:

Environmental interventions

This approach makes alcohol harder to get—for example, by raising the price of alcohol and keeping the minimum drinking age at 21. Enacting zero-tolerance laws that outlaw driving after any amount of drinking for people under 21 also can help prevent problems.

Individual-level interventions

This approach seeks to change the way young people think about alcohol, so they are better able to resist pressures to drink.

School-based interventions

These are programs that provide students with the knowledge, skills, motivation, and opportunities they need to remain alcohol free.

Family-based interventions

These are efforts to empower parents to set and enforce clear rules against drinking, as well as improve communication between children and parents about alcohol.

The Role Parents Play

Parents and teachers can play a big role in shaping young people's attitudes toward drinking.

Parents in particular can have either a positive or negative influence.

Parents can help their children avoid alcohol problems by:

- Talking about the dangers of drinking
- Drinking responsibly, if they choose to drink
- Serving as positive role models in general
- Not making alcohol available

- Getting to know their children's friends
- Having regular conversations about life in general
- Connecting with other parents about sending clear messages about the importance of not drinking alcohol
- Supervising all parties to make sure there is no alcohol
- Encouraging kids to participate in healthy and fun activities that do not involve alcohol

Research shows that children whose parents are actively involved in their lives are less likely to drink alcohol.

On the other hand, research shows that a child with a parent who binge drinks is much more likely to binge drink than a child whose parents do not binge drink.

Warning Signs of Underage Drinking

Adolescence is a time of change and growth, including behavior changes. These changes usually are a normal part of growing up but sometimes can point to an alcohol problem. Parents and teachers should pay close attention to the following warning signs that may indicate underage drinking:

- Changes in mood, including anger and irritability
- Academic and/or behavioral problems in school
- Rebelliousness
- Changing groups of friends
- Low energy level
- Less interest in activities and/or care in appearance
- Finding alcohol among a young person's things
- Smelling alcohol on a young person's breath
- Problems concentrating and/or remembering
- Slurred speech
- Coordination problems

Treating Underage Drinking Problems

Screening young people for alcohol use and alcohol use disorder is very important and may avoid problems down the road. Screening by a health practitioner (e.g., pediatrician) provides an opportunity to identify problems early and address them before they escalate. It also allows young people to ask questions of a knowledgeable adult. NIAAA and the American Academy of Pediatrics both recommend that all youth be regularly screened for alcohol use.

Some young people can experience serious problems as a result of drinking, including alcohol use disorder, which require intervention by trained professionals. Professional treatment options include:

- Seeing a counselor, psychologist, psychiatrist, or other trained professional
- Participating in outpatient or inpatient treatment at a substance abuse treatment facility or other licensed program

References

1. Substance Abuse and Mental Health Services Administration (SAMHSA). *2015 National Survey on Drug Use and Health (NSDUH)*. Table 2.19B: Alcohol Use in Lifetime, Past Year, and Past Month, by Detailed Age Category: Percentages, 2014 and 2015. Rockville, MD: SAMHSA, 2016. Available at: http://www.samhsa.gov/data/sites/default/files/NSDUH-DetTabs-2015/NSDUH-DetTabs-2015/NSDUH-DetTabs-2015.htm#tab2-19b. Accessed 1/20/17.

2. Substance Abuse and Mental Health Services Administration (SAMHSA). *2015 Key Substance Use and Mental Health Indicators in the United States: Results from the 2015 National Survey on Drug Use and Health*. Figure 24. Rockville, MD: SAMHSA, 2016. Available at: http://www.samhsa.gov/data/sites/default/files/NSDUH-FFR1-2015/NSDUH-FFR1-2015/NSDUH-FFR1-2015.htm#fig24. Accessed 1/20/17.

3. Centers for Disease Control and Prevention (CDC). *Fact Sheets: Underage Drinking*. Atlanta, GA: CDC, 2016. Available at: http://www.cdc.gov/alcohol/fact-sheets/underage-drinking.htm. Accessed 1/20/17.

4. Centers for Disease Control and Prevention (CDC). *Alcohol and Public Health: Alcohol-Related Disease Impact (ARDI)*. Atlanta, GA: CDC, 2016. Available at: http://go.usa.gov/xkde2. Accessed 1/20/17.

5. Substance Abuse and Mental Health Services Administration (SAMHSA), Center for Behavioral Health Statistics and Quality. *The DAWN Report: Highlights of the 2014 Drug Abuse Warning Network (DAWN) Findings on Drug-Related Emergency Department Visits*. Rockville, MD: SAMHSA, 2014. Available at: http://www.samhsa.gov/data/sites/default/files/spot143-underage-drinking-2014/spot143-underage-drinking-2014/spot143-underage-drinking-2014.pdf. Accessed 1/20/17.

6. Substance Abuse and Mental Health Services Administration (SAMHSA). *2015 National Survey*

on Drug Use and Health (NSDUH). Table 6.70B: Source Where Alcohol Was Obtained for Most Recent Use in Past Month among Past Month Alcohol Users Aged 12 to 20, by Age Group: Percentages, 2014 and 2015. Rockville, MD: SAMHSA, 2016. Available at: http://www.samhsa.gov/data/sites/default/files/NSDUH-DetTabs-2015/NSDUH-DetTabs-2015/NSDUH-DetTabs-2015.htm#tab6-70b. Accessed 1/20/17.

7. National Institute on Alcohol Abuse and Alcoholism (NIAAA). Underage drinking: Why do adolescents drink, what are the risks, and how can underage drinking be prevented? *Alcohol Alert*, No. 67. Rockville, MD: NIAAA, January 2006. Available at: http://pubs.niaaa.nih.gov/publicai tions/AA67/AA67.htm. Accessed 1/20/17.

THE NATIONAL INSTITUTE ON ALCOHOL ABUSE AND ALCOHOL-ISM supports and conducts research on the impact of alcohol use on human health and well-being. It aims to reduce alcohol-related problems through research, collaborating with institutions engaged in public health, and by disseminating research findings to health practitioners.

Jeffrey A. Tucker

➜ **NO**

Lower the Drinking Age!

It's rush time for fraternities and sororities on college campuses right now. That means dressing up, networking, socializing, attending parties, and staying up late nights. It also means, whether parents know it (or like it) or not, astonishing amounts of drinking of very potent liquor. One of the most famous "drinks" is called "jungle juice": trash barrels filled with random spirits and mixtures, consumed one red cup at a time.

Many of these kids are away from home for the first time, able to drink to their heart's content. A huge culture as grown up around this practice, including a full vocabulary, games, and rituals. Mostly it is just fun, but it can also lead to serious trouble for everyone involved. Let's not be

squeamish: it leads to very un-adult-like amounts of personal abuse and, often, the abuse of others.

Most of these kids have never been socialized in what it means to drink responsibly. They are living for the thrill that comes with defiance. The combination of new freedom, liquor, and sexual opportunity leads to potentially damaged lives.

How do these kids get away with this? In fraternities and sororities, it all happens on private property, not public and commercial spaces, and so campus police can look the other way. Most everyone does.

Indeed, being able to drink with friends, and unhampered by authority, is a major appeal of the Greek system on campus. It's a way to get around the preposterously

high drinking age. Getting around this law will consume a major part of the energy and creativity of these kids for the next three years.

As for everyone else who cannot afford to join, it's all about a life of sneaking around, getting to know older friends, lying and hiding, pregaming before parties just in case there is no liquor there, and generally adopting a life of bingeing and purging, blackouts and hangovers, rising and repeating. And so on it goes for years until finally the dawn of what the state considers adulthood.

For an entire class of people, it's the Roaring Twenties all over again.

It's all part of Prohibition's legacy and a reflection of this country's strange attitudes toward drinking in general. The drinking age in the United States (21), adopted in 1984, is one of the highest in the world. Countries that compare in severity are only a few, including Indonesia, Kazakhstan, Cameroon, Oman, Pakistan, Qatar, Sri Lanka, Tajikistan.

Most of the rest of the world has settled on 18 for liquor and 16 for beer and wine. In practice, most European countries have very low enforcement of even that. Somehow it works just fine for them.

The consequences of this draconian law have been terrible for American society. Teenage drinking is a gigantic part of American life, all done surreptitiously and mostly without responsible oversight. The market for fake IDs is ubiquitous and diffuse. Everyone in the United States has a story of kids and their abusive habits, their strategizing, their hidden flasks and risky games, their constant maneuvering to do what they know they are not supposed to do.

The drinking-age law would surely be a winner in a competition for the least obeyed law. The notion that this law is accomplishing anything to actually stop or even curb teen drinking is preposterous. Instead, we see all the unintended effects of Prohibition: over-indulgence, anti-social behavior, disrespect for the law, secrecy and sneaking, and a massive diversion of human energy.

People speak of a rape crisis on campus, and whatever the scope of the problem, the fact that women under 21 must retreat to dorm rooms and frat houses to drink puts them all in a vulnerable situation. It's hard to imagine that consent is really there when people are falling down, passing out, and feeling mortified the next day about what happened. In fact, the law represents a true danger to women in particular because it prohibits legal access to safe public places to drink responsibly, and go home to a safe environment afterward.

There is an organization of college administrators who are fed up. It is called the Amethyst Initiative.

Currently, 135 colleges have signed support for a lower drinking age. Their goal is not to encourage more drinking but to recognize the unreality of the current law, and how it has led to perverse consequences on campus.

You know the situation has to be extremely serious to get this risk-averse crowd on board. Their statement reads:

A culture of dangerous, clandestine "binge-drinking"—often conducted off-campus—has developed. Alcohol education that mandates abstinence as the only legal option has not resulted in significant constructive behavioral change among our students.

Adults under 21 are deemed capable of voting, signing contracts, serving on juries and enlisting in the military, but are told they are not mature enough to have a beer. By choosing to use fake IDs, students make ethical compromises that erode respect for the law.

Beyond the Campus

It's not just about campus. It's about teens and drinking in general. The law requires them to hide in private places. Such clandestine meetings can lead to compromising and dangerous situations without reliable public oversight.

It's also about business. Convenience stores and bars, in particular, have been put in a strange position. They have been enlisted to become the enforcement arm of an unenforceable policy, which has meant haranguing customers, inventing new systems for ferreting out violators, turning the servers into cops, confiscating IDs, and creating an environment of snooping and threats in a place that should be about service and fun.

Why isn't something done to change this? Those who are most affected have the least political power. By the time they figure out the ropes in American political life, they are turning 21 and so no longer have to deal with the problem. In practice, this means that there is no real constituency pushing for reform of these laws. That's why they have persisted for 30 years without serious pressure to change, despite the obvious failure they have been.

There is some movement at the state level. In Missouri, longtime state representative Rep. Phyllis Kahn has worked for a lowering of the drinking age in her state. She has an interesting take on whether this would mean that the state would have to give up 10% of federal highway funds (the threat that the feds used to force states to raise their drinking ages). In 2012, a Supreme Court ruling on Medicaid clearly stated that the federal government could not coerce states by withdrawing funding to force legislative action at the state level.

Other activists have said that even if the federal highway funding is cut, the increase in revenue from alcohol sales (and decline in enforcement costs) could make up a lot of the difference.

Regardless of the financing issues, current drinking-age law is unenforceable and destructive. The reality is that kids are going to drink. Denying that and imposing ever more draconian punishments doesn't fix the real problems with alcohol.

What we need is a normal environment of parental and community supervision so that such drinking can occur in a responsible way. Yes, kids will probably drink more often, and yes, more kids will probably try alcohol, but they can do so in an environment of safety and responsibility.

Bringing it into the light, rather than driving it underground, is the best way to solve binging and abuse.

Doubling down on a bad rule, rooted in the idea that laws can change human desire, is not a workable solution.

The choice between virtue and vice is a human choice. Relying on the government to make this choice for us disables the social order's internal mechanisms for bringing about and rewarding responsible behavior. It seems like a paradox, but it is true: The only path toward restoring sanity in teenage drinking is greater liberty.

Jeffrey A. Tucker is Director of Content for the Foundation for Economic Education, an organization that "strives to bring about a world in which the economic, ethical, and legal principles of a free society are familiar and credible to the rising generation." Mr. Tucker writes and speaks on economics and individual liberty.

EXPLORING THE ISSUE

Should the Legal Drinking Age Stay at 21 to Decrease Underage Alcohol Use?

Critical Thinking and Reflection

1. Is alcohol consumption a "right" or a "privilege"?
2. Why is alcohol consumption more of a public health and personal concern for younger people than for older people?
3. Should a standard drinking age be established in the United States? If so, what age would you select and why?
4. If the drinking age is lowered to 18, what effect would that have on teenagers aged 15, 16, and 17? Would there be an increase in this age group consuming alcohol? Would 18-year-olds provide alcohol to younger teens?
5. What is "binge drinking" and why is it a problem for young people? How might lowering or removing the drinking age of 21 influence binge-drinking behavior?

Is There Common Ground?

The debate on the drinking age in the United States is linked to binge drinking behavior. As noted in the YES section, the National Institute on Alcohol Abuse and Alcoholism (NIAAA) defines "binge drinking" as, "a pattern of drinking that brings blood alcohol concentration (BAC) levels to 0.08 g/dL. This typically occurs after 4 drinks for women and 5 drinks for men—in about 2 hours." The Substance Abuse and Mental Health Services Administration (SAMHSA), defines it as, "drinking 5 or more alcoholic drinks on the same occasion on at least 1 day in the past 30 days." More simply put, binge drinking is the heavy consumption of alcohol over a short period of time.

According to the NIAA, about 4 of 5 college students drink alcohol. Of those that drink, half consume their alcohol through binge drinking. High schools, colleges, and universities across the United States have focused on binge drinking prevention and education—educating on the dangers of binge drinking, helping people develop strategies to avoid it, and training on tools to handle high-risk situations. Despite this emphasis, binge drinking persists. The Monitoring the Future survey indicates that the percentage of high school students who see "great risk" in consuming five or more drinks in a row is around 40% and over 25% of these students do not disapprove of this drinking behavior.

Why do people, especially high school and college students, binge drink? One explanation is a curiosity to

know what it's like to drink. Another explanation is a focus on the belief that it will make them feel better, neglecting to consider or minimizing the likelihood that it will make them feel sick or hungover. Peer pressure can contribute to binge drinking—a desire to conform and fit in. It could be viewed as a ritual that students often see as an integral part of their college experience. Others binge drink to decrease stress and anxiety. This could be stress and anxiety with day-to-day life or a psychological disorder, it could also be stress and anxiety associated with risky social and sexual behavior.

Additional Resources

Brown, S.A. et al. (2008). A Developmental Perspective on Alcohol and Youths 16 to 20 Years of Age. *Pediatrics* 121: S290–S310. The authors review the normative neurologic, cognitive, and social changes that typically occur in late adolescence, and discuss the evidence for the impact of these transitions on individual drinking trajectories.

Martinez, J.A., Sher, K.J. & Wood, P.J. (2009). Is heavy drinking really associated with attrition from college? The alcohol–attrition paradox. *Psychology of Addictive Behavior* 22(3): 450–456. Researchers from the University of Missouri examined drinking behavior and class performance in college students. They report that heavy drinking predicts attrition from college.

Shelton, C.D. (2012) *Teenagers and Alcohol: A Tale of Teenage Drinking & Driving*. Choice PH. This is a fictional tale of teen drinking and driving and how alcohol use and have a life-long impact.

U.S. Department of Health and Human Services. (2007) *The Surgeon General's Call to Action To Prevent and Reduce Underage Drinking: A Guide to Action for Educators*. U.S. Department of Health and Human Services, Office of the Surgeon General. The report highlights key issues related to underage drinking, a major public health and safety issue.

Welch, B. & Vecsey, G. (1991) *Five O'Clock Comes Early: A Cy Young Award-Winner Recounts His Greatest Victory*. Fireside. Award-winning baseball player Bob Welch, formerly of the Los Angeles Dodgers and Oakland Athletics, describes his experience with alcoholism as a young professional athlete.

Internet References . . .

Anheuser-Busch – Family Talk on Teen Drinking

http://www.familytalkaboutdrinking.com/

Monitoring the Future

http://www.monitoringthefuture.org/

Foundation for Economic Education

https://fee.org/

National Institute on Alcohol Abuse and Alcoholism

http://www.niaaa.nih.gov

U.S. Department of Health and Human Services—The Substance Abuse and Mental Health Services Administration—Too Smart to Start: Help Prevent Underage Alcohol Use

http://toosmarttostart.samhsa.gov

Selected, Edited, and with Issue Framing Material by:
Dennis K. Miller, *University of Missouri*

ISSUE

Are Energy Drinks with Alcohol Dangerous Enough to Ban?

YES: Don Troop, from "Four Loko Does Its Job with Efficiency and Economy, Students Say," *The Chronicle of Higher Education* (2010)

NO: Jacob Sullum, from "Loco Over Four Loko," *Reason Magazine* (2011)

Learning Outcomes
After reading this issue, you should be able to:
• Discuss the health implications of energy drinks.
• Discuss the argument that energy drinks should be banned from sale and distribution.
• Assess the reason for the popularity of energy drinks among college students.

ISSUE SUMMARY

YES: *The Chronicle of Higher Education* journalist Don Troop argues that the combination of caffeine and alcohol is extremely dangerous and should not be sold or marketed to college students and young people.

NO: Journalist and editor of *Reason Magazine* Jacob Sullum disagrees and claims that alcoholic energy drinks should not have been targeted and banned since many other products are far more dangerous.

Energy drinks such as Four Loko are alcoholic beverages that originally also contained caffeine and other stimulants. These products have been the object of legal, ethical, and health concerns related to companies supposedly marketing them to underaged consumers and the alleged danger of combining alcohol and caffeine. After the beverage was banned in several states, a product reintroduction in December 2010 removed caffeine and the malt beverage is no longer marketed as an energy drink.

In 2009, companies that produced and sold caffeinated alcohol beverages were investigated, on the grounds that their products were being inappropriately advertised to an underage audience and that the drinks had possible health risks by masking feelings of intoxication due to the caffeine content. Energy drinks came under major fire in 2010, as colleges and universities across the United States began to see injuries and blackouts related to the

drinks' consumption. Colleges such as the University of Rhode Island banned this product from their campus that year. The state of Washington banned Four Loko after nine university students, all under 20, from Central Washington University became ill after consuming the beverage at a nearby house party. The Central Washington college students were hospitalized and one student, with extremely high blood alcohol content, nearly died.

Following the hospitalization of 17 students and 6 visitors in 2010, Ramapo College of New Jersey banned the possession and consumption of Four Loko on its campus. Several other colleges also prohibited the sale of the beverages. Many colleges and universities sent out notices informing their students to avoid the drinks because of the risk associated with their consumption.

Other efforts to control the use of energy drinks have been under way. The Pennsylvania Liquor Control Board sent letters to all liquor stores urging distributors to discontinue the sale of the drink. The PLCB also sent letters to all colleges and universities warning them of the dangers of the product. While the board has stopped short of a ban, it has asked retailers to stop selling the drink until U.S. Food and Drug Administration (FDA) findings prove the products are safe. Several grocery chains have voluntarily removed energy beverages from their stores. In Oregon, the sale of the restricted products carried a penalty of 30-day suspension of liquor license.

The U.S. FDA issued a warning letter in 2010 to four manufacturers of caffeinated alcohol beverages stating that the caffeine added to their malt alcoholic beverages is an "unsafe food additive" and said that further action, including seizure of their products, may occur under federal law. The FDA determined that beverages that combine caffeine with alcohol, such as Four Loko energy drinks, are a "public health concern" and couldn't stay on the market in their current form. The FDA also stated that concerns have been raised that caffeine can mask some of the sensory cues individuals might normally rely on to determine their level of intoxication. Warning letters were issued to each of the four companies requiring them to provide to the FDA in writing within 15 days of the specific steps the firms will be taking. Prior to the FDA ruling, many consumers bought and hoarded large quantities of the beverage. This buying frenzy created a black market for energy drinks, with some sellers charging inflated prices. A reformulated version of the drink was put on shelves in late 2010. The new product had exactly the same design as the original, but the caffeine had been removed.

Effective February 2013, cans of Four Loko carry an "Alcohol Facts" label. The label change is part of a final settlement between the Federal Trade Commission and Phusion Projects, the manufacturer of Four Loko. The company still disagrees with the commission's allegations, but said in a statement that the agreement provides a practical way for the company to move ahead. The FTC claimed that ads for Four Loko inaccurately claimed that a 23.5-ounce can contain the alcohol equivalent of one to two cans of beer. In fact, the FTC says, it's more like four to five beers. In the YES selection, Don Troop argues that the combination of caffeine and alcohol is extremely dangerous and should not be sold or marketed to college students and young people. In the NO selection, journalist and editor of *Reason Magazine* Jacob Sullum disagrees and claims that alcoholic energy drinks should not have been targeted and banned since many other products are far more dangerous.

YES ↩

Don Troop

Four Loko Does Its Job with Efficiency and Economy, Students Say

It's Friday night in this steep-hilled college town, and if anyone needs an excuse to party, here are two: In 30 minutes the Mountaineers football team will kick off against the UConn Huskies in East Hartford, Conn., and tonight begins the three-day Halloween weekend.

A few blocks from the West Virginia University campus, young people crowd the aisles of Ashebrooke Liquor Outlet, an airy shop that is popular among students. One rack in the chilled-beverage cooler is nearly empty, the one that is usually filled with 23.5-ounce cans of Four Loko, a fruity malt beverage that combines the caffeine of two cups of coffee with the buzz factor of four to six beers.

"That's what everyone's buying these days," says a liquor store employee, "Loko and Burnett's vodka," a line of distilled spirits that are commonly mixed with nonalcoholic energy drinks like Red Bull and Monster to create fruity cocktails with a stimulating kick.

Four Loko's name comes from its four primary ingredients—alcohol (12 percent by volume), caffeine, taurine, and guarana. Although it is among dozens of caffeinated alcoholic drinks on the market, Four Loko has come to symbolize the dangers of such beverages because of its role in binge-drinking incidents this fall involving students at New Jersey's Ramapo College and at Central Washington University. Ramapo and Central Washington have banned Four Loko from their campuses, and several other colleges have sent urgent e-mail messages advising students not to drink it. But whether Four Loko is really "blackout in a can" or just the highest-profile social lubricant of the moment is unclear.

Just uphill from Ashebrooke Liquor Outlet, four young men stand on a porch sipping cans of Four Loko—fruit punch and cranberry-lemonade. All are upperclassmen except for one, Philip Donnachie, who graduated in May. He says most Four Loko drinkers he knows like to guzzle a can of it at home before meeting up with friends, a custom that researchers in the field call "predrinking."

"Everyone that's going to go out for the night, they're going to start with a Four Loko first," Mr. Donnachie says, adding that he generally switches to beer.

A student named Tony says he paid $5.28 at Ashebrooke for two Lokos—a bargain whether the goal is to get tipsy or flat-out drunk. Before the drink became infamous, he says, he would see students bring cans of it into classrooms. "The teachers didn't know what it was," Tony says, and if they asked, the student would casually reply, "It's an energy drink."

Farther uphill, on the sidewalk along Grant Avenue, the Tin Man from *The Wizard of Oz* carries a Loko—watermelon flavor, judging by its color. Down the block a keg party spills out onto the front porch, where guests sprawl on a sofa and flick cigarette ashes over the railing. No one here is drinking Four Loko, but most are eager to talk about the product because they've heard that it could be banned by the federal government as a result of the student illnesses.

Research Gap

That's not likely to happen anytime soon, according to the Food and Drug Administration.

"The FDA's decision regarding the regulatory status of caffeine added to various alcoholic beverages will be a high priority for the agency," Michael L. Herndon, an FDA spokesman, wrote in an e-mail message. "However, a decision regarding the use of caffeine in alcoholic beverages could take some time." The FDA does not consider such drinks to be "generally recognized as safe." A year ago the agency gave 27 manufacturers 30 days to provide evidence to the contrary, if it existed. Only 19 of the companies have responded.

Dennis L. Thombs is chairman of the Department of Social and Behavioral Sciences at the University of North Texas Health Science Center, in Fort Worth. He knows a great deal about the drinking habits of young people.

Last year he was the lead author on a paper submitted to the journal *Addictive Behaviors* that described his team's study of bar patrons' consumption of energy drinks and alcohol in the college town of Gainesville, Fla. After interviewing 802 patrons and testing their blood-alcohol content, Mr. Thombs and his fellow researchers concluded that energy drinks' labels should clearly describe the ingredients, their amounts, and the potential risks involved in using the products.

But Mr. Thombs says the government should have more data before it decides what to do about alcoholic energy drinks.

"There's still a big gap in this research," he says. "We need to get better pharmacological measures in natural drinking environments" like bars.

He says he has submitted a grant application to the National Institutes of Health in hopes of doing just that.

"Liquid Crack"

Back at the keg party in Morgantown, a student wearing Freddy Krueger's brown fedora and razor-blade glove calls Four Loko "liquid crack" and says he prefers not to buy it for his underage friends. "I'll buy them something else," he says, "but not Four Loko."

Dipsy from the *Teletubbies* says the people abusing Four Loko are younger students, mostly 17- and 18-year-olds. He calls the students who became ill at Ramapo and Central Washington "a bunch of kids that don't know how to drink."

Two freshmen at the party, Gabrielle and Meredith, appear to confirm that assertion.

"I like Four Loko because it's cheap and it gets me drunk," says Gabrielle, 19, who seems well on her way to getting drunk tonight, Four Loko or not. "Especially for concerts. I drink two Four Lokos before going, and then I don't have to spend $14 on a couple drinks at the stadium."

Meredith, 18 and equally intoxicated, says that although she drinks Four Loko, she favors a ban. "They're 600 calories, and they're gross."

An interview with Alex, a 19-year-old student at a religiously affiliated college in the Pacific Northwest, suggests one reason that the drink might be popular among a younger crowd. In his state and many others, the laws that govern the sale of Four Loko and beer are less stringent than those for hard liquor.

That eases the hassle for older friends who buy for Alex. These days that's not a concern, though. He stopped drinking Four Loko because of how it made him feel the next day.

"Every time I drank it I got, like, a blackout," says Alex. "Now I usually just drink beer."

DON TROOP is a senior editor of the *Chronicles of Higher Education,* which covers state policy, as well as economic development, town-and-gown relations, fund raising and endowments, and other financial issues at the campus level.

Jacob Sullum    **NO**

Loco Over Four Loko

In a column at the end of October, *The New York Times* restaurant critic Frank Bruni looked down his nose at Four Loko, a fruity, bubbly, brightly colored malt beverage with a lower alcohol content than Chardonnay and less caffeine per ounce than Red Bull. "It's a malt liquor in confectionery drag," Bruni wrote, "not only raising questions about the marketing strategy behind it but also serving as the clearest possible reminder that many drinkers aren't seeking any particular culinary or aesthetic enjoyment. They're taking a drug. The more festively it's dressed and the more vacuously it goes down, the better."

Less than two weeks after Bruni panned Four Loko and its déclassé drinkers, he wrote admiringly of the "ambition and thought" reflected in hoity-toity coffee cocktails offered by the Randolph at Broome, a boutique bar in downtown Manhattan. He conceded that "there is a long if not entirely glorious history of caffeine and alcohol joining forces, of whiskey or liqueurs poured into after-dinner coffee by adults looking for the same sort of effect that Four Loko fans seek: an extension of the night without a surrender of the buzz."

Like Bruni's distaste for Four Loko, the moral panic that led the Food and Drug Administration (FDA) to ban the beverage and others like it in November, just two years after it was introduced, cannot be explained in pharmacological terms. As Brum admitted and as the drink's Chicago-based manufacturer, Phusion Projects, kept pointing out to no avail, there is nothing new about mixing alcohol with caffeine. What made this particular formulation intolerable—indeed "adulterated," according to the FDA—was not its chemical composition but its class connotations: the wild and crazy name, the garish packaging, the low cost, the eight color-coded flavors, and the drink's popularity among young partiers who see "blackout in a can" as a recommendation. Those attributes made Four Loko offensive to the guardians of public health and morals in a way that Irish coffee, rum and cola, and even Red Bull and vodka never were.

The FDA itself conceded that the combination of alcohol and caffeine, a feature of many drinks, that remain legal, was not the real issue. Rather, the agency complained that "the marketing of the caffeinated versions of this class of alcoholic beverage appears to be specifically directed to young adults," who are "especially vulnerable" to "combined ingestion of caffeine and alcohol."

Because Four Loko was presumed to be unacceptably hazardous, the FDA did not feel a need to present much in the way of scientific evidence. A grand total of two studies have found that college-students who drink alcoholic beverages containing caffeine (typically bar- or home-mixed cocktails unaffected by the FDA's ban) tend to drink more and are more prone to risky behavior than college students who drink alcohol by itself. Neither study clarified whether the differences were due to the psychoactive effects of caffeine or to the predispositions of hearty partiers attracted to drinks they believe will help keep them going all night. But that distinction did not matter to panic-promoting politicians and their publicists in the press, who breathlessly advertised Four Loko while marveling at its rising popularity.

This dual function of publicity about an officially condemned intoxicant is familiar to anyone who has witnessed or read about previous scare campaigns against stigmatized substances, ranging from absinthe to *Salvia divinorum*. So is the evidentiary standard employed by Four Loko alarmists: If something bad happens and Four Loko is anywhere in the vicinity, blame Four Loko.

The National Highway Traffic Safety Administration counted 13,800 alcohol-related fatalities in 2008. It did not place crashes involving Four Loko drinkers in a special category. But news organizations around the country, primed to perceive the drink as unusually dangerous, routinely did. Three days before the FDA declared Four Loko illegal, a 14-year-old stole his parents' SUV and crashed it into a guardrail on Interstate 35 in Denton, Texas. His girlfriend, who was not wearing a seat belt, was ejected from the car and killed. Police, who said they found a 12-pack of beer and five cans of Four Loko in the SUV, charged the boy with intoxication manslaughter. Here is how the local Fox station headlined its story: "'Four Loko' Found in Deadly Teen Crash."

Likewise, college students were getting sick after drinking too much long before Four Loko was introduced in August 2008. According to the federal government's Drug Abuse Warning Network, more than 100,000 18-to-20-year-olds make alcohol-related visits to American emergency rooms every year. Yet 15 students at two colleges who were treated for alcohol poisoning after consuming excessive amounts of Four Loko were repeatedly held up as examples of the drink's unique dangers.

If all alcoholic beverages had to satisfy the reckless college student test, all of them would be banned. In a sense, then, we should be grateful for the government's inconsistency. With Four Loko, as with other taboo tipples and illegal drugs, there is little logic to the process by which the scapegoat is selected, but there are noticeable patterns. Once an intoxicant has been identified with a disfavored group—in this case, heedless, hedonistic "young adults"—everything about it is viewed in that light. Soon the wildest charges seem plausible: Four Loko is "a recipe for disaster," "a death wish disguised as an energy drink," a "witch's brew" that drives you mad, makes you shoot yourself in the head, and compels you to steal vehicles and crash them into things.

The timeline that follows shows how quickly a legal product can be transformed into contraband once it becomes the target of such over-the-top opprobrium. Although it's too late for Four Loko, lessons gleaned from the story of its demise could help prevent the next panicky prohibition by scaremongers who criminalize first and ask questions later.

June 2008: Anheuser-Busch, under pressure from 11 attorneys general who are investigating the brewing giant for selling the caffeinated malt beverages Tilt and Bud Extra, agrees to decaffeinate the drinks. "Drinking is not a sport, a race, or an endurance test," says New York Attorney General Andrew Cuomo, who will later be elected governor. "Adding alcohol to energy drinks sends exactly the wrong message about responsible drinking, most especially to young people."

August 2008: Phusion Projects, a Chicago company founded in 2005 by three recent graduates of Ohio State University, introduces Four Loko, which has an alcohol content of up to 12 percent (depending on state regulations); comes in brightly colored, 23.5-ounce cans; contains the familiar energy-drink ingredients caffeine, guarana, and taurine; and is eventually available in eight fruity, neon-hued varieties.

September 2008: The Center for Science in the Public Interest (CSPI), a pro-regulation group that is proud of being known as "the food police," sues MillerCoors Brewing Company over its malt beverage Sparks, arguing that the caffeine and guarana in the drink are additives that have not been approved by the FDA. "Mix alcohol and stimulants with a young person's sense of invincibility," says CSPI's George Hacker, "and you have a recipe for disaster. Sparks is a drink designed to mask feelings of drunkenness and to encourage people to keep drinking past the point atwhich they otherwise would have stopped. The end result is more drunk driving, more injuries, and more sexual assaults."

December 2008: In a deal with 13 attorneys general and the city of San Francisco, MillerCoors agrees to reformulate Sparks, removing the caffeine, guarana, taurine, and ginseng. Cuomo says caffeinated alcoholic beverages are "fundamentally dangerous and put drinkers of all ages at risk."

July 2009: *The Wall Street Journal* reports that Cuomo, Connecticut Attorney General Richard Blumenthal (now a U.S. senator), California Attorney General Jerry Brown (now governor), and their counterparts in several other states are investigating Four Loko and Joose, a close competitor. The National Association of Convenience Stores says the two brands are growing fast now that Tilt and Sparks have left the caffeinated malt beverage market.

August 2009: To demonstrate the threat that Four Loko poses to the youth of America, Blumenthal cites an online testimonial from a fan of the drink: "You just gotta drink it and drink it and drink it and drink it and not even worry about it because it's awesome and you're just partying and having fun and getting wild and drinking it." *The Chicago Tribune* cannot locate that particular comment on Phusion Projects' website, but it does find this: "I'm having a weird reaction to Four that makes me want to dance in my bra and panties. Please advise."

September 2009: Eighteen attorneys general ask the FDA to investigate the safety of alcoholic beverages containing caffeine.

November 2009: The FDA sends letters to 27 companies known to sell caffeinated alcoholic beverages, warning them that the combination has never been officially approved and asking them to submit evidence that it is "generally recognized as safe," as required by the Food, Drug, and Cosmetic Act. In addition to Phusion Projects, the recipients include Joose's manufacturer, United Brands; Charge Beverages, which sells similar products; the PINK Spirits Company, which makes caffeinated vodka, rum, gin, whiskey, and sake; and even the Ithaca Beer Company, which at one point made a special-edition stout brewed with coffee. "I continue to be very concerned that these drinks are extremely dangerous," says Illinois Attorney General Lisa Madigan, "especially in the hands of young people."

February 2010: In a feature story carried by several newspapers under headlines such as "Alcopops Only Look Innocent and Can Hook Kids," Kim Hone-McMahan of the *Akron Beacon Journal* outlines one scenario in which these extremely dangerous drinks might end up in tiny hands: "Intentionally or by accident, a child could grab an alcoholic beverage that looks like an energy drink, and hand it to Mom to pay for at the register. Without taking a closer look at the label, Mom may think it's just another brand of nonalcoholic energy beverage." It does seem like the sort of mistake that Hone-McMahan, who confuses fermented malt beverages with distilled spirits and warns parents about an alcoholic energy drink that was never actually introduced, might make. She explains that the combination of alcohol and caffeine "can confuse the nervous system," producing "wired, wide-awake drunks."

July 12, 2010: Sen. Charles Schumer (D-N.Y.) urges the Federal Trade Commission to investigate Four Loko and products like it. "It is my understanding that caffeine-infused, flavored malt beverages are becoming increasingly popular among teenagers," he writes. "The style and promotion of these products is extremely troubling." Schumer complains that the packaging of Joose and Four Loko is "designed to appear hip with flashy colors and funky designs that could appeal to younger consumers."

July 29, 2010: Schumer, joined by Sens. Dianne Feinstein (D-Calif.), Amy Klobuchar (D-Minn.), and Jeff Merkley (D-Ore.), urges the FDA to complete its investigation. "The FDA needs to determine once and for all if these drinks are safe, and if they're not, they ought to be banned," says Schumer, right before telling the FDA the conclusion it should reach: "Caffeine and alcohol are a dangerous mix, especially for young people."

August 1, 2010: After a crash in St. Petersburg, Florida, that kills four visitors from Orlando, police arrest 20-year-old Demetrius Jordan and charge him with drunk driving and manslaughter. The *St. Petersburg Times* reports that Jordan, who "had been drinking liquor and a caffeinated alcoholic beverage and smoking marijuana prior to the crash," "may have been going in excess of 80 mph when he crashed into the other vehicle." It notes that a "can of Four Loko was found on the floor of the back seat."

August 5, 2010: In a follow-up story, the *St. Petersburg Times* reports that "Four Loko, the caffeine-fueled malt liquor that police say Demetrius Jordan downed before he was accused of driving drunk and killing four people, is part of a new breed of beverages stirring controversy across the country." It quotes Bruce Goldberger, a toxicologist at the University of Florida, who declares, "I don't think there's a place for these beverages in the marketplace." The headline: "Alcohol, Caffeine: A Deadly Combo?"

August 12, 2010: The *Orlando Sentinel*, catching up with the *St. Petersburg Times,* shows it can quote Goldberger too. "It's a very bad combination having alcohol, plus caffeine, plus the brain of a young person," he says. "It's like a perfect storm." The headline: "Did High-Octane Drink Fuel Deadly Crash?"

September 2010: Peter Mercer, president of Ramapo College in Mahwah, New Jersey, bans Four Loko and other caffeinated malt beverages from campus after several incidents in which a total of 23 students were hospitalized for alcohol poisoning. Just six of the students were drinking Four Loko. Mercer later tells the Associated Press, "There's no redeeming social purpose to be served by having the beverage."

October 9, 2010: In a story about nine gang members who tied up and tortured a gay man after luring him to an abandoned building in the Bronx by telling him they were having a party, the *New York Daily News* plays up the detail that they "forced him to guzzle four cans" of the Four Loko he had brought with him. "The sodomized man couldn't give police a clear account of what he'd gone through," the paper reports, "possibly because of the Four Loko he was forced to drink."

October 10, 2010: In a follow-up story, the *Daily News* reports that Four Loko, a "wild drink full of caffeine and booze," "is causing controversy from coast to coast," citing the deadly crash in St. Petersburg.

October 13, 2010: Police in New Port Richey, Florida, arrest Justin Barker, 21, after he breaks into an old woman's home, trashes the place, strips naked, defecates on the floor, and then breaks into another house, where he falls asleep on the couch. Barker says Four Loko made him do it.

October 15, 2010: Calling Four Loko "a quick and intense high that has been dubbed 'blackout in a can,'" the Passaic County, New Jersey, *Herald News* notes the Ramapo College ban and quotes Mahwah Police Chief James Batelli. "The bottom line on the product is it gets you very drunk, very quick," he says. "To me, Four Loko is just a dangerous substance." The "blackout in a can" sobriquet, obviously hyperbolic when applied to a beverage that contains less alcohol per container than a bottle of wine, originated with Four Loko fans who considered it high praise; one of their Facebook pages is titled "four lokos are blackouts in a can and the end of my morals."

October 19, 2010: Bruce Goldberger, who co-authored one of the two studies linking caffeinated alcohol to risky behavior, tells the *Pittsburgh Post-Gazette* "the science is clear that consumption of alcohol with caffeine leads to risky behaviors." Mary Claire O'Brien, the Wake Forest University researcher who co-authored the other study, expresses her anger at the FDA. "I'm mad as a hornet that they didn't do something in the first place," she says, "and I'm mad as a hornet that they haven't done anything yet."

October 20, 2010: Based on a single case of a 19-year-old who came to Temple University Hospital in Philadelphia with chest pains after drinking Four Loko, ABC News warns that the stuff, which contains about one-third as much caffeine per ounce as coffee, can cause fatal heart attacks in perfectly healthy people. "That was the only explanation we had," says the doctor who treated the 19-year-old, before extrapolating further from his sample of one: "This is a dangerous product from what we've seen. It doesn't have to be chronic use. I think it could happen to somebody on a first-time use."

October 25, 2010: Citing the hospitalization of nine Central Washington University students for alcohol poisoning following an October 8 party in Roslyn where they drank Four Loko along with beer, rum, and vodka, Washington Attorney General Rob McKenna calls for a ban on caffeinated malt liquor. "The wide availability of the alcoholic energy drinks means that a single mistake can be deadly," he says. "They're marketed to kids by using fruit flavors that mask the taste of alcohol, and they have such high levels of stimulants that people have no idea how inebriated they really are." McKenna's office cites Ken Briggs, chairman of the university's physical education department, who says Four Loko is known as "liquid cocaine" as well as "blackout in a can," and with good reason, since it is "a binge drinker's dream."

October 26, 2010: McKenna's reaction to college students who drank too much Four Loko, like Peter Mercer's at Ramapo, attracts national attention. A Pennsylvania E.R. doctor quoted by *The New York Times* calls Four Loko "a recipe for disaster" and "one of the most dangerous new alcohol concoctions I have ever seen."

November 1, 2010: The Pennsylvania Liquor Control Board asks retailers to stop selling Four Loko, which is produced at the former Rolling Rock brewery in Latrobe, because it may "pose a significant threat to the health of all Pennsylvanians." State Rep. Robert Donatucci (D-Philadelphia) says "there is overriding circumstantial evidence that this combination may be very dangerous," and "until we can determine its effect on people and what kind of danger it may present, it should be yanked from the shelves."

November 3, 2010: Two Chicago aldermen propose an ordinance that would ban Four Loko from the city where its manufacturer is based. "I think it is completely irresponsible," says one, "to manufacture and market a product that can make young people so intoxicated so fast."

November 4, 2010: The Michigan Liquor Control Commission bans 55 "alcohol energy drinks," including Four Loko, Joose, a "hard" iced tea that no longer exists, a cola-flavored variety of Jack Daniel's Country Cocktails, and an India pale ale brewed with yerba mate. "With all the things that are happening, it's very alarming," explains commission chairwoman Nida Samona. "It's more serious than any of us ever imagined."

November 8, 2010: Oklahoma's Alcoholic Beverage Laws Enforcement Commission bans Four Loko from the state "in light of the growing scientific evidence against alcohol energy drinks, and the October 8th incident involving Four Loko in Roslyn, Washington."

November 9, 2010: NPR quotes Washington State University student Jarod Franklin as an authority on Four Loko's effects. "We would start to lose those inhibitions," he says, "and then [it would be like], 'How did you get a broken knuckle?' 'Oh, I punched through a three-inch layer of ice [because] you bet me I couldn't.'"

November 10, 2010: The Washington State Liquor Control Board bans beverages that "combine beer, strong beer, or malt liquor with caffeine, guarana, taurine, or other similar substances." Gov. Christine Gregoire, who recommended the ban, explains her reasoning: "I was particularly concerned that these drinks tend to target young people. Reports of inexperienced or underage drinkers consuming them in reckless amounts have given us cause for concern. . . . By taking these drinks off the shelves we are saying 'no' to irresponsible drinking and taking steps to prevent incidents like the one that made these college students so ill."

Sen. Schumer urges the New York State Liquor Authority to "immediately ban caffeinated alcoholic beverages." He says drinks like Four Loko "are a toxic, dangerous mix of caffeine and alcohol, and they are spreading like a plague across the country." Schumer claims "studies have shown that caffeinated alcoholic beverages raise unique and disturbing safety concerns, especially for younger drinkers." While they "can be extremely hazardous for teens and adults alike," he says, they "pose a unique danger because they target young people" with their "vibrantly colored aluminum can colors and funky designs."

November 12, 2010: A CBS station in Baltimore reports that two cans of Four Loko caused a 21-year-old Maryland woman to "lose her mind," steal a friend's pickup truck, and crash it into a telephone pole, killing herself.

A CBS station in Philadelphia reports that a middle-aged suburban dad "spiraled into a hallucinogenic frenzy" featuring "nightmarish delusions" after drinking a can and a half of Four Loko. "It was like he was stuck inside a horror movie and he couldn't get out and I couldn't get him out," the man's wife says. "In his mind, he had harmed all of our kids and he had to kill me and kill himself so that we could go to heaven to take care of them. Next thing I know, he was having convulsions [and] making gurgling sounds as if someone were choking him, and then he stopped breathing."

Connecticut Attorney General Blumenthal urges the FDA to "impose a nationwide ban on these dangerous and potentially deadly drinks."

November 14, 2010: Under pressure from Gov. David Paterson and the state liquor authority, Phusion Projects agrees to stop shipping Four Loko to New York. "We have an obligation to keep products that are potentially hazardous off the shelves," says the liquor authority's chairman.

Bruce Goldberger tells the *New Haven Register* Four Loko is "a very significant problem" for the "instant gratification generation." The kids today, he says, "text, they have iPhones, and they can access the Internet any minute of their life. And now, they can get drunk for literally less than $5, and they can get drunk very rapidly."

November 15, 2010: WBZ, the CBS affiliate in Boston, reports that the Massachusetts Alcoholic Beverages Control Commission plans to ban Four Loko. According to WBZ, commission officials say the drink—a fermented malt beverage with an alcohol content of 12 percent, compared to 40 percent or more for distilled spirits—"is really not a malt liquor, but a much more potent form of hard liquor, like vodka." The commission's chairman explains that the ban is aimed at protecting consumers who cannot read: "We are concerned that people who are drinking these alcoholic beverages are not aware of the ingredients which are contained in them."

The New York Times reports that Four Loko "has been blamed for several deaths over the last several months," including that of a 20-year-old sophomore at Florida State University in Tallahassee who "started playing with a gun and fatally shot himself after drinking several cans of Four Loko over a number of hours." Richard Blumenthal tells the *Times* "there's just no excuse for the delay in applying

standards that clearly should bar this kind of witch's brew." Mary Claire O'Brien argues that Four Loko is guilty until proven innocent: "The addition of the caffeine impairs the ability of the drinker to tell when they're drunk. What is the level at which it becomes dangerous? We don't know that, and until we can figure it out, the answer is that no level is safe."

November 16, 2010: Phusion Projects says it will reformulate Four Loko, removing the caffeine, guarana, and taurine. "We have repeatedly contended—and still believe, as do many people throughout the country—that the combination of alcohol and caffeine is safe," the company's founders say. "We are taking this step after trying—unsuccessfully—to navigate a difficult and politically charged regulatory environment at both the state and federal levels."

The Arizona Republic reports that an "extremely intoxicated" 18-year-old from Mesa crashed her SUV into a tree after "playing 'beer pong' with the controversial caffeinated alcoholic beverage Four Loko." The headline: "Caffeine, Alcohol Drink Tied to Crash."

Reporting on a lawsuit against Phusion Projects by the parents of the FSU student who shot himself after drinking Four Loko, ABC News quotes Schumer, who avers, "It's almost a death wish disguised as an energy drink."

November 17, 2010: The FDA and the Federal Trade Commission send warning letters to Phusion Projects, United Brands, Charge Beverages, and New Century Brewing Company, which makes a caffeinated lager called Moonshot. The agency says their products are "adulterated," and therefore illegal under the Food, Drug, and Cosmetic Act, because they contain an additive, caffeine, that is not generally recognized as safe in this context. But the FDA does not conclude that all beverages combining alcohol and caffeine are inherently unsafe. It focuses on these particular companies because they "seemingly target the young adult user." Federal drug czar Gil Kerlikowske approves the FDA's marketing-based definition of adulteration, saying "these products are designed, branded, and promoted to encourage binge drinking."

NPR correspondent Tovia Smith reports that "many college students say they agree with the FDA that alcoholic energy drinks do result in more risky behavior, like drunk driving or sexual assaults." Smith presents one such student, Ali Burak of Boston College, who says "it seems like every time someone wakes up in the morning and regrets the night before it's usually because they had Four Loko."

November 20, 2010: In a *Huffington Post* essay, David Katz, director of Yale University's Prevention Research Center, explains why "anyone who is for sanity and safety in marketing" should welcome the FDA's ban. "Combining alcohol and caffeine is—in one word—crazy," he writes. "Don't do it! It has an excellent chance of hurting you, and a fairly good chance of killing you." His evidence: the Maryland car crash in which a woman who had been drinking Four Loko died after colliding with a telephone pole. "It's hard to imagine any argument for such products," Katz concludes. "It's also hard to imagine anyone objecting to a ban of such products."

JACOB SULLUM is a journalist and editor of *Reason Magazine*.

EXPLORING THE ISSUE

Are Energy Drinks with Alcohol Dangerous Enough to Ban?

Critical Thinking and Reflection

1. Why were energy drinks with caffeine banned?
2. Why are caffeinated energy drinks so popular among college students?
3. Describe why the drinks are dangerous and how they contributed to deaths among some college students.

Is There Common Ground?

Four Loko and other energy drinks provide the effects of caffeine and sugar, but there is little or no evidence that a wide variety of other ingredients have any impact on the body. A variety of physiological and psychological effects, however, have been blamed on energy drinks and their components. Excess use of energy drinks may produce mild-to-moderate euphoria primarily due to the stimulant properties of caffeine. The drinks may also cause agitation, anxiety, irritability, and sleeplessness.

Ingestion of a single energy drink will not lead to excessive caffeine intake, but consumption of two or more drinks over the course of a day can. Ginseng, guarana, and other stimulants are often added to energy drinks and may bolster the effects of caffeine. Negative effects associated with caffeine consumption in amounts greater than 400 mg include nervousness, irritability, sleeplessness, increased urination, abnormal heart rhythms, and upset stomach. By comparison, a cup of drip coffee contains about 150 mg of caffeine. Caffeine in energy drinks can cause the excretion of water from the body to dilute high concentrations of sugar entering the blood stream, leading to dehydration.

In the United States, energy drinks have been linked with reports of emergency room visits due to heart palpitations and anxiety. The beverages have been associated with seizures due to the crash following the high energy that occurs after ingestion. In the United States, caffeine dosage is not required to be on the product label for food, unlike drugs, but some advocates are urging the FDA to change this practice.

Drinking one 24-ounce can of Four Loko provides the alcoholic kick of four beers and the caffeine buzz of a strong cup of coffee. Drinking one quickly makes someone pretty drunk and reasonably awake, and able to drink more. As a result, college students seem particularly drawn to it, which has landed some in hospitals. But should Four Loko be banned state-by-state as a result? Banning Four Loko might prevent some people, especially some college students, from hurting themselves or others. But does banning Four Loko and similar beverages improve people's judgment or otherwise empower them to protect themselves?

Additional Resources

The party's over. (2010, November 25). *Nature, 475*.

Siegel, S. (2011). The Four-Loko effect. *Perspectives on Psychological Science, 6*(4), 357–362.

Wood, D. B. (2010, November 19). Four Loko: Does FDA's caffeinated alcoholic beverage ban go too far? *Christian Science Monitor*, p. N.PAG.

Internet References . . .

Energy Drinks—American Association of Poison Control Centers

www.aapcc.org/alerts/energy-drinks

Food and Drug Administration

www.fda.gov

National Institute on Drug Abuse (NIDA)

www.nida.nih.gov

Selected, Edited, and with Issue Framing Material by:
Dennis K. Miller, *University of Missouri*

ISSUE

Should Smoking Be Banned from Public Places?

YES: Sheelah A. Feinberg, from "No-Smoking, Please," *Huffington Post* (2013)

NO: John Stossel, from "Control Freaks Still Targeting Tobacco," *Reason Magazine* (2014)

Learning Outcomes

After reading this issue, you will be able to:

- Identify the health risks associated with tobacco smoking and environmental tobacco smoke.
- Consider the balance between the rights of the individual smoker and the rights of the nonsmoker.
- Evaluate the roles of federal, state, and local governments in establishing drug use policies.

ISSUE SUMMARY

YES: Environmental tobacco smoke (a.k.a., "secondhand smoke") is classified as a carcinogen and government agencies declared that there are no safe exposure levels. Many communities have banned smoking in public areas (e.g., bars, restaurants, and parks) to minimize secondhand smoke exposure, including New York. Sheelah A. Feinberg, director of New York's Coalition for a Smoke-Free City, reports that her city's ban on public smoking has improved health and quality of life.

NO: Journalist John Stossel disagrees with this position in his opinion piece in *Reason Magazine* and believes that bans on public smoking are indicative of increased government control over American's lives.

The primary pharmacologically active ingredient in a tobacco cigarette is nicotine. While there are other tobacco alkaloids that might contribute to the psychological and physiological effects of tobacco, it is clear that smokers use a tobacco cigarette as a nicotine delivery vehicle. There is little doubt today that nicotine is a reinforcer (i.e., it increases the behavior) and access to nicotine controls smoking behavior. Humans are sensitive to the concentration of nicotine in a cigarette and adjust smoking behavior (e.g., the depth of a puff on a cigarette and rate of taking puffs) accordingly to low- and high-nicotine content cigarettes.

Many smokers find tobacco and nicotine to be pleasurable. In laboratory studies, smokers report nicotine to produce liking and subjective effects similar to those caused by opiates and amphetamines. They report that smoking produces a "rush," a "buzz," or a "high" shortly after taking a puff from a cigarette. Smokers may report

that tobacco smoking increases pleasure from drinking alcohol and dining, and smoking has been an important part of our popular culture. Many cultural icons, such as Groucho Marx, Arnold Schwarzenegger, and John Wayne, are closely associated in the public's memories with smoking a cigarette, cigar, or pipe. Nicotine improves fine motor abilities, increases attention, and expands the capacity and efficiency of short term memory. It can improve various aspects of cognitive function, such as reaction time, including in patients with Alzheimer's disease. In fact, nicotine-like drugs are being investigated to minimize the symptoms of neurodegenerative diseases.

It is also clear that tobacco use may be compulsive. When smokers are unable to use tobacco, a withdrawal syndrome is present. Nicotine withdrawal is not as physically severe as the symptoms reported following heroin withdrawal, but it can be just as psychologically unpleasant. Anecdotally, some heroin users report that it is harder to try to quit smoking tobacco than to quit using the opiate. The nicotine withdrawal symptoms can be unpleasant enough to reinitiate and maintain smoking behavior. Although rates of tobacco in the United States have declined from the middle part of the twentieth century, the prevalence of tobacco smoking among adults is around 20 percent. This means that there are likely 40–45 million smokers in the United States.

A key factor in the decline of tobacco smoking in the United States was the Surgeon General's Report of 1964. This report linked, for the first time, smoking to cancer and other diseases. Smoking is responsible for one-third of all cancer deaths in the United States, according to the American Cancer Society and the National Cancer Institute. Furthermore, the risk of developing lung cancer is 15–25 times higher in smokers than in nonsmokers. Tobacco smoking also increases the risks for other cancers, including cancer of the mouth, throat, stomach, and blood (leukemia). The precise mechanism through which tobacco smoking is carcinogenic is unclear; however, tobacco smoke contains a number of known carcinogens.

Smoking also increases the risk of heart and lung disease and dysfunction. Particles and gasses in tobacco smoke cause air passages in the lungs to be obstructed, restricting air flow. The ash and tars from tobacco smoke can accumulate on the membranes inside the lung, altering the passage of oxygen and carbon dioxide in and out of the blood. Furthermore, carbon monoxide, present in tobacco smoke, reduces the ability of the blood to carry oxygen when it is inhaled into the lungs. Chronic obstructive pulmonary disease (COPD)—chronic bronchitis, emphysema, and/or both conditions—is one of the leading causes of death in the United States and smoking is one of the leading causes of COPD.

Tobacco smoking is unhealthy; however, because it is difficult to quit, the smoker continues the behavior and the exposure to tobacco smoke. Tobacco smoking can also be unhealthy for people who live and work with the smoker.

Environmental tobacco smoke (ETS) is the smoke from someone else's cigarette, cigar, or pipe. It is also known as "secondhand smoke" and is the material in indoor air that originates from tobacco smoke. Within ETS, the smoke that is inhaled and exhaled from the smoker's lungs is called mainstream smoke (MS). Sidestream smoke (SS) is the smoke that enters the air directly from the burning end of a cigarette, cigar, or pipe. ETS is composed of both MS and SS. Although ETS can be diluted in the air, nicotine, carbon monoxide, and other smoke-related chemicals have been found in the body fluids of nonsmokers exposed to ETS. Both smokers and nonsmokers may actually have similar exposure to the toxicants found in tobacco smoke (e.g., the known carcinogens

formaldehyde and vinyl chloride) because nearly 85 percent of ETS in a room comes from SS. Various studies suggest that passive exposure to ETS over an eight-hour day is comparable to directly smoking one to three cigarettes.

ETS is classified as a known human carcinogen by the U.S. federal government. Inhaling secondhand smoke causes lung cancer in nonsmoking adults and the U.S. Surgeon General estimates that living with a smoker increases a nonsmoker's chances of developing lung cancer by 20 to 30 percent. Exposure to ETS irritates the airways and has immediate harmful effects on a person's heart and blood vessels. It may increase the risk of heart disease by 25 to 30 percent and is thought to cause about 46,000 heart disease deaths each year.

According to the National Cancer Institute, there is no safe level of exposure to ETS: Even low levels of ETS can be harmful. As such, the only way to fully protect nonsmokers from ETS is to completely eliminate smoking in indoor spaces. Separating smokers from nonsmokers, cleaning the air, and ventilating buildings cannot completely eliminate exposure to secondhand smoke.

Several laws restricting smoking in public places have been passed at the federal level in the United States. Federal law bans smoking on domestic airline flights, nearly all flights between the United States and foreign destinations, interstate buses, and most trains. Smoking is also banned in most federally owned buildings, as well as in most public buildings by law or by choice of the building manager. The Pro-Children Act of 1994 prohibits smoking in facilities that routinely provide federally funded services to children. At the state and local level, many governments have passed laws prohibiting smoking in public facilities, as well as private workplaces, including restaurants and bars. Some states have passed laws regulating smoking in multiunit housing and cars. More than half of the states have enacted statewide bans on workplace smoking.

The articles address the issue, should smoking be banned from public places? In the YES selection, Oklahoma businessman Don Millican supports a ban on tobacco smoking in all public places in his state. He acknowledges that a smoker has the right to smoke a cigarette, but the smoker does not have the right to damage the nonsmoker's health through ETS. As such, Mr. Millican believes smoking should be banned from public places. Television journalist John Stossel disagrees in the NO selection. He acknowledges that he selfishly likes smoking bans, but he does not believe the government should force private business people from eliminating smoking from their bars and restaurants. To Stossel, the decision to make a venue smoking or nonsmoking should be up to the individual and the government should stay out.

YES ↵

Sheelah A. Feinberg

"No-Smoking, Please"

"No-smoking, please." Ten years ago today, you no longer had to say that when you went to dinner in a New York City restaurant. Also, if you tended bar or worked in a restaurant, you no longer had to breathe in toxic second-hand smoke while you worked your shift.

Today marks the tenth anniversary of the NYC Smoke-Free Air Act, a landmark piece of legislation that has helped New Yorkers breathe easier and live longer. Thanks to this bold health policy, New Yorkers are able to breathe clean, smoke-free air in the workplace, regardless of whether they work in a high-rise office or neighborhood restaurant or bar.

We often forget that just 10 years ago, many New Yorkers couldn't earn a living without risking their lives. Waiters and waitresses, bartenders and nightclub performers, maître-des and bus boys all went to work every day in smoke-filled bars, restaurants and nightclubs. These workers are the backbone of the service industry and essential to our city's economy. They deserve the right to do their job in a smoke-free environment. The right to breathe is more important than the perceived right to pollute. The NYC Smoke-Free Air Act protected all New Yorkers' right to breathe smoke-free air at work.

New York City is recognized as a leader in protecting public health, and New Yorkers have embraced cleaner air and sharply declining smoking rates. The smoking rate among adults decreased from 21.5 percent in 2002 to 14.8 percent in 2011 and from 17.5 percent to 8.5 percent among youth. In spite of those who predicted that protecting New Yorkers' health would hurt the economy, we have seen significant increases in business and employment in our bars and restaurants and the tourism sector. Also, when was the last time you heard someone complain about the lack of smoke-filled offices or restaurants?

New York City is a beacon across the country and around the world. Following our lead, more than 500 U.S. municipalities and 49 countries have passed smoke-free laws since 2003, affecting more than 1.5 billion people.

Smoke-free workplace laws protect workers, save lives, and made smoking less socially acceptable.

We have made great strides in protecting all New Yorkers' health and a real difference in our city. But more work needs to be done. Smoking rates among teens have dropped considerably over the last decade, but the rate of decline has ground to a halt in recent years. Youth smoking in New York City reached a historic low of 8.5 percent in 2007, but it has remained level since then. That's still 19,000 NYC public high school students under the age of 18 who currently smoke; one-third of them will die prematurely as a result of smoking.

The battle against tobacco is far from over, and tobacco companies remain as ruthless as ever in targeting our kids, the replacement smokers they need for the more than 400,000 Americans killed by tobacco use each year.

That's why we applaud Mayor Bloomberg and New York City Council for proposing two bold and historic tobacco control bills that will reduce youth smoking. The "Tobacco Product Display Restriction" bill would make New York City the first in the nation to prohibit retailers from displaying tobacco products prominently and in plain view of youth and other customers. We know that the more tobacco product displays kids see, the more likely they are to smoke. The proposed bill will help protect youth from being bombarded by tobacco displays at all New York City retail outlets.

A new set of "Sensible Tobacco Enforcement and Pricing" (STEP) initiatives was also proposed. STEP would increase the fines and penalties for selling untaxed tobacco, restrict the use of coupons and price discounts, and create a price floor for a pack of cigarettes or little cigars. These measures will not only reduce youth access to tobacco products, but through increased enforcement of illegal sales and tobacco tax evasion, will level the playing field for local businesses that play by the rules.

These proposed policies will help save lives and potentially millions of dollars in health care costs. As we look back and celebrate 10 years of smoke-free workplaces in New York, let's not rest on our laurels. We have a long way to go. We are committed to providing all New Yorkers with the resources they need to quit smoking and preventing our youth from ever starting to light up.

These new initiatives will solidify New York City's legacy as an innovative national and global public health leader and help even more New Yorkers live longer, healthier lives.

SHEELAH A. FEINBERG is the director of the New York City Coalition for a Smoke-Free City. She has conducted successful advocacy campaigns in economic self-sufficiency, parks development, workforce and community development, and public health. Ms. Feinberg served in the Clinton Administration in the White House as deputy associate director of Presidential Personnel.

John Stossel → **NO**

Control Freaks Still Targeting Tobacco

Rule-makers always want *more*.

Control freaks want to run your life. They call themselves "public servants." But whether student council president, environmental bureaucrat, or member of Congress, most believe they know how to run your life better than you do.

I admit I was once guilty of this kind of thinking. As a young consumer reporter, I researched what doctors said was bad for us and what products might harm us. Then I demanded that the state pass rules to protect us from those things. The concept of *individual freedom* was not yet on my radar screen. I apologize. I was ignorant and arrogant.

But at least I had no real power. I couldn't force consumers to avoid unhealthy things or pay for certain kinds of health care. I couldn't force any business to stop selling something. Only government can do that. Only government can use force.

Sadly, government is filled with people just as ignorant and arrogant as I was.

Economist Matthew Mitchell of the Mercatus Center likes to point out that governments impose regulations without acknowledging that the new rules will have unintended consequences.

Bans on smoking in restaurants and bars is one of the control freaks' favorite campaigns. "A recent Cornell University of Wisconsin study," Mitchell says on my show this week, "found that in those areas where they introduced bans on smoking, you saw an increase in accidents related to alcohol. The theory is that people drive longer distances in order to find bars that either have outside seating or are outside the jurisdiction."

I selfishly like smoking bans. I don't like breathing others' smoke. But the majority of us shouldn't force our preferences on the minority, even if they do things that are dangerous. Smokers ought to be allowed to smoke in some bars, if the bar owners allow it. But today in about half the states, no one may smoke in any bar.

It's totalitarianism from the health police. If secondhand smoke were dangerous enough to threaten nonsmokers, the control freaks would have a point, but it isn't. It barely has any detectable health effect at all.

Rule-makers always want *more*. At first, they just asked for bans on TV's cigarette ads. Then they demanded no-smoking sections in restaurants. Then bans in airplanes, schools, workplaces, entire restaurants. Then bars, too. Now sometimes even apartments and outdoor spaces. Can't smokers have some places?

So far, smokers just . . . take it. But maybe that's changing. The town of Westminster, Massachusetts, recently held hearings on whether to ban the sale of tobacco products altogether, and 500 angry people showed up.

One said, "I find smoking one of the most disgusting habits anybody could possibly do. On top of that, I find this proposal to be even more of a disgusting thing." Good for him.

Mitchell warns that "we are accustomed to thinking about the federal government and federal overreach. But a lot of the most intrusive regulations happen at the local level," as in Westminster.

In Fort Lauderdale, Florida, police charged two pastors and a 90-year-old volunteer with giving food to poor people in public. Florida law declares it illegal to give away food in an outdoor location without providing public toilets. The restrictions were instated in the name of "public health and safety."

In New Jersey, churches were forced to stop offering Thanksgiving dinners to poor people because they didn't have "properly licensed commercial kitchens."

A court threw out a soft drink ban imposed on my city, New York, by then-mayor Bloomberg, but my new control-freak mayor, Bill de Blasio, plans to reinstate the ban.

The rules keep coming. Another New York regulation, banning trans fats in restaurants, led to stringent bans on which foods people were allowed to donate to the hungry. I'd think the poor have bigger problems than trans fats. Their biggest problem is the same one we all have: too much government.

JOHN STOSSEL is a consumer television personality, author, and libertarian pundit. He is the host of *Stossel*, a weekly talk show on political, social, and economic issues, which airs on the FOX Business Network and FOX News. He is the author of *Give Me a Break* and *Myths, Lies,* and *Downright Stupidity*.

EXPLORING THE ISSUE

Should Smoking Be Banned from Public Places?

Critical Thinking and Reflection

1. In the YES selection, Stossel refers to government antismoking advocates as "control freaks." Where should government regulation of personal behavior be limited, if anywhere?
2. What other personal behaviors might have an influence on others' health and well-being? Should these be regulated or limited by government?
3. Is government regulation necessary to limit nonsmokers' exposure to ETS?
4. Do nonsmokers have the *right* to be free from ETS? Do smokers have the *right* to generate ETS?
5. Considering the health risks of tobacco smoking from MS and SS, should the government ban tobacco smoking completely—in public and in private?

Is There Common Ground?

Should smoking be banned from public places? The rationale for public smoking bans is that tobacco smoking is optional habit where the individual accepts the known risks of smoking and chooses to perform the behavior. However, breathing is not an optional behavior and the nonsmoker should not be forced to accept the known and unknown risks associated with tobacco smoking. As such, smoking bans are enforced to protect people from the effects of environmental tobacco smoke (ETS), which include an increased risk of heart disease, cancer, emphysema, and other diseases. Many states and communities in the United States have implemented bans on indoor and outdoor smoking.

In polls, over half of Americans favor completely smoke-free restaurants, while a significant minority supports smoke-free hotels and bars. Many studies have documented health and economic benefits following public smoking bans. Smoking bans are generally acknowledged to reduce rates of smoking, smoke-free workplaces reduce smoking rates among workers, and restrictions upon smoking in public places reduce general smoking rates. Ahead of smoking bans in a community restaurant and bar owners are concerned with the ban's impact on their customers; however, the majority studies have found no negative economic impact associated with smoking restrictions. Many findings indicate there may be a positive effect on local businesses, with increased revenue.

A basic principle of libertarian politics is that the actions of individuals should only be limited to prevent harm to others. According to John Stuart Mill (*On Liberty*, 1859), "the only purpose for which [government] power can be rightfully exercised over any member of a civilized community, against his will, is to prevent harm to others." What truly is the harm of smoking and ETS to another individual? If someone doesn't like or want to be exposed to ETS, they can go somewhere else. While the government may be free to regulate smoking in public areas (e.g., a government building), bar and restaurant owners should determine if they want to allow smoking or prevent smoking in their private establishment. In the YES selection for this issue, John Stossel argues that smoking bans are not about public health and ETS, but "totalitarianism from the health police."

The conflict between smoker and nonsmoker represents a very basic conflict between individual freedom and public health.

Additional Resources

Jackson, J. (2010). A dozen reasons to stub out the smoking ban. *Spiked*. http://www.spiked-online.com/newsite/article/9278#.VQ7R6fnF98H.

British pop musician Joe Jackson ("Steppin' Out" and "You Can't Get What You Want (Till You Know What You Want)") strongly opposes bans on smoking in bars and clubs in the United Kingdom.

Lauterstein, D. et al., (2014). The changing face of tobacco use among United States youth. *Current Drug Abuse Reviews*. 7(1): 29–43.

This review paper shows that the decline in cigarette use in the United States has been accompanied by an upsurge in adolescent and young adult use of new, non-cigarette tobacco and nicotine-delivery products (e.g., e-cigarettes).

McIntire, R. T., et al. (2015). Secondhand smoke exposure and other correlates of susceptibility to smoking: A propensity score matching approach. *Addictive Behaviors*. 48: 36–43.

The researchers from Indiana University show that children exposed to environmental tobacco smoke are more likely to smoke in adolescence.

Mill, J. S. (1859). *On Liberty*. London: The Walter Scott Publishing Co., Ltd. https://www.gutenberg.org/files/34901/34901-h/34901-h.htm.

British philosopher John Stuart Mill established standards for the relationship between authority and liberty and emphasized the importance of individuality in *On Liberty*. This book is one of the bases for Stossel's position in the YES argument in this issue.

McKee, M. et al. (2004). Why we need to ban smoking in public places now. *Journal of Public Health*. 26(4): 325–326.

The authors, who are from London, report that there is widespread public support for action to eliminate smoking from public areas (e.g., restaurants and bars) and that members of the public health community should pressure politicians and political leaders to enact bans to eliminate ETS exposure.

Internet References . . .

American Cancer Society—Secondhand Smoke

http://www.cancer.org/cancer/cancercauses/tobaccocancer/secondhand-smoke

Americans for Non-Smokers' Rights

http://www.no-smoke.org/

Citizens for Tobacco Rights

http://www.tobaccorights.com/

National Institutes of Health—National Cancer Institute: Secondhand Smoke and Cancer

http://www.cancer.gov/about-cancer/causes-prevention/risk/tobacco/second-hand-smoke-fact-sheet

New York City Coalition for a Smoke-Free City

http://www.nycsmokefree.org/

Philip Morris International

http://www.pmi.com/

Selected, Edited, and with Issue Framing Material by:
Dennis K. Miller, *University of Missouri*

ISSUE

Should Health Care Plans Cover Naturopathic Remedies?

YES: **Mary Flynn**, from "Naturopathic Doctors Fighting for Inclusion Under Health Reform Insurance Policies," *California Health Report* (2014)

NO: **Brian Palmer**, from "Quacking All the Way to the Bank," *Slate* (2014)

Learning Outcomes

After reading this issue, you will be able to:

- Define and describe naturopathic medicine and compare it to traditional medicine.
- Identify the potential strengths of naturopathic medicine and understand the perspectives of those critical of naturopathy.
- Understand differences between drugs and natural products used to manage the symptoms of diseases and disorders.
- Consider the role of culture and politics in developing and managing government-controlled and private health care plans.

ISSUE SUMMARY

YES: Naturopathy, or naturopathic medicine, emphasizes prevention, treatment, and optimal health via methods that stimulate self-healing processes. Mary Flynn, a reporter for *California Health Report*, describes efforts in California to have visits to naturopathic doctors covered in her state's new insurance marketplace.

NO: Brian Palmer, who writes for *Slate*, is concerned that taxpayers are forced to support, through state and federal public medical plans, alternative approaches that have little efficacy.

P opular television shows and magazines (e.g., *Dr. Oz* and *Prevention*) tout the benefits of "alternative medicine" to manage the symptoms of or cure varied diseases and disorders. Alternative medicine is generally defined as a medical practice that is used to have healing effects, but is not based on evidence gained through the scientific method. Examples include chiropractic care, homeopathy, Ayurvedic medicine, and forms of acupuncture. Alternative medicine can be used in cooperation with traditional evidence-based medicine, called complementary medicine and complementary and alternative medicine (CAM).

Supporters of alternative medicine point to its focus on the whole person. Traditional medical approaches tend to view disease as an object distinct from entire individual.

As such, the traditional physician will focus on the one small part of individual, rather than the whole which has many healthy interacting systems. Practitioners of alternative medicine often focus on "whole body" care. With a "whole body" approach, alternative medicine will be more likely to be concerned with the individual's overall emotional and spiritual health and well-being. With a holistic approach, an alternative medicine practitioner will likely give personal attention and one-on-one care. Finally, alternative medicine focuses on disease prevention, rather than strictly focusing on treating distinct diseases or disorders already present.

Naturopathy, or naturopathic medicine, is a form of alternative medicine. It emphasizes prevention, treatment, and optimal health via methods that stimulate self-healing processes. Naturopathy is based in the principle that the body can heal itself through a "vital spark" or "vital force" that guides the body's processes. When a patient has a disease or disorder, the naturopath will help the patient to take steps to stimulate the body's natural ability to heal. The stimulatory methods may include herbs and vitamins, physical medicine or kinesiology, and acupuncture. These treatments seek to minimize the risk of side effects and use the least force necessary to diagnose and treat symptoms. An important principle of naturopathy is "do no harm"—using the least invasive and toxic treatments. Naturopathic physicians do not perform major surgery, and while they can be trained to prescribe drugs, their emphasis is on natural healing agents.

An emphasis for naturopathy is prevention. A naturopath will seek to identify and eliminate the underlying causes of diseases and disorders before they affect function, rather than strictly focusing on removing or minimizing symptoms once they appear. Naturopathic practitioners seek to look beyond symptoms to identify underlying causes, and education is a key part of the relationship between the patient and physician to learn steps to achieve and maintain good health. Prevention should lead to optimum health, which will then be followed by overall wellness—a state characterized by positive emotion, thought, and action. Naturopaths believe that if wellness is recognized and experienced by an individual, they will be less likely to experience disease and/or will heal more quickly from a disease.

There are several naturopathic medical schools in the United States and Canada, accredited by the Association of Accredited Naturopathic Medical Schools (AAMMC). The naturopathic medical schools are typically a four-year graduate program where students earn a naturopathic medicine degree (ND). The training includes general medicine, as well as naturopathic approaches (e.g., herbalism, physical medicine, acupuncture, and counseling). In their practice, naturopathic physicians are generally considered as primary care providers, the first contact for a person with an undiagnosed health concern as well as continuing care of varied medical conditions. In the United States and Canada licensure for naturopathic physicians varies—some states/provinces offer licensure to naturopathic physicians, while others do not. Some states prohibit its practice.

Alternative and naturopathic medicine has been criticized strongly because it is not founded on evidence gathered by the scientific method. Critics note that the alternative treatments and approaches are not as well researched as those used in conventional medicine. Furthermore, the research literature supporting alternative

treatments is inconclusive, with poorly designed studies and conclusions that extend well beyond the limited observations and effects reported. As mentioned, naturopathy is based on healing through an individual's "vital spark" or "vital force" that guides the body's processes. The existence of these sparks or forces has never been proven and is not compatible with a modern medical, biological, and neural models based on scientific research.

While scientific studies generally do not support the efficacy of alternative and naturopathic medicine, many patients report that it is successful to minimize disease and improve health. Support for naturopathy often comes from testimonials such as, "I don't know how it works. I don't know why it works. But it works." Testimonials are anecdotal evidence—the type of information that should be rejected in the scientific evaluation of the efficacy of a treatment. One explanation for the successful reports from anecdotes is the "placebo effect," a perceived or actual improvement in a medical condition following a simulated or otherwise medically ineffectual treatment. The response to placebo is pervasive in medicine, accounting for as much as two-thirds of a response to a drug in some studies, and is considered part of the active response when considering overall treatment outcomes. In traditional medical research, a placebo is typically included in some way in the research design as a control condition. The placebo effect is related to the patient's expectation and is linked to neural motivation circuits that can influence the body's activity (e.g., the immune response) through a "top-down" control. Some supporters of alternative medicine, however, consider the placebo effect as support for a naturopathic approach because it supports the important role of belief, expectancy, and perceptions of well-being in positive health.

Critics note that a treatment that is scientifically ineffective, such as naturopathy, can be harmful beyond the minimal loss of some time and money. When ineffective or unproven treatments are applied at an early stage, the severity of the illness can progress. A disorder that could have been managed at an early stage may reach a status where even traditional treatments are ineffective. Should someone adopt a naturopathic approach to manage cancer? Britt Marie Hermes, a former naturopathic doctor, describes the interaction between naturopathy and a diagnosis of cancer on her website Naturopathic Diaries (available at http://www.naturopathicdiaries.com/finding-cancer-as-a-young-naturopathic-doctor/).

Despite the criticisms from traditional medicine, naturopathy is popular and widely practiced throughout North America. It has appeal to patients that want an alternative to traditional medicine and are seeking a holistic approach to overall health and well-being. This has created a conflict with health care reform at the national and local level. Should health care plans be required to cover naturopathic remedies? Many seek to use some form of alternative medicine to manage acute and chronic conditions, but these alternatives might not be covered by public or private health care plans. In the United States, the Affordable Care Act mandates that insurers do not discriminate against licensed health care providers, including naturopaths. However, insurers may limit coverage deemed experimental or unnecessary

to manage illness symptoms. Considering the lack of support for alternative medicine from scientific research and the emphasis of naturopathy on prevention and overall well-being, where does this leave naturopathic treatments?

In the YES selection Mary Flynn, a reporter for *California Health Report*, describes efforts in California to have visits to naturopathic doctors covered in her state's new insurance marketplace. In the NO selection Brian Palmer, writing in *Slate*, is concerned that taxpayers are forced to support, through state and federal public medical plans, alternative approaches that have little efficacy.

YES ↵

Mary Flynn

Naturopathic Doctors Fighting for Inclusion Under Health Reform Insurance Policies

As more people gained access to insurance and primary care under the Affordable Care Act this year, naturopathic doctors hoped that their role in medicine might become more mainstream as well.

But that has generally not been the case, and services by these holistic practitioners are often not covered by health plans, particularly those purchased on Covered California, the state's new insurance marketplace.

Naturopathic doctors, whose four-year graduate training focuses on primary care from a holistic perspective, feel that they are uniquely positioned to help meet the demands of the impending shortage of primary-care physicians in California. But physicians and regulators say they're not sure the holistic doctors have the right training, despite the need for more providers.

Still, naturopathic doctors say they're qualified to do some procedures and checkups, such as well-woman exams, and they want to be reimbursed by insurers for these services. There are a few naturopathic doctors that are listed as in-network providers with insurance plans known as preferred provider organizations, or PPOs, but most plans don't include naturopathic benefits.

"In terms of annual exams, preventive care, chronic disease management, ND's are filling a gap," even if they're not getting reimbursed by insurers for it, said Jacqui McGrath, a naturopathic doctor.

The California Association of Health Plans, which represents health insurers in the state, declined to comment for this story, instead referring questions back to the insurance companies. Anthem Blue Cross, Blue Shield, Health Net and Kaiser Permanente—the four largest insurers who participated in Covered California, the state's insurance marketplace—also declined to explain why they generally don't cover naturopathic services or did not return calls seeking comment. Blue Shield said it does include the alternative therapy of acupuncture as an out-of-network benefit in its Affordable Care Act plans, but naturopathic services aren't covered.

Debate over Qualifications

Under current regulations, naturopathic doctors are somewhat limited in what they can do under their license. The California Naturopathic Doctors Association is trying to expand the scope of what these practitioners are allowed to do.

But the California Medical Association said it's concerned that naturopathic doctors don't have enough education to do many primary-care exams and procedures.

"Naturopaths do not have equivalent training to physicians," said Yvonne Choong, senior director for the Association's Center for Medical and Regulatory Policy.

She pointed out that the content of a physician and naturopathic do ctor's four years of medical school is different. In addition, most physicians complete an additional three to seven years of residency training, whereas naturopathic doctors are not required to complete residency training, she said.

But many naturopathic doctors say their graduate training does provide them with enough training to perform at least some primary-care exams—something they're already doing but often not getting insurance reimbursement for. According to Bastyr University, an accredited school of naturopathic medicine, naturopathy is a system of primary health care that emphasizes prevention and the body's ability to heal itself using natural therapies, with a focus on the underlying cause of disease, rather than treating only the symptoms.

Trying to Expand Their Scope

The National Institute of Health categorizes naturopathy under the heading of "complementary and alternative medicine," a term that also includes meditation, chiropractic care and acupuncture. According to a 2007 survey conducted by the Institute, approximately 38 percent of adults and 12 percent of children have used some form of alternative medicine.

As part of their practice, naturopathic doctors can provide many of the same primary care services one might receive at a conventional doctor's office—except that the services often aren't covered by insurance.

"We do some things that are different, but we do the same: I order the same complete blood count, chem panel, lipid panel, blood sugar, thyroid testing, I can prescribe medicines," said Aimée Gould Shunney, a naturopathic doctor practicing in Santa Cruz. She added that her own practice focuses on women's health and gynecology, so STD testing and prescribing birth control pills also fall under her scope.

However, naturopathic doctors can only prescribe medications under the supervision of a medical doctor, said Dhurga Reddy, a naturopathic doctor and chair of the state Naturopathic Association's insurance committee. According to Reddy, naturopathic doctors originally opted to limit their scope of what they could do in order to gain licensure, more than 10 years ago. Reddy said they made certain concessions to their scope, with the hope they would be able to expand it down the road.

If a naturopathic physician does not have a supervisory relationship with a medical doctor, and the patient requires medication, the patient must then go to a conventional doctor for the prescription. "That creates a lot of redundancy," Reddy said, which is one reason insurers might be reluctant to contract with naturopathic doctors.

Naturopathic doctors instead want to be allowed to prescribe certain drugs without supervision. It is one part of a four-part change they are hoping to bring to their scope of practice through state legislation.

They're also seeking to be able to perform minor office procedures consistent with their training (such as the removal of a suspicious mole for biopsy), give orders to allied health professionals (such as order a nurse practitioner to start an IV on a patient) and perform joint manipulation consistent with naturopathic medical training.

Patients Seek Coverage

Many alternative providers had hoped that part of the Affordable Care Act, section 2706, would allow including practitioners like chiropractors and naturopathic doctors

to be widely reimbursed by insurers. Sometimes called the "non-discrimination clause," the section says that insurance companies "shall not discriminate with respect to participation under the plan or coverage against any health care provider who is acting within the scope of that provider's license or certification under applicable state law."

However, many insurance companies do not reimburse patients for services provided by alternative practitioners and they may not be legally required to after all. A 2013 guidance report issued by the U.S. Department of Health and Human Services that clarifies that the nondiscrimination clause "does not require plans or issuers to accept all types of providers into a network."

Naturopathic doctors, meanwhile, are left to sort out exactly how federal health reform may apply to them and whether it will help their patients get insurance that covers their services.

Kirsten Smith, 43, is an accountant who has insurance offered through her employer, but the plan doesn't cover naturopathic services. She's worked with a naturopathic doctor in the past and said she would appreciate the services being covered in some capacity.

Smith said the naturopathic doctor she saw spent a significant amount of time talking with her about things like her eating and sleeping habits, and where she worked.

"I felt like it was a whole picture, rather than just a 15-minute 'Go see the doctor,'" she said, adding that she takes supplements, and has regular visits for acupuncture and chiropractic care, the costs of which come out of her own pocket.

"I'm really big on empowering people to make choices for their own health care, rather than the insurance companies dictating who we can see and what's going to be in our best interest," she said. "Because nobody at the insurance company knows my health situation. It's the doctors that I choose and that are in my area that do, and so, putting the empowerment back into the hands of the patient and the doctor."

MARY FLYNN is a multimedia journalist based in the San Francisco Bay Area. She spent 8 years in the Army National Guard, serving two year-long deployments working in public affairs. In her personal website (http://www.bymaryflynn.com/), she writes and produces video documentaries on stories that deal with women's issues, the military (including veterans' issues), and public health.

Brian Palmer

 **NO**

Quacking All the Way to the Bank

Naturopaths are winning insurance coverage for medical nonsense.

Legislators in Washington state refuse to live in a world where only the wealthy can afford care from poorly trained health care providers who practice unproven medicine. This year Washington joined Oregon and Vermont in covering naturopathic care under Medicaid. Now every Washingtonian, regardless of means, has the right to life, liberty, and the pursuit of quackery. And taxpayers are footing the bill.

Medicaid coverage is the result of a series of anti-scientific decisions many states have made. The whole mess began with an argument within the community of naturopaths. Many acupuncturists, herbalists, and practitioners of ayurveda have been working for decades without formal training or licensure. As it became clear that there was money to be made in the field, four-year naturopathic colleges sprang up and expanded. Their graduates, who can spend more than $150,000 for their educations, wanted to distinguish themselves from untrained naturopaths, so they lobbied state legislatures to create a licensing system. Many states acquiesced—over the objections of traditional naturopaths—believing that they were protecting consumers. Currently, 18 states and the District of Columbia license naturopaths.

This was a serious mistake. Naturopathic medicine isn't a coherent discipline like otolaryngology or gastroenterology. Take a look at the curriculum at Bastyr University, one of five U.S. schools accredited by the Association of Accredited Naturopathic Medical Colleges. Botanical medicine, homeopathy, acupuncture, and ayurvedic sciences are all on the course list. The only thing that these approaches to medicine share in common is that they lack a sound basis in evidence. Differentiating between trained quacks and untrained quacks is not actually a consumer protection measure.

Once state governments recognized naturopathic medicine as a legitimate practice, the naturopaths wanted more. They are now lobbying hard for what they call "non-discrimination" among health care specialists. Since they're licensed like real doctors and nurses, naturopaths want to charge like real doctors and nurses and get reimbursed like real doctors and nurses. This is an exploitation of the word "discrimination." Treating things that are fundamentally different in a different manner—for example, covering proven therapies but not disproven or unproven therapies—isn't discriminatory, it's sensible. To equate it with real discrimination is an insult to people who have actually suffered.

The tactic, however absurd, has succeeded in Washington, Oregon, and Vermont. Now naturopathic lobbyists are working their black magic on the federal level. Their man in Congress is Iowa Sen. Tom Harkin, one of quackery's best friends on the Hill. Harkin was the driving force behind the creation of the National Center for Complementary and Alternative Medicine. Harkin's monster devours money that could be used for cancer, infectious disease, and neuroscience research and gives undeserved credibility to long-disproven therapies. (That's not the federal agency's official mission statement—I'm interpreting it for you.) Harkin also apparently micromanaged the process to ensure that actual science didn't undermine his agenda. When Joseph Jacobs, who ran a previous version of NCCAM in the 1990s, resigned his post, he told *Science* magazine that Harkin had pressured the agency to fund pet projects and ignore the evidence. In fairness, Harkin isn't a hypocrite—he really believes in this nonsense. He once claimed that bee pollen cured his hay fever. The manufacturer of his miracle cure was later fined by the Federal Trade Commission for false claims (surprise!), but that doesn't seem to have deterred the indefatigable Harkin.

Sorry, I've gotten sidetracked making fun of Tom Harkin again. Where was I? Right, Harkin slipped a "non-discrimination" provision into the Affordable Care Act, at a late stage of the legislative process, when it would not be reviewed in committee. The provision states that health insurance providers "shall not discriminate . . . against any health care provider who is acting within the scope of that provider's license."

Federal agencies have struggled to interpret the provision. Last year a joint document issued by several federal departments suggested that insurers may legally exclude some providers from coverage if the decision is consistent with "reasonable medical management." Harkin's Senate committee rejected the interpretation, which would allow insurers to "exclude from participation whole categories of providers." Regulators are now trying to decide how to reconcile their view of evidence-based medicine with Harkin's vision for medical care.

As a point of clarification, there is little chance that private insurers will be required by law to pay for herbal medications or acupuncture. Medical doctors wouldn't receive reimbursement if they delivered those services, so denying reimbursement to naturopaths doesn't represent "discrimination" in Harkin's world. The problem is that insurers may be forced to pay naturopaths to provide the kinds of services currently provided by actual medical doctors—consultations and the like. A recent article in the *Seattle Times* told the story of a couple now saving $95 under Medicaid each time they take their toddler son to a naturopath, and it noted that Washington's naturopaths are licensed to prescribe antibiotics.

Exposing the holes in naturopathic medicine is a bit like taking candy from a baby, but this is a super-annoying baby, so let's have some fun. The widely respected Cochrane Collaboration has produced dozens of articles comprehensively reviewing the evidence for alternative medical practices. In virtually all of the assessments, the authors conclude that the evidence is too weak to say whether the therapies have any effect. In 2011, for example, the group assessed the validity of ayurvedic medicine in treating diabetes—exactly the kind of chronic ailment for which some people seek out a naturopath. The researchers found that a handful of studies suggested that ayurvedic herbs may lower blood glucose levels, but those studies were methodologically flawed. "There is insufficient evidence at present," they concluded, "to recommend the use of these interventions in routine clinical practice."

Many naturopaths insist that their expertise is preventive medicine—a selling point of the Affordable Care Act—but most of those claims are either untestable or wrong. Many naturopaths encourage their patients to take antioxidant supplements to stave off cancer. The large-scale studies that have addressed this issue overwhelmingly show that the strategy doesn't work. Green tea, another darling of naturopaths, is similarly ineffective at preventing cancer. Consult the Cochrane database for further debunking enjoyment.

I'm all for choice, but we share the cost of health care collectively. People who contribute to Medicaid and private insurance pools should know that their money is going to good use. We can't say that for naturopathic medicine. If people want to see a medical practitioner who lacks appropriate training and advocates for unproven treatments, they should pay for it with their own money.

BRIAN PALMER is a regular columnist for *Slate Magazine* ("Explainer") and *The Washington Post* ("How and Why" and "Ecologic"). He writes about science, medicine, and the environment.

EXPLORING THE ISSUE

Should Health Care Plans Cover Naturopathic Remedies?

Critical Thinking and Reflection

1. When might you recommend someone visit a naturopathic physician? When might you encourage someone to avoid naturopathy?
2. What evidence would be required for you to accept naturopathy as an appropriate approach to help improve overall wellness or manage the symptoms of a disease?
3. What regulations, if any, should be present to limit naturopathic medicine in your community? What is the balance between an individual's right to choose medical treatment appropriate for them versus evidence from scientific research?
4. Why are naturopathic treatments appealing to many? Can traditional approaches apply any principles from naturopathy or alternative medicine, or are they incompatible?
5. How should government or private health care plans evaluate treatments that should and should not be covered? What is an appropriate balance between the preferences of the individuals and the costs to the public or private health plan?

Is There Common Ground?

Many patients find alternative treatments, such as naturopathy, appealing. They focus on the entire person, and not a single diseased part of the body. They promote prevention, healthy living, and overall wellness. They consider the needs of the individual patient, rather than employing a "one size fits all" model that is associated with traditional medicine and large, impersonal health centers. If it is right for the individual's situation, it should be used.

However, critics of alternative medicine comment that the term "alternative" is a misnomer. Medicine should focus on what treatments work, and reject treatments that do not work. The treatments associated with alternative medicine do not work, according to the scientific literature, and should be rejected. Naturopathy is "quackery" and should be rejected.

These approaches have clashed recently with concerns on health care costs and the political and social debates on the Affordable Care Act. Where do individual rights to choose treatment stop and restrictions for coverage based on cost or scientific studies begin? If an individual is contributing to a health care plan through taxes, insurance premiums, and co-payments, shouldn't they have the right to decide what treatment is best for them?

Additional Resources

Ahmad A., et al. (2015). Molecular targets of naturopathy in cancer research: Bridge to modern medicine. *Nutrients*. 7(1): 321–334.

The authors discuss the anticancer potential of nutraceuticals that have translational potential as a naturopathic approach for the management of cancers.

Atwood IV, K. C. (2004). Naturopathy, pseudoscience, and medicine: Myths and fallacies vs truth. *Medscape General Medicine*. 6(1): 33.

Physician Atwood responds to common arguments and pieces of evidence to support naturopathy.

Elder, C. R. (2013). Integrating naturopathy: Can we move forward? *The Permanente Journal*. 17(4): 80–83.

This essay provides a discussion of the potential benefits of naturopathic medicine, as well as an overview of current obstacles to its integration.

Ventola, C. L. (2010). Current issues regarding complementary and alternative medicine (CAM) in the United States Part 1: The widespread use of CAM and the need for better-informed health care professionals to provide patient counseling. *Pharmacy and Therapeutics*. 35(8): 461–468.

This is first in a series of three articles in the Journal *Pharmacy and Therapeutics* on the use of complementary and alternative medicine (CAM) and dietary supplements. Part 2 will discuss

regulation, drug interactions, and other safety issues, as well as sources of information about dietary supplements. The third article in this series will focus on the policies and practices regarding CAM and integrative medicine in health care facilities.

Internet References . . .

The American Association of Naturopathic Physicians

> http://www.naturopathic.org/

The Association of Accredited Naturopathic Medical Colleges

> http://aanmc.org/

National Institutes of Health—The National Center for Complementary and Integrative Health

> https://nccih.nih.gov/

Naturopathic Diaries—Confessions of a Former Naturopath

> http://www.naturopathicdiaries.com/

Quackwatch—Your Guide to Quackery, Health Fraud, and Intelligent Decisions

> http://www.quackwatch.com/

Selected, Edited, and with Issue Framing Material by:
Dennis K. Miller, *University of Missouri*

ISSUE

Does China Have an Effective Approach to Combat Drug Addiction?

YES: Sheldon X. Zhang and Ko-lin Chin, from "A People's War: China's Struggle to Contain Its Illicit Drug Problem," *Foreign Policy at Brookings* (2016)

NO: Yingxi Bi, from "On the Death Penalty for Drug-related Crime in China," *Human Rights and Drugs* (2012)

Learning Outcomes

After reading this issue, you will be able to:

- Assess the status of drug use and addiction in modern China.
- Describe the problems associated with drug use and trafficking that are unique to China.
- Compare anti-drug approaches in China to those in other countries.
- Evaluate the use of capital punishment to combat drug addiction in China and in the United States.

ISSUE SUMMARY

YES: Sheldon X. Zhang and Ko-Lin Chin provide an overview of China's approaches and its successes and failures in combating illicit drugs, including the use of capital punishment for severe offenses.

NO: Yingxi Bi examines the factors that have led to a relatively large number of Chinese citizens and non-citizens being subject to the death penalty.

China is the world's most heavily populated nation with a population close to 1.4 billion people. The current People's Republic of China was established in 1949 as a socialist state that is ruled by the Communist Party of China. China's economy is second in size to the United States', and has grown rapidly since the late 1970s when it increased trade worldwide. With the growth in trade came an increase in the trafficking of illicit drugs and their chemical precursors.

The production and distribution of drugs play an important part of China's history. Opium was introduced to China during the sixth century and was used for medicinal purposes. But, it was the habit of smoking opium (mixed with tobacco) that created great demand for the narcotic in the eighteenth century and for its importation. By the early nineteenth century the imperial Chinese government banned opium import, considering the drug a harm that undermines good culture and morality. The ban was minimally effective because of intense demand from recreational users and those addicted to opium. Moreover, the ban led to military conflict (the two Opium Wars, 1839–1860) with Britain, whose economic interests in Asia were based on the exchange of opium for Chinese goods.

Opium smoking did not decrease in China after the Opium Wars, as importation was replaced with cultivation of the poppy. Opium and heroin export from China, especially Shanghai, followed in the early twentieth century. When the Communists assumed control of the government in 1949 opium addiction was a significant public health and economic concern. The new government eliminated the problem by using the planned agricultural economy to replace poppy cultivation with other crops, by massive public education programs on the dangers of opium, and by treating addiction as a medical disease. Low-level drug traffickers were given jobs in the economy. However, high-level opium traffickers were treated as enemies of the people and given severe punishments, including life in prison and public execution.

In modern China alcohol and tobacco consumption are public health concerns. Both are legal, widely available, and use rates are going to meet or exceed those in the United States and Europe. Regarding tobacco, according to the World Health Organization (WHO), nearly one-third of the world's tobacco smokers are Chinese and nearly one-third (28%) of the population smokes. In comparison to China, only one-seventh (15%) of the American population smokes, according to the Centers for Disease Control. Tobacco is relatively cheap in China, as the price of a pack of cigarettes is less than two dollars (10–15 renminbi) and tobacco taxes are much lower in China (<40%) than in the United States (>70%). The Chinese health system faces increased expenses as challenges due to smoking-related illnesses, such as heart disease, cancer, and respiratory diseases. The WHO notes someone because of tobacco use dies approximately every 30 seconds in China—around 3000 people every day.

What about illicit drugs, such as cocaine, methamphetamine, marijuana and heroin in modern China? The authors of both the YES and NO sections of this issue acknowledge that China faces a growing problem of illicit drug use. Since opening its borders to trade in the late 1970s and early 1980s, the flow of illicit drugs into and out of China has grown.

In contrast to extensive growth of the poppy plant for opium and heroin in the early twentieth century, there is very little illegal cultivation of opium in China today. This is due, in part, to the strong regulation of land use by the government. The majority of heroin used in China is trafficked through the southern border with Myanmar (Burma), Laos and Vietnam. As in the United States, there has been an increase in heroin and other narcotic addiction among Chinese young people in the last ten years. China has a large chemical industry and products can be diverted for the illicit synthesis of methamphetamine, 3,4-Methylenedioxymethamphetamine (MDMA), sedatives, ketamine, and narcotics. Synthetic drug use is on the rise in China and these drugs can also be exported from China through the rest of Asia.

Estimates of the scope of illicit drug addiction in China vary. Data in the article for the YES section indicate 2.5 million registered addicts. Unofficial estimates suggest that the real number of people with addiction might be as many as 25 million. Despite this large problem, there are few voluntary rehabilitation centers and the demand for treatment likely well exceeds the available resources. Compulsory treatment is more common than voluntary rehabilitation, and treatment is administered through the criminal justice system, not the medical community.

Penalties for drug distribution and trafficking are harsh in China and can include capital punishment, also known as the death penalty. According to Amnesty International, China executes the highest number of people annually, with over 1000 executions in 2016 for all offenses. There is a short delay, often less than sixth months, between sentencing and application of capital punishment in China.

The Criminal Law of the People's Republic of China allows capital punishment for the following offenses.

- use of arms or violence to cover up drug trafficking crimes or to resist arrest or detention
- opium (more than 1 kg), methamphetamine (more than 50 g), heroin (more than 50 g), or large quantities of narcotic drugs are involved
- individuals are participants in international drug smuggling, leaders of trafficking groups, or government officials who divert state-controlled drugs for illegal sale

Capital punishment for drug offenses gained worldwide notoriety in 2010 when a Colombian citizen was arrested in Guangzhou trying to smuggle almost 4 kg of cocaine into China. Despite pleas for commutation of the punishment and a stay of execution, Ismael Enrique Arciniegas was executed by lethal injection in February 2017. Citizens of South Korea, the Philippines, the United Kingdom and Canada have also been executed in China for crimes related to drug trafficking.

Support for the death penalty by Chinese citizens is high overall. Part of the support is culturally based. A popular Chinese saying is, "to repay a tooth with a tooth and to pay back blood with blood." In the past 50 years there have been periods where real, or perceived, increases in crime were met with a strong public response from the government. *Yanda* ("strike hard") campaigns in 1983, 1996, 2001, and 2010 were performed to crack down and curb rising crime—including drug offenses—and to decrease social conflict. A 2008 survey by the Max Planck Institute indicated close to sixty percent of the population supported capital punishment for drug trafficking.

There are arguments for and against capital punishment. Proponents of capital punishment argue that it guarantees that perpetrators will not commit more crimes, it deters crime, it is less cruel than life imprisonment, it provides investigators and prosecutors a tool to leverage cooperation with coconspirators, and it satisfies a need for vengeance and retribution. Those opposed to capital punishment note that it can condemn an innocent person to death, it is cruel, it does not allow an individual the opportunity to make amends to their victim, it is not a deterrent against overall crime, and that it is applied unfairly to minorities and the poor.

It is important to note that the death penalty is not mandatory for any offense and China is not the only country where capital punishment can be applied for drug offenses. The death penalty *may* be applied for drug trafficking in the United States in severe offenses against the state. Still, humanitarian groups have consistently noted that China has exceedingly high numbers of executions.

YES ↵

Sheldon X. Zhang and Ko-lin Chin

A People's War: China's Struggle to Contain Its Illicit Drug Problem

An Ever-Expanding Addict Population

Like its red hot economy, China also witnesses the use of illicit drugs growing at an unprecedented speed.[1] Practically all psychedelic drugs known in the West have found their consumers in the country. Illicit drug dealing and consumption are highly stigmatized in China because of its bitter history. All Chinese governments in the past 150 years, irrespective of their political persuasions, have tried various harsh measures in curtailing drug use and trade, and the society at large holds drug addicts in disrepute and considers it a failure of the family. Still the problem persists.

China fought and lost two wars over opium in the 19th century. Following its defeat, China succumbed to large scale opium consumption by its populace. Historians claimed that by 1906, China was producing 85 percent of the world's opium, some 35,000 tons,[2] and more than a quarter of its adult male population regularly used opium.[3] After the communists took over China in 1949, eradication wiped out the largest ever cultivation of poppy in the world, opium dens were shut down, opium manufacturing facilities closed, drug traffickers summarily executed or imprisoned, and drug addicts sent to labor camps. The massive prohibition campaign, widely supported by the public, was so effective that in less than three years the communist government declared China a drug-free country.[4] Following China's open-door policy and economic reform in the 1980s, illicit drugs quickly returned, starting in Yunnan Province bordering Myanmar and the rest of the infamous Golden Triangle. It should be noted that opium cultivation has not returned.

Although attempting to stamp out the problem quietly in the early years of its economic reform, the Chinese government in the past two decades has openly acknowledged that illicit drug consumption has infested every province. The central government has been issuing an annual report since 1998, through its National Narcotics Control Commission, publicizing information on the trends, law enforcement activities, and intervention activities of its narcotic control efforts.

One unique practice in China's attempt to control illicit drugs is the extensive use of its criminal justice system, from combatting drug trafficking activities to treating drug addicts. Police agencies across the country are required to identify and register all drug users with whom they come in contact. A national registry has been established where all local police agencies routinely submit statistics on their drug enforcement activities including arrests, seizures, investigations, and contacts with drug addicts. Although somewhat inconsistent in its format as well as content, the official drug enforcement data are published in the *Annual Report on Drug Control in China*. To provide an idea of the extent of drug abuse in China, Table 1 is constructed using the data published in the official annual reports since 2001.

Table 1

	Total registered addicts	Total heroin addicts	% heroin addicts	% users ≤ 35 years old
2001	901,100	745,000	82.7%	77.0%
2002	1,000,000	876,000	87.6%	75.2%
2003	1,050,000	740,000	70.5%	72.2%
2004	1,140,400	924,864	81.1%	70.4%
2005	1,160,000	700,000	78.3%	68.1%
2006	*	*	*	*
2007	957,000	746,460	78.0%	62.1%
2008	1,126,700	877,736	77.9%	59.7%
2009	1,335,00	978,000	73.3%	58.1%
2010	1,545,000	1,065,000	68.9%	*
2011	1,794,000	1,156,000	64.5%	67.8%
2012	2,098,000	1,272,000	60.6%	*
2013	2,475,000	1,326,000	53.6%	*

Officially registered drug addicts in China

Source: Annual Report on Drug Control in China, 2001 through 2014.
* Total figures not reported.

There are two clear patterns: (1) the total number of addicts is on a steady increase, and (2) the proportion of heroin using addicts is on a steady decrease. It is estimated that China, together with the Russian Federation and the United States, account for 46 percent of all intravenous drug users in the world.[5] Ever since the drug user registration was established in the 1990s, the official figures have been on a continuous climb, some years more rapidly than others. Heroin is still the number one illicit drug in China, although the proportion of heroin users in the total addict population has been on a steady, albeit slow, decline over the past ten years. In comparison, the number of registered users who were abusing synthetic drugs has been on a steady rise. Crystal methamphetamine (commonly known in China as *bingdu* or "ice drug") and ketamine are the top two choices in synthetic drugs. Our field observations and interviews with community informants corroborate the official claims that these amphetamine-type stimulants are mostly consumed by groups of youths and often found in night clubs and karaoke bars.

In a recent survey of drug addicts in compulsory drug treatment centers, Huang et al. found that addicts were mostly young male and adults, unemployed and with an education of less than high school.[6] These findings are consistent with those found with U.S. drug users.[7] Huang et al. also found that Chinese drug users were likely to be single and come from poor families. Heroin was the most commonly consumed drug, followed by methamphetamine.[8] In comparison, in the United States, the most commonly used drug reported by prison inmates and the general population is marijuana, followed by cocaine (crack and powder).[9] Such differences in the choice of drugs may be due to geographical differences in the source of productions and supplies. While Southeast Asia has a long history of opium poppy cultivation, which provides the raw material for heroin production, coca leaves are mostly cultivated in the American continent. Synthetic drugs (e.g., methamphetamine and ketamine), however, are made with chemical precursors widely available in legitimate products, which are less constrained via global trades.

Another interesting trend revealed by China's annual anti-narcotic reports is the proportion of registered users under the age of 35. As shown in Table 1, drug addicts appear to be aging. At the beginning of the decade, the vast majority of registered users were under the age of 35. By 2009, the proportion decreased to 58.1 percent. No official explanations have been provided as to why drug users appear to be getting older when the number of synthetic drug (or club drug) users has been on an increase. After

2011, the Chinese government stopped reporting the age figure.

Chinese authorities claimed to have great confidence in their counts of active drug users, particularly the heroin users. One high ranking official at the Narcotics Control Bureau of China's Ministry of Public Security claimed that:

> I can tell you the registration of heroin users is highly reliable because of our local police work. Community-oriented policing is far more efficient than that of the U.S. because of our residential registration system. We comb through the neighborhoods of the entire country and knock on doors to interview residents to find out who the drug users are. Neighbors and even family members also tell us who the heroin users are. It is hard for them to escape the police attention.

> However, the same can't be said of synthetic drug users—those taking head-shaking pills (ecstasy), crystal meth, or ketamine—because these drugs are often consumed in entertainment facilities such as bars, karaoke clubs, and restaurants. Even when family members suspect their children are using drugs, they are never sure because these children often only tell their parents that they are going out with friends. For heroin users, their physical signs and living conditions easily give away their addiction problems. Synthetic drug users are often in good spirits and leave few physical traces. Therefore, we have great confidence on the number of heroin users in China. I would venture to say the accuracy is above 90 percent. But we don't have an accurate count of stimulant drug users.

. . .

Drug Treatment in China: Struggling to Keep Up

The Chinese government is fully aware of the serious social and public health challenges posed by its expanding addict population. It was estimated that 50–70 percent of heroin users were injection drug users (IDUs).[10] IDUs are now considered the most important source of Hepatitis C and HIV infections in China.[11] More than a decade ago, at the turn of the millennium, 72.1 percent of all confirmed HIV cases were attributed to intravenous heroin injection.[12] Needle sharing was a common practice among heroin users. Even after years of public campaigns and the expanding needle exchange programs, intravenous heroin injection continues to be a major contributor to the spread of HIV, accounting for 24.3 percent of all newly reported cases.[13]

Although private facilities exist in urban areas, drug treatment remains mostly under the control of the criminal justice system. Use of illicit drugs is considered an administrative offense and police make frequent detentions of anyone identified as a drug user. Individuals detained by the police, especially those involved in property crimes, are routinely interrogated for possible drug use. A female heroin addict and dealer in Yunnan Province that we talked to during our field work in 2005 described how the police identified drug users: "In the old time, police just asked you to roll up your sleeve and they looked for injection marks on your arm. So I learned to inject in the veins in my thighs because I knew the police wouldn't check there. Now they use urine tests all the time if they suspect you are using drugs." Aside from drug raids and property crime suspects, police also employ other strategies to screen for and rope in drug addicts, such as use of informants and neighborhood committees.

There are two main strategies for treating addiction in China: (1) enrollment in compulsory detoxification centers, and (2) sentencing to "education through labor" camps. Both involve locked-up residential stays, but the former typically lasts up to six months and the latter can last for one to three years. While first-timers are typically sent to the compulsory detoxification centers, repeat offenders are to enter labor camps for a longer "treatment," regardless of how they are brought to the attention of law enforcement agencies (e.g., arrested for crimes, turned in by relatives). These treatment facilities are typically walled off from the outside world. "Patient" movement is restricted and daily schedules are highly regimented. All treatment facilities impose a paramilitary routine, along with manual labor, physical exercise, and education.

Addicts brought to the compulsory treatment center are kept in isolation for the initial seven to ten days to "cleanse their system." Basic medical services are available at the better-financed facilities. Addicts going through withdrawal are supervised by medical staff and receive doctor visits and medications. In economically deprived regions, however, addicts are often forced to go through so-called "dry detoxification" (without any medication to alleviate physical pains). After "detoxification," addicts undergo rehabilitation, which mainly involves physical labor, education, and group discussions featuring mostly self-criticism. Treatment usually lasts about three to six months at these centers.

Few compulsory treatment facilities offer Western-style counseling or behavioral therapy. In our interactions with public health officials as well as administrators in charge of the treatment centers, the need for psychosocial intervention was widely expressed. However, psychotherapy is underdeveloped in most such treatment facilities. For instance, during our field activities, we inquired about any systematic measurement of the severity of addiction for client assessment at intake. There were none. Clinical assessment tools commonly used in the West, such as the Addiction Severity Index and Hopkins Symptom Check, were unheard of in these government-run facilities. Instead, physical labor remained the most common treatment protocol. Addicts were required to participate in various production activities (e.g., growing crops, raising livestock, and manufacturing electronics), supposedly serving to distract from yearning for drugs as well as to support the facility financially.

For addicts who have gone through the compulsory detoxification centers once and are caught again by police, labor camps are the "treatment" option. These camps last anywhere from one to three years, and are usually located away from the cities. Most labor camps involve some form of farming activity, and are controlled by correctional agencies (as opposed to the police). Information on rehabilitation activities at these labor camps is scarce but is believed to be similar to that found at the compulsory detoxification centers. Starting in 2009, Chinese authorities declared that labor camps were no longer available for drug treatment purposes. Instead, chronic addicts are now "committed to community-based treatment programs" and reported as such in the *Annual Report on Drug Control in China*.

Central to drug treatment protocols in all government-run facilities is physical labor. All incarcerated people in China, whether in prison for a criminal offense or in government-run drug treatment centers, must work to support themselves and their facilities. In our visits to drug treatment facilities, we were told that these "patients" were not paid a wage and their "collective" income was used to pay for their food and other amenities such as exercise equipment. Depending on the resourcefulness of the administrators, some treatment facilities have more money-making opportunities than others and the standard of living and equipment in the dorms thus vary enormously.

The effectiveness of these compulsory detoxification centers and labor camps has not been examined either by the government or independent researchers. We are not aware of any national depository of data related to substance abuse treatment or addiction research. However, in 2010 the National Narcotics Control Commission began to report the number of addicts who had not used drugs in the past three years.[14] Only a total figure of those who "stopped using in the past three years" was provided, without any contextual information as to how many others of the same cohort were still using. The figure is nonetheless a step forward in the gradual improvement of the national report on drug treatment outcome assessment. Much more research is needed to assess the efficacy of these large scale compulsory drug treatment facilities on the nation's drug use.

Upon completing the compulsory treatment or the labor camp, addicts are released back into the community where after support services range from inadequate to non-existent. In recent years, the Chinese government has stepped up its effort to improve re-entry efforts and to establish the so-called "drug-free communities" (also called drug-free counties, drug-free cities, or drug-free districts) by implementing surveillance of released addicts, organizing support groups, and sponsoring various anti-drug education campaigns. Community-based organizations that are not affiliated with government agencies have begun to appear in urban areas to assist addiction recovery and coordinate "self-help" groups.

. . .

The cost of delivering treatment appears to be a key factor in the development of effective substance abuse treatment in China, as drug addiction does not receive much sympathy from the public and thus lacks urgency in government funding priorities. With limited funding, the chronically anemic treatment community struggles to cope with the throngs of drug addicts who are mostly destitute and looked down upon by the society in general as well as by their own families.

The Struggle to Combat Illicit Drugs: A People's War

Annual public campaigns. Much in line with the political tradition of the communist party, propaganda campaigns are regularly launched in China as the main venue to indoctrinate and mobilize the masses to combat illicit drugs. The government has always portrayed its fight against illicit drugs as a people's war, stirring up public sentiments and enlisting participation from the public. While some political campaigns may be met with skepticism and faked enthusiasm, anti-narcotic activities in general receive widespread support because of the cultural taboo toward drug addiction and the fact that Chinese people, young and old, have long been taught of the national humiliation brought about by the two Opium Wars. School-aged populations aside, governments in different parts of the country also design and organize anti-narcotic campaigns targeting specific geographical regions, such as

villagers in rural areas and migrant laborers in the cities. It was estimated that in 2011, these mass-based outreach activities distributed more than 30 million copies of campaign materials such as pamphlets and covered more than 110 million people.[15]

The Chinese government is particularly enthusiastic about launching national campaigns against drugs around June 26 each year, the International Day against Drug Abuse and Illicit Trafficking, to show-case its resolve to combat drug problems. Massive events are held across the country, featuring visits by high-level government officials to drug treatment facilities and drug enforcement police units, public display and destruction of seized drugs, public gatherings, media blitz of major drug raids, presentations by former addicts, and public trials of drug traffickers.[16]

Each year one or more pieces of the central government's drug policy are promulgated, while other themes are reiterated in these national campaigns. For instance, the main feature of the 2011 anti-narcotics campaign was the promulgation of the newly published Regulations on Drug Rehabilitation, which delineates the roles and responsibilities of all stake-holders in the identification and treatment of drug users. Other themes regularly appearing include: establishing and strengthening drug-free communities, and community-based drug treatment facilities. Most of the anti-narcotic slogans remain the same from year to year, casting the government in a paternalistic position that asks society in general to save the drug addicts and then urges drug abusers to treasure their lives and strive to become productive citizens. On and around June 26, the Chinese government also releases its *Annual Report on Drug Control*, summarizing major accomplishments for the previous year such as drug seizures, number of suspects arrested and prosecuted, addicts registered, and treatment facilities established. These annual reports and other accompanying announcements are typically delivered by ranking officials in the Ministry of Public Security in Beijing and carried by all major news media outlets in China.

Severe punishment as deterrence. Drug trafficking is among the few criminal offenses that that qualifies for the death penalty in China, and the threshold for the capital punishment is relatively low. According to Chinese criminal law, people who smuggle, sell, transport, or manufacture heroin or methamphetamine in an amount greater than 50 grams can be sentenced to 15 years in prison, life imprisonment, or death. Aside from the weight factor, other aggravating circumstances include being the head of a trafficking organization, using armed protection during transportation, or engaging in violent resistance against police inspection.

In the past, the death penalty was typically carried out in an open field as a public spectacle, where the condemned was forced to kneel and then shot in close range with a rifle.[17] Lethal injection is now the standard procedure and the execution is held away from public view. Prior to the execution, the condemned is allowed to have a final face-to-face meeting with his immediate family. On the final day, the inmate is allowed to order his favorite meal and pick out his favorite clothes before being sent away. A 45-year-old inmate we interviewed in a city in southern China, who was sentenced to death with a two-year reprieve for his role in trafficking 60 kilograms of heroin from Myanmar, described the final hours he spent with his brother-in-law, the leader of the trafficking ring:

> On the day of the execution, my sister, her two children and I went to meet my brother-in-law. There were four groups of families in the visiting room. We had breakfast together. None of us were interested in eating. My brother-in-law was calm. He talked to us as if he was leaving on a long trip, asking his children to listen to his mother, to look after each other, and to never ever touch drugs. I think most of them on the death row would tell their families never to get involved in the drug business before they were executed. My brother-in-law was put to death by lethal injection.

Nobody knows how many are executed each year for drug offenses. Watts claimed that China executes 1,700 to 10,000 people each year, which account for seven out of every 10 executions in the world.[18] The last time the Chinese government mentioned executing drug traffickers was in its 2000 annual report, in which brief statements were made on 54 executions in different parts of the country.[19] The Chinese government has since stopped publishing any statistics on the executions of drug traffickers in its annual reports. However, one can still find local news outlets reporting on drug traffickers being sentenced to death. From time to time, stories of executions for drug offenses are also reported in official news outlets in foreign languages.[20]

Three circles of barriers to combat drug trafficking. Based on our interviews with police officials, China's anti-drug trafficking strategies at the tactical level rely on three major lines of defense, which one provincial official called the "three circles of barriers." The front-line is along the borders, where border patrols and customs inspections strive to stop the traffickers from entering the country. For the second line of defense, the police attempt to set up blocks along major highways extending from the borders

to all other provinces, such as Guangxi, Guangdong, and Guizhou. Around-the-clock checkpoints and random mobile inspections are strategically positioned to stop drugs from further traveling along major highways. Finally, the police establish inspections at all major ports of exits to other provinces and countries, including airports and train stations. One provincial official described that at these barriers: "We rely on a host of measures to catch drug traffickers: human inspectors, machines, drug sniffing dogs, and intelligence."

Professionalization of drug enforcement. The first police force in China specifically trained and assigned to drug details was in 1982 in Yunnan Province. This was mostly due to the rampant influx of heroin because of Yunnan's geographical vicinity to the Golden Triangle. As a result, Yunnan's drug police are probably among the most advanced and well organized in China, as one senior provincial police official noted:

> We have a special responsibility in this field. Since the 1980s till now, we have had 20 to 23 years of experience. In comparison, most other provinces started a lot later. We were the first to have a special anti-narcotics police force; many other provinces didn't even have such specialized police forces until very recently.

However, complaints were frequently voiced by front line police officials over the poor equipment and inadequate firepower. Because of their early and frequent encounters with transborder drug traffickers, drug police in Yunnan have arguably engaged in the most firefights and also suffered the most relative to police agencies in other parts of the country. According one news source, since the establishment in 1982, more than 360 police officers were injured and 40 died on drug enforcement duties.[21] Relative to their Western counterparts, China's drug enforcement is underfunded. For instance, despite decades of anti-narcotic efforts, China was only able to establish in 2010 a fully operational lab to conduct chemical assays of seized drugs; and the current analysis is limited to major drug ingredients such as opioids and amphetamine-type stimulants.[22]

Drug trafficking organizations in China. With a large addict population, illicit drugs need to move from the border regions into the interior. Needless to say, there are numerous groups of drug traffickers in China that are willing to risk their lives to supply the drug market. However, our field work and existing literature suggest that most drug trafficking groups are loosely affiliated individuals with little hierarchical structure; these are mostly entrepreneurs who utilize their social networks and often times fortuitous opportunities to move drugs.[23] Once any drug trafficking groups come into the investigative focus of the authorities, few can escape the eventual harsh punishment. Large trafficking groups, especially those with any name recognition in the drug business, are surely inviting attention from the authorities. With all the drug enforcement strategies in China, nothing commands a higher priority than identifying and breaking up criminal organizations in drug trafficking. As a totalitarian society, nothing poses a greater threat to the political establishment than extralegal organizations, let alone ones that engage in illicit drugs.

Almost without exception, crackdowns of major drug trafficking organizations are announced around June 26 each year to coincide with the rollout of annual counternarcotic campaigns. For instance in 2011, China broke up a 52-member criminal gang that organized HIV-positive people and juveniles to transport drugs. The group leader, Liu Fucheng, was sentenced to death.[24] One unique feature in the drug trafficking business in China is the absence of widespread violence. Sporadic violence erupts when drug traffickers of large consignments are cornered by police; these traffickers may resort to violent resistance to avoid the certain death sentence. Though statistics on drug-related homicides are not available, violent rivalries or fights among drug traffickers or street vendors are almost unheard of. Unlike their counterparts in Latin America that are known for extreme violence and openly challenging the authorities, Chinese drug trafficking organizations consist mostly of low-key entrepreneurs who are doing everything possible to avoid detection by and confrontation with the police or each other. Making money quietly is their motto.

Extensive use of confidential informants. Most drug enforcement officials in China will be quick to admit that they operate an extensive network of informants, many of whom are developed from the arrested traffickers. These informants provide vital information about the flow of drugs and names of major players in the region. All officials we interviewed in this study agreed that without intelligence development and maintenance of large networks of informants, drug enforcement will not likely make any progress. . . .

A Look into the Future: Reforms in China's Drug Control Policy

Because of its growing drug addict population, China is struggling to stem the rising trends in both consumption and sales of illicit drugs. There are many things China can do better. Domestically, China needs to establish a reliable drug market forecast system, which combines chemical composition analysis, reports and urine tests of arrested drug abusing offenders, and community informants on the trends of illicit drug use and pricing information. These vital signs are critical in understanding the direction of the illicit drug market and mobilizing resources.

In addition to drug use forecast, centralized efforts are also needed develop a treatment framework that is not only culturally sensitive but can also withstand rigorous empirical assessment. The Chinese government has recognized that a community of researchers and treatment professionals specialized in drug treatment and recovery is needed to augment the police-led compulsory treatment and labor camp approach in dealing with addicts. Moreover, China has banned the use of labor camps for the purpose of rehabilitating drug addicts. Needle exchange programs and medical treatment such as methadone maintenance clinics should be greatly expanded under the auspices of public health agencies not only because they are far more humane than the traditional compulsory treatment facilities but also because they reduce risks to public health for a host of infectious diseases. Systematic and rigorous research is of vital importance to assessing any treatment and recovery services. There are two major shortcomings in current drug treatment in China: (1) a lack of venues for practitioners and researchers to share and exchange ideas and experiences; and (2) a general lack of capacity in conducting rigorous clinical tests and assessment of treatment protocols in practice. Drug treatment in China remains either a fringe enterprise endeavored by a few do-gooders in the community or by the criminal justice system that believes in the simple method of manual labor and deprivation of personal freedom.

Internationally, China can improve its collaboration with neighboring countries and the United States by minimizing political interference. For years China has worked to increase collaboration with its neighboring countries to combat cross-border trafficking activities, such training drug enforcement police officers and providing financial incentives to encourage farmers to grow replacement crops in place of opium poppy. China also pressures its neighboring countries to be more forceful in eliminating opium cultivation and the trafficking of heroin and other drugs across their borders into China. Despite its eagerness to seek cooperation from neighboring countries to help reduce the influx of illicit drugs, China's growing economic and political power in the region also make these neighbors nervous. Many of these neighboring countries have long been weary of China's growing influence in the region. However, our interviews with the regional law enforcement representatives also suggest that when it comes to drug trafficking in Southeast Asia, it is difficult to avoid running into Chinese criminal organizations. Trafficking groups made up of ethnic Chinese rely on their extensive contacts within the Chinese enclaves in the region to purchase and transport drugs to places where profits can be made.[25]

As a result, international collaboration is critically important in China's effort to combat drug trafficking. However, such international efforts are often clumsy and bureaucratic. Although every provincial police agency has a foreign affairs office assigned to coordinate and assist with investigations involving international matters, all activities must go through the central government in Beijing. This significantly increases the complexity and burdens of all parties involved.

Despite the relentless and draconian counter measures, China's drug problem does not seem to have subsided much. After a few years of progress in the mid-2000s, the Chinese government is now acknowledging that the country has a long way to go in controlling illicit drugs and faces increasing challenges from transborder drug traffickers because of its geographical proximity to the two most significant drug producing regions in the world—the Golden Triangle and the Golden Crescent. In short, China is surrounded by ample supplies of heroin and amphetamine-type stimulants (ATS) drugs.

The future of drug trafficking in China is caught between two conflicting forces. On the one hand, China's booming economy and the frenzy among the populace to become rich will undoubtedly encourage entrepreneurship in all types of commercial trade, licit or illicit. Drug trafficking, with its tremendous profits, will continue to draw risk-takers who are limited in conventional opportunities for any substantial material prosperity. China is surrounded by cheap supplies of heroin and ATS drugs. Coupled with a growing economy and greater convenience in travel and commerce, it would be naïve to believe that the drug situation can improve quickly. On the other hand, the strong social stigma surrounding illicit drugs, coupled with an unforgiving penal system and totalitarian government, will likely limit the growth of the addict population and the number of daring entrepreneurs. There is little moral ambiguity about illicit drugs in China. Therefore, China's anti-narcotic measures may seem draconian by Western standards, such as the use of the death penalty for drug traffickers and compulsory detoxification centers and labor camps. The question becomes what price is China willing to pay to curtail its drug problems? Harsh legal sanctions to scare off prospective risk-takers coupled with draconian treatment conditions to deter drug users are their current strategies in combatting the drug problem. However, neither seems to have worked particularly

well, judging from the ever increasing size of addict population and amounts of drugs seized by police. While not a silver bullet, perhaps China perhaps should also consider experimenting with a more compassionate approach oriented toward harm reduction.

Notes

1. Portions of this paper have been previously presented and published.

2. Alfred W. McCoy, "From Free Trade to Prohibition: A Critical History of the Modern Asian Opium Trade," *Fordham Urban Law Journal* 28, no. 1 (2000): 307–49, http://ir.lawnet.fordham.edu/cgi/viewcontent.cgi?article=1804&context=ulj.

3. Yangwen Zheng, *The Social Life of Opium in China* (New York: Cambridge University Press, 2005).

4. Chongde Zhang and Chen Yuan, *China's Battle Against Narcotics* (Beijing: New Star Publishers, 1998).

5. United Nations Office on Drugs and Crime, *World Drug Report 2014* (Vienna: United Nations, 2014), http://www.unodc.org/documents/wdr2014/World_Drug_Report_2014_web.pdf.

6. Kaicheng Huang et al., "Chinese Narcotics Trafficking: A Preliminary Report," *International Journal of Offender Therapy and Comparative Criminology* 56 (2010): 134–52.

7. Substance Abuse and Mental Health Services Administration (SAMHSA), *Results From the 2009 National Survey on Drug Use and Health: Volume I. Summary of National Findings* (Rockville, MD: Office of Applied Studies, SAMHSA, 2010), http://www.oas.samhsa.gov/NSDUH/2k9NSDUH/2k9ResultsP.pdf.

8. Huang et al., "Chinese Narcotics Trafficking: A Preliminary Report."

9. SAMHSA, *Results From the 2009 National Survey on Drug Use and Health: Volume I. Summary of National Findings.*

10. Lin Lu, Yuxia Fang, and Xi Wang, "Drug Abuse in China: Past, Present and Future," *Cellular and Molecular Neurobiology* 28, no. 4 (2008): 479–90; YiLang Tang and Wei Hao, "Improving Drug Addiction Treatment in China," *Addiction* 102, no. 7 (2007): 1057–63.

11. Masahiro Tanaka et al., "Hepatitis B and C Virus Infection and Hepatocellular Carcinoma in China: A Review of Epidemiology and Control Measures," *Journal of Epidemiology* 21, no. 6 (2011): 401–16, https://www.jstage.jst.go.jp/article/jea/21/6/21_JE20100190/_pdf; and Xuyi Wang et al., "HCV and HIV Infection among Heroin Addicts in Methadone Maintenance Treatment (MMT) and Not in MMT in Changsha and Wuhan, China," *PLoS ONE* 7, no. 9 (2012): 1–5, http://www.plosone.org/article/

fetchObject.action?uri=info:doi/10.1371/journal.pone.0045632&representation=PDF.

12. National Narcotics Control Commission, *Annual Report on Drug Control in China, 2000* (Beijing: National Narcotics Control Commission, 2000), http://www.mps.gov.cn/n16/n80209/n80481/n804535/804639.html.

13. National Narcotics Control Commission, *Annual Report on Drug Control in China, 2011* (Beijing: National Narcotics Control Commission, 2011), http://www.bjjdzx.org/157/2011-10-14/45547.htm.

14. Huang et al., "Chinese Narcotics Trafficking: A Preliminary Report."

15. National Narcotics Control Commission, *Annual Report on Drug Control in China, 2012* (Beijing: National Narcotics Control Commission, 2012), http://www.bjjdzx.org/157/2011-10-14/45547.htm.

16. Chang Ting, *China Always Says "No" to Narcotics* (Beijing: Foreign Languages Press, 2004).

17. Jonathan Watts, "Akmal Shaikh's Final Hours: Convicted Drug Smuggler Was First European to Be Executed in China in More than Half a Century," *The Guardian*, December 29, 2009, http://www.guardian.co.uk/world/2009/dec/29/akmal-shaikh-final-hours-china.

18. Ibid.

19. National Narcotics Control Commission, *Annual Report on Drug Control in China, 2000.*

20. See, for example, "Drug Traffickers Sentenced in China," Xinhua, June 26, 2012, http://news.xinhuanet.com/english/china/2012-06-26/c_131677349. HYPERLINK "http://news.xinhuanet.com/english/china/2012-06-26/c_131677349.htm".

21. Muyang Cui, "Drug Enforcement Police and Their Sacrifices," *Beijing News*, May 14, 2012, http://epaper.bjnews.com.cn/html/2012-05-14/content_338310.htm?div=-1.

22. National Narcotics Control Commission, *Annual Report on Drug Control in China, 2012.*

23. Ko-lin Chin and Sheldon X. Zhang, "The Chinese Connection: Cross-Border Drug Trafficking Between Myanmar and China" (Final report to the U.S. Department of Justice, National Institute of Justice, Grant # 2004-IJ-CX-0023, 2007), https://www.ncjrs.gov/pdffiles1/nij/grants/218254.pdf.

24. "China Focus: China Faces Drug Control Challenge," *Xinhua*, June 26, 2012, http://news.xinhuanet.com/english/china/2012-06-26/c_131677326.htm.

25. Ko-lin Chin, *The Golden Triangle: Inside Southeast Asia's Drug Trade* (Ithaca, NY: Cornell University Press, 2009).

Bibliography

Chin, Ko-lin. *The Golden Triangle: Inside Southeast Asia's Drug Trade*. Ithaca, NY: Cornell University Press, 2009.

Chin, Ko-lin, and Sheldon X. Zhang. "The Chinese Connection: Cross-Border Drug Trafficking Between Myanmar and China." Final report to the U.S. Department of Justice, National Institute of Justice, Grant # 2004-IJ-CX-0023, 2007. https://www.ncjrs.gov/pdffiles1/nij/grants/218254.pdf.

"China Focus: China Faces Drug Control Challenge." *Xinhua*, June 26, 2012. http://news.xinhuanet.com/english/china/2012-06-26/c_131677326.htm.

"China Warns of Severe Battle against Cross-Border Drug Trafficking." *Xinhua*, June 6, 2012. http://news.xinhuanet.com/english/china/2012-06-05/c_131633203.htm.

Cui, Muyang. "Drug Enforcement Police and Their Sacrifices." *Beijing News*, May 14, 2012, sec. A06. http://epaper.bjnews.com.cn/html/2012-05-14/content_338310.htm?div=-1.

"Drug Traffickers Sentenced in China." *Xinhua*, June 26, 2012. http://news.xinhuanet.com/english/china/2012-06-26/c_131677349.htm.

Gao, F., Y. S. Zhu, S. G. Wei, S. B. Li, and J. H. Lai. "Polymorphism G861C of 5-HT Receptor Subtype 1B Is Associated with Heroin Dependence in Han Chinese." *Biochemical and Biophysical Research Communications* 412, no. 3 (2011): 450–53. http://ww2.biol.sc.edu/~elygen/biol303/2011%20papers/heroin%20addiction.pdf.

Huang, Kaicheng, Jianhong Liu, Ruohui Zhao, and Paul Friday. "Chinese Narcotics Trafficking: A Preliminary Report." *International Journal of Offender Therapy and Comparative Criminology* 56 (2010): 134–52.

Li, Lei, Rassamee Sangthong, Virasakdi Chongsuvivatwong, Edward McNeil, and Jianhua Li. "Lifetime Multiple Substance Use Pattern Among Heroin Users Before Entering Methadone Maintenance Treatment Clinic in Yunnan, China." *Drug and Alcohol Review* 29, no. 4 (2010): 420–25.

Li, Lei, Rassamee Sangthong, Edward McNeil, and Jianhua Li. "Multiple Substance Use Among Heroin-Dependent Patients Before and During Attendance at Methadone Maintenance Treatment Program, Yunnan, China." *Drug and Alcohol Dependence* 116 (2011): 246–49.

Liu, Zhimin, Zhi Lian, and Chengzheng Zhao. "Drug Use and HIV/AIDS in China." *Drug and Alcohol Review* 25, no. 2 (2006): 173–75.

Lu, Lin, Yuxia Fang, and Xi Wang. "Drug Abuse in China: Past, Present and Future." *Cellular and Molecular Neurobiology* 28, no. 4 (2008): 479–90.

McCoy, Alfred W. "From Free Trade to Prohibition: A Critical History of the Modern Asian Opium Trade." *Fordham Urban Law Journal* 28, no. 1 (2000): 307–49. http://ir.lawnet.fordham.edu/cgi/viewcontent.cgi?article=1804&context=ulj.

National Narcotics Control Commission. *Annual Report on Drug Control in China, 2000*. Beijing: National Narcotics Control Commission, 2000. http://www.mps.gov.cn/n16/n80209/n80481/n804535/804639.html.

National Narcotics Control Commission. *Annual Report on Drug Control in China, 2011*. Beijing: National Narcotics Control Commission, 2011. http://www.bjjdzx.org/157/2011-10-14/45547.htm.

National Narcotics Control Commission. *Annual Report on Drug Control in China, 2012*. Beijing: National Narcotics Control Commission, 2012. http://www.bjjdzx.org/157/2011-10-14/45547.htm.

National Narcotics Control Commission. *Annual Report on Drug Control in China, 2014*. Beijing: National Narcotics Control Commission, 2014. http://blog.sina.com.cn/s/blog_52215ca80102uwbt.html.

Substance Abuse and Mental Health Services Administration (SAMHSA). *Results From the 2009 National Survey on Drug Use and Health: Volume I. Summary of National Findings*. Rockville, MD: Office of Applied Studies, SAMHSA, 2010. http://www.oas.samhsa.gov/NSDUH/2k9NSDUH/2k9ResultsP.pdf.

Tanaka, Masahiro, Francisco Katayama, Hideaki Kato, Hideo Tanaka, Jianbing Wang, You Lin Qiao, and Manami Inoue. "Hepatitis B and C Virus Infection and Hepatocellular Carcinoma in China: A Review of Epidemiology and Control Measures." *Journal of Epidemiology* 21, no. 6 (2011): 401–16. https://www.jstage.jst.go.jp/article/jea/21/6/21_JE20100190/_pdf.

Tang, Yi-Lang, and Wei Hao. "Improving Drug Addiction Treatment in China." *Addiction* 102, no. 7 (2007): 1057–63.

Ting, Chang. *China Always Says "No" to Narcotics*. Beijing: Foreign Languages Press, 2004.

United Nations Office on Drugs and Crime. *World Drug Report 2014*. Vienna: United Nations, 2014. http://www.unodc.org/documents/wdr2014/World_Drug_Report_2014_web.pdf.

Wang, Xuyi, Linxiang Tan, Yi Li, Yao Zhang, Dongyi Zhou, Tieqiao Liu, and Wei Hao. "HCV and HIV Infection Among Heroin Addicts in Methadone Maintenance Treatment (MMT) and Not in MMT in Changsha and Wuhan, China." *PLoS ONE* 7, no. 9 (2012): 1–5. http://www.plosone.org/article/fetchObject.action?uri=info:doi/10.1371/journal.pone.0045632&representation=PDF.

Watts, Jonathan. "Akmal Shaikh's Final Hours: Convicted Drug Smuggler Was First European to Be Executed in China in More than Half a Century." *The Guardian*, December 29, 2009. http://www.guardian.co.uk/world/2009/dec/29/akmal-shaikh-final-hours-china.

Zhang, Chongde, and Chen Yuan. *China's Battle Against Narcotics*. Beijing: New Star Publishers, 1998.

Zheng, Yangwen. *The Social Life of Opium in China*. New York: Cambridge University Press, 2005.

Dr. Sheldon Zhang is a Professor in the Department of Sociology at San Diego State University. His research assesses the effectiveness of community reentry programs for ex-offenders and understanding transnational organized crime.

Dr. Ko-lin Chin studies organized crime and gangs as a Professor of Criminal Justice at Rutgers University, and is the author of several books on immigrant smuggling in China.

Yingxi Bi

 **NO**

On the Death Penalty for Drug-related Crime in China

I. Grounds for Imposing the Death Penalty to Drug-Related Offences in China

This section will examine some of the main factors that have led to a large number of individuals charged with drug offences being subjected to the death penalty in China, including the criminal legislation, the criminal justice system, and the situation of drug-related crime in China.

Criminal Legislation

The handing down of death sentences is made possible by the stringent criminal legislation which has been put in place to punish drug-related crimes, namely drug trafficking. Offences and sanctions related to drug offences are prescribed under Section Seven of the *Criminal Law of the People's Republic of China*, Article 347 which states that,

> Whoever smuggles, traffics in, transports or manufactures narcotic drugs, and commits any of the following acts shall be sentenced to fixed-term imprisonment of fifteen years, life imprisonment or death, and concurrently be sentenced to confiscation of property:
>
> (1) smuggling, trafficking in, transporting or manufacturing opium of not less than 1,000 grams, or heroin or methyl Benzedrine of not less than 50 grams or other narcotic drugs of large quantities;
> (2) being ringleaders of gangs engaged in smuggling, trafficking in, transporting or manufacturing of narcotic drugs;
> (3) shielding with arms the smuggling, trafficking in, transporting or manufacturing of narcotic drugs;
> (4) violently resisting inspection, detention or arrest with serious circumstances; or
> (5) involved in organized international drug trafficking.[1]

According to the law, 'persons who smuggle, traffic in, transport or manufacture opium of not less than 1,000 grams, heroin or methylaniline of not less than 50 grams

or other narcotic drugs of large quantities' can be sentenced to death.[2] Under the legislation, there are two specific elements that make a sentence of death more likely to be imposed for drug offences.

One of the elements of the legislation that prejudices the accused is its employment of a quantitative model when assessing whether the offence reaches the threshold of severity necessary to impose the death penalty. In practice, this means that the purity of the drug is not taken into consideration, but instead that all substances are treated the same regardless of their content or harmfulness. According to the law,

> The term 'narcotic drugs' as used in this Law means opium, heroin, methylaniline (ice), morphine, marijuana, cocaine and other narcotic and psychotropic substances that can make people addicted to their use and are controlled under State regulations.
>
> The quantity of narcotic drugs smuggled, trafficked in, transported, manufactured or illegally possessed shall be calculated on the basis of the verified amount and shall not be converted according to its purity.[3]

The second is that for the purposes of sentencing, penalties are calculated cumulatively. According to article 347:

> With respect to persons who have repeatedly smuggled, trafficked in, transported or manufactured narcotic drugs and have not been dealt with, the quantity of narcotic drugs thus involved shall be computed cumulatively.[4]

This approach increases the possibility of the death penalty being imposed, as a series of minor drug convictions may together meet the quantity threshold necessary for capital punishment.

Further adding to the likelihood of a death sentence being imposed for drug crimes is the enacting of legislation that provides for the possibility of more severe punishment in the case of repeat offences. Article 65 of the *Criminal Law* already prescribes legislation allowing more severe punishment in cases of recidivism.[5] However,

Article 356 applies this concept specifically within the context of drug-related crimes, stating that,

> Any person who was punished for the crime of smuggling, trafficking in, transporting, manufacturing or illegally possessing narcotic drugs commits again any of the crimes mentioned in this Section shall be given a heavier punishment.[6]

As a consequence of these factors, China's legislative framework creates comparatively high possibility for the imposition of the death penalty in cases of drug-related offences. China's continuance of the policy is regressive in light of the fact that many countries whose legislation at one time provided for the death penalty for drug-related crimes have subsequently abolished it. In others, the legitimacy of applying the death penalty for drug offences is a topic of hot debate. For instance, in countries such as Viet Nam, Bahrain and Libya, official proposals to abolish the death penalty for drug offences have been considered. The high courts of both Singapore and Indonesia have heard legal actions challenging the constitutionality of the death penalty in drug-related cases.[7] Many other states whose legislation retains the death penalty for drug offences are either observing moratoria, decline to apply death penalty or seldom carry out executions.[8] For example, in Cuba, 'there have been no reported executions for drug offences' since 2003.[9] Also for some Asian countries, like Sri Lanka, no judicial executions have been carried out since 1979.[10]

Criminal Justice System

In China, the Supreme Court's judicial interpretation plays a major role in guiding the District Court, which is usually the main court involved in the sentencing of drug-related crimes. For example, the Supreme Court has pronounced upon drug-related crimes in *The Seminar on Drug-related Crime for Part of the National Court* (2008), the *National Court on the Seminar of Drug-related Crime* (2000) and *The Interpretation of the Standards Related to the Trial Issues for Conviction and Sentencing of Drug Cases* (2000). In doing so, the Supreme Court has called upon the judicial system to adhere to a 'crackdown policy' for drug-related crimes. The Supreme Court has conveyed that the District Court should focus on combating the criminal 'kingpins' at the top of the drug trafficking industry. It has approved the sentencing to death of major drug traffickers, recidivists, repeat offenders, habitual offenders and those who were armed or whose offences included violence causing serious harm. All of these documents have paved the way for a system in favour of severe punishments for drug offenders.

In addition, some District Courts have developed their own standards for sentencing drug offenders, based on the local situation regarding drug crime. For example, one of the municipalities issued regulations imposing a sentence of death for the sale of 100 grams of ecstasy.[11] In addition, the District Court in the judicial process often functions in a dogmatic manner. For example, the judiciary has leaned towards applying the death penalty in cases in which the quantity of drugs has reached a level that has been determined to attract such a sentence, there are no mitigating circumstances and the defendant has not surrendered to the court. This problem has been further heightened by the fact that within the system, the judiciary has been quick to apply the death sentence to cases involving the smuggling, trafficking, transporting and manufacturing of drugs. For example, a recent survey found that 89.5% of judges among the respondents supported the imposition of the death penalty, while 92.6% of prosecutors, 93.7% of policemen and 94.7% of lawyers were also in favour of it.[12]

Since 1 January 2007 it has become mandatory for all death sentences to be reviewed by the Supreme People's Court. Namely, 'all the death penalty cases, which not sentenced by the Supreme People's Court, should submit to Supreme People's Court for approval.'[13] This change was made in order to avoid inconsistent applications of the death penalty in various cases. This development is considered a major step towards securing procedural justice in death penalty cases and promoting human rights in China. One Chinese scholar has pointed out that, '[A]fter the right reverted to the Supreme Court to approve the death penalty, the number of death penalty in China will be significantly decreased, a decline of at least 20%'.[14] It has been reported that Yunnan Province, well known for drug trafficking, observed a one-third reduction in death sentences following the implementation of the judicial review by the Supreme Court of death penalty cases.[15] However, the degree to which these developments have or will affect the death penalty for drug-related crime in China is difficult to ascertain because for the past four years, no accurate official statistical information on executions has been made available.

Drug-related Crime

Also contributing to the application of severe punishments for drug-related crimes in China, such as the death penalty, are the large number of drug cases, and the increased trend of drug-related crime. Drug-related crime is considered to be a threat not only to the Chinese population, but also for the country's development and security. The belief that these threats are increasing has been used as the basis upon which to promote the 'crackdown' policy for drug-related crime. This policy is underpinned by the idea that the harsher the punishment for the crime, the more likely it is to deter individuals from engaging in it.

. . .

II. Debate on the Application of the Death Penalty for Drug-Related Offences

Despite the high rates of drug-related crime in China and the concerns this raises, the death penalty for drug-related crime is not justified. The following section will focus on debates both for and against the death penalty for drug-related offences.

Retentionist arguments on the death penalty for drug-related offences

Those who support the use of the death penalty for drug-related offences generally ground their position in consequentialist justifications.[16] This argument contends that drugs kill victims and cause unnecessary social harm that cannot be tolerated. In some communities, drugs are considered one of the most dangerous threats to society. This is particularly true amongst the Chinese population who, as a result of historical events, view trafficking in drugs as a grave crime. Drug-related crime is seen as heinous, grievous and odious, disrupting traditional values, affecting social stability and consuming a large amount of social wealth. Thus, even though drug-related offences are often non-violent crimes that do not result in direct death or severe injury, many still consider it appropriate to use death penalty in response.[17]

In this context, it is important to note that the application of the death penalty for nonviolent offences is not unusual. As compared with other retentionist jurisdictions where the death penalty is not applied for nonviolent crimes, in China there are many nonviolent crimes, separate from those related to drug offences, also attracting the death penalty under criminal law. Under the 1997 Criminal Code, which was in force prior to the abolition of capital punishment for thirteen nonviolent offences in 2011, there were as many as forty-four non-violent crimes for which the statutory maximum penalty was death, accounting for 69% of all death penalty offences.[18] These include provisions such as Article 170 (counterfeiting) and Article 383 (embezzlement).[19] Given this context, in which the law prescribes harsh punishments for even

relatively minor offences, it is easy to avoid debate on the abolition of the death penalty for drug offences, given the public perception on the harmfulness of drugs.

Opposition to the use of the death penalty for the punishment of drug-related crimes

Despite the above, there are strong arguments in favour of abolishing the death penalty for drug-related crimes. These arguments derive largely from the perspectives of penology and human rights.

Penology perspective

During the 20th century, many penology and criminology scholars have analysed the death penalty through the lens of both its effectiveness in preventing crime, and the notion of retribution in punishment. Therefore, to determine whether it is reasonable to apply the death penalty for a certain crime, one must determine whether this punishment best meets the demands of retribution and plays an effective role in the prevention and deterrence of future offenses.

In simple terms, the retribution perspective reflects the notion of 'an eye for an eye', or that 'the punishment must fit the crime', the central idea being that there should be an equivalence between the severity of the punishment and the harmfulness of the criminal act. The penalty should adapt to the harm inflicted by the crime, but should not exceed it.[20] In 2006 the Malaysian Prime Minister argued that the death penalty is the 'right kind of punishment' for drug trafficking, as '[i]t is a threat to the well-being of our society'.[21]

From a criminal law perspective, drug-related crime in and of itself is non violent, and does not directly endanger human life or cause injury. Absent any specific violent act associated with the drug offence, drug-related crimes are therefore not on a par with murder, terrorism or other acts resulting in death or serious injury. Even within the Chinese *Criminal Law*, drug-related offences are categorised under Chapter VI, which are 'Crimes of Obstructing the Administration of Public Order'. Also included in this category are 'Crimes of Impairing Judicial Activities', 'Crimes of Undermining Protection of Environmental Resources', and six others that are all nonviolent.[22] Thus, it would seem that the punishment for drug-related crimes, if it is to reflect the gravity of the act, should be more lenient than that prescribed for crimes of murder or similar acts causing physical injury. Punishing drug crimes with the deprivation of life undermines the basic balance between crime and punishment. It does not meet the standards of equivalence and rationality.

Gravity is a necessary, but insufficient condition for the application of the death penalty. Determinations as to whether to apply the death penalty must consider the purpose of the penalty and analyse the necessity of prevention. Therefore further analysis must be undertaken as to the preventative value of the death penalty. There are numerous arguments that examine why the application of the death penalty for drug-related crime in China is not an effective instrument in relation to general or special deterrence. For example, the application of the death penalty to drug-related crime is intended by lawmakers to have the effect of deterring potential offenders from engaging in the drug trade. However, it can be argued that such efforts, if successful, will result in the reduced availability of drugs in the community, resulting in an increase in price and related profit margins. This situation, in turn, would create greater financial incentives for people to engage in this activity. Rather than creating a situation of deterrence, it instead creates one of encouragement. As Beccaria stated in the 19th century, '[a] proper sentence is a sentence that is just sufficient enough to deter crime.'[23] It is only when the penalty for an offence is tailored to meet the needs of prevention that the deterrent effect will be maximised and consistent with the rationality requirement of the penalty.

In addition, data on drugs offences in China in recent years do not reveal the type of decline in crime one would expect if the death penalty policy was an effective deterrent. According to the *Annual Report on Drug Control in China*, the number of criminal suspects in drug cases has increased from 73,400 in 2008, to 91,000 in 2009 and 101,000 in 2010.[24] Chinese authorities investigated 89,000 drug-related crimes in 2010, which represents an increase of 14.5% since the previous year's figures.[25] Imposing the death penalty to prevent and curb drug-related crime, in practice, to be ineffective.

Human rights perspective

There is a strong argument that judicial killings for drug-related crimes violate international human rights law.[26] Although capital punishment is not absolutely prohibited under international law, its lawful application is limited under Article 6(2) of the International Covenant on Civil and Political Rights to only 'the most serious crimes'.[27] The UN Human Rights Committee has noted in its General Comment on the Right to Life that 'the expression "most serious crimes" must be read restrictively to mean that the death penalty should be a quite exceptional measure'.[28] There is little evidence to suggest that drug-related offences meet this threshold.

The jurisprudence of the UN Human Rights Committee indicates that only crimes which directly result

in death could be considered as 'most serious',[29] and, as pointed out by Manfred Nowak in his commentary on the Covenant, '[I]n no event was the death penalty to be provided for crimes of property, economic crimes, political crimes or in general for offenses not involving the use of force.'[30] The UN High Commissioner for Human Rights noted in a March 2009 statement that, '[T]he application of the death penalty to those convicted solely of drug-related offenses raises serious human rights concerns.'[31] In his 2010 report to the General Assembly, the UN Special Rapporteur on the Right to Health also affirmed that the death penalty for drug-related offences violates international human rights law.[32] The United Nations Office on Drugs and Crime (UNODC) also acknowledged in a 2010 report that, 'As an entity of the United Nations system, UNODC advocates the abolition of the death penalty and calls upon Member States to follow international standards concerning prohibition of the death penalty for offenses of a drug-related or purely economic nature.'[33]

III. The Way Forward

The prospects for abolishing death penalty on drug related crimes in China

According to the 2011 Report from the Secretary-General of United Nations on the 'Question of the death penalty',[34] as of June 2011, 140 of the 192 Members of the United Nations are believed to have abolished the death penalty or introduced a moratorium either legally or in practice. . . .

With this worldwide trend towards the abolition of the death penalty, and following the welcome news that China abolished thirteen capital offences in 2011—nearly one in five of all death penalty offences in China—it would be easy to argue that it is inevitable that the death penalty will be abolished for drug related crimes. However, this argument is undermined by the reality of the situation in China.

Typically, the abolition of the death penalty requires law reform and/or changes in state practice. Law reform could include new legislation abolishing or restricting its scope, or the ratification of international instruments that provide for the abolition of the death penalty. Practical changes might include the introduction of a new non-legislative practice limiting the use of the death penalty, such as announcing a moratorium on executions even while the death penalty is retained in law. In the case of China, it is not unrealistic to hope for any or all of these achievements, but significant uncertainty exists regarding if or when such changes will take place.

. . .

Given the current situation in China, it is unlikely the government will announce a moratorium application of the death penalty, especially for drug-related offences. As Mou Xinsheng, a member of the National People's Congress Standing Committee, has said,

> It is the international trend to abolish death penalty. China, as a developing country, is in the period of social conflict prominent, with intense criminal offence, and some are serious crimes. It is not reality for China to abolish death penalty now, but to reduce the number of death penalty offences is suitable.[35]

During a seminar entitled 'The strict application of death penalty to drug related crime', held in China in March 2011, Ma Yukong, vice chairman of Intermediate People's Court in Kunming, Yunan province, stated that '[I]t is reckless to abolish death penalty for some drug-related crimes. Even though it is the international trend to abolish death penalty, China has to be cautious to take the step now, the reality of China should be considered'.[36] In addition, findings of 'Professionals Attitude Towards Death Penalty' in China shows significant support for death penalty for drug-related offences amongst professional groups.[37] In all, 75.7% of the respondents believed that the death penalty needed to be applied to drug trafficking. By way of comparison, 90.1% supported the application of the death penalty to intentional homicide.[38]

Support for the death penalty for drug-related offences is found among the general public. In 1995, the Law Institute of Chinese Academy of Social Science and the National Bureau of Statistics of China conducted a public opinion survey in three Chinese provinces on attitudes toward the death penalty. The survey found that over 95% of the respondents supported capital punishment.[39] A more recent survey conducted by the Research Center for Contemporary China at Peking University found that 57.8% of respondents were favour of death penalty.[40] Even though these figures suggest a decline in overall support for the death penalty, the support of death penalty for drug offences remains high, with 59.2% of respondents supporting the application of capital punishment for 'drug dealing'.[41] The survey found that the level of support for the death penalty for drug dealing was just below that for murder and for intentional injury resulting in death.[42]

The widespread public support for capital punishment is one of the main barriers to abolishing the death penalty in China. For example, in response to the question, 'Which group's opinions mainly affect the death penalty system in China?', 62.6% considered public opinion to be a main reason for maintaining the death penalty.[43] Tian Wenchang, one of the most famous criminal defence lawyers in China, has also noted that the 'death penalty could play a role of balancing the mass emotion. Chinese people are not ready to tolerate murderers not be sentenced to death.'[44]

Restricting the death penalty for drug-related offences

Although it is unlikely that China will abolish the death penalty for drug-related offences in the near future, there are possibilities for the continued restriction of its use in drug cases. If the trend towards restricting the use of the death penalty is to be continued, as evidenced by the recent removal of thirteen offences from the list of capital crimes, then safeguards for the protection of the rights of those facing the death penalty must be expanded and guaranteed.

. . .

China has adopted a policy of 'less kills, cautious kills', which requires the application of high evidentiary standards and fair trial guarantees in capital cases. The so-called 'less kills' provision applies specifically to reducing executions, while the notion of 'cautious kills' means that the death penalty must be carefully used, that stringent evidentiary standards must be applied and that mistakes must not be made.[45]

. . .

Before China abolishes the death penalty for drug offences, the trial process itself must scrupulously observe the international and domestic standards for the protection of the rights of people facing capital punishment. Proceedings leading to the imposition of death sentences must conform to the highest standards of independence, objectivity and impartiality. Competent defense counsel must be provided at every stage of the process. The gathering and assessment of evidence must meet the highest standards, and all mitigating factors must be taken into account in sentencing. Finally, it is necessary to work towards ensuring that people facing the death penalty are given the opportunity to seek pardons. Working to increase the human rights standards of the judicial system in death penalty cases is an important aspect of progress in restricting and abolishing capital punishment.

References

1. *Criminal Law of People's Republic of China 1997*, (adopted at the Second Session of the Fifth National People's Congress on July 1, 1979, revised at the Fifth Session of the Eighth National People's Congress on March 14, 1997 and promulgated by Order No.83 of the President of the People's Republic of China on March 14, 1997), Section 7, art. 347, available online at http://www.

npc.gov.cn/englishnpc/Law/2007-12/13/content_1384075.htm (date of last access 29 January 2012).

2. ibid, art. 347(1).

3. ibid, art. 357.

4. ibid, art. 347.

5. ibid, art. 65.

6. ibid, art. 356.

7. Patrick Gallahue and Rick Lines, *The Death Penalty for Drug Offences Global Overview 2010*, International Harm Reduction Association, 2010, p. 8.

8. ibid, p. 18.

9. ibid, p. 39.

10. Daniel Johnson D and Franklin Zimring, *The Next Frontier: National Development, Political Change and the Death Penalty in Asia*, Oxford University Press, 2009, p. 323.

11. PENG Xuhui, LI Kun, 'On the death penalty application in drug crime cases', *Journal of Central South University of Technology*, vol. 12, no. 2, April 2006.

12. 武汉大学刑事法研究中心与德国马普外国刑法与国际刑法研究所编辑。中国死刑态度调查报告 ('Opinion survey report on China's death penalty'). 中国台湾：元照出版公司，2010.6. p. 85 [Criminal Law Study Centre of Wu Han University and Max Planck Institute for Foreign and International Criminal Law Editor, 'Opinion survey report on China's death penalty', Taiwan China, YUANGZHAO Publication, June 2010].

13. *Organic law of the People's Courts of the People's Republic of China*, available online at http://www.china.org.cn/english/government/207253.htm (date of last access 20 December 2011) art. 13.

14. 死刑核准权自 2007 年1月1日起收归最高人民法院 available online at http://news.xinhuanet.com/legal/2006-10/31/content_5272293.htm (date of last access 20 December 2011). ['Death penalty reverted to the Supreme Court for approval from January 1st, 2007', XINHUA NEWS]. [Translated by the author].

15. Johnson and Zimring (n 10) p. 281. For a discussion on the decrease of executions in China, see also Jim Yardley, 'With new law, China reports drop in executions', *New York Times*, 9 June 2007.

16. ibid., vol. 8, no. 4, 616–619.

17. Griffith Edwards, et al. 'Drug Trafficking: Time to Abolish the Death Penalty', *International Journal of Mental Health and Addiction*, vol. 8, no. 4, p. 617.; 莫关耀．从死刑的存废谈毒品犯罪死刑的限制．云南警官学院学报 2007 年第一期 [MO Guangyao, 'Talk about the restriction of the death penalty for drug-related crimes from the perspective of retention or abolition', Journal of Yunnan Police Officer Academy].

18. 死刑之争："民众向左，专家向右"．京师刑事法治网，(2010-11-13, available online at http://www.deathpenalty.cn/criminal/Info/showpage.asp?showhead=S&ProgramID=1740&pkID=28863&keyword= (date of last access 29 January 2012) ['Debate on Death Penalty', College for Criminal Law Science of Beijing Normal University].

19. *Criminal Law of People's Republic of China* (n 1).

20. 莫洪宪，陈金林，'论毒品犯罪死刑限制适用' 法学杂志，2010 年第一期 [Mo Hongxian, Chen Jinlin, 'On the application of the death penalty for drug-related crime', Law Science Magazine, 2010].

21. 'Abdullah defends death penalty for drug traffickers', *Bernama—Malaysian National News Agency*, 22 February 2006, cited in Rick Lines, 'The death penalty for drug offences: A violation of international human rights law', International Harm Reduction Association, 2007, p. 12.

22. *Criminal Law of People's Republic of China* (n 1).

23. Cesare Bonesana, Marchese Beccaria, *Of Crime and Punishments*, translated by Edward D Ingraham, 2nd edn., Philadelphia, 1819, p. 26.

24. *Annual Report on Drug Control in China (2009, 2010, 2011)*, available online (in Chinese) on the website of Narcotics Control Bureau of the Ministry of Public Security of People's Republic of China, (Chinese) http://www.mps.gov.cn/n16/n80209/n80481/n804535/index.html (date of last access 20 April 2012).

25. 2011 *Annual Report on Drug Control in China* (n 19).

26. See, for example, Rick Lines, 'A "most serious crime"?—The death penalty for drug offences and international human rights law', *Amicus Law Journal*, issue 21, 2010, p 21–28.

27. International Covenant on Civil and Political Rights (adopted 16 December 1966) 999 UNTS 171 (ICCPR), art. 6(2).

28. UN Human Rights Committee, 'General Comment No. 06: The Right to Life (art.6)' (30 April 1982) (adopted at the Sixteenth Session of the Human Rights Committee), para. 7.

29. UN Human Rights Committee, 'Concluding Observations of the Human Rights Committee: Iran' (29 July 1993) Doc. No. CCPR/C/79/Add.25, para. 8.

30. Manfred Nowak, *UN Covenant on Civil Political Rights: CCPR Commentary*, N.P. Engel Verlag, Germany, p. 141.

31. UN High Commissioner for Human Rights, 'High Commissioner calls for focus on human rights and harm reduction in international drug policy' (10 March 2009).

32. UN General Assembly, 'Right of everyone to the enjoyment of the highest attainable standard of physical and mental health' (6 August 2010) UN Doc. No A/65/255, para. 17.

33. Commission on Narcotic Drugs, 'Drug control, crime prevention and criminal justice: A human rights perspective. Note by the Executive Director' (3 March 2010) UN Doc. E/CN.7/2010/CRP.6, para. 26.

34. Human Rights Council, 'Question of the death penalty: Report of the Secretary-General' (4 July 2011) UN Doc. No. A/HRC/18.20, para. 4.

35. 全国人大常委会组成人员聚集消减死刑罪名 (n 45). [Translated by the author]

36. 毒品犯罪死刑的限制适用. 马豫昆等, available online at http://www.death-penalty.cn/criminal/Info/showpage.asp?showhead=S&pkID=30247 (date of last access 9 January 2012) [`Restriction on the application of the death penalty for drug-related crime', Global Centre on Death Penalty Study, Beijing Normal University].[Translated by the author].

37. The professionals mentioned in the survey include judges, prosecutors, police, officers from legal departments and criminal defence lawyers whose work is related to death penalty cases. See 武汉大学刑事法研究中心与德国马普外国刑法与国际刑法研究所编辑。中国死刑态度调查报 告 Opinion survey report on China's death penalty. 中国台湾: 元照出版公司 (2010), p. 63. [Criminal Law Study Centre of Wu Han University and Max Planck Institute for Foreign and International Criminal Law Editor, `Opinion survey report on China's death penalty', Taiwan China, YUANGZHAO Publication]. [Translated by the author]

38. ibid, p. 70.

39. Dietrich Oberwittler and Shenghui Qi, 'Public opinion on the Death Penalty in China: Results from a general population survey conducted in three province in 2007/2008', Max Planck Institute for Foreign and International Criminal Law, 2009, p. 4.

40. ibid, p. 10.

41. For the Chinese version of the survey, 'drug dealing' can be translated as 'drug trafficking' as well, which the author believes to be the more appropriate translation, as trafficking is considered more severe than drug dealing, which usually is used to describe the sale of small quantities by individuals. See 武汉大学刑事法研究中心与德国马普外国刑法与国际刑法研究所编辑。中国死刑态度调查报告 Opinion survey report on China's death penalty. 中国台湾: 元照出版公司 (2010), p. 13. [Criminal Law Study Centre of Wu Han University and Max Planck Institute for Foreign and International Criminal Law Editor, `Opinion survey report on China's death penalty', Taiwan China, YUANGZHAO Publication]. [Translated by the author].

42. Oberwittler and Qi (n 53) p. 13.

43. 武汉大学刑事法研究中心与德国马普外国刑法与国际刑法研究所编辑。中国死刑态度调查报告 (n 50) p. 63. [Criminal Law Study Centre of Wu Han University and Max Planck Institute for Foreign and International Criminal Law Editor, `Opinion survey report on China's death penalty', Taiwan China, YUANGZHAO Publication]. [Translated by the author].

44. ibid.

45. 袁林. 王力理, `毒品犯罪死刑配置的理性思考', 东岳论丛 [YUAN Lin, WANG lili, `Rational thinking on the configuration of the death Penalty for drug-related crimes', Dong Yue Tribune, vol. 31, no. 2, Feb. 2010].

DR. YINGXI BI is a Senior Research Associate at the International Centre on Human Rights and Drug Policy. Dr. Bi studies and writes about the development of a human rights-based approach to drug policy and the death penalty for crimes in China.

EXPLORING THE ISSUE

Does China Have an Effective Approach to Combat Drug Addiction?

Critical Thinking and Reflection

1. How are the problems with drug use and trafficking in China similar to and different from the problems in the United States?
2. Describe the approaches taken by the Chinese government to combat drug trafficking and addiction. Are they effective?
3. What are the arguments for and against the death penalty? When do you think it is appropriate for a nation to use capital punishment?
4. What is the best approach for a country to combat drug trafficking? What is the best approach to combat drug addiction?

Is There Common Ground?

United States President Richard Nixon declared a "War on Drugs" in 1971 with the goal of eliminating the production, distribution, and consumption of addictive drugs. President Nixon said drug abuse is "public enemy number one." Both Republican (e.g., Ronald Reagan and George H. Bush) and Democrat (e.g., Bill Clinton and Barak Obama) administrations have continued the fight against drugs. Phases of the War have included harm reduction and drug-treatment programs that have helped those addicted to heroin, cocaine and methamphetamine. However, the War has also included stiff criminal penalties domestically and military actions (e.g., Operation Just Cause in Panama in 1989) overseas that have led to deaths.

What is the most effective way to decrease drug trafficking and use, and the deleterious impact of drug addiction on society? Should capital punishment be used to punish those responsible for importing and distributing large drug quantities or who target vulnerable populations, such as children and adolescents, for use? In the NO section, Dr. Yngxi Bi presents arguments in favor of abolishing the death penalty for drug-related crimes that are derived from perspectives of penology and human rights.

China's criminal law allows capital punishment for the use of arms during drug trafficking crimes, distribution of relatively large quantities of drugs, and corruption related trafficking. Capital punishment can be used for drug-related crimes in thirty four other countries, including the United States; however, China executes largest

number of people annually. While the application of the death penalty has decreased in recent years, President Xi Jinping has not expressed plans to eliminate capital punishment in China.

Additional Resources

Chin, K.-l. & Zhang, S.X. (2015) *The Chinese Heroin Trade: Cross-Border Drug Trafficking in Southeast Asia and Beyond*. NYU Press. The authors of the YES section for this issue examine heroin trafficking in China and the Golden Triangle. Drug use, policies and perspectives in China are compared to those of other countries.

Leechaianan, Y. & Longmire, D. R. (2013) The use of the death penalty for drug trafficking in the United States, Singapore, Malaysia, Indonesia and Thailand: A comparative legal analysis. *Laws* 2: 115–149. This review article assesses the use of capital punishment for drug trafficking and related crimes in the Golden Triangle, one of the world's leading drug markets.

Ropp, P.S. (2010) *China in World History*. Oxford University Press. Dr. Ropp provides a fascinating introduction to the long history of China, from the beginnings of civilization through modern times. Interactions with and comparisons to other cultures are provided to help the reader appreciate the dynamics of China's three thousand year (plus) history.

Yuqun, L. (2010) *Traditional Chinese Medicine: Understanding Its Principles and Practices*. China Intercontinental Press. This brief guide provides an overview of how traditional Chinese medicine, an approach with little connection with Western science, exists and is used in the modern era.

Zoccatelli, G. (2014) "It was fun, it was dangerous": Heroin, young urbanites and opening reforms in China's borderlands. *International Journal of Drug Policy* 25: 762–768. The author from the University of London examines the causes of increased heroin use in China in the 1990s.

Internet References . . .

Amnesty International

https://www.amnesty.org/en/

Central Intelligence Agency World Factbook—China

https://www.cia.gov/library/publications/the-world-factbook/geos/ch.html

Death Penalty Information Center

https://deathpenaltyinfo.org/

The State Council of the People's Republic of China

http://english.gov.cn/

United Nations Office on Drugs and Crime

https://www.unodc.org/unodc

Unit 2

UNIT

Drugs and Social Policy

*S*igns on the front of a local high school may designate it as a "drug free zone." A politician may say that she is going to "eliminate drugs from her community if reelected." However, none of us live lives that are unaffected by drugs. Many of us use psychoactive therapeutic drugs to manage the symptoms of a short- or long-term psychological disorder, such as oxycodone after surgery or methylphenidate to minimize the symptoms of a hyperactivity disorder. Drugs are more than heroin sold by a stereotypical drug pusher or cocaine used by a libertine.

<bpu_tn>The issues in this Unit address questions related to drugs that most experience on a day-to-day basis in their community. For example, many communities are debating the legal status of marijuana? Should laws that place strong prohibitions against and penalty for possession and use of marijuana result in severe punishments? Should someone face a long jail sentence for using marijuana, which might minimize their anxiety and pain? If these penalties are minimized or eliminated, what impact might they have on recreational or compulsive marijuana use? Will a liberalization of marijuana laws lead to increased use of harder drugs, like cocaine and heroin?

Selected, Edited, and with Issue Framing Material by:
Dennis K. Miller, *University of Missouri*

ISSUE

Are Opiates Overprescribed?

YES: Graeme Wood, from "Drug Dealers Aren't to Blame for the Heroin Boom. Doctors Are," *The New Republic* (2014)

NO: Carol M. Ostrom, from "New Pain-Management Rules Leave Patients Hurting," *The Seattle Times* (2011)

Learning Outcomes

After reading this issue, you will be able to:

- Understand the challenges faced by those experiencing chronic pain and health professionals that manage pain.
- Describe the laws used to regulate opiate availability.
- Consider perspectives taken by those who view opiates primarily as drugs to manage pain and those who view these drugs primarily as addictive.
- Appraise the policies used to manage pain and conceive new approaches that would balance those concerned with opiate misuse and those focused on pain management.

ISSUE SUMMARY

YES: Graeme Wood, a contributing editor at *The New Republic*, draws on his personal experience using potent opiates after dental surgery to explain the prevalence of opiate addiction. He describes an American medical system that precipitates opiate abuse and dependence.

NO: Carol Ostrom, who writes for *The Seattle Times*, acknowledges that prescription opiate addiction and drug diversion are important concerns; however, these concerns could be inflated. As a consequence, those who need opiates are denied appropriate management of their pain.

Opiates are a large class of drugs that produce analgesia, a decreased sensitivity to a painful stimulus, and cause sleep. They are also referred to as narcotics, drugs that cause sleep or drugs that are habit-forming. There are a number of different opiate analgesics that are widely used to manage the pain. However, opiate drugs are reinforcing, via both positive and negative reinforcement, and can have a high abuse and dependence liability.

Opiates are classified into categories based on their source. For example, opium is the sap collected from the *Papaver somniferum* and it contains the pharmacologically active ingredients morphine and codeine. Heroin is a more-potent form of morphine because it has been chemically altered to speed its absorption into the brain. The opium poppy can also provide the source material for oxycodone—an opiate found in Percocet, Percodan, and OxyContin—and hydrocodone—an opiate found in Vicodin. Opiates produce their effect on behavior by mimicking the activity of opiate-like substances produced naturally in the body called endorphins.

Endorphins and opiates produce their analgesic effect primarily in the central nervous system—the brain and spinal cord—in regions that regulate the sensation and perception of temperature, physical damage to the muscles and skin, and damage to organs. While using an opiate the user may report that the pain is present, but they feel comfortable and are able to tolerate the aversive experience. In addition, opiates can produce analgesia without inducing a loss of consciousness. Some opiates decrease the emotional aspects of pain, including anxiety and dysphoria, and induce feelings of extreme pleasure and enjoyment. Some opiate users report relieved tension and euphoria with their initial drug experiences. These effects of opiates, to take away pain and induce pleasure, are related to the drugs' abuse potentials.

With repeated opiate use tolerance, withdrawal and dependence may develop. Tolerance is a decrease in a drug's effectiveness that leads to the necessity of increasing the drug dose. Once tolerance has developed, an individual may experience withdrawal symptoms, aversive physiological or psychological changes, when opiate use is stopped or the opiate dose is decreased. Withdrawal symptoms are the opposite of the pharmacological effects of the opiate. For example, opiate administration produces analgesia, but pain and irritability may be experienced when the opiate is not available. While using an opiate the individual may experience euphoria, but dysphoria, anxiety, and depression might be experienced during opiate withdrawal. Some of the withdrawal symptoms are physiological, such as diarrhea, pupillary dilation, and chills. While the withdrawal symptoms are aversive, they are not considered to be life threatening. An opiate user may be motivated to use the drug to prevent or minimize withdrawal symptoms, a state referred to as dependence.

When we consider opiate addiction, heroin is the drug that most frequently comes to mind. As mentioned, heroin is produced through a slight modification of morphine's chemical structure. Heroin is also known as *diacetylmorphine*. After it is smoked, sniffed, or injected, heroin rapidly enters the brain where it produces an intense rush of euphoria that is followed by a twilight state of sleep. In the United States, heroin is classified as a Schedule I drug under the Controlled Substances Act, which means it has a high abuse potential and no currently accepted medical use. Heroin has many street names (e.g., "smack," "chiva," and "big H") and it is illicitly imported into the United States as "black tar" from Mexico and white heroin from Colombia.

While heroin is the opiate that is most frequently associated with addiction in the United States, a rapidly emerging concern is misuse and abuse of prescription medications. The Department of Justice reports that more accidental deaths are now caused by prescription drug overdoses than by car accidents. According to the National Survey on Drug Use and Health (2011), conducted by the Substance Abuse and Mental Health Services Administration (SAMHS), more than six million Americans abuse prescription drugs. More than 70 percent of people abusing prescription pain relievers got them through friends or relatives. The Drug Enforcement Agency (DEA) refers to this as diversion—the use of prescription drugs for recreational purposes. According to the SAMHS, the most common diversion is receiving the opiate from a friend or family member for free. Others steal or purchase opiates from friends, relative, drug dealers, or strangers. Opiates can be diverted by visiting multiple doctors with the same pain symptoms (i.e., "doctor shopping") or by stealing them from clinics and pharmacies. A small, but significant, concern in the United States is buying opiates through the internet.

Several opiate preparations are of concern for diversion.

- Hydrocodone is often formulated (e.g., Vicodin and Lortab) in preparations with the non-opiate analgesic acetaminophen. It is one of the most commonly prescribed—and commonly diverted and abused—opiate preparations.
- Oxycodone (e.g., Percodan and OxyContin) is frequently used for the management of acute and chronic pain. On the street, OxyContin is known as "poor man's heroin" and "hillbilly heroin," as its pills are snorted, smoked or injected, like heroin, to induce euphoria or minimize the dysphoria associated with opiate withdrawal.
- Meperidine (e.g., Demerol) is considered to be less potent than morphine, but is widely-used for its analgesic effects. Individuals addicted to heroin use meperidine as an opiate substitute, as it can produce a heroin-like psychological state and diminish opiate withdrawal symptoms.

Increases in opiate abuse and dependence may be an unintended consequence of efforts to use these drugs to manage pain. As such, addiction could follow well-intended efforts by health practitioners to actively manage the discomfort and dysphoria associated with chronic pain. Government agencies, such as the DEA and Food and Drug Administration, have taken steps to limit opiate diversion. Pharmaceutical companies have focused on developing new opiate formulations that effectively manage pain, but minimize the risk of abuse and dependence. New non-opiate analgesics that may lack opiates' reinforcing properties have been developed. Law enforcement and regulatory agencies have investigated and prosecuted pharmacies and clinics that may contribute to diversion by overprescribing opiates to their community. Finally, health practitioners have been educated on the symptoms of opiate abuse and dependence and have been encouraged to decrease the number of opiate prescriptions written and choose less-potent opiates for pain management.

Prescription opiate abuse and dependence has created a conflict: How can we help individuals minimize their pain, while preventing opiate diversion, abuse, and dependence? Have anti-diversion efforts left patients experiencing pain that could be effectively minimized by available opiates? How do we help individuals that became dependent on opiates through the management of their acute or chronic pain?

In the article for the YES selection, Graeme Wood, a journalist and lecturer, describes how potent opiates, such as hydorocodone, are widely prescribed and freely available in the United States. As a consequence, many people could become addicted to drugs as strong as heroin. Historically, our medical system has placed few limits on the availability of opiates and has encouraged health practitioners to dispense these drugs liberally, which is a cause of the current high rates of opiate abuse and dependence. Wood reports, "A physician in California told me he could easily end up with a long line of paying patients out his door, if he just let word out to addicts that OxyContin flowed freely from his prescription pad."

In the article for the NO selection, journalist Carol M. Ostrom describes the consequence of policies that restrict access to opiates on people that experience chronic pain. Ostrom notes that many doctors may refuse to see pain patients rather than risk the discipline or legal liability that could come with violation of new anti-diversion policies.

YES ↵

Graeme Wood

Drug Dealers Aren't to Blame for the Heroin Boom. Doctors Are.

In 2010, a dentist extracted my wisdom teeth, told me to gargle with salt water, and sent me home with a prescription for a Costco-sized bottle of hydrocodone pills. During the procedure, she knocked me out with propofol—the same drug that killed Michael Jackson—and afterward I felt no pain. After a few hours, I popped one hydrocodone, more out of politeness than need. Weeks later, I still felt fine, but I popped two more, just to see what it was like. Hydrocodone's dreamy, pain-dulling effect was impressive: I bit my cheek hard enough to draw blood, and it didn't hurt at all. But the pills made me woozy. I then put the remaining 57 or so of them into my medicine cabinet, and I have no idea what happened to them after that. Lost in a move, I guess.

Heroin epidemics don't come and go randomly, like the McRib. They have clearly identifiable causes—and in this case, by far the largest cause is doctor-prescribed pills. Every year since 2007, doctors have written more than 200 million prescriptions for opioid painkillers. (Consider that there are 240 million adults in the country.) And about four in five new heroin addicts report that they got addicted to prescription pills before they ever took heroin.

My experience was typical: Most people who try opiates don't get addicted. But enough do. Since 2002, the total number of monthly heroin abusers has doubled to 335,000 nationwide. Some of the addicts get the pills through a well-meaning doctor or dentist, and many others swipe leftover pills from their friends or family members. The result for an addict is the same: Once the pills or money run out, heroin is still available—and cheap. At about $10 per hit, it can be half the street cost of pills.

"We seeded the population with opiates," says Robert DuPont, an addiction doctor who served as drug czar under Presidents Nixon and Ford and who is now a harsh critic of opiate over-prescription. The supply shock from easy access to prescription drugs has pushed heroin use out of cities and into rural and suburban and middle-class areas. Massachusetts reported a staggering 185 heroin deaths

outside its major cities since November, and Peter Shumlin, the governor of Vermont, spent his entire "state-of-the-state" address talking about the nearly eightfold increase in people seeking opiate treatment there since 2000. "What started as an OxyContin and prescription-drug addiction problem in Vermont has now grown into a full-blown heroin crisis," he said.

Just 30 years ago, the pills were barely available in the United States, and the only way to get addicted to opiates was to shoot or snort heroin, probably bought on a street corner from a man carrying a weapon. DuPont observed a heroin boom in the late '60s in Washington, D.C., when users consisted primarily of young black men with criminal backgrounds. Dupont says these users chose heroin as their first drug, skipping more benign highs like marijuana. That wave gained energy when American servicemen began returning from Vietnam, where pure Golden Triangle heroin—the granddaddy of all smack—could be bought cheap. "Through 1992, if you went to a methadone program, that's who you'd see," DuPont says. "It was an aging population of people who began their addiction in the 1970s."

It took the intervention of doctors to bring heroin back, with the demographic switcheroo we see coming to fruition today. In 2000, the Joint Commission on Hospital Accreditation released a report concluding that doctors were undertreating chronic pain and that thousands of patients were suffering needlessly. Pharmaceutical companies welcomed the medical profession's decision to supply those patients with previously unobtainable prescription opiates. Companies zealously promoted these drugs and underplayed their potential to turn patients—and any bored friend or relative who decided to play prescription roulette with the contents of their medicine cabinets—into junkies.

Over the last two decades, pain doctors have been competing with each other to win the business of addicts. At one point, 25 of the top 50 prescribers of opiates in the United States practiced in Broward County, Florida.

Some of them boasted that they didn't even require patients to show ID—a frank admission that the clinics welcomed doctor-shopping addicts and their money. In many cases, they advertised a "No Pill, No Pay" policy. Some doctors still dispense opioids like Pez, and patients know exactly where to find them. "Physicians get their practices reviewed on Yelp, and people who don't get their opiates give bad reviews," says Michael Ostacher, an addiction psychiatrist at Stanford.

Until recently, the system was rigged to encourage doctors and dentists to give out opioids with reckless abandon. "Most things in health care that seem crazy become explicable if you look at the incentive structure," says Keith Humphreys, a psychologist who worked in the Office of Drug Control Policy from 2009 to 2010. "If you are a dentist and you give someone thirty Vicodins, they won't bother you again. And if they develop a problem, no one blames you." A physician in California told me he could easily end up with a long line of paying patients out his door, if he just let word out to addicts that OxyContin flowed freely from his prescription pad. Better medical education and tighter regulation have at least begun to slow down the pill flow.

"The result of this is that you probably have opioids in your medicine cabinet right now," says Humphreys. "And who knows that? People who are addicted to opioids." Realtors now advise people selling their homes to clear out their medicine cabinets before an open house, because of the high risk that addicts will attend the showing solely to swipe pills. "You don't have to go to a drug dealer anymore," says DuPont. "You just have to know some college friend who had his wisdom teeth pulled."

For the addict and his or her family, the addiction can of course be hellish, no matter how it started. But there are two silver linings to this epidemic, relative to the previous ones. First, there is a movement to increase public access to Naloxone (brand name: Narcan), an "anti-O.D." drug that first responders can stick up a victim's nose. Naloxone strips

opioids off the receptors in the addict's nervous system, and if used in time can keep the addict breathing long enough to survive. Some worry that the availability of Naloxone will lead addicts to take more risks—opiate enthusiasts have been known to wear "Got Narcan?" t-shirts, using the "Got Milk?" logo—but already the drug has saved lives, and there's no evidence yet that it makes people inject heroin more than they already are.

Second, we can take slight comfort in knowing that the origins of this epidemic at least aren't directly tied up in gang violence, or in a psychologically and morally scarring war in Indochina. If you can choose which addict to have in your life, the one who starts by furtively gobbling pills, or the one who is surrounded by violence and one day decides to drive a spike into his vein and inject a substance sold to him by a street-corner pusher, you definitely want the former. Docility and passivity are virtues in an addict, and in previous heroin booms, the gateways to addiction opened more readily for criminals and killers than for suburban kids poking through their grandparents' bathrooms.

So while the addicts are more numerous than a decade ago (still only 0.14 percent of Americans), they are also significantly less scary and perhaps more likely to survive long enough to be helped. Unfortunately, modern medicine hasn't yet figured out a universally effective way to wean abusers off long-term addiction; some will be sidling up to a methadone-clinic window every morning for the rest of their lives. And their addictions will continue the way they began, just as the doctor ordered.

GRAEME WOOD is a journalist and lecturer who is a contributing editor to *The Atlantic* and *The New Republic*. He is a lecturer in political Science at Yale and has received fellowships from the Social Sciences Research Council, the East-West Center, and the U.S. Holocaust Memorial Museum's Center for the Prevention of Genocide.

Carol M. Ostrom

New Pain-Management Rules Leave Patients Hurting

Denis Murphy's last doctor got suspicious when he saw him sitting in a restaurant.

Murphy, 72, who contracted a painful nerve disorder after a case of shingles, had told the doctor his condition is so painful he often has to stand up.

At his next appointment, the doctor accused him of flimflamming him: making up a story to score narcotic pain relievers.

Murphy, a retired IRS pension-plan examiner and manager from Edmonds, was humiliated. Now, he has a new doctor and a new prescription—but also a growing fear that he could suddenly lose the only relief he's found in six years.

Then, he worries, he'll find himself back in the throes of pain he describes as "a blowtorch to my testicles."

He has reason to worry.

Over the last several months, an effort in Washington to curb a steep rise in prescription-drug overdose deaths—the most ambitious crackdown in the nation—has prompted a number of doctors and clinics to stop taking new chronic-pain patients on opiates, and in some cases to cut off current pain patients.

The hard new line marks the end of a period of relatively liberal—some would say lax—prescribing that began in the late 1980s.

Before then, studies showed that pain was being seriously undertreated, even in dying patients. The statistics and stories fueled assisted-death campaigns in Washington and Oregon and prompted medical boards to reassure doctors not to fear discipline for relieving pain.

But as opiate prescribing increased, so did the deaths—to alarming levels.

Last year, Washington lawmakers attempted to reverse the trend, requiring licensing boards to craft tougher rules for treating pain patients, except for those with injuries, surgery, cancer or who are dying.

The rules don't take effect until Jan. 1 but already, many doctors say they will mean a lot of work, requiring them to gather records, check emergency-room reports,

sign pain contracts with patients and arrange consultations as they try to assess an invisible affliction.

For now, the effort has engendered more questions than answers.

Are doctors simply using the new law as an excuse to dump pain patients, who can be needy and demanding—and, in some cases, addicted?

Will the new rules cut down on overdose deaths—or just make life unbearable for the many patients who are legitimately hurting?

In the South Puget Sound area, a University of Washington Medicine neighborhood clinic stopped taking new chronic-pain patients on opiates about two months ago, after patients flooded in, saying their doctors had cut them off.

"A lot of it is because other providers have stopped doing it," said Dr. Peter McGough, chief medical officer for UW Medicine's Neighborhood Clinics. "I think there's been a fair amount of patient abandonment going on."

McGough calls the new law and rules helpful and important, saying many pain patients weren't previously well managed.

"That said, a lot of physicians are saying it's more trouble than it's worth, so I'm just going to send my patients away."

The swift reaction by doctors and clinics to the new rules has startled even critics who expected some negative fallout for patients.

"We did not see coming that entire hospitals, ERs and clinics would have anti-opioid policies coming down the pike; we didn't see that coming," said Elin Björling, Washington state policy specialist for the American Pain Foundation, a patient-advocacy group.

Request to Amend Rules

Two large statewide physician groups have asked the state's medical-licensing board to amend the rules, saying they are so detailed that doctors could face discipline or legal liability if they don't dot every "i" and cross every "t."

The result, warned the Washington State Medical Association and the Washington Academy of Family Physicians, likely will be that many doctors simply refuse to see pain patients. The board has declined to act.

Dr. Carl Olden, head of the family practitioners' group, said pain-management specialists in Yakima are overwhelmed with pain patients, particularly those on Medicaid, who say their primary-care doctors no longer prescribe the meds they seek.

Linda Van De Bogart, 62, an Eastern Washington resident who has an often-painful genetic defect called Ehlers-Danlos Syndrome, as well as ADD, has been on pain meds for 25 years.

But after being dismissed by her doctor when she and her husband had fallen behind on their clinic bills, she's had no success finding a new provider after calling dozens of doctors and clinics, she says.

"This law has got to be unconstitutional," she says. "It's taking away my life."

Dr. Robert Stevens Singer, a Kirkland neurologist, said he, too, has seen an increasing number of headache-pain patients saying their doctors stopped prescribing opiates. He understands why that might happen.

"It's kind of like saying 'We are no longer going to let you eat liver anymore,'" Singer said. "You didn't want to do it in the first place, and now you've been given an opportunity to escape."

Lax Prescribing Seen

What lawmakers wanted to do was to stop the dying.

The graphs and charts were ominous, and testimony by Dr. Alex Cahana, head of the UW's Division of Pain Medicine, among others, drew a grim picture of patients addicted or dying from lax prescribing.

Cahana, chief proponent of the new regulations, thinks many doctors have been too quick with the pills, in part because they have little training in other modes of relief, a situation he is working to change at the UW.

"Since when does good pain management equal opioids? Since when has the whole practice been reduced to just prescribing a pill?" says Cahana.

"The U.S. is the only country in the world where overtreatment is the new undertreatment."

In a report this year, the federal Institute of Medicine estimated that chronic pain affects 116 million American adults and that relieving it should be a national priority.

But on the ground, practical realities rule.

At Country Doctor Community Health Centers, Dr. Hal Moore, clinic site director, said providers decided they were spending too much energy on pain patients.

"Is the pain real, are they drug seeking, is mental health a factor? There are all these factors you have to consider," he said, and the rules added another layer. As a result, Moore said, new pain patients no longer will get opiates at those clinics.

Dr. Marcus Rempel, medical director for Neighborcare Health, said providers were disturbed to find that many of the patients inundating its six local clinics seeking narcotic pain relief weren't 50- or 60-year-old workers with back injuries, but young adults of 25 or 30, asking for long-term opiate medication.

"We felt like we were in a situation where we were contributing to a public-health problem," said Rempel, whose clinics closed to new pain patients on opiates.

Community Health Care's five Pierce County clinics stopped prescribing opiates for most new or current chronic-pain patients after two died last year, said Dr. Jeff Smith, medical director.

Other providers say they'll still see pain patients, but under stricter conditions.

"Anyone who says there's not a problem out there has their head in the sand," says Dr. Warren Fein, primary-care medical director for Swedish Medical Group.

The regulations have prompted a new, standardized opiate policy there, adding paperwork such as patient contracts and requiring urine tests for all pain patients.

Fear of Being Cut Off

For some pain patients, the changes are unnerving.

"I'm living in fear of cutoff," says Denis Murphy, despite being what his wife, Judy Murphy, calls a career rule-follower with no history of abuse.

He understands that doctors are afraid of being disciplined, so he endures the random urine tests, although "at the age of 70-plus, it's no fun to go down to one of these druggie centers and stand in line with all these guys with tattoos and pee in a bottle."

Judy Murphy recalls the day in the previous physician's office when her husband was mortified by the doctor's suspicion. "I thought Denis was going to melt into this puddle of humiliation," she said. "He was ready to run or cry or dissolve."

Others say they know they need to reduce their medication but say they haven't been given help to do so.

Eric, a Mercer Island father who has had severe back pain for years after several failed surgeries, said he wants to cut back on his opiate dose but doesn't know how he'd get pain relief during the process.

"When I don't have my pain meds, I sit in the corner shaking and doubled over in pain that makes me cry," he said.

Targeted Approach

Some statistics hint that a more targeted approach might be more fruitful.

In King County, UW researcher Caleb Banta-Green has shown that the vast majority of prescription-overdose deaths aren't from single prescriptions but narcotics combined with other drugs or alcohol.

Across the state, more than half of those who died were patients on Medicaid, according to state figures, and the most common pain drug was methadone, increasingly prescribed for Medicaid patients after the state restricted other medications.

Many providers said they expect the new rules will ultimately prove helpful but worry that some patients may try risky alternatives in the meantime, taking dangerous levels of acetaminophen or ibuprofen, or even buying opiates on the street.

"It happens, and it's a scenario I've heard too often," Banta-Green says.

Dr. Kimber Rotchford, a Port Townsend pain and addiction specialist, puts it bluntly: "The new law promotes the illicit traffic of opioids" while doing nothing to increase access to mental-health help or alternative pain-relief treatments.

Legitimate patients should not be held hostage to "a few losers," says Singer, the neurologist. "What we need is some balance here."

CAROL M. OSTROM was a reporter for *The Seattle Times* from 1980–2014 who focused on religion, values and ethics, health insurance, and health reform.

EXPLORING THE ISSUE

Are Opiates Overprescribed?

Critical Thinking and Reflection

1. What is the relationship between pain and addiction? How might a drug that diminishes physical pain produce drug addiction?
2. Why do opiates have a high abuse and dependence potential?
3. Are the current federal and state government polices effective to allow health practitioners to help their patients experiencing pain, while curtailing drug diversion? What new policies or laws would you propose?
4. What could you do as a physician or pharmacist to decrease the chance your patients will divert prescription opiates for abuse? What could you do to help a patient that is dependent on an opiate?

Is There Common Ground?

Opiates have been cultivated and used to manage pain for at least seven thousand years, as there are archaeological records of their use in ancient cultures in the Middle East, Europe, and North Africa. Recently, there has been a dramatic increase in prescription drug abuse. This increase has led to a corresponding increase in admissions to drug treatment programs for drug addictions, emergency room visits because of overdoses, and new programs and policies to prevent diversion.

The initial decision to take prescription drugs is voluntary, and desired, with opiates, to manage pain, stress, and anxiety. However, changes in the brain caused by repeated drug abuse over a period of time affect a person's self-control and ability to make sound decisions. When the opiate is not accessible, the user may experience withdrawal symptoms including pain, irritability, dysphoria, depression, and hostility. The user may be motivated to continue using opiates to escape or avoid these aversive symptoms.

There are a number of potential reasons for why prescription opiate abuse is on the rise. One reason is that doctors report writing more opiate prescriptions for managing acute and chronic pain. However, health practitioners are then left to consider, "How can we help individuals minimize their pain, while preventing opiate diversion, abuse, and dependence?"

Additional Resources

Bender, E. (2014). Growing percentage of admissions attributed to opiate abuse. *Psychiatric News*. http://psychnews.psychiatryonline.org/doi/full/10.1176/pn.42.20.0017a.

This article reports on the prevalence of drug-related emergency room admissions related to opiate misuse.

Dalrymple, T. (2006). *Romancing Opiates*. Encounter Books.

Theodore Dalrymple argues that opiate addiction is not a disease and that withdrawal from opiates is not medically serious.

Manchikanti, L., et al. (2010). Therapeutic Use, Abuse, and Nonmedical Use of Opioids: A Ten-Year Perspective. *Pain Physician*. 13(5): 401.

Dr. Manchikanti and colleagues provide an updated 10-year perspective on therapeutic use, abuse, and nonmedical use of opioids and their consequences

McQuay, H. (1999). Opioids in pain management. *The Lancet*. 353(9171): 22–29.

This review article provides a basic overview of the pharmacological properties of opioids used to manage pain.

Internet References . . .

National Association of Drug Diversion Investigators

http://www.naddi.org/aws/NADDI/pt/sp/home_page

National Institutes of Drug Abuse: Prescription Drug Abuse

http://www.drugabuse.gov/publications/research -reports/prescription-drugs/director

National Library of Medicine: Opiate Withdrawal

http://www.nlm.nih.gov/medlineplus/ency/article /000949.htm

United States Drug Enforcement Adminstration: Office of Diversion Control

http://www.deadiversion.usdoj.gov/

Web MD: Opiate Analgesics

http://www.webmd.com/drugs/condition-3079-Pain .aspx

Selected, Edited, and with Issue Framing Material by:
Dennis K. Miller, *University of Missouri*

ISSUE

Is Opiate Addiction Truly Debilitating?

YES: **Heather Lynn Peters**, from "Young Father Details Heroin-Addiction Nightmare: 'It's the Worst Sickness You Can Imagine,'" *Michigan Live Media Group* (2015)

NO: **Theodore Dalrymple**, from "Withdrawal from Heroin Is a Trivial Matter," *The Spectator* (2009)

Learning Outcomes

After reading this issue, you should be able to:

- Explain which drugs are classified, pharmacologically, as narcotics and describe their effects on behavior.
- Describe the physical and psychological symptoms of opiate withdrawal.
- Explain how withdrawal symptoms could be so debilitating to cause continued drug use.
- Refer to different treatments that are available to manage opiate dependence.

ISSUE SUMMARY

YES: A heroin addict stays a heroin addict to avoid the misery of withdrawal, a sickness where the addict is unable to function: This is the experience of young man in Michigan who is dependent on opiates. The article by Heath Lynn Peters describes how addiction to heroin and other opiates has torn apart a community.

NO: Theodore Dalrymple is the pen name of Anthony Daniels, a retired prison doctor and psychiatrist. He reports that opiate withdrawal is medically trivial and the withdrawal symptoms are overstated. Dalrymple states, "the great majority, though not quite all, of the suffering caused by withdrawal from opiates, insofar as it is real and not feigned, is psychological in origin and caused by the mythology surrounding it."

Darren Aronofsky's film "Requiem for a Dream," based on the novel by Hubert Selby, Jr., depicts the lives of three young New Yorkers. At the start of the movie, Harry (portrayed by Jared Leto) plans to start a business. His girlfriend, Marion (Jennifer Connelly), is following-through on her goal of opening a high-end boutique. Their friend Tyrone (Marlon Wayans) wants to grow into a man that his late mother would respect. However, each is addicted to the narcotic heroin: They compulsively use the drug and go to extraordinary lengths to attain it. Early in the story the three begin distributing heroin, but they quickly begin to use what they intended to sell. By the end of the movie Harry's left arm, infected from repeated intravenous heroin injection, is amputated. Tyrone is sentenced

to prison where he is forced to do hard labor under racist guards. Marion is supplied with drugs in exchange for sex and her performance in a graphic sex show. Each character struggles with despair, depression, and hopelessness caused by heroin addiction.

"Requiem for a Dream" is one of many pieces of popular media describing the experience of narcotic addiction. These books, films, and songs depict characters that cannot stop taking the drug because of the insurmountable withdrawal symptoms that enslave the addict to the drug. However, narcotic addiction and the corresponding withdrawal symptoms are among the most controversial areas in the study of drug use.

In the legal system, "narcotic" refers to any illicit and habit-forming drug (e.g., heroin, as well as cocaine him. We made contact there in (the Oceana County) jail and he showed up in church one Sunday when I was preaching," Harden said.

"He's a charming young man and people are drawn to him. He had a tremendous amount of potential. He knows apart from the power of God, he has the power to overcome things. Addiction is a very powerful thing for people to deal with." Harden said

Nelson sent Harden a letter from jail recently, asking to speak with him again.

"It says, 'I miss you dearly and all I want is to do good again,'" Harden said from his Oceana County home. "I'm looking at a picture of him now."

Harden said he plans to reach out to Nelson and possibly attempt to see him at the rehab center. He is fearful that if the rehabilitation program doesn't work, the young father could end up in prison, or worse: another casualty of drug use.

According to Oceana County Prosecutor Joseph Bizon, Nelson's criminal history there dates back to 2008 through 2014 and includes convictions for: possession of marijuana; receiving and concealing stolen firearms; allowing a person to violate the motor vehicle code; delivery/manufacturing marijuana; operating while intoxicated; and domestic violence.

Harden said when the drugs take hold of Nelson, he just isn't the same person.

"That heroin addiction," Harden says, "He knows he can't handle it, but when everything else falls apart, he goes back."

Heather Lynn Peters is a journalist for the Muskegon (Michigan) Chronicle. A graduate of Central Michigan University, Ms. Peters covers police and fire, as well as cooking.

Selected, Edited, and with Issue Framing Material by:
Dennis K. Miller, *University of Missouri*

ISSUE

Is Opiate Addiction Truly Debilitating?

YES: Heather Lynn Peters, from "Young Father Details Heroin-Addiction Nightmare: 'It's the Worst Sickness You Can Imagine,'" *Michigan Live Media Group* (2015)

NO: Theodore Dalrymple, from "Withdrawal from Heroin Is a Trivial Matter," *The Spectator* (2009)

Learning Outcomes

After reading this issue, you should be able to:

- Explain which drugs are classified, pharmacologically, as narcotics and describe their effects on behavior.
- Describe the physical and psychological symptoms of opiate withdrawal.
- Explain how withdrawal symptoms could be so debilitating to cause continued drug use.
- Refer to different treatments that are available to manage opiate dependence.

ISSUE SUMMARY

YES: A heroin addict stays a heroin addict to avoid the misery of withdrawal, a sickness where the addict is unable to function: This is the experience of young man in Michigan who is dependent on opiates. The article by Heath Lynn Peters describes how addiction to heroin and other opiates has torn apart a community.

NO: Theodore Dalrymple is the pen name of Anthony Daniels, a retired prison doctor and psychiatrist. He reports that opiate withdrawal is medically trivial and the withdrawal symptoms are overstated. Dalrymple states, "the great majority, though not quite all, of the suffering caused by withdrawal from opiates, insofar as it is real and not feigned, is psychological in origin and caused by the mythology surrounding it."

Darren Aronofsky's film "Requiem for a Dream," based on the novel by Hubert Selby, Jr., depicts the lives of three young New Yorkers. At the start of the movie, Harry (portrayed by Jared Leto) plans to start a business. His girlfriend, Marion (Jennifer Connelly), is following-through on her goal of opening a high-end boutique. Their friend Tyrone (Marlon Wayans) wants to grow into a man that his late mother would respect. However, each is addicted to the narcotic heroin: They compulsively use the drug and go to extraordinary lengths to attain it. Early in the story the three begin distributing heroin, but they quickly begin to use what they intended to sell. By the end of the movie Harry's left arm, infected from repeated intravenous heroin injection, is amputated. Tyrone is sentenced to prison where he is forced to do hard labor under racist guards. Marion is supplied with drugs in exchange for sex and her performance in a graphic sex show. Each character struggles with despair, depression, and hopelessness caused by heroin addiction.

"Requiem for a Dream" is one of many pieces of popular media describing the experience of narcotic addiction. These books, films, and songs depict characters that cannot stop taking the drug because of the insurmountable withdrawal symptoms that enslave the addict to the drug. However, narcotic addiction and the corresponding withdrawal symptoms are among the most controversial areas in the study of drug use.

In the legal system, "narcotic" refers to any illicit and habit-forming drug (e.g., heroin, as well as cocaine and marijuana); however, pharmacologists use the term "narcotic" to refer to "opiates," a class of drugs with pharmacological properties similar to opium. Opiates have an analgesic effect (i.e., they decrease sensitivity to pain) and they induce sleep. As such, they are effective to decrease the unpleasant emotional experiences of pain and help an individual rest and relax. Some report that they are still aware of their pain after using an opiate, but the pain is no longer uncomfortable.

While heroin is the opiate that is most frequently associated with addiction in the United States, a rapidly-emerging concern is misuse and abuse of prescription medications. Opiate abuse and dependence may be an unintended consequence of efforts to use these drugs to manage pain. Addiction could follow well-intended efforts by health practitioners to actively and appropriately manage chronic pain.

A number of different opiates are used by people clinically and/or recreationally and have an addiction liability, including codeine, morphine, oxycodone, meperidine, and heroin.

- Codeine is a refined from opium, a sap from the poppy plant, and is used to treat pain and suppress a cough.
- Morphine is also refined from the poppy and is used to minimize acute and chronic pain.
- Oxycodone is synthesized in the laboratory from opium and is used for relief of moderate and severe pain. It is available in different clinical preparations including OxyContin.
- Meperidine is a synthetic, or man-made, opiate that is available as Demerol and has been used for moderate pain.
- Heroin is synthesized from morphine and has strong analgesic properties.

With recurrent use, tolerance can develop to many of the physical and psychological effects of opiates—that is, the drug experience may diminish. If a specific dose of an opiate is used for its analgesic properties, then that dose will likely become ineffective when it is to be used again-and-again for chronic pain. The same diminution is likely with the euphoric properties sought by someone using a narcotic to get "high." To compensate for the development of tolerance, the user may increase his intake. For example, within a few months, consumption of oxycodone may increase 10 times, or more, to achieve the desired analgesic effects. Someone tolerant to an opiate may consume a drug dose that would be sufficient to kill a naïve user.

If the user must increase opiate use to surmount tolerance, what happens when the drug is not available? Along with the development of drug tolerance is the development of withdrawal symptoms and dependence. When someone has used a high narcotic dose for a prolonged period of time, withdrawal symptoms may appear when the effects of those high drug doses wear off. As indicated, opiate withdrawal is one of the most controversial areas in the study of drugs and behavior. According to the popular media, such as "Requiem for a Dream," the symptoms are severe enough to motivate criminal behavior or even cause death.

Clinical and preclinical research indicates that the symptoms of heroin withdrawal follow a standard pattern. Within the first few hours of withdrawal, the individual experiences anxiety, malaise, and depression. Later, extreme yawning, sweats or excessive perspiration, a runny nose, and teary eyes occur. By the end of the first day of narcotic withdrawal, the individual will also experience pupil dilation, "goose pimples" or "goose flesh," muscle twitches or tremors, aching bones and muscles, hot and cold flashes, and a loss of appetite. During the second day of withdrawal the symptoms include insomnia; increased blood pressure, respiratory rate, and body temperature; and nausea, vomiting, and diarrhea. These symptoms are similar to what people experience during a case of intestinal flu. While they can be extremely unpleasant and create a general sense of misery, they are rarely life-threatening. The intensity and duration of the symptoms depend on the degree of tolerance that developed and the amount of narcotic that had been consumed.

The symptoms listed above represent physiological withdrawal and are compared to a case of the flu. What about psychological withdrawal symptoms, also known as drug craving? During the first few hours of narcotic withdrawal the individual experiences anxiety, depression, and malaise—and a strong craving for the drug. The craving has been described as a hunger or intense yearning for the drug. Part of it could be a desire to reexperience the sense of pleasure that comes with the narcotic "high," while the other part could be a desire to escape or avoid the uncomfortable anxiety and depression.

As the physiological and psychological symptoms develop after only a few hours of withdrawal, the individual addicted to a narcotic is on a tight schedule or acquiring and using the drug on a regular basis. Three or four administrations may be desired each day to surmount withdrawal symptoms. The addict may become preoccupied with "taking care of business" or obtaining, taking, and recovering from the drug. The narcotic can become the center of the addict's attention, time, and money, leaving few resources for anything else in life. Narcotics, like heroin and oxycodone, are scheduled by the Drug Enforcement Administration (DEA). In the case of heroin, the drug cannot be dispensed legally for any use, and in the case of oxycodone and many other narcotics, they can only be dispensed with a prescription. The DEA and many states have increased their review and regulation of narcotic prescriptions by doctors and pharmacists to cut down on drug diversion from limited pain management to illicit street use. As a consequence, narcotics can be expensive and difficult to find. The film "Requiem for a Dream" depicts the criminal behavior—theft and prostitution—associated with narcotic dependence, as users find ways to acquire the drug.

But, does the media depict only the worst case situation? Is heroin addiction truly debilitating? In the YES selection, Heather Lynn Peters describes the extreme pain of heroin withdrawal and how these symptoms are strong enough to motivate individuals to continue using the drug, despite the consequences. In her article she describes experiences in her community of people developing an addiction to narcotics after using prescription painkillers. Theodore Dalrymple states that the severity of narcotic (heroin) withdrawal is overstated. In the NO selection, Dalrymple writes, "The evidence is pretty conclusive that the great majority, though not quite all of the suffering caused by withdrawal from opiates, insofar as it is real and not feigned, is psychological in origin and caused by the mythology surrounding it."

YES ⬅

Heather Lynn Peters

Young Father Details Heroin-Addiction Nightmare: "It's the Worst Sickness You Can Imagine"

Daniel Nelson talks about falling back into heroin addiction

MUSKEGON, MI—Daniel Nelson's desperation is palpable.

The 24-year-old Shelby man takes full responsibility for ending up back behind bars, while his girlfriend raises their young son alone.

He knows he's considered a failure, a letdown to his son, his girlfriend, the northern pastor who tried to save him. He was a former high school athlete and threw it all away. He gets it.

He understands, to the public, he's just another statistic, another heroin addict who fell into the firm clutches of Muskegon County's growing drug problem. He's an exhausted addict who discovered a heroin-addict's honey pot: Muskegon County—where the heroin is plentiful, affordable and easily to obtain.

"I found heroin in Muskegon. I was 20," Nelson said during a recent jail interview. "The heroin is so strong now. They can sniff it or smoke it and get high as a kite."

Hitting Rock Bottom

Nelson was several days into withdrawal at the Muskegon County Jail when he agreed to share his struggle with the MLive. On the date of the interview, Nelson had been there 32 days.

He told a judge that he pleaded with his probation officer to send him back to jail. He wasn't ready to face temptation again. He's too tired to chase that dreamy, numbing sensation of heroin running through his veins. He finds comfort confined behind the bars of the county jail.

"When you shoot it up, there's no better feeling. There's no better feeling. You feel a warm feeling. It's like

an orgasm that runs through your whole body. It numbs all pain. All the problems, they are numbed," he said.

That is, until the start of withdrawal. Then that numbing sensation turns to true horror—an absolute living hell for those who hit rock bottom, he said.

"At first you can't function on it, but then you can't live without it. It turns into the only thing you can function with. You don't work anymore," Nelson said.

"It's really terrible. I know what it does to me every time I do it. The problem with heroin is the withdrawal. You say, 'I don't want that sickness today. I'll deal with it tomorrow.' Two or three weeks go by and you're not able to function. The withdrawal—it's the worst sickness you can imagine."

And that, Nelson swears, is why an addict stays an addict: To avoid the misery of withdrawal. Addicts run from the withdrawal, he said, and it's easier to function high.

"No one wants to get off it. Every morning you wake up to the worst sickness ever. It lasts for about a month. You don't gain your weight back. Your functions still aren't working well. It's about 90 days that you come back out of it," he said.

Prescription Drugs Led to Addiction

Nelson, who attended Shelby High School, was a high school wrestler who had overcome some significant odds as a child. His father died when he was 5, and he was primarily raised by his grandparents, he said. His mother struggled with her own demons.

While living with his grandmother, he suffered a pulled muscle while wrestling and found one of her Norco pills.

Heather Lynn Peters, from "Young father details heroin-addiction nightmare: 'It's the worst sickness you can imagine,'" Michigan Live Media Group (May 26, 2015). Used with permission.

"I couldn't feel any pain. I liked the way I felt. I continued taking them. I could work out harder and my recovery time was faster. But in 10th grade I started having withdrawal and was throwing up. I didn't know what was going on. Then I started buying them off the street and then started getting them from my doctor," Nelson said. "I had all kind of excuses to get them."

But by the time he was a junior in high school, he was getting anxious and built up a tolerance to the Norco. He was having a difficult time obtaining a higher quantity of them.

"There was a real change going on in me. Someone said a methadone clinic would help me. This is when my whole life started to change. I went from Norco to a methadone clinic," Nelson said.

Nelson said he went to the clinic six days a week. He would receive liquid doses of methadone and continued that process for months. He turned 18, found himself addicted to methadone, and tangled with law enforcement on more than one occasion.

He says he bartered marijuana for a couple of hunting rifles one year that later came up stolen.

It resulted in his first felony charge. He knew he wasn't going to get into college on a wrestling scholarship with a felony conviction on his record.

"Everything changed. I was in trouble. Everything went downhill," Nelson said.

The years that followed included him dropping out of high school his senior year, a breakup with a steady girlfriend, a stint at a rehab center where he got in a fight and was subsequently released.

But he managed to detox during that time. He thought he kicked his addiction to methadone, but then life happened. He had a son with his current girlfriend, he got into more trouble with Oceana County law enforcement, and finally decided he couldn't handle it anymore.

"I tried to get clean. I had a lot of responsibilities and overwhelming stuff. I had great intentions. I started the methadone again, but I couldn't get funding to go back to the clinic," Nelson said.

So, he found heroin in Muskegon, and from that point forward, his life spiraled out of control.

"I knew I had to get clean. I just had a kid. I did a year in the Oceana County Jail. I do really good when I get out. But it had been five years of being in and out of jail and just using drugs and I didn't know how to live in society without using drugs. Every time I start having problems, I try and try and I fall back into it," Nelson said.

"I would get on probation and get on drugs again. I got back on heroin, so I told my probation officer that I needed to be locked up and I needed a detox, I need help," Nelson said.

Nelson went back to jail for 14 days, detoxed while in jail and promised himself that this time it would be different. He went to church when he got out, made contact with a former pastor who he had previously met in the Oceana County Jail, and that pastor, Elden Harden, took Nelson under his wing.

"He changed my whole life," Nelson said.

Nelson said Harden got him various jobs, worked to keep him in church and helped him wean off the drugs. But then Nelson got kidney stones and Norco was back in his life to ease the pain, and shortly after, he was hooked again on heroin.

That's what landed him in the Muskegon County Jail. Nelson said he was found with drugs on his person in Muskegon during a trip to Muskegon Heights to buy heroin.

Casualties of Addiction

Nelson, now charged as a third-time habitual offender, is slated to be sentenced on June 8 in Muskegon for one count of controlled substance, less than 25 grams. As of May 21, court officials confirmed that Nelson is at the Salvation Army Adult Rehabilitation Center in Grand Rapids, and about 30 days into that program.

As a patient there, he cannot speak to anyone in the first 30 days of treatment, according to a Salvation Army official. That official said facility representatives are not allowed to confirm whether Nelson is a patient there for privacy reasons.

Nelson's girlfriend, Kailee Perez, 22, who says she is pregnant with Nelson's second child, said the rehab facility is his only hope. Perez said she understands his struggle with heroin, as she too was addicted after the birth of their first son, who is now 2½. Perez and her son currently live with Perez's mother.

Perez said she watched Nelson wrestle with the addiction for years. It was no surprise then that she too became immersed in that lifestyle as well.

"It was horrible. We spent all our tax money on heroin because we were both doing it. It's a struggle. We had our first son and he has made changes since we had him. But when (Nelson) hangs around the wrong crowd, he falls off," Perez said.

The retired pastor, who spent years working with Nelson and staying in contact with Perez as well, says he too is pulling for Nelson. He confirmed the struggles Nelson had growing up without a father and that, deep down, Nelson does yearn for a better life.

"There was a real breakdown with his family, and since then, Danny has had a ton of people reach out to him. We made contact there in (the Oceana County) jail and he showed up in church one Sunday when I was preaching," Harden said.

"He's a charming young man and people are drawn to him. He had a tremendous amount of potential. He knows apart from the power of God, he has the power to overcome things. Addiction is a very powerful thing for people to deal with." Harden said

Nelson sent Harden a letter from jail recently, asking to speak with him again.

"It says, 'I miss you dearly and all I want is to do good again,'" Harden said from his Oceana County home. "I'm looking at a picture of him now."

Harden said he plans to reach out to Nelson and possibly attempt to see him at the rehab center. He is fearful that if the rehabilitation program doesn't work, the young father could end up in prison, or worse: another casualty of drug use.

According to Oceana County Prosecutor Joseph Bizon, Nelson's criminal history there dates back to 2008 through 2014 and includes convictions for: possession of marijuana; receiving and concealing stolen firearms; allowing a person to violate the motor vehicle code; delivery/manufacturing marijuana; operating while intoxicated; and domestic violence.

Harden said when the drugs take hold of Nelson, he just isn't the same person.

"That heroin addiction," Harden says, "He knows he can't handle it, but when everything else falls apart, he goes back."

Heather Lynn Peters is a journalist for the Muskegon (Michigan) Chronicle. A graduate of Central Michigan University, Ms. Peters covers police and fire, as well as cooking.

[handwritten note] ✱ Look up research on over indulgent personality

Theodore Dalrymple   ➡ **NO**

Withdrawal from Heroin Is a Trivial Matter

We live in Keynesian times: the answer to the economic problems created by a mountain of debt frittered away on trifles is clearly a whole mountain range of debt frittered away on trifles. In the circumstances it is good to know that a judge has done his bit to stimulate the general improvidence—sorry, the British economy. He has awarded £11,000 each to three prisoners in Winchester Prison who underwent withdrawal from heroin without benefit of further doses of heroin or of methadone and other heroin substitutes. It was against their human rights, he said.

This is indeed odd. It is doubtful whether anyone ever dies from withdrawal of opiates alone. In reviewing the medical literature between 1875 and 1968, the doctors and researchers Glaser and Ball were unable to find a single case of death from withdrawal of opiates, despite the fact that the literature covered many thousands of cases.

Indeed, such withdrawal is medically trival, unlike that from alcohol and barbiturates (and sometimes even benzodiazepines such as valium). Let me quote Niesink, Jaspers, Kornet and van Ree's book, *Drugs of Abuse and Addiction: Neurobehavioral Toxicology:* "[Withdrawal] is time limited . . . and not life-threatening, thus can be easily controlled by reassurance, personal attention and general nursing care without any need for pharmacotherapy."

By contrast, 2,845 people died of methadone poisoning in Great Britain between 1996 and 2005. In 2006, 241 died of methadone, and 713 of heroin or morphine poisoning. In 2007, the figures were 325 and 829 respectively. In Dublin, more people die of methadone poisoning than of heroin poisoning.

I repeat, no one dies of opiate withdrawal. I might add also that doctors have a very long history of treating the trivial condition of withdrawal from opiates in a dangerous, indeed fatal fashion.

It goes without saying that we are all furious at Mr Putin's treatment of Georgia, but few of us realise that the drug addicts of the country whose president brokered a ceasefire between Russia and Georgia—France—have caused far more harm to the population of that country than Mr Putin's Russia.

They have systematically diverted the drug with which their heroin addiction is "treated," buprenorphine, to Georgia (as well as to Finland, incidentally), where scores of thousands of Georgians have addicted themselves to it. The fact that the French addicts have diverted it in this fashion is eloquent testimony to how much they needed it in the first place, and how easily they were able to deceive doctors.

It might, I suppose, be argued that such drugs as heroin, methadone and buprenorphine are potentially safe when given under strict medical supervision; but such supervision is extremely difficult to enforce, given the levels of duplicity, deviousness and dishonesty among the population for whom they are prescribed. In one Canadian case, for example, a woman in a prison prescribed methadone for her withdrawal symptoms vomited it to sell it to another prisoner, who then died of an overdose. Guess whom the relatives of the dead woman sued?

The evidence is pretty conclusive that the great majority, though not quite all, of the suffering caused by withdrawal from opiates, insofar as it is real and not feigned, is psychological in origin and caused by the mythology surrounding it. In the 1930s, experiments were done demonstrating that morphine addicts could not reliably distinguish between injections of water and morphine: when they received water thinking it was morphine, their symptoms abated, but when they received morphine thinking it was water, they grew worse.

It has also been established that the distress of withdrawal is not correlated with the physical severity of withdrawal symptoms, and is often at its worst before, not during, withdrawal.

Even accepting the ludicrous, corrupt and corrupting doctrine of human rights, it is difficult to see how it can be a human right to have a non-life-threatening condition transformed into a life-threatening one by supposed (and ineffectual) treatment. The old medical adage, first do no harm, ought to take precedence, and therefore the presumption must always be against, not for, treatment for withdrawal. That so evident and unassailable a point did not prevail in court, instead landing the British taxpayer with a total bill that no doubt ran into hundreds of thousands of pounds, is deeply emblematic of the moral and intellectual decadence into which we have fallen.

This is not an isolated instance of it, either, even in the relatively small question of how we conceive of heroin addiction. The Sentencing Guidelines Council last week suggested that first-time offenders who steal from the vulnerable should be given stiffer sentences than they currently receive, but that courts should not send drug addicts who steal to "feed their habits" to prison, but should consider instead drug or alcohol treatment programmes.

The Sentencing Guidelines Council was attempting, as it has so often done in the past, to mislead the British public into thinking that the law has become harder on criminals when in fact it is becoming more lenient. The class of the former type of offender—the first-timers who target the vulnerable—is of course very much smaller than the second class, the addicted thief, robber or burglar.

Thus, despite the impression given by headlines that say "Stiffer sentences for first-time offenders," what is being proposed is a reduction in severity of sentencing.

Now it does not follow from the fact that many thieves and burglars are drug-addicted that they are thieves and burglars because they are addicted. In fact, the evidence suggests that the relationship is the other way round: that whatever causes them to become criminals causes them to become addicts.

In a survey in the prison in which I worked, I found that the great majority of heroin addicts sentenced to imprisonment had been imprisoned for the first time well before they ever took heroin. Since most people are convicted about ten times before they are sent to prison, and the clear-up rate of crimes is about 5 percent (and even that, thanks to police dishonesty,

is an exaggeration), it is likely that many of them had committed dozens, perhaps hundreds, of crimes before they ever took heroin. Therefore, it cannot be that they are criminals because they are addicted.

Heroin addicts are not "hooked" by heroin, as fishermen take fish; they "hook" heroin. Most of them take it intermittently for quite a time before they take it regularly and become physiologically addicted to it. Moreover, taking opiates by injection is not incompatible with normal working. In the 1930s, the majority of morphine addicts in America went to work normally.

Moreover, the Sentencing Guidelines Council must know that the Audit Commission recently found that 75 percent of addicts did not even comply with the kind of community sentences that they recommend, and that Home Office research found that the re-conviction rate within two years of people given such sentences was 90 percent, i.e. the re-offending rate must be close to 100 percent.

The Sentencing Guidelines Council is therefore aiding and abetting crime on a huge scale, and ought to be disbanded forthwith. Addiction should be treated as an aggravating circumstance, and an automatic additional five or ten years ought to be added to addicts' sentences: that is, if the peace of the poor, who are the primary victims of crime, is to be protected by the government and the criminal justice system.

THEODORE DALRYMPLE is the pen name of Anthony Daniels, a retired doctor and psychiatrist who practiced in a British inner-city hospital and prison. He is a fellow at the Manhattan Institute, a contributing editor of *City Journal*, and an author of several books, including *Romancing Opiates*.

EXPLORING THE ISSUE

Is Opiate Addiction Truly Debilitating?

Critical Thinking and Reflection

1. Is opiate addiction debilitating or is it a function of our culture's perceptions of narcotics?
2. This issue made a distinction between physiological and psychological withdrawal symptoms. Can we separate the two, and how do they reflect the same processes in the body and brain?
3. Our nation's laws have strong prohibitions against narcotics, yet they are widely used. How could we change laws and policies to minimize the impact of narcotic addiction on society and the individual?
4. There is a correlation between drug use and crime. What are the other factors or variables that could contribute to this relationship?
5. Considering the risk of narcotic addition described in the YES selection for this issue, what questions or concerns should have practitioners have when prescribing narcotics?

Is There Common Ground?

One misconception about narcotics, especially heroin, is that one "hit" of the drug leads to a lifetime addiction, similar to what is depicted in "Requiem for a Dream." However, preclinical and clinical research indicates that this perception is false. The development of narcotic dependence takes time and persistence from the user. While withdrawal symptoms may be evident after a few days' use, physical dependence severe enough to induce craving requires a longer period of time.

There are many individuals who use narcotics but are not dependent on them. "Chippers," or those with an "ice cream habit," use narcotics occasionally, when the drug and opportunities to take it are available. The number of chippers in the United States is not known, and research focuses on how chippers differ from those who are physically dependent on narcotics.

Being a narcotic addict can be dangerous. Much of the harm comes from the lifestyles that individuals addicted to narcotics live. Many of the drugs are expensive and it requires money to sustain the habit. Other life priorities, such as nutrition and health, become secondary and suffer. Loved ones of those addicted, including their children, can suffer from the effects of narcotic addiction.

Additional Resources

Adams, T. (2013). *Opiate Addiction—The Painkiller Addiction Epidemic, Heroin Addiction and the Way Out. St.* Petersburg FL: Rapid Response Press.

This book offers information for people addicted to opiates with information on how to manage its symptoms and overcome dependence. While the focus of the book is on heroin, it offers insight into the transition from prescription narcotics (e.g., OxyContin) to heroin.

Anderson, K. (2014). *Opiate Addiction: The Ultimate Guide to Overcoming Opiate Addiction for Life*. Seattle WA: Amazon Digital Services.

The eBook provides insight to help an individual overcome opiate addiction. It describes the basics of the biological basis of addiction, opiate withdrawal, and addiction treatments in an easy-to-read and understand format.

Dalrymple, T. (2006). *Romancing Opiates*. New York: Encounter Books.

Theodore Dalrymple argues that opiate addiction is not a disease and that withdrawal from opiates is not medically serious.

Reed, B. et al. (2014). Genetics of opiate addiction. *Current Psychiatry Reports.* 16(11): 504–516.

This review article describes how genetics could contribute to susceptibility to narcotic addiction. The research presented is from the pharmacology literature, and is translated into the clinical realm to help health practitioners.

Reed, K. et al. (2015). Pharmacological treatments for drug misuse and dependence. *Expert Opinion in Pharmacotherapy.* 16(3): 325–333.

This paper provides an up-to-date overview on the pharmacological treatments that are available to combat drug addiction, including narcotics.

Internet References . . .

American Psychiatric Association—Addiction

http://www.psychiatry.org
/addiction

Foundation for a Drug-Free World—Heroin

http://www.drugfreeworld.org
/drugfacts/heroin.html

National Institutes of Health—National Institute on Drug Abuse: Opioids

http://www.drugabuse.gov/publications
/research-reports/prescription-drugs/opioids

National Library of Medicine: Opiate Withdrawal

http://www.nlm.nih.gov/medlineplus/ency
/article/000949.htm

Selected, Edited, and with Issue Framing Material by:
Dennis K. Miller, *University of Missouri*

ISSUE

Should Laws Prohibiting Marijuana Use Be Relaxed?

YES: **Kevin Drum**, from "The Patriot's Guide to Legalization," *Mother Jones* (2009)

NO: **National Institute on Drug Abuse**, from "Marijuana Abuse," *National Institute on Drug Abuse Research Report* (2010)

Learning Outcomes
After reading this issue, you will be able to:
• Explain the history of laws against marijuana use in the United States and the rationale behind these laws.
• Provide arguments in favor of and opposed to legalization and decriminalization of marijuana.
• Identify the medical benefits of marijuana and describe research on marijuana's abuse and dependence liability.
• Understand the relationship between a drug's legal status—licit or illicit—and its use in a community.

ISSUE SUMMARY

YES: Political columnist Kevin Drum contends that medical marijuana is now legal in more than a dozen states without any major serious problems or increased usage.

NO: The research report from the National Institute on Drug Abuse identifies various deleterious effects associated with marijuana. For example, marijuana alters perception and time, impairs memory and learning, and compromises academic performance. This report also notes that long-term marijuana use can lead to addiction and negatively affect the fetuses of women who used marijuana while pregnant.

Despite the fact that marijuana is the most commonly used illegal drug in the United States, the federal government maintains that it is a potentially dangerous substance. Also, its use represents a danger, not just to the user, but to others. The government claims that marijuana can be addictive and that more young people are in treatment for marijuana than for other illegal drugs. Thus, the federal government does not advocate relaxing laws regarding marijuana.

The federal government argues that relaxing laws against marijuana use, even for medical purposes, is unwarranted. However, since the mid-1990s voters in California, Arizona, Oregon, Colorado, and other states have passed referenda to legalize marijuana for medical and recreational purposes. Despite the position of these voters, however, the federal government does not support the medical use of marijuana, and federal laws take precedence over state laws. A major concern of opponents of these referenda is that legalization of marijuana for medical purposes will lead to its use for recreational purposes.

The use of marijuana dates at least 5000 years ago. It was utilized medically as far back as 2737 B.C., when Chinese emperor Shen Nung recommended marijuana, or cannabis, for medical use. By the 1890s some medical reports had stated that cannabis was useful as a pain reliever. However, despite its historical significance, the use of marijuana for medical treatment is still a widely debated and controversial topic. The easing of marijuana laws, despite the drug's possible medical benefits, is viewed as a slippery slope. If marijuana is used medically, then its nonmedical use may increase. Opponents argue that there has not been an increase in recreational marijuana use in those states where marijuana has been legalized for medical purposes.

Many of the concerns about the effects of marijuana date back to the 1930s when movies such as *Reefer Madness* were produced. Marijuana was painted as a drug that caused sexual perversions and violent behavior. In the absence of research, many people believed that marijuana was an evil drug that resulted in these horrendous acts. When the Marijuana Tax Act was enacted in 1937, there was only small opposition to the law.

In more current times, marijuana is purported to cause mental illness and addiction. It is believed that marijuana affects academic achievement. Moreover, it is considered a gateway drug leading to other and more dangerous drugs. Kevin Drum in the YES selection for this issue argues that these assumptions are untrue. He maintains that the federal government has not scientifically proven these assumptions to be valid. Proponents of marijuana claim that the research is lacking. Moreover, proponents for relaxing marijuana laws indicate that marijuana does not cause significant problems for individuals in European countries where marijuana is used.

Advocates for relaxing marijuana laws feel that the drug is unfairly labeled as a dangerous drug. For example, many more people throughout the world die from tobacco smoking and alcohol than from marijuana. Yet, adults using those products do not go to jail or a deprived of rights that other citizens enjoy There are as many people in jail today for marijuana offenses as from cocaine, heroin, methamphetamine, Ecstasy, and all other illegal drugs combined.

Another point raised by those people in favor of relaxing marijuana laws is that it would be easier to educate young people about marijuana's effects if it was legal. By simply keeping the drug illegal, the message is "Don't use marijuana," rather than how to reduce harms associated with it. Marijuana proponents do not advocate the unregulated use of marijuana. They favor a more reasoned, controlled approach. They feel governmental resources could be better used on stopping serious criminal activity.

In the YES selection, Kevin Drum asserts that the federal government is overzealous in its enforcement of marijuana laws. The federal government, according to Drum, continues to perpetuate myths regarding the dangers of marijuana use such as marijuana leading to other, more dangerous drug. In the NO selection, the National Institute on Drug Abuse (NIDA) argues that marijuana is far more dangerous that many young people realize. NIDA tries to dispel many of the myths associated with marijuana and maintains that marijuana can lead to physical and mental problems, and birth defects.

YES ↵   **Kevin Drum**

The Patriot's Guide to Legalization

Have you ever looked at our marijuana policy? I mean, *really* looked at it?

When we think of the drug war, it's the heavy-duty narcotics like heroin and cocaine that get most of the attention. And why not? That's where the action is. It's not marijuana that is sustaining the Taliban in Afghanistan, after all. When Crips and Bloods descend into gun battles in the streets of Los Angeles, they're not usually fighting over pot. The junkie who breaks into your house and steals your Blu-ray player isn't doing it so he can score a couple of spliffs.

No, the marijuana trade is more genteel than that. At least, I used to think it was. Then, like a lot of people, I started reading about the open warfare that has erupted among the narcotraffickers in Mexico and is now spilling across the American border. Stories of drugs coming north and arsenals of guns going south. Thousands of people brutally murdered. Entire towns terrorized. And this was a war not just over cocaine and meth, but marijuana as well.

And I began to wonder: Maybe the war against pot is about to get a lot uglier. After all, in the 1920s, Prohibition gave us Al Capone and the St. Valentine's Day Massacre, and that was over plain old whiskey and rum. Are we about to start paying the same price for marijuana?

If so, it might eventually start to affect me, too. Indirectly, sure, but that's more than it ever has before. I've never smoked a joint in my life. I've only seen one once, and that was 30 years ago. I barely drink, I don't smoke, and I don't like coffee. When it comes to mood altering substances, I live the life of a monk. I never really cared much if marijuana was legal or not.

But if a war is breaking out over the stuff, I figured maybe I should start looking at the evidence on whether marijuana prohibition is worth it. Not the spin from the drug czar at one end or the hemp hucksters at the other. Just the facts, as best as I could figure them out. So I did. Here's what I found.

In 1972, the report of the National Commission on Marihuana and Drug Abuse urged that possession of marijuana for personal use be decriminalized. A small wave of states followed this recommendation, but most refused; in Washington, President Carter called for eliminating penalties for small-time possession, but Congress stonewalled. And that's the way things have stayed since the late '70s. Some states have decriminalized, most haven't, and possession is still a criminal offense under federal law. So how has that worked out?

I won't give away the ending just yet, but one thing to know is this: On virtually every subject related to cannabis (an inclusive term that refers to both the sativa and indica varieties of the marijuana plant, as well as hashish, bhang, and other derivatives), the evidence is ambiguous. Sometimes even mysterious. So let's start with the obvious question.

Does Decriminalizing Cannabis Have Any Effect at All?

It's remarkably hard to tell—in part because drug use is faddish. Cannabis use among teens in the United States, for example, went down sharply in the '80s, bounced back in the early '90s, and has declined moderately since. Nobody really knows why.

We do, however, have studies that compare rates of cannabis use in states that have decriminalized vs. states that haven't. And the somewhat surprising conclusion, in the words of Robert MacCoun, a professor of law and public policy at the University of California-Berkeley, is simple: "Most of the evidence suggests that decriminalization has no effect."

But decriminalization is not legalization. In places that have decriminalized, simple possession is still illegal; it's just treated as an administrative offense, like a traffic ticket. And production and distribution remain felonies. What would happen if cannabis use were fully legalized?

No country has ever done this, so we don't know. The closest example is the Netherlands, where possession and sale of small amounts of marijuana is de facto legal in the famous coffeehouses. MacCoun and a colleague, Peter Reuter of the University of Maryland, have studied the Dutch experience and concluded that while legalization at first had little effect, once the coffeehouses began advertising and promoting themselves more aggressively in the 1980s, cannabis use more than doubled in a decade. Then

From *Mother Jones*, July/August 2009. Copyright ©2009 by Mother Jones. Reprinted by permission of the Foundation for National Progress.

again, cannabis use in Europe has gone up and down in waves, and some of the Dutch increase (as well as a later decrease, which followed a tightening of the coffeehouse laws in the mid-'90s) may have simply been part of those larger waves.

The most likely conclusion from the overall data is that if you fully legalized cannabis, use would almost certainly go up, but probably not enormously. MacCoun guesses that it might rise by half—say, from around 15 percent of the population to a little more than 20 percent. "It's not going to triple," he says. "Most people who want to use marijuana are already finding a way to use marijuana."

Still, there would be a cost. For one thing, a much higher increase isn't out of the question if companies like Philip Morris or R.J. Reynolds set their finest minds on the promotion of dope. And much of the increase would likely come among the heaviest users. "One person smoking eight joints a day is worth more to the industry than fifty people each smoking a joint a week," says Mark Kleiman, a drug policy expert at UCLA. "If the cannabis industry were to expand greatly, it couldn't do so by increasing the number of casual users. It would have to create and maintain more chronic zonkers." And that's a problem. Chronic use can lead to dependence and even long-term cognitive impairment. Heavy cannabis users are more likely to be in auto accidents. There have been scattered reports of respiratory and fetal development problems. Still, sensible regulation can limit the commercialization of pot, and compared to other illicit drugs (and alcohol), its health effects are fairly mild. Even a 50 percent increase in cannabis use might be a net benefit if it led to lower rates of use of other drugs.

So Would People Just Smoke More and Drink Less?

Maybe. The generic term for this effect in the economics literature is "substitute goods," and it simply means that some things replace other things. If the total demand for transportation is generally steady, an increase in sales of SUVs will lead to a decrease in the sales of sedans. Likewise, if the total demand for intoxicants is steady, an increase in the use of one drug should lead to a decrease in others.

Several years ago, John DiNardo, an economist now at the University of Michigan, found a clever way to test this via a natural experiment. Back in the 1980s, the Reagan administration pushed states to raise the drinking age to 21. Some states did this early in the decade, some later, and this gave DiNardo the idea of comparing data from the various states to see if the Reagan policy worked.

He found that raising the drinking age did lead to lower alcohol consumption; the effect was modest but real.

But then DiNardo hit on another analysis—comparing cannabis use in states that raised the drinking age early with those that did it later. And he found that indeed, there seemed to be a substitution effect. On average, among high school seniors, a 4.5 percent decrease in drinking produced a 2.4 percent increase in getting high.

But what we really want to know is whether the effect works in the other direction: Would increased marijuana use lead to less drinking? "What goes up should go down," DiNardo told me cheerfully, but he admits that in the absence of empirical evidence this hypothesis depends on your faith in basic economic models.

Some other studies are less encouraging than DiNardo's, but even if the substitute goods effect is smaller than his research suggests—if, say, a 30 percent increase in cannabis use led to a 5 or 10 percent drop in drinking—it would still be a strong argument in favor of legalization. After all, excessive drinking causes nearly 80,000 deaths per year in the United States, compared to virtually none for pot. Trading alcohol consumption for cannabis use might be a pretty attractive deal.

But What About the Gateway Effect?

This has been a perennial bogeyman of the drug warriors. Kids who use pot, the TV ads tell us, will graduate to ecstasy, then coke, then meth, and then—who knows? Maybe even talk radio.

Is there anything to this? There are two plausible pathways for the gateway theory. The first is that drug use of any kind creates an affinity for increasingly intense narcotic experiences. The second is that when cannabis is illegal, the only place to get it is from dealers who also sell other stuff.

The evidence for the first pathway is mixed. Research in New Zealand, for example, suggests that regular cannabis use is correlated with higher rates of other illicit drug use, especially in teenagers. A Norwegian study comes to similar conclusions, but only for a small segment of "troubled" teenagers. Other research, however, suggests that these correlations aren't caused by gateway effects at all, but by the simple fact that kids who like drugs do drugs. All kinds of drugs.

The second pathway was deliberately targeted by the Dutch when they began their coffeehouse experiment in the '70s in part to sever the connection of cannabis with the illicit drug market. The evidence suggests that it worked: Even with cannabis freely available, Dutch cannabis use is currently about average among developed countries and use of other illicit drugs is about average, too. Easy access to marijuana, outside the dealer network for harder drugs, doesn't seem to have led to greater use of cocaine or heroin.

So, to recap: Decriminalization of simple possession appears to have little effect on cannabis consumption. Full legalization would likely increase use only moderately as long as heavy commercialization is prohibited, although the effect on chronic users might be more substantial. It would increase heroin and cocaine use only slightly if at all, and it might decrease alcohol consumption by a small amount. Which leads to the question:

HIGH SIERRAS

The woods are lovely, dark, and . . .
full of gun-toting narcofarmers.

Early one morning in August 2005, a small team of game wardens and deputies climbed through coyote brush and manzanita in the Sierra Azul Open Space Preserve outside San Jose, California, searching for an illegal pot farm. As they crested a ridge, they discovered densely planted rows of cannabis stalks. Suddenly, a high-powered rifle cracked and an officer fell to the ground, shot through both legs. Seconds later, another deputy shot and killed a man wielding a sawed-off shotgun. "It was literally like a jungle firefight," recalls warden John Nores, who fired at the other shooter before he escaped into the woods. Left behind in a meadow just minutes from the heart of Silicon Valley were 22,000 marijuana plants worth some $88 million.

Over the past decade, marijuana patches known as "grows" or "gardens" have sprung up on public lands across the West, including a third of California's national parks and nearly 40 percent of all national forests. Where hippies once grew just enough weed to peace out, traffickers now cultivate more than 100,000 plants at a time on 30-acre terraces irrigated by plastic pipe, laced with illegal pesticides, and guarded by men with MAC-10S and Uzis. Grows have turned up everywhere from the deepest backcountry to the edges of suburban subdivisions. Farming pot on public land can be more profitable than smuggling it across the increasingly militarized border. The 3.1 million pot plants seized in national forests in the year prior to last September had an estimated street value of $12.4 billion.

Rangers and game wardens say pot growers are a major threat to California's 23,500 square miles of wilderness (which doesn't include state or regional lands). "These guys literally create cities within your national forests," says Laura Mark, a special agent with the US Forest Service. Growers clear land year-round, plant crops in the spring, and haul out the harvest in the fall, often leaving behind mounds of trash and dead animals, denuded hillsides, and streams full of sediment and human waste. Last year, the community of Snow Creek, California, traced feces in its water treatment plant to a grow in the nearby San Bernardino National Forest. Restoring the 10,000 acres of national forest fouled by pot farms could cost more than $30 million.

Pot farmers who till public lands avoid the risk of forfeiting their property if they're busted, but they must also ward off competitors. "They are going to point guns at you first and ask questions later," says Troy Bolen, the Bureau of Land Management's head of law enforcement in California. In the past decade, growers have killed two people who have stumbled upon their fields, held nature lovers at gunpoint, and had numerous shoot-outs with cops. Last year, in California's national forests the state's anti-grow task force killed one grower and arrested 177, 80 percent of whom were Mexican citizens.

Officials believe that Mexican drug cartels control the grows, but proving that is tough. Last year, Nores caught a pot grower who revealed almost everything about his operation but said he didn't know whom he worked for. "They're kind of set up like terrorist cells," he observes. After the bloody 2005 ambush, he says, his team now treats raids like potential battles, bringing along medics and keeping air support on standby—just in case.

—Josh Harkinson

Can We Still Afford Prohibition?

The consequences of legalization, after all, must be compared to the cost of the status quo. Unsurprisingly, this too is hard to quantify. The worst effects of the drug war, including property crime and gang warfare, are mostly associated with cocaine, heroin, and meth. Likewise, most drug-law enforcement is aimed at harder drugs, not cannabis; contrary to conventional wisdom, only about 44,000 people are currently serving prison time on cannabis charges—and most of those are there for dealing and distribution, not possession.

Still, the University of Maryland's Reuter points out that about 800,000 people are arrested for cannabis possession every year in the United States. And even though very few end up being sentenced to prison, a study of three counties in Maryland following a recent marijuana crackdown suggests that a third spend at least one pretrial night in jail and a sixth spend more than ten days. That takes a substantial human toll. Overall, Harvard economist Jeffrey Miron estimates the cost of cannabis prohibition in the United States at $13 billion annually and the lost tax revenue at nearly $7 billion.

So What Are the Odds of Legalization?

Slim. For starters, the United States, along with virtually every other country in the world, is a signatory to the 1961 Single Convention on Narcotic Drugs (and its 1988 successor), which flatly prohibits legalization of cannabis. The only way around this is to unilaterally withdraw from the treaties or to withdraw and then reenter with reservations. That's not going to happen.

At the federal level, there's virtually no appetite for legalizing cannabis either. Though public opinion has made steady strides, increasing from around 20 percent favoring marijuana legalization in the Reagan era to nearly 40 percent favoring it today, the only policy change in Washington has been Attorney General Eric Holder's announcement in March that the Obama administration planned to end raids on distributors of medical marijuana. (Applications for pot dispensaries promptly surged in Los Angeles County.)

The real action in cannabis legalization is at the state level. More than a dozen states now have effective medical marijuana laws, most notably California. Medical marijuana dispensaries are dotted all over the state, and it's common knowledge that the "medical" part is in many cases a thin fiction. Like the Dutch coffeehouses, California's dispensaries are now a de facto legal distribution network that severs the link between cannabis and other illicit drugs for a significant number of adults (albeit still only a fraction of total users). And the result? Nothing. "We've had this experiment for a decade and the sky hasn't fallen," says Paul Armentano, deputy director of the National Organization for the Reform of Marijuana Laws. California Assemblyman Tom Ammiano has even introduced a bill that would legalize, tax, and regulate marijuana; it has gained the endorsement of the head of the state's tax collection agency, which informally estimates it could collect $1.3 billion a year from cannabis sales. Still, the legislation hasn't found a single cosponsor, and isn't scheduled for so much as a hearing.

Which is too bad. Going into this assignment, I didn't care much personally about cannabis legalization. I just had a vague sense that if other people wanted to do it, why not let them? But the evidence suggests pretty clearly that we ought to significantly soften our laws on marijuana. Too many lives have been ruined and too much money spent for a social benefit that, if not zero, certainly isn't very high.

And it may actually happen. If attitudes continue to soften; if the Obama administration turns down the volume on anti-pot propaganda; if medical dispensaries avoid heavy commercialization; if drug use remains stable; and if emergency rooms don't start filling up with drug-related traumas while all this is happening, California's experience could go a long way toward destigmatizing cannabis use. That's a lot of ifs.

Still, things are changing. Even GOP icon Arnold Schwarzenegger now says, "I think it's time for a debate." That doesn't mean he's in favor of legalizing pot right this minute, but it might mean we're getting close to a tipping point. Ten years from now, as the flower power generation enters its 70s, you might finally be able to smoke a fully legal, taxed, and regulated joint.

JUST SAY KNOW

Dust off your short-term memory and test your drug war knowledge, with a quiz based on Ryan Grim's new book, *This Is Your Country on Drugs: The Secret History of Getting High in America*.

1. A 1918 *New York Times* article suggested Germany was trying to make Americans "cokeys" and "hop fiends" with . . .
   A. Drugs mixed into sausage
   B. Drugs in toothpaste and teething syrup
   C. Narco-polkas

2. How much "ditchweed"—wild hemp with no psychoactive properties—did the DEA destroy in 2005?
   A. 219 plants
   B. 219,000 plants
   C. 219 million plants

3. During the late 19th century, most opium addicts were first turned on to the drug by . . .
   A. Doctors
   B. Hobos
   C. Chinese opium dens

4. Which of the following did *not* support efforts to criminalize marijuana in the 1930s?
   A. Pharmaceutical industry
   B. American Medical Association
   C. Liquor industry

5. Which president first declared cocaine "the most dangerous drug problem that the US ever faced"?
   A. William Taft
   B. Ronald Reagan
   C. George W. Bush

6. In 2004, the White House buried a study that found that a $1.4 billion anti-pot ad campaign had . . .
   A. Increased first-time pot use among 14- to 16-year-olds
   B. Increased first-time pot use among whites
   C. Both A and B

(Answers: 1-B, 2-C, 3-A, 4-B, 5-A, 6-C)

Kevin Drum is a political blogger for *Mother Jones* (http://www.motherjones.com/authors/kevin-drum). In addition to writing on political issues—including energy, education, and liberal politics—he is a pioneer in cat-blogging, the practice of posting pictures of cats, in typical cat postures and expressions.

National Institute on Drug Abuse

➜ **NO**

Marijuana Abuse

How Does Marijuana Use Affect Your Brain and Body?

Effects on the Brain

As THC enters the brain, it causes the user to feel euphoric—or high—by acting on the brain's reward system, which is made up of regions that govern the response to pleasurable things like sex and chocolate, as well as to most drugs of abuse. THC activates the reward system in the same way that nearly all drugs of abuse do: by stimulating brain cells to release the chemical dopamine.

Along with euphoria, relaxation is another frequently reported effect in human studies. Other effects, which vary dramatically among different users, include heightened sensory perception (e.g., brighter colors), laughter, altered perception of time, and increased appetite. After a while, the euphoria subsides, and the user may feel sleepy or depressed. Occasionally, marijuana use may produce anxiety, fear, distrust, or panic.

Marijuana use impairs a person's ability to form new memories and to shift focus. THC also disrupts coordination and balance by binding to receptors in the cerebellum and basal ganglia—parts of the brain that regulate balance, posture, coordination, and reaction time. Therefore, learning, doing complicated tasks, participating in athletics, and driving are also affected.

Marijuana users who have taken large doses of the drug may experience an acute psychosis, which includes hallucinations, delusions, and a loss of the sense of personal identity. Although the specific causes of these symptoms remain unknown, they appear to occur more frequently when a high dose of cannabis is consumed in food or drink rather than smoked. Such short-term psychotic reactions to high concentrations of THC are distinct from longer-lasting, schizophrenia-like disorders that have been associated with the use of cannabis in vulnerable individuals. (See section on the link between marijuana use and mental illness.)

Our understanding of marijuana's long-term brain effects is limited. Research findings on how chronic cannabis use affects brain *structure*, for example, have been inconsistent. It may be that the effects are too subtle for reliable detection by current techniques. A similar challenge arises in studies of the effects of chronic marijuana use on brain *function*. Although imaging studies (functional MRI; fMRI) in chronic users do show some consistent alterations, the relation of these changes to cognitive functioning is less clear. This uncertainty may stem from confounding factors such as other drug use, residual drug effects (which can occur for at least 24 hours in chronic users), or withdrawal symptoms in long-term chronic users.

An enduring question in the field is whether individuals who quit marijuana, even after long-term, heavy use, can recover some of their cognitive abilities. One study reports that the ability of long-term heavy marijuana users to recall words from a list was still impaired 1 week after they quit using, but returned to normal by 4 weeks. However, another study found that marijuana's effects on the brain can build up and deteriorate critical life skills over time. Such effects may be worse in those with other mental disorders, or simply by virtue of the normal aging process.

Effects on General Physical Health

Within a few minutes after inhaling marijuana smoke, an individual's heart rate speeds up, the bronchial passages relax and become enlarged, and blood vessels in the eyes expand, making the eyes look red. The heart rate—normally 70 to 80 beats per minute—may increase by 20 to 50 beats per minute, or may even double in some cases. Taking other drugs with marijuana can amplify this effect.

Limited evidence suggests that a person's risk of heart attack during the first hour after smoking marijuana is four times his or her usual risk. This observation could be partly explained by marijuana raising blood pressure (in some cases) and heart rate and reducing the blood's capacity to carry oxygen. Such possibilities need to be examined more closely, particularly since current marijuana users include adults from the baby boomer generation, who may have other cardiovascular risks that may increase their vulnerability.

The smoke of marijuana, like that of tobacco, consists of a toxic mixture of gases and particulates, many of which are known to be harmful to the lungs. Someone who smokes marijuana regularly may have many of the same respiratory problems that tobacco smokers do, such as daily cough and phlegm production, more frequent acute chest illnesses, and a greater risk of lung infections. Even infrequent marijuana use can cause burning and stinging of the mouth and throat, often accompanied by a heavy cough. One study found that extra sick days used by frequent marijuana smokers were often because of respiratory illnesses.

In addition, marijuana has the *potential* to promote cancer of the lungs and other parts of the respiratory tract because it contains irritants and carcinogens—up to 70 percent more than tobacco smoke. It also induces high levels of an enzyme that converts certain hydrocarbons into their cancer-causing form, which could accelerate the changes that ultimately produce malignant cells. And since marijuana smokers generally inhale more deeply and hold their breath longer than tobacco smokers, the lungs are exposed longer to carcinogenic smoke. However, while several lines of evidence have suggested that marijuana use may lead to lung cancer, the supporting evidence is inconclusive. The presence of an unidentified active ingredient in cannabis smoke having protective properties—if corroborated and properly characterized—could help explain the inconsistencies and modest findings.

CONSEQUENCES OF MARIJUANA ABUSE

Acute (present during intoxication)
- Impairs short-term memory
- Impairs attention, judgment, and other congnitive functions
- Impairs coordination and balance
- Increases heart rate
- Psychotic episodes

Persistent (lasting longer than intoxication, but may not be permanent)
- Impairs memory and learning skills
- Sleep impairment

Long-term (cumulative effects of chronic abuse)
- Can lead to addiction
- Increases risk of chronic cough, bronchitis
- Increases risk of schizophrenia in vulnerable individuals
- May increase risk of anxiety, depression, and amotivational syndrome*

*These are often reported co-occurring symptoms/disorders with chronic marijuana use. However, research has not yet determined whether marijuana is causal or just associated with these mental problems.

A significant body of research demonstrates negative effects of THC on the function of various immune cells, both in vitro in cells and in vivo with test animals. However, no studies to date connect marijuana's suspected immune system suppression with greater incidence of infections or immune disorders in humans. One short (3-week) study found marijuana smoking to be associated with a few statistically significant negative effects on the immune function of AIDS patients; a second small study of college students also suggested the possibility of marijuana having adverse effects on immune system functioning. Thus, the combined evidence from animal studies plus the limited human data available, seem to warrant additional research on the impact of marijuana on the immune system.

Is There a Link Between Marijuana Use and Mental Illness?

Research in the past decade has focused on whether marijuana use actually causes other mental illnesses. The strongest evidence to date suggests a link between cannabis use and psychosis. For example, a series of large prospective studies that followed a group of people over time showed a relationship between marijuana use and later development of psychosis. Marijuana use also worsens the course of illness in patients with schizophrenia and can produce a brief psychotic reaction in some users that fades as the drug wears off. The amount of drug used, the age at first use, and genetic vulnerability can all influence this relationship. One example is a study that found an increased risk of psychosis among adults who had used marijuana in adolescence *and* who also carried a specific variant of the gene for catechol-O-methyltransferase (COMT), an enzyme that degrades neurotransmitters such as dopamine and norepinephrine.

In addition to the observed links between marijuana use and schizophrenia, other less consistent associations have been reported between marijuana use and depression, anxiety, suicidal thoughts among adolescents, and personality disturbances. One of the most frequently cited, albeit still controversial, is an amotivational syndrome, defined as a diminished or absent drive to engage in typically rewarding activities. Because of the role of the endocannabinoid system in regulating mood, these associations make a certain amount of sense; however, more research is needed to confirm and better understand these linkages.

Is Marijuana Addictive?

Long-term marijuana use can lead to addiction; that is, people have difficulty controlling their drug use and cannot stop even though it interferes with many aspects of their lives. It is estimated that 9 percent of people who use marijuana will become dependent on it. The number goes up to about 1 in 6 in those who start using young (in their teens) and to 25–50 percent among daily users. Moreover, a study of over 300 fraternal and identical twin pairs found that the twin who had used marijuana before the age of 17 had elevated rates of other drug use and drug problems later on, compared with their twin who did not use before age 17.

According to the 2008 NSDUH, marijuana accounted for 4.2 million of the estimated 7 million Americans dependent on or abusing illicit drugs. In 2008, approximately 15 percent of people entering drug abuse treatment programs reported marijuana as their primary drug of abuse; 61 percent of persons under 15 reported marijuana as their primary drug of abuse, as did 56 percent of those 15 to 19 years old.

Marijuana addiction is also linked to a withdrawal syndrome similar to that of nicotine withdrawal, which can make it hard to quit. People trying to quit report irritability, sleeping difficulties, craving, and anxiety. They also show increased aggression on psychological tests, peaking approximately 1 week after they last used the drug.

How Does Marijuana Use Affect School, Work, and Social Life?

Research has shown that marijuana's negative effects on attention, memory, and learning can last for days or weeks after the acute effects of the drug wear off. Consequently, someone who smokes marijuana daily may be functioning at a reduced intellectual level most or all of the time. Not surprisingly, evidence suggests that, compared with their nonsmoking peers, students who smoke marijuana tend to get lower grades and are more likely to drop out of high school. A meta-analysis of 48 relevant studies—one of the most thorough performed to date—found cannabis use to be associated consistently with reduced educational attainment (e.g., grades and chances of graduating). However, a *causal* relationship is not yet proven between cannabis use by young people and psychosocial harm.

That said, marijuana users themselves report poor outcomes on a variety of life satisfaction and achievement measures. One study compared current and former long-term heavy users of marijuana with a control group who reported smoking cannabis at least once in their lives but not more than 50 times. Despite similar education and income backgrounds, significant differences were found

in educational attainment: fewer of the heavy users of cannabis completed college, and more had yearly household incomes of less than $30,000. When asked how marijuana affected their cognitive abilities, career achievements, social lives, and physical and mental health, the majority of heavy cannabis users reported the drug's negative effects on all of these measures. In addition, several studies have linked workers' marijuana smoking with increased absences, tardiness, accidents, workers' compensation claims, and job turnover. For example, a study among postal workers found that employees who tested positive for marijuana on a pre-employment urine drug test had 55 percent more industrial accidents, 85 percent more injuries, and a 75-percent increase in absenteeism compared with those who tested negative for marijuana use.

Does Marijuana Use Affect Driving?

Because marijuana impairs judgment and motor coordination and slows reaction time, an intoxicated person has an increased chance of being involved in and being responsible for an accident. According to the National Highway Traffic Safety Administration, drugs other than alcohol (e.g., marijuana and cocaine) are involved in about 18 percent of motor vehicle driver deaths. A recent survey found that 6.8 percent of drivers, mostly under 35, who were involved in accidents tested positive for THC; alcohol levels above the legal limit were found in 21 percent of such drivers.

Can Marijuana Use During Pregnancy Harm the Baby?

Animal research suggests that the body's endocannabinoid system plays a role in the control of brain maturation, particularly in the development of emotional responses. It is conceivable that even low concentrations of THC, when administered during the perinatal period, could have profound and long-lasting consequences for both brain and behavior. Research has shown that some babies born to women who used marijuana during their pregnancies display altered responses to visual stimuli, increased tremulousness, and a high-pitched cry, which could indicate problems with neurological development. In school, marijuana-exposed children are more likely to show gaps in problem-solving skills, memory, and the ability to remain attentive. More research is needed, however, to disentangle the drug-specific factors from the environmental ones.

Available Treatments for Marijuana Use Disorders

Marijuana dependence appears to be very similar to other substance dependence disorders, although the long-term clinical outcomes may be less severe. On average, adults seeking treatment for marijuana abuse or dependence have used marijuana nearly every day for more than 10 years and have attempted to quit more than six times. It is important to note that marijuana dependence is most prevalent among patients suffering from other psychiatric disorders, particularly among adolescent and young adult populations. Also, marijuana abuse or dependence typically co-occurs with use of other drugs, such as cocaine and alcohol. Available studies indicate that effectively treating the mental health disorder with standard treatments involving medications and behavioral therapies may help reduce cannabis use, particularly among heavy users and those with more chronic mental disorders. Behavioral treatments, such as motivational enhancement therapy (MET), group or individual cognitive-behavioral therapy (CBT), and contingency management (CM), as well as family-based treatments, have shown promise.

Unfortunately, the success rates of treatment are rather modest. Even with the most effective treatment for adults, only about 50 percent of enrollees achieve an initial 2-week period of abstinence, and among those who do, approximately half will resume use within a year. Across studies, 1-year abstinence rates have ranged between 10 and 30 percent for the various behavioral approaches. As with other addictions, these data suggest that a chronic care model should be considered for marijuana addiction, with treatment intensity stepped up or down based on need, comorbid addictions or other mental disorders, and the availability of family and other supports.

Currently, no medications are available to treat marijuana abuse, but research is active in this area. Most of the studies to date have targeted the marijuana withdrawal syndrome. For example, a recent human laboratory study showed that a combination of a cannabinoid agonist medication with lofexidine (a medication approved in the United Kingdom for the treatment of opioid withdrawal) produced more robust improvements in sleep and decreased marijuana withdrawal, craving, and relapse in daily marijuana smokers relative to either medication alone. Recent discoveries about the inner workings of the endogenous cannabinoid system raise the future possibility of a medication able to block THC's intoxicating effects, which could help prevent relapse by reducing or eliminating marijuana's appeal.

The mission of the **NATIONAL INSTITUTE ON DRUG ABUSE** is to lead the nation in bringing the power of science to bear on drug abuse and addiction. It supports and conducts research across a broad range of disciplines and ensures the rapid and effective dissemination of the results of that research to significantly improve prevention and treatment.

EXPLORING THE ISSUE

Should Laws Prohibiting Marijuana Use Be Relaxed?

Critical Thinking and Reflection

1. Historically, what were the arguments used against marijuana use? Which arguments lacked validity and have not been supported? Which arguments do you consider valid?
2. How much do a drug's legal status and criminal penalties associated with its possession and use influence whether someone will or will not use a drug?
3. If marijuana were legal, what limits would you support on its access and use (e.g., age for purchase and exposure to second-hand smoke)?
4. If an easing of the laws resulted in much abuse and physical or psychological problems, how easy would it be to return to more restrictive marijuana laws?
5. Is marijuana a "gateway drug"? In other words, does early marijuana use increase the chance that someone will move on to using "harder" drugs like cocaine or heroin? What logic or information supports or refutes the classification of marijuana as a "gateway drug"?

Is There Common Ground?

The restrictive laws against marijuana have resulted in a burgeoning number of people in prison for marijuana offenses. In the YES selection Kevin Drum maintains that the scientific proof demonstrating that marijuana is harmful is lacking. Nonetheless, politicians have shown little interest in overturning the laws banning marijuana. Drum does not contend that marijuana is a safe drug, but that legalizing it would enable officials to have better control over its use. The government's objection to marijuana, says Drum, is based more on politics than scientific evidence.

Despite its popularity, the federal government notes that parents should and can assert more influence on their children's desire to use marijuana. The government claims that marijuana is not the harmless drug that many proponents believe. Marijuana can have adverse effects, on mental health, physical well-being, and academic performance. In addition, thousands of young people enter substance abuse treatment for their addiction to marijuana. It is important, states the National Institute on Drug Abuse, to counteract how culture trivializes the dangers of marijuana use.

Many marijuana proponents contend that the effort to prevent the legalization of marijuana for medical use and nonmedical use is purely a political battle. Detractors maintain that the issue is purely scientific— that the data supporting marijuana's medical usefulness are inconclusive and scientifically unsubstantiated. And

although the chief administrative law judge of the Drug Enforcement Administration (DEA) made a recommendation to change the status of marijuana from Schedule I to Schedule II, the DEA and other federal agencies are not compelled to do so and they have resisted any change in federal law.

Additional Resources

Hagerty, S. L. et al. (2015). The cannabis conundrum: Thinking outside the THC box. *The Journal of Clinical Pharmacology*. PMID: 25855064.

In this commentary and review paper the authors identify limitations with respect to previous research on cannabis, discuss the genesis and implications of these limitations, and offer suggestions for future research.

Hill, K. P. (2015). *Marijuana: The Unbiased Truth about the World's Most Popular Weed*. Center City MI: Hazelden Publishing.

Dr. Hill provides a comprehensive guide to understanding the drug through research-based historical, scientific, and medical information.

Kandel, D. & Kandel, E. (2015). The Gateway Hypothesis of substance abuse: Developmental, biological, and societal perspectives. *Acta Paediatrica*. 104(2): 130–137.

This animal study conducted, in part, by Nobel Prize winner Eric Kandel, assessed the gateway hypothesis of drug addiction using a mouse model.

Phillips, K. T. et al., (2015). Marijuana use, craving, and academic motivation and performance among college students: An in-the-moment study. *Addictive Behaviors*. 47: 42–47.

This research study assessed college students who use marijuana and their academic motivation, effort, and success. The authors observed that heavy marijuana use is negatively associated with academic outcomes.

Sznitman, S. R. & Zolotov, Y. (2015). Cannabis for therapeutic purposes and public health and safety: A systematic and critical review. *International Journal of Drug Policy*. 26(1): 20–29.

The authors summarize public health literature related to medical cannabis legalization and conclude that additional research and monitoring is needed on the interaction between therapeutic and recreational marijuana use.

Internet References . . .

Foundation for a Drug-Free World—What is marijuana?

http://www.drugfreeworld.org/drugfacts/marijuana.html

Internet Archive—Reefer Madness

https://archive.org/details/reefer_madness1938

National Institutes of Health—National Institute on Drug Abuse

http://www.drugabuse.gov/

NORML: Working to Reform Marijuana Laws

http://norml.org/

Office of National Drug Control Policy—Marijuana Resource Center

https://www.whitehouse.gov/ondcp/marijuanainfo/

Selected, Edited, and with Issue Framing Material by:
Dennis K. Miller, *University of Missouri*

ISSUE

Can Ecstasy or Molly (3,4-Methylenedioxy-Methamphetamine, MDMA) Effectively Treat Psychological Disorders?

YES: Kelley McMillan, from "Is Ecstasy the Key to Treating Women with PTSD?," *Marie Claire* (2015)

NO: Rachel Patel and Daniel Titheradge, from "MDMA for the Treatment of Mood Disorder: All Talk No Substance?" *Therapeutic Advances in Psychopharmacology* (2015)

Learning Outcomes

After reading this issue, you will be able to:

- Describe the pharmacological properties of MDMA and the symptoms of post-traumatic stress disorder (PTSD).
- Explain how MDMA can be used in psychotherapy to help people with PTSD, depression, and anxiety.
- Identify the adverse effects of MDMA on the body and brain, as well as the risks associated with its use.
- Evaluate the benefits of MDMA-aided psychotherapy and potential problems with using a recreational drug in the psychiatric clinic.

ISSUE SUMMARY

YES: 3,4-Methylenedioxy-methamphetamine (MDMA) is a synthetic drug that is similar to both stimulants and hallucinogens and is associated with the club scene where it is known as "Ecstasy" and "Molly". Kelley McMillan in "Is Ecstasy the Key to Treating Women with PTSD?" notes the potential clinical benefits of MDMA to help those with the anxiety disorder and post-traumatic stress disorder.

NO: Rachel Patel and Daniel Titheradge reviewed preclinical and clinical literature on MDMA and conclude that, "the pharmacology of MDMA offers a promising target as a rapid-onset agent"; however, they note neurotoxicity and safety concerns for MDMA. These limit its wide adoption to help manage the symptoms of psychological disorders.

The terms "ecstasy" and "molly" typically refer to 3,4-methylenedioxy-methamphetamine (MDMA), a drug that shares chemical properties with the stimulant methamphetamine and the psychedelic mescaline. MDMA was first synthesized in 1912 by chemists at the Merck pharmaceutical company as a substance to stop internal bleeding.

It was generally ignored by pharmacologists until the late 1950s and early 1960s when it was rediscovered for its psychedelic (produce hallucinations and apparent expansion of consciousness), entactogenic (produce experiences of emotional relatedness and openness), and empathogenic (produce the ability to understand and share the feelings of another) properties.

During the late 1960s and early 1970s, MDMA and drugs that are structurally-related to it (e.g., N-ethyl-3,4-methylenedioxy-amphetamine, MDEA; and 3,4-methylenedioxyamphetamine, MDA) were manufactured in clandestine labs for recreational and nascent psychotherapeutic purposes. MDMA can be synthesized relatively easily by home "chemists" from materials readily available. Many websites and YouTube videos today provide easy-to-follow recipes that can be completed by those with only high-school level chemistry experience.

Ecstasy and molly are sold in tablets that may be marked with a brand or symbol and contain about 50–150 mg of MDMA and/or its related compounds (e.g., MDEA or MDA). It is taken orally and remains in the body for a long period of time as it has a biologic half-life of about eight hours. Psychological effects may persist several days after single administration. In the nervous system MDMA increases the release of the monoamine neurotransmitters dopamine, serotonin, and norepinephrine. This neurochemical activity leads to increased body temperature, perspiration, and headache. Bruxism (teeth grinding), jaw clinching, and muscle tension is also observed.

Psychologically, MDMA produces a sense of well-being, increased empathy and feelings of closeness to others, a sense of inner peace, relaxation, and decreased anxiety. Some report that it makes them feel "wonderful—one of life's great experiences". These effects led MDMA to be considered and used as a recreational drug. It is classified as a "club drug", used by teens and young adults at dance parties and raves or to enhance sexual experiences and activities. However, the emotional and cognitive effects also led some psychologists and psychiatrists to consider MDMA as an adjunct to psychotherapy for marital problems, anxiety and depression.

In the 1970s MDMA was explored to eliminate fear responses and increase communication in people with psychological disorders, including post-traumatic stress disorder (PTSD). PTSD is a disorder that develops in some people who have experienced a shocking, scary, or dangerous event. Most people experience a range of reactions after trauma, but recover from initial symptoms naturally. Individuals with PTSD continue to experience problems. They may feel stressed or frightened even when they are not in danger. People with PTSD display the following symptoms.

- reexperiencing symptoms, such as bad dreams, frightening thoughts, or flashbacks (reliving the trauma again and again)
- avoidance symptoms, such as staying away from places or objects that are reminders of the trauma, or avoiding thoughts related to the initiating event
- arousal and reactivity symptoms, including being easily startled, being angered easily, feeling tense and "on edge", and difficulty sleeping
- cognition and mood symptoms, such as trouble remembering, negative thoughts about oneself, feelings of guilt and blame, and anhedonia

Treatments for PTSD include cognitive-behavioral therapy where the therapist helps the patient with PTSD understand and change how they think about the trauma and its aftermath. The patient learns to understand how certain thoughts about their trauma cause them stress and make symptoms worse. In exposure therapy, the patient talks repeatedly to the therapist about the trauma. While discussions may be difficult at first, over time the patient feels less overwhelmed and less afraid of the memories. Pharmacotherapy with antidepressants (e.g., Zoloft or Lexapro) or anxiolytics (e.g., Xanax or Valium) may be used.

In the YES section for this issue Kelley McMillian describes the use of MDMA to help a woman, Roxxann Murphy, experiencing PTSD after the death of her husband in a violent traffic incident. MDMA-assisted psychotherapy helped Murphy move beyond the reexperiencing and arousal symptoms of her PTSD. It is important to note that MDMA does not cure the symptoms of PTSD or any other psychological disorder. Rather, MDMA is used as an adjunct to assist and aid psychotherapy. Unlike treatment with antidepressants or anxiolytics that are used consistently (e.g., once- or twice-daily administration) and long-term, MDMA is only administered a few times and only within the context of therapeutic treatment with a counselor. Proponents of MDMA psychotherapy note the drug makes it easier for patients to be comfortable and move away from the extreme fear and avoidance of PTSD. While using MDMA the patient may be more receptive to behavioral therapeutic techniques. They gain insight to their fear, anger and grief, but are not overwhelmed by intense, negative emotions.

Many scholarly articles, including those performed with strong research designs and cited in both the YES and NO sections for this issue, support the use of MDMA to help with PTSD, anxiety disorders, and depression. So, why is there resistance to the use of MDMA in therapy?

The growing use of MDMA in the 1970s led to increased scrutiny of its addictive and toxic properties by the United States Drug Enforcement Administration (DEA) in the early 1980s. MDMA is currently classified as a Schedule I drug under the Controlled Substances Act, which means that the drug is considered to have no accepted medical use and a high potential for abuse. Other examples of Schedule I drugs are heroin, marijuana and lysergic acid diethylamide (LSD). The Schedule I classification severely limits government funds available for research on potential therapeutic benefits. MDMA is legally controlled in most countries worldwide with severe restrictions and prohibitions against its synthesis, trafficking, and use.

A second reason why there is this resistance to MDMA use in therapy is the drug's negative effects after short- and long-term use. These are described in the NO section for this issue. While the drug is on board the user may experience nausea, muscle cramping, bruxism, blurred vision, and chills. MDMA has a low therapeutic index (ratio between drug doses that are lethal and doses that produce the intended therapeutic or recreational

effect). Death may result from hyperthermia and hyponatremia abnormally low sodium in the body after a single administration. These are compounded by the dehydration, and increased heart rate, blood pressure, and perspiration induced by the drug. The popular media of the 1990s and early 2000s contained many reports of young people that died after using MDMA at a club or party.

MDMA may also produce long-term adverse effects such as irritability, depression, sleep problems, anxiety, and anhedonia. There is considerable evidence from animal and human studies that after increasing neurotransmitter levels, MDMA produces a long-lasting depletion of dopamine, norepinephrine, and serotonin in the brain. Depletion of the latter chemical may contribute to the anxiety and depression "burn out" some long-term users experience, as well as memory impairments.

YES ↰

Kelley McMillan

Is Ecstasy the Key to Treating Women with PTSD?

Some say yes—and that the prescription could come as early as 2021.

On a bright, sunny morning in June 2012, 36-year-old massage therapist Roxxann Murphy and her husband, David, 34, were driving to Oklahoma City's Myriad Botanical Gardens with their 18-month-old daughter, Romy. Almost as soon as David—blond and handsome, with light-blue eyes—turned their Honda Fit onto the highway, they saw a man waving wildly for assistance on the right side of the road. Eager to help, David slowed down and parked the car. It turned out to be a domestic disturbance between the man and his female companion; after making sure the couple was OK, David began walking back toward Murphy, the flat plains framing his athletic build.

Suddenly, a car swerved from the highway at 70 miles per hour, striking David and another man who had stopped to help. Murphy recalls watching the stranger fly through the air upside down. *He's not going to survive*, she thought. Then she saw David's body roll to a stop in the grass that lined the highway. "David! David!" she screamed, before grabbing Romy from her car seat and running to his side. He was unconscious by the time she reached him, with blood seeping from a deep gash in his forehead and nose. She knelt beside him, gently stroking his head and body with one arm while breast-feeding Romy in the other, the only thing that would soothe her crying daughter. Sunlight streamed down and small crickets hopped over David's body as Murphy begged him not to leave her. An hour later, they were still waiting for an ambulance to arrive. "I felt him dying," Murphy says. Soon, he was gone.

Immediately after the accident, Murphy began having flashbacks. She jumped at noises. She hallucinated that shadowy, hulking men stood by her bed. She lost 25 pounds and rarely slept; when she did, she dreamed of blood, gore, and body parts. Her waking hours were spent

in a zombielike state. Mostly, she fantasized about bashing her brain with a hammer; but she had to stick around for Romy, which made her resentful.

So a few weeks after David's death, she began seeing a cognitive behavioral therapist at the University of Oklahoma. He diagnosed her with post-traumatic stress disorder, or PTSD, a condition characterized by flashbacks, feelings of hopelessness, and emotional numbing that affects 8 million U.S. adults (81 percent of them women) and can occur when someone experiences a traumatic event like military combat or sexual assault. But even with weekly therapy, Murphy was still suicidal two years after the accident. Desperate for something that would keep her alive for her daughter, she sought out alternative PTSD treatments online, and finally, as a last-ditch effort, took a weeklong trip to Boulder, Colorado, to join a progressive clinical trial that would eventually save her life: a psychotherapy session catalyzed by the hallucinogen MDMA.

Better known by its street names, Molly or Ecstasy, and long viewed as a party drug, 3,4-methylenedioxy-methamphetamine, or MDMA, is currently being studied as a treatment for chronic, treatment-resistant PTSD in four FDA-approved, phase-two clinical studies: in Boulder; Charleston, South Carolina; Vancouver, British Columbia; and Beer Yaakov, Israel (international studies can be used in the FDA-approval process). Over the course of about five months, the trials' 98 subjects, including 54 women, ingest between 75 and 188 milligrams of MDMA during three- to five-day psychotherapy sessions (comparable to a street dose), supplemented by about 20 hours of non-drug-enhanced talk therapy with mental-health professionals. Lauded for its ability to break down emotional barriers, enhance communication skills, and promote deep introspection, the drug acts not as a medication, but as a catalyst to psychotherapy, many times achieving in a few sessions what might take years in traditional therapeutic settings.

Results from an earlier phase-two study in Charleston completed in 2008 (there are three stages for a medication to get FDA approval) showed great promise: After just two sessions of MDMA-assisted psychotherapy, 83 percent of participants no longer qualified for a PTSD diagnosis, compared with only 25 percent who were cured from talk therapy alone. If these current trials are successful, MDMA-assisted psychotherapy may become a prescription treatment for PTSD and radically change how we treat a wide range of psychiatric illnesses, like autism, anxiety, and anorexia.

Though it's frequently associated with war veterans, PTSD is common in civilian women; one in 10 women will experience it in their lifetime, owing, in part, to the fact that women are more likely to suffer sexual trauma, the type of incident that most frequently leads to the disorder. Standard treatments for PTSD include antidepressants and talk therapy, but their efficacy is mediocre at best: In clinical trials, these therapies were ineffective for about 25 to 50 percent of patients.

About two years after David's death, Murphy sat in the bright, airy office of therapist Marcela Ot'alora, the Boulder study's lead investigator, preparing to embark on her first MDMA-assisted psychotherapy session. She was nervous to take the hallucinogen in front of a therapist, especially one she didn't know. Rhythmic drumming played on the stereo in the background. Lit candles adorned a table where Murphy placed a photo of her and David kissing in a field of goldenrod.

Twenty minutes after Murphy swallowed her capsule of MDMA, the drug took hold. Murphy envisioned herself rocketing through the earth's atmosphere toward space, where she came upon David, illuminated like a zodiac drawing among the stars. They spoke about the mundane—her travel hiccups getting from Oklahoma to Boulder—and the profound. She updated him on his family, shared her worries about Romy's future, and expressed anger with him for leaving her to raise their daughter alone. He nodded knowingly and assured her with his big *Aw, shucks* smile. Then Murphy asked him a question: "How big *are* you?" David threw open his arms, which unfurled into wings that stretched across the entirety of the universe. After two years of terror and grief, Murphy finally felt peace.

MDMA-assisted psychotherapy may seem like a novel treatment born of the medical-marijuana age. But this new round of research is, in fact, revisiting old ground. Before it was co-opted by club-goers, MDMA was used by therapists during similar intensive, daylong therapy sessions in the late 1970s and early 1980s. California therapist and pioneer of the psychedelic psychotherapy movement Leo Zeff coined it "penicillin for the soul." In 1985, the Drug Enforcement Administration (DEA) classified it as a schedule I substance, along with heroin and LSD—a designation given to "drugs with no currently accepted medical use and a high potential for abuse."

That kicked off years of bad publicity for MDMA, including inaccurate claims that MDMA causes Parkinson's disease and holes in the brain, and permanently damages serotonin reserves. In reality, no studies have shown that clinical usage—that is, taking pure MDMA in moderate doses under medical supervision a limited number of times—leads to long- term cognitive damage, according to Matthew Johnson, associate professor of psychiatry and behavioral sciences at Johns Hopkins Medicine. MDMA has been administered in various studies to more than 1,113 subjects, with only one report of a serious, drug-related adverse event, which ended once the drug wore off. (A subject was admitted to the hospital with an irregular heartbeat and was released the next day.)

Recreational and pharmaceutical MDMA barely resemble each other, however. While the terms *MDMA*, *Ecstasy*, and *Molly* are used interchangeably, Molly or Ecstasy bought on the street is often misrepresented or cut with dangerous adulterants, like methamphetamine, and rarely contains actual MDMA. (Only 9 percent of the Molly the DEA collected in New York state in 2013 contained the pure form of the drug.) And using even pure MDMA in a nonmedical setting, like a club, can be risky: The drug increases blood pressure and heart rate and can cause hyperthermia, or overheating, which can lead to liver, kidney, muscle, and heart failure.

Ranging in age from 23 to 66, the 54 women in the six phase-two studies are mothers, teachers, professional athletes, military veterans, police officers, psychotherapists, and office managers. They have survived combat, rape, physical and sexual torture, and more. Each has taken the DSM-IV Clinician- Administered PTSD scale, or CAPS test, the standard for diagnosing the disorder. (The maximum score is 136; anything above 60 is considered severe PTSD. The average score among the studies' participants is 82.) For these women, participation is oftentimes their final attempt to reclaim their lives.

Rachel Hope, a 43-year-old writer from Los Angeles, endured a troubled childhood: At 4 years old, she was physically and sexually abused, then hit by a truck at age 11, which left her partially paralyzed for a year and requiring four surgeries and years of physical therapy. As a result of the various traumas, Hope suffered from debilitating, treatment-resistant PTSD, which manifested as extreme irritable bowel syndrome (IBS), acute anxiety, night terrors, panic attacks, and insomnia, among other symptoms, and left her malnourished and unable to maintain romantic relationships or to work outside the home. "It was a monstrous existence," she says. At one point, she was on 15 medications before enrolling in the Charleston study in 2005. "I was dying," she says of her choice to join the study. "I had nothing to lose."

Brenda, a 38-year-old teacher from the Denver area, who was physically and sexually tortured by her father from ages 3 to 12, was so clinically depressed from PTSD that she was left suicidal and unable to teach her elementary school classes. (She asked not to use her last name to protect her family and career.) She tried 11 medications and was in weekly therapy for 15 years before enrolling in a study. "I entered the Boulder study with a CAPS score of 87, on meds," she says. "That's bullshit. That's me doing everything I'm supposed to do, everything that these therapists are taught to do in school, and it's not helping." She was wary of using a so-called party drug to treat her condition, but she was desperate. "I was really in a fight for my life," Brenda says. "The fear of the stigma associated with using MDMA was far less than the fear of continuing to feel the PTSD symptoms for the rest of my life."

The sessions are not high-flying, blissed-out psychedelic drug trips, but intense feelings of "connection," or love for oneself and others, do pervade the experience. "My husband and I have been married 17 years, and it was the first time I understood how much he must love me and how I deserve that love," explains Brenda, who says MDMA opened up a world of new emotions for her. "I was able to feel. I think that's the biggest takeaway. While on the MDMA, I had access to feelings that I hadn't ever had access to before." The drug, which lasts three to six hours, produces an objective state in which one is able to revisit difficult emotions and experiences, and able to do so without being overwhelmed by them. "I was terrified a lot of the time. I was reliving it," says Murphy, who regularly went back to the scene of the trauma. "I actually saw all of the accident, but it didn't overwhelm me because I was outside of it somehow."

This sense of peace is typical of the MDMA sessions. "Instead of feeling hyperaroused or overstimulated, I felt a tremendous calm and had reduced anxiety," says Hope. Despite the enhanced sensory perception that is a hallmark of the psychedelic experience (things like light appearing more crystalline, the sensation of air currents wafting over skin), participants are extremely focused on the task at hand: healing. "Even though MDMA is a psychedelic, I didn't feel like I was tripping," says Hope. "I didn't feel

fucked up. I felt really empowered, like I could direct my mind where I needed to."

There's a chemical explanation for all of this. MDMA triggers a massive release of serotonin, a neurotransmitter critical to mood regulation; dopamine, which modulates emotional response; and oxytocin, the hormone of bonding, trust, and intimacy. "Patients are awake, alert, connected. They want to talk. They want to explore. They feel calm enough and their fear is extinguished enough that they can actually process the trauma," says psychiatrist Dr. Julie Holland, author of *Ecstasy: The Complete Guide: A Comprehensive Look at the Risks and Benefits of MDMA*. "You basically couldn't design a molecule that is better for therapy than MDMA."

MRI brain scans suggest that one way MDMA works is by decreasing activity in the amygdala, the brain's fear center, while increasing activity in the prefrontal cortex, regions associated with memory and higher functioning. In the PTSD brain, activities in these areas are out of balance. Researchers believe MDMA's effects on the amygdala and prefrontal cortex allow people to understand a trauma without being overwhelmed by negative emotions. "It's almost like anesthesia for surgery," says Holland. "It allows you to dig and get to the malignant thing that needs to be pulled out and examined. It takes years in psychotherapy to dig around the trauma and start to get to it. This is a way for people to process the core issue in order to move forward."

Accessing traumatic memories allows patients to re-remember them, a process called memory reconsolidation, in which memories can be changed if they are reactivated and updated with new information. "You're actually manipulating that memory, and when it gets stored again, what's stored again is a little different than what you pulled out," says Johnson. This is key for people with PTSD, whose brains haven't properly worked through trauma. "I felt as if I was literally reprogramming my brain and confronting all of the fixed thought patterns and belief structures that were keeping the PTSD in place, that were making me relive the past over and over again. I was able to file those memories in the past," says Hope.

From June through October 2014, Murphy underwent three 8-hour MDMA treatments. After her first session, her sleep improved. After her second, she stopped wanting to kill herself; her flashbacks began to subside. "It felt like burdens were lifted off my shoulders," Murphy says. By the end of her participation in the study, her CAPS score had fallen from 114 to 37, meaning she no longer qualified for a PTSD diagnosis. "It saved me," she says of the treatment. "It delivered me back to my good life and delivered my daughter her mother."

Brenda also credits MDMA-assisted psychotherapy with saving her life. "I spent 35 years suicidal, and I'm not anymore, because of the MDMA and two really skilled therapists," she says. She is now off all her medications and teaching full-time again for the first time in seven years. "I'm the healthiest I've ever been, because I have so much clarity." And more than 10 years after enrolling in the first study in Charleston, Hope says she is still cured of PTSD and has not suffered IBS, flashbacks, or night terrors since her first MDMA session.

Whereas psychiatric medications such as Zoloft try to address so-called biological imbalances, they act as a temporary Band-Aid to suffering, say researchers. MDMA may heal it altogether. And MDMA may be safer than psychiatric medications, in part because you don't have to take it every day. "If used carefully, it could be safer simply because your side effects are time-limited," says Johnson. Zoloft and Paxil, traditional treatments for PTSD, can cause weight gain, sexual dysfunction, and suicidal thoughts, whereas a single dose of medical-grade MDMA may only cause increases in heart rate and blood pressure during the session, and fatigue, loss of appetite, and low mood for a day or so afterward. For people like Murphy, Brenda, and Hope, the insights and emotional shifts gleaned from their MDMA sessions have profoundly changed their lives. Brenda says, "It's really like stepping outside into a whole new world and breathing fresh air."

MDMA research has helped pave the way for psychiatry's current psychedelic resurgence. Scientists at Johns Hopkins, Imperial College London, and the University of New Mexico are studying LSD and psilocybin, the psychoactive compound in magic mushrooms, as antidotes to addiction, anxiety, depression, and more. In the future, MDMA researchers hope to see the no-longer-experimental treatment administered by specially trained and licensed therapists in mental health clinics around the globe.

But Bertha Madras, Ph.D., a professor of psychobiology at Harvard Medical School, fears that legalizing MDMA for medical use is just the first step in decriminalizing serious drugs in the United States. "The illicit hallucinogens MDMA, LSD, and psilocybin are the next wave of drugs being promoted as 'medicines,' with the long-term view of normalizing their use for psychoactive purposes," she says. "At present, there is insufficient evidence to support the use of MDMA for therapeutic purposes." Dr. Joseph Lee, medical director of Hazelden Betty Ford Foundation Youth Continuum, a rehab facility in Minnesota, believes MDMA may have therapeutic properties but worries about the greater ramifications of legalizing MDMA-assisted psychotherapy. "My concern is that somehow this conversation about researching MDMA for PTSD will bleed into people justifying recreational use or minimizing misuse. We've seen that happen with prescription drugs," says Lee. He also cautions against overuse of MDMA. "We routinely see kids every year who used too much MDMA or for whatever reason had a side effect from the MDMA and needed to be psychiatrically hospitalized before coming to treatment," he says, touching on another concern of MDMA—that it may trigger latent psychiatric issues. (Prospective participants for the MDMA-assisted psychotherapy trials are screened for any psychological issues—like bipolar disorder and schizophrenia—that may be of concern.)

One of the biggest obstacles standing in the way of developing MDMA into an FDA-approved medication is funding. The process is a $20 million endeavor and one that relies completely on the fundraising efforts of MAPS, the Multidisciplinary Association for Psychedelic Studies, a nonprofit research and educational organization that studies and develops therapeutic applications for psychedelic drugs—partly because pharmaceutical companies have little interest in developing a drug administered only a few times. In 2016, MAPS will move MDMA-assisted psychotherapy one step closer to legalization when it begins phase-three clinical trials, which will involve more than 400 participants and last five years. If those trials are successful, psychiatrists may be prescribing the treatment by 2021.

In the meantime, MDMA has caught the attention of those at the highest levels of the military; 22 veterans per day commit suicide. The National Center for PTSD, in the Department of Veterans Affairs, has been consulting with MAPS concerning an upcoming study, which will look at MDMA-assisted couples therapy involving veterans and top VA-affiliated psychologists, and will begin at the end of this year. Based on the results, Rick Doblin, MAPS founder and executive director, is hopeful the Department of Defense may fund further studies and allow MAPS to work with active-duty soldiers.

Today, Murphy lives with Romy on a quiet street in Norman, Oklahoma, and is thriving. In June, she traveled to Northern California, where she lived with David for two years, to scatter his ashes at Muir Woods, a stretch of lush redwood forest near the Pacific that they frequented and loved. She brought along her new boyfriend, who, coincidentally, is also named David; they met after Murphy's second MDMA-assisted psychotherapy session. They are talking about a life together, something she never could have imagined before the experimental treatment. For the first time in years, she is hopeful about what lies ahead.

"I'm able to make a life for us now, and he's right here with me," she says of her late husband. "I feel blessed that I ever got to be with him in the first place." Some days, when she's out in her yard with Romy, a bird will fly by and Murphy will reach up to the sky and say, "Daddy's birds." Her daughter smiles, knowing her father is close by, and, at long last, so does Murphy. "It's still sad," she says. "But I can access those memories, and see him in my daughter, and I rejoice in it."

KELLEY MCMILLAN is a freelance journalist whose work on health, skiing, and adventure travel has appeared in the *New York Times*, *Marie Claire*, and *Vogue*.

Rachel Patel and Daniel Titheradge

MDMA for the Treatment of Mood Disorder: All Talk No Substance?

Introduction

3,4-Methylene-dioxymethamphetamine (MDMA), the active component of 'ecstasy', is a recreational drug which has recently been proposed to exhibit antidepressant properties [Riedlinger and Montagne, 2001; Sessa and Nutt, 2007]. This postulate is based on the acute pharmacology of MDMA and is consistent with the hallmark theory of depression, the monoamine hypothesis [Krishnan and Nestler, 2008]. MDMA rapidly increases availability of extracellular 5-hydroxytryptamine (5-HT) at the synapse, mirroring the action of commonly prescribed antidepressants. However, current first-line treatments for depression, such as selective serotonin reuptake inhibitors (SSRIs), typically take about 6 weeks to produce optimum therapeutic change [Frazer and Benmansour, 2002]; MDMA could offer instantaneous relief. This rapid onset is an attractive prospect for treatment-resistant depression (TRD), where currently the only therapeutic option is electroconvulsive therapy (ECT). Although there is a theoretical basis, at present experimental evidence of antidepressant action of MDMA is low, with just one rodent [Majumder *et al.* 2011] and one volunteer study [Majumder *et al.* 2012] suggesting direct rapid-onset antidepressant action.

MDMA is a controlled substance in most countries, typically in the most restrictive category (Class A in the UK). Despite this, MDMA is already in clinical trials for anxiety disorders such as post-traumatic stress disorder (PTSD), as an adjunct to psychotherapy where it is thought to assist therapy sessions by strengthening the therapeutic relationships between patient and therapist [MAPS, 2015; Mithoefer *et al.* 2011, 2013; Oehen *et al.* 2013]. Psychotherapy, in the form of cognitive behavioural therapy (CBT), is one of the most effective treatments for depression, indicating that the translation of MDMA-assisted therapy to depression may also be beneficial.

To date, experiments using MDMA have been of limited scope, in part due to its Class A scheduling, as well as concerns over its safety and neuro-toxicity profile. Through recreational use, it has garnered a reputation for being dangerous in the media, with reports focused on the rare deaths of young adults; and in the scientific literature through demonstration of neurotoxicity in animals. In humans, MDMA overdose can produce hyperthermia, with subsequent muscle break down resulting in hyperkalaemia and organ failure [Carvalho *et al.* 2012]. However, the doses required for these effects are excessive and thus reports of death solely from MDMA overdose are scarce; MDMA is more commonly linked to death as a contributing factor in a polydrug environment [Kaye *et al.* 2009]. To date, there are no published studies demonstrating neurotoxicity of repeated low dose MDMA in drug-naïve volunteers; indeed this regimen is in use in PTSD trials and has been postulated to have antidepressant activity [Sessa and Nutt, 2007].

Animal studies highlight physiological and psychological changes that occur after MDMA exposure, but these studies are limited, employing aggressive dose regimes over intense time periods that do not reflect patterns of human recreational use or those utilized in clinical trials [Mithoefer *et al.* 2011, 2013; Oehen *et al.* 2013]. Data from recreational users are also inadequate, restricted by retrospective design that cannot rule out premorbid differences, as well as reliance on self-reported variables of time and dose. Additionally, such data are confounded by polydrug use and ambiguity over whether 'ecstasy' tablets contain MDMA; a recent government report states that 'most ecstasy tablets sold in the UK do not contain MDMA [Jones *et al.* 2011]. If MDMA is to be assessed for its antidepressant properties, there is an urgent need to eliminate equivocal data, as interpretation and relevant translation to patient populations is currently impossible. In this article we examine the conclusions of both animal and human literature to assess whether MDMA could prove a safe and effective therapy for TRD.

MDMA pharmacology

Positive indications

MDMA is an amphetamine derivative, capable of crossing the blood–brain barrier to the central nervous system, where its major substrates are the vesicular and presynaptic monoamine transporters [Elliott and Beveridge, 2005]. Early work identifying MDMA substrates, using *post mortem* brain material, or *in vitro* tissue samples, concluded that MDMA acts to reverse transport across these proteins, inducing a rapid, dose-dependent, nonexocytic monoamine release into the synapse [Schmidt, 1987; Rudnick and Wall, 1992; Rothman and Baumann, 2002]. These finding have been recapitulated in conscious rats [Baumann *et al.* 2005].

Of the monoamines, MDMA has highest efficacy for 5-HT release *via* the serotonin reuptake transporter (SERT) [Steele *et al.* 1987; Elliott and Beveridge, 2005]. Thus, MDMA acts to increase 5-HT availability in the acute setting, as SSRIs do chronically. Indeed, many of MDMA's effects are abolished in SERT-deficient mice [Bengel *et al.* 1998; Fox *et al.* 2007], as well as by SSRIs, which act as competitive antagonists to SERT [Schmidt and Taylor, 1987]. In humans, SSRIs also diminish the effects of MDMA [Liechti and Vollenweider, 2000], an important consideration when thinking about use as a rapid-onset antidepressant or augmentation therapy. That is, giving MDMA in conjunction with commonly used antidepressants may prevent the therapeutic effects of MDMA, due to substrate competition [Hysek *et al.* 2012]. In addition to monoamine modulation itself, MDMA-induced 5-HT release acts to increase oxytocin in humans [Dumont *et al.* 2009]. Oxytocin characteristically precipitates prosocial behaviours and an improved ability to infer the mental state of others [Domes *et al.* 2007]; this has the potential to offer a gateway to successful psychotherapy.

Negative indications

Following acute MDMA-induced 5-HT release from serotonergic terminals, in conjunction with inhibition of 5-HT reuptake, marked depletions in 5-HT and its metabolite, 5-hydroxyindoleacetic acid (5-HIAA), have been reported in *post mortem* brain tissue of animals and humans [Schmidt *et al.* 1986], as well as in *vivo* from cerebrospinal fluid (CSF) measurements [Ricaurte *et al.* 1990; Taffe *et al.* 2003]. This does not bode well for use as an antidepressant following the monoamine theory of depression. Yet, these data are

not definitive; rodent studies drawing such conclusions have used single doses, more than 10 times greater than an average recreational dose [Schmidt *et al.* 1986] or multiple high doses in rapid succession [Wallinga *et al.* 2011]. Primate data follow similar regimes [Ali *et al.* 1993].

. . .

Although current studies are heavily confounded, the evidence currently highlights a discrepancy between the acute and chronic pharmacology of MDMA. Acutely, MDMA works to increase 5-HT availability, suggestive of rapid-onset antidepressant properties and positive changes to emotion, but this transient effect may be accompanied by later depletions of 5-HT. However, studies examining long-term effects are inadequate and thus it cannot be concluded that MDMA significantly depletes 5-HT stores at doses that would be used therapeutically.

. . .

Despite MDMA passing safety measures for its use in clinical trials of PTSD, we believe that until discrepancies in neurotoxicity data are resolved, it is unlikely that MDMA will be explored as a rapid-onset antidepressant because of the emphasis in both depression pathophysiology and MDMA neurotoxicity on 5-HT. MDMA is the second most popular illicit substance in Europe, peaking in popularity in the 1980s, and thus if MDMA use posed a chronic, detrimental effect, a resultant epidemic should emerge shortly. As of yet this does not appear to have surfaced and thus it might be hypothesized to be unlikely that MDMA has a noticeable lasting effect.

Psychological effects of MDMA

. . .

Numerous studies have compiled data from recreational users to investigate the relationship between MDMA and mood in humans. In one self-reported study, it was stated that the feeling of depression post-MDMA exposure in a cohort of 20 'ecstasy' users was 55% [Davison and Parrott, 1997]. In a larger study, 52 frequent 'ecstasy' users were questioned, and the prevalence of depression reported was just 4% [De Almeida and Silva, 2003]. It is difficult to determine which figure is more representative as both studies used retrospective designs lacking biochemical analysis to confirm MDMA or other drug use. Furthermore, in humans, there is an argument that the environment in which MDMA is taken, rather than MDMA itself, causes negative changes to long-term mood, a factor that these self-reported studies do not consider. Indeed, it is suggested that reduced quality of sleep following recreational MDMA use, rather than the use itself, can lead to depression, anxiety and aggression [Scott *et al.* 2013].

Prospective studies have also been conducted, attempting to clarify whether MDMA use precipitates depression, or whether the drug is used recreationally as self-medication. One such study investigated behavioural outcomes of MDMA use in an initially MDMA-naïve population who were likely to use MDMA in the near future [De Win *et al.* 2006]. These volunteers underwent a number of behavioural tests over a mean period of 16 months, with data suggesting that premorbid depression did not predict MDMA use. In addition, this study found that depression post-MDMA was not significantly increased. However, these findings are not consistent across the prospective study literature [Lieb *et al.* 2002; Huizink *et al.* 2006; Briere *et al.* 2012].

A large Dutch population study explored the relationship between behavioural traits exhibited by school children and their future MDMA use, assessed 14 years later via questionnaire [Huizink *et al.* 2006]. The work found that the children who had fulfilled the criteria for anxious or depressed childhood behaviours were significantly more likely to used MDMA as they grew up and into young adulthood. A 4-year prospective study of 14–24 year olds from Munich demonstrated that ecstasy users had a 3-fold odds increase in the presence of mental disorders compared with nondrug users and a 2-fold odds increase compared with non-ecstasy users [Lieb *et al.* 2002]. As a prospective study the temporal nature of this relationship was investigated and it was demonstrated that, in 80.4% of ecstasy users with mental disorders, the presence of mental illness predated ecstasy use. Major depressive disorder was associated with increased ecstasy use and, within the cohort of ecstasy users with comorbid depression, the diagnosis of depression predated ecstasy use in 44.5%. In both these studies the authors proposed that these data were evidence that mental illness leads to increased rates of ecstasy use, in fitting with a hypothesis of self-medication. Differences between prospective studies still leave ambiguity, likely due to confounding factors such as polydrug use, dose and compound uncertainty.

Research into MDMA and its biochemical and/or behavioural effects on healthy volunteers now has considerable statistical power, with about 900 people having partaken in clinical trials. Kirkpatrick and colleagues undertook an analysis of data of the effects of MDMA across three different laboratories, with 220 healthy volunteers [Kirkpatrick *et al.* 2014a]. They demonstrated consistent subjective effects, as well as physical changes. The subjective effects were assessed using visual analogue scales and covered perception of a drug effect, liking of drug effect, closeness to others and feelings of anxiety. Significant positive shifts were demonstrated on each of these factors. Physical changes related to an increase in both heart rate

and blood pressure, resulting in a significant cardiovascular profile, which may prove problematic for patients in older age and those with pre-existing medical health problems. The overarching conclusion of this work is that the measured subjective and physical effects of MDMA are reproducible, irrelevant of population, demographic and experimental methodology.

In 1998, Vollenweider and colleagues safely conducted the first trial examining the effects of MDMA on nonpatient volunteers [Vollenweider *et al.* 1998]. Recently, a number of studies have furthered this work to characterize the acute effects of MDMA in a controlled environment [Hartman *et al.* 2013; Carhart-Harris *et al.* 2014a, 2014b; De Sousa Fernandes Perna *et al.* 2014; Frye *et al.* 2014; Hysek *et al.* 2014; Kirkpatrick *et al.* 2014b, 2014c; Kuypers *et al.* 2014; Schmid *et al.* 2014, 2015; Seibert *et al.* 2014; Spronk *et al.* 2014; Wardle and De Wit, 2014; Yubero-Lahoz *et al.* 2014; Clark *et al.* 2015].Two papers of note, examining the psychological effects of MDMA were published by the groups of Nutt and De Wit respectively [Carhart-Harris *et al.* 2014b; Frye *et al.* 2014]. Nutt's group looked at the effects of a modest MDMA dose on the recall of emotionally important memories, using functional magnetic resonance imaging (fMRI) and subjective ratings [Carhart-Harris *et al.* 2014a. De Wit's group investigated the effects of MDMA on the perception of social rejection using a computer simulated task and subjective ratings [Frye *et al.* 2014a]. In both studies, MDMA was shown to enhance positivity. In the work by Nutt's group, participants reported that during the use of MDMA, worst memories, such as the death of a close friend, were significantly less negative, whilst favourite memories were more positive, vivid and emotionally intense. In the study by De Wit's group, enhanced positivity is demonstrated by a decreased subjective response to rejection. These two papers address differing areas of MDMA's psychopharmacology, with effects of enhanced positivity apparently appearing consistent across both autobiographical recollection and contemporaneous subjective experience. These findings are highly supportive of the putative use of MDMA in depression for elevating mood, as well as further supporting the use of MDMA as an adjunct to psychotherapy. A modulation enabling increased positivity has the potential to increase engagement in the therapeutic process, to assist in the exploration of the underlying cognitions and to create a platform for subsequent behavioural change.

These studies have paved the way for exploration of the acute effects of MDMA on psychology. For the purposes of an antidepressant therapy, it will be important in the future to explore whether the positive changes in psychology demonstrated can persist beyond the duration of the acute actions of MDMA. In addition, translation to patient groups will need to be addressed. We have found one study looking at the effects of MDMA on mood in a putative target population [Majumder *et al.* 2012], which reported that in a population of MDMA users, with and without a predisposition of depression, the administration of the drug decreases depressive symptoms. The authors argue that this effect could underlie the popularity of MDMA as a form of self-medication; we would argue that this further supports the hypothesis that MDMA may provide a helpful therapy in depression.

Recreational drugs as clinical therapies

Rapid-onset antidepressants

In the 1940s, the first antidepressant, amphetamine, was used for its rapid-acting pharmacology. In his excellent book, *On Speed: The Many Lives of Amphetamine*, Rasmussen discusses the history of amphetamines and their rise to fame as wonder drugs that claimed to cure a whole host of ailments from obesity to mood disorders [Rasmussen, 2008]. Today the use of amphetamine has clearly fallen out of vogue, in part due to the prolific side effects observed from prescription and their highly addictive nature that led to the patterns of abuse that built up around them. Taboo now shrouds the conversion of illicit substances to clinical therapy; nevertheless, ketamine is in a number of clinical trials for TRD [Murrough and Charney, 2012]. Ketamine's therapeutic use in anaesthesia ensures safety margins are established, but it is still significant that it is being considered as a rapid-onset antidepressant. Many trials of ketamine as a novel antidepressant have taken place in the past year, including a small naturalistic open label study by Diamond and colleagues looking at the efficacy and safety of delivering ketamine treatment within an NHS clinic setting [Diamond *et al.* 2014]. The model used a regime of once weekly intravenous (IV) doses of ketamine for 3 weeks, followed by twice weekly doses for a further 3 weeks, demonstrating a potential model for the safe clinical use of controlled substances which could be applied to MDMA.

Initial evidence supports ketamine's role as a therapy for TRD, but this substance is markedly psychotropic, which may not be desirable for severely ill patients. MDMA is not overtly psychotropic and thus may provide a more attractive therapy. Alternatively, specific analogues to these drugs, lacking unwanted effects, can be developed. One group has synthesized a ketamine analogue for use in TRD [Burgdorf *et al.* 2013] and UWA-101, an MDMA analogue, has also been developed for use in Parkinson's disease. UWA-apparently lacks cytotoxicity in primates [Johnston *et al.* 2012]. This could be applied to TRD if the monoaminergic actions of MDMA are decreed to be antidepressant as a designer agent will be less controversial and neurotoxic.

Psychotherapy adjuncts

In the middle of the last century, the precedent was set for the use of psychostimulants as rapid acting antidepressants and a simultaneous interest into the use of psychedelics as adjuncts to psychotherapy developed. In 1967, Naranjo and colleagues published a paper on MDA, a substance structurally related to MDMA, and its potential as an adjunct to psychotherapy on the basis of its ability to heighten affect, increase emotional empathy and increase self-insight, without the distracting perceptual alterations of LSD [Naranjo *et al.* 1967]. In 1986, Grinspoon and Bakalar discussed the history of drug use for the enhancement of psychotherapy and highlighted MDMA as one of the most promising agents of interest [Grinspoon and Bakalar, 1986]. Modern trials of MDMA as an augmentation strategy in cognitive therapies have been initiated with treatment-resistant PTSD patients. PTSD is an anxiety disorder, related and often comorbid with depression, and the protocols from the groups researching the efficacy of MDMA assisted psychotherapy in PTSD could be translated into work on depression. Current protocols consist of a number of MDMA-assisted sessions interspersed with nondrug based psychotherapy sessions, with an overnight inpatient stay following MDMA assisted-sessions to ensure safety [Oehen *et al.* 2013].

It is worth considering that many patients undergoing psychotherapy are on a variety of psychotropic medications and some data suggest that current antidepressants combined with CBT may have reduced effects on outcome. SSRIs negatively affect amygdala function, which is thought to be one of the structural targets of psychotherapy [Browning *et al.* 2011]. Episodic memory, mediated in part by the amygdala, is thought to be impaired in depression and hyperactive responses in the amygdala, to neutral stimuli, are well-documented in depressed subjects [Nestler *et al.* 2002]. MDMA acutely reduces activity in the amygdala [Gamma *et al.* 2000], suggesting that it may help overcome the cognitive insufficiencies linked to depression in addition to correcting monoamine imbalances. However, whether a reduction in amygdala function, as a result of MDMA exposure, affects psychotherapy outcomes, is unknown.

Conclusion

MDMA has the potential to act as a rapid-onset antidepressant *via* its modulation of the 5-HT system and as an augmentation strategy in cognitive therapy. Acutely, MDMA acts to increase extracellular 5-HT availability, portraying an ideal antidepressant agent according to the monoamine hypothesis. A single rodent study has confirmed this acute effect, but use as an antidepressant is restricted by inadequate experimental evidence and safety uncertainties. A precedent for the safe use of MDMA has been set by its use in clinical trials of PTSD, but a more concrete analysis needs to be resolved through human volunteer studies. Large doses appear neurotoxic in animals, thus small doses of subrecreational values, are most appropriate for use in initial trials. . . . Once a safety profile and therapeutic index are concluded, the next step will be to look definitively at the antidepressant action of MDMA. There is no doubt that MDMA acutely causes feelings of empathy in almost all users. However, if antidepressant properties are tested, it should be remembered that when healthy volunteers are administered SSRIs, noticeable effects on mood are not recorded and thus it is important to emphasize studies on patients rather than healthy volunteers. In conclusion, the data from PTSD trials of MDMA assisted psychotherapy set a promising precedent that can likely be applied to depression. The use of MDMA as a standalone rapid-onset antidepressant is theoretically well-grounded, but lacks proof of concept.

Funding

This research received no specific grant from any funding agency in the public, commercial, or not-for-profit sectors.

Conflict of interest statement

The authors declare no conflicts of interest in preparing this article.

References

Ali, S., Newport, G., Scallet, A., Binienda, Z., Ferguson, S., Bailey, J. *et al.* (1993) Oral Administration of 3,4-methylenedioxymethamphetamine (MDMA) produces selective serotonergic depletion in the nonhuman primate. *Neurotoxicol Teratol* 15: 91–96.

Baumann, M., Clark, R., Budzynski, A., Partilla, J., Blough, B. and Rothman, R. (2005) N-substituted piperazines abused by humans mimic the molecular mechanism of 3,4-methylenedioxymethamphetamine (MDMA, or 'ecstasy'). *Neuropsychopharmacology* 30: 550–560.

Bengel, D., Murphy, D., Andrews, A., Wichems, C., Feltner, D., Heils, A. *et al.* (1998) Altered brain serotonin homeostasis and locomotor insensitivity to 3, 4-methylenedioxymethamphetamine ('ecstasy') in serotonin transporter-deficient mice. *Mol Pharmacol* 53: 649–655.

Briere, F., Fallu, J., Janosz, M. and Pagani, L. (2012) Prospective associations between meth/amphetamine (speed) and MDMA (ecstasy) use and depressive symptoms in secondary school students. *J Epidemiol Community Health* 66: 990–994.

Browning, M., Grol, M., Ly, V., Goodwin, G., Holmes, E. and Harmer, C. (2011) Using an experimental medicine model to explore combination effects of pharmacological and cognitive interventions for depression and anxiety. *Neuropsychopharmacology* 36: 2689–2697.

Burgdorf, J., Zhang, X., Nicholson, K., Balster, R., Leander, J., Stanton, P. *et al.* (2013) GLYX-13, a NMDA receptor glycine-site functional partial agonist, induces antidepressant-like effects without ketamine-like side effects. *Neuropsychopharmacology* 38: 729–742.

Carhart-Harris, R., Murphy, K., Leech, R., Erritzoe, D., Wall, M., Ferguson, B. *et al.* (2014a) The effects of acutely administered 3,4-methylenedioxymethamphetamine on spontaneous brain function in healthy volunteers measured with arterial spin labeling and blood oxygen level-dependent resting state functional connectivity. *Biol Psychiatry*. DOI: 10.1016/j.biopsych.2013.12.015.

Carhart-Harris, R., Wall, M., Erritzoe, D., Kaelen, M., Ferguson, B., De Meer, I. *et al.* (2014b) The effect of acutely administered MDMA on subjective and bold-fMRI responses to favourite and worst autobiographical memories. *Int J Neuropsychopharmacol* 17: 527–540.

Carvalho, M., Carmo, H., Costa, V., Capela, J., Pontes, H., Remiao, F. *et al.* (2012) Toxicity of amphetamines: an update. *Arch Toxicol* 86: 1167–1231.

Clark, C., Frye, C., Wardle, M., Norman, G. and De Wit, H. (2015) Acute effects of MDMA on autonomic cardiac activity and their relation to subjective prosocial and stimulant effects. *Psychophysiology* 52: 429–435.

Davison, D. and Parrott, A. (1997) Ecstasy (MDMA) in recreational users: self-reported psychological and physiological effects. *Human Psychopharmacol Clin Exp* 12: 221–226.

De Almeida, S. and Silva, M. (2003) Ecstasy (MDMA): effects and patterns of use reported by users in Sao Paulo. *Rev Bras Psiquiatr* 25: 11–17.

De Sousa Fernandes Perna, E., Theunissen, E., Kuypers, K., Heckman, P., De La Torre, R., Farre, M. *et al.* (2014) Memory and mood during MDMA intoxication, with and without memantine pretreatment. *Neuropharmacology* 87: 198–205.

De Win, M., Schilt, T., Reneman, L., Vervaeke, H., Jager, G., Dijkink, S. *et al.* (2006) Ecstasy use and self-reported depression, impulsivity, and sensation seeking: a prospective cohort study. *J Psychopharmacol* 20: 226–235.

Diamond, P., Farmery, A., Atkinson, S., Haldar, J., Williams, N., Cowen, P. *et al.* (2014) Ketamine infusions for treatment resistant depression: a series of 28 patients treated weekly or twice weekly in an ECT clinic. *J Psychopharmacol* 28: 536–544.

Domes, G., Heinrichs, M., Michel, A., Berger, C. and Herpertz, S. (2007) Oxytocin improves 'mindreading' in humans. *Biol Psychiatry* 61: 731–733.

Dumont, G., Sweep, F., van Der Steen, R., Hermsen, R., Donders, A., Touw, D. *et al.* (2009) Increased oxytocin concentrations and prosocial feelings in humans after ecstasy (3,4-methylenedioxymethamphetamine) administration. *Soc Neurosci* 4: 359–366.

Elliott, J. and Beveridge, T. (2005) psychostimulants and monoamine transporters: upsetting the balance. *Curr Opin Pharmacol* 5: 94–100.

Fox, M., Andrews, A., Wendland, J., Lesch, K., Holmes, A. and Murphy, D. (2007) A pharmacological analysis of mice with a targeted disruption of the serotonin transporter. *Psychopharmacology* 195: 147–166.

Frazer, A. and Benmansour, S. (2002) Delayed pharmacological effects of antidepressants. *Mol Psychiatry* 7(Suppl. 1): S23–S28.

Frye, C., Wardle, M., Norman, G. and De Wit, H. (2014) MDMA decreases the effects of simulated social rejection. *Pharmacol Biochem Behav* 117: 1–6.

Gamma, A., Buck, A., Berthold, T., Liechti, M. and Vollenweider, F. (2000) 3,4-Methylenedioxymethamphetamine (MDMA) modulates cortical and limbic brain activity as measured by [H(2)(15)O]-PET in healthy humans. *Neuropsychopharmacology* 23: 388–395.

Grinspoon, L. and Bakalar, J. (1986) Can drugs be used to enhance the psychotherapeutic process? *Am J Psychother* 40: 393–404.

Hartman, R., Desrosiers, N., Barnes, A., Yun, K., Scheidweiler, K., Kolbrich-Spargo, E. *et al.* (2013) 3,4-Methylenedioxymethamphetamine (MDMA) and metabolites disposition in blood and plasma following controlled oral administration. *Anal Bioanal Chem.* 15 November 2013. [Epub ahead of print]

Huizink, A., Ferdinand, R., Van Der Ende, J. and Verhulst, F. (2006) Symptoms of anxiety and depression in childhood and use of MDMA: prospective, population based study. *Br Med J* 332: 825–828.

Hysek, C., Domes, G. and Liechti, M. (2012) MDMA enhances 'mind reading' of positive emotions and impairs 'mind reading' of negative emotions. *Psychopharmacology* 222: 293–302.

Hysek, C., Simmler, L., Schillinger, N., Meyer, N., Schmid, Y., Donzelli, M. *et al.* (2014) Pharmacokinetic and pharmacodynamic effects of methylphenidate and MDMA administered alone or in combination. *Int J Neuropsychopharmacol* 17: 371–381.

Johnston, T., Millar, Z., Huot, P., Wagg, K., Thiele, S., Salomonczyk, D. *et al.* (2012) A novel MDMA analogue, UWA-101, that lacks psychoactivity and cytotoxicity, enhances L-DOPA benefit in Parkinsonian primates. *FASEB J* 26: 2154–2163.

Jones, L., Bates, G., Bellis, M., Beynon, C., Duffy, P., Evans-Brown, M. *et al.* (2011) A summary of the health harms of drugs. London: Department of Health.

Kaye, S., Darke, S. and Duflou, J. (2009) Methylenedioxymethamphetamine (MDMA)-related fatalities in Australia: demographics, circumstances, toxicology and major organ pathology. *Drug Alcohol Depend* 104: 254–261.

Kirkpatrick, M., Baggott, M., Mendelson, J., Galloway, G., Liechti, M., Hysek, C. *et al.* (2014a) MDMA effects consistent across laboratories. *Psychopharmacology* 231: 3899–3905.

Kirkpatrick, M., Francis, S., Lee, R., De Wit, H. and Jacob, S. (2014b) Plasma oxytocin concentrations following MDMA or intranasal oxytocin in humans. *Psychoneuroendocrinology* 46: 23–31.

Kirkpatrick, M., Lee, R., Wardle, M., Jacob, S. and De Wit, H. (2014c) Effects of MDMA and intranasal oxytocin on social and emotional processing. *Neuropsychopharmacology* 39: 1654–1663.

Krishnan, V. and Nestler, E. (2008) The molecular neurobiology of depression. *Nature* 455: 894–902.

Kuypers, K., De La Torre, R., Farre, M., Yubero-Lahoz, S., Dziobek, I., Van Den Bos, W. *et al.* (2014) No evidence that MDMA-induced enhancement of emotional empathy is related to peripheral oxytocin levels or 5-HT1a receptor activation. *PLoS One* 9: e100719.

Lieb, R., Schuetz, C., Pfister, H., Von Sydow, K. and Wittchen, H. (2002) Mental disorders in ecstasy users: a prospective-longitudinal investigation. *Drug Alcohol Depend* 68: 195–207.

Liechti, M. and Vollenweider, F. (2000) The serotonin uptake inhibitor citalopram reduces acute cardiovascular and vegetative effects of 3,4-methylenedioxymethamphetamine ('ecstasy') in healthy volunteers. *J Psychopharmacol* 14: 269–274.

Majumder, I., White, J. and Irvine, R. (2011) Antidepressant-like effects of 3,4-methylenedioxymethamphetamine in an animal model of depression. *Behav Pharmacol* 22: 758–765.

Majumder, I., White, J. and Irvine, R. (2012) antidepressant-like effects of ecstasy in subjects with a predisposition to depression. *Addict Behav* 37: 1189–1192.

MAPS (2015) 3,4-methylenedioxymethamphetamine (MDMA) Annual Report IND# 63,384. Multidisciplinary Association for Psychedelic Studies.

Mithoefer, M., Wagner, M., Mithoefer, A., Jerome, L. and Doblin, R. (2011) The safety and efficacy of {+/-}3,4-methylenedioxymethamphetamine-assisted psychotherapy in subjects with chronic, treatment-resistant posttraumatic stress disorder: the first randomized controlled pilot study. *J Psychopharmacol* 25: 439–452.

Mithoefer, M., Wagner, M., Mithoefer, A., Jerome, L., Martin, S., Yazar-Klosinski, B. *et al.* (2013) Durability of improvement in post-traumatic stress disorder symptoms and absence of harmful effects or drug dependency after 3,4-methylenedioxymethamphetamine-assisted psychotherapy: a prospective

long-term follow-up study. *J Psychopharmacol* 27: 28–39.

Murrough, J. and Charney, D. (2012) Is there anything really novel on the antidepressant horizon? *Curr Psychiatry* Rep 14: 643–649.

Naranjo, C., Shulgin, A. and Sargent, T. (1967) Evaluation of 3,4-methylenedioxyamphetamine (MDA) as an adjunct to psychotherapy. *Med Pharmacol Exp Int J Exp Med* 17: 359–364.

Nestler, E., Barrot, M., Dileone, R., Eisch, A., Gold, S. and Monteggia, L. (2002) Neurobiology of depression. *Neuron* 34: 13–25.

Oehen, P., Traber, R., Widmer, V. and Schnyder, U. (2013) A randomized, controlled pilot study of MDMA (+/- 3,4-methylenedioxymethamphetamine)-assisted psychotherapy for treatment of resistant, chronic post-traumatic stress disorder (PTSD). *J Psychopharmacol* 27: 40–52.

Rasmussen, N. (2008) *On Speed: The Many Lives of Amphetamine*. New York: New York University Press.

Ricaurte, G., Finnegan, K., Irwin, I. and Langston, J. (1990) Aminergic metabolites in cerebrospinal fluid of humans previously exposed to MDMA: preliminary observations. *Ann N Y Acad Sci* 600: 699–708; discussion 708–610.

Riedlinger, J. and Montagne, M. (2001) Potential clinical uses for MDMA. In: Holland, J. (ed.), *Ecstasy: The Complete Guide: A Comprehensive Review of the Risks and Benefits of MDMA*. Rochester, VT: Park Street Press, pp. 243–247.

Rothman, R. and Baumann, M. (2002) Serotonin releasing agents. Neurochemical, therapeutic and adverse effects. *Pharmacol Biochem Behav* 71: 825–836.

Rudnick, G. and Wall, S. (1992) The molecular mechanism of 'ecstasy' [3,4-methylenedioxy-methamphetamine (MDMA)]: serotonin transporters are targets for MDMA-induced serotonin release. *Proc Natl Acad Sci U S A* 89: 1817–1821.

Schmid, Y., Hysek, C., Preller, K., Bosch, O., Bilderbeck, A., Rogers, R. *et al.* (2015) Effects of methylphenidate and MDMA on appraisal of erotic stimuli and intimate relationships. *Eur Neuropsychopharmacol* 25: 17–25.

Schmid, Y., Hysek, C., Simmler, L., Crockett, M., Quednow, B. and Liechti, M. (2014) Differential effects of MDMA and methylphenidate on social cognition. *J Psychopharmacol* 28: 847–856.

Schmidt, C. (1987) Acute administration of methylenedioxymethamphetamine: comparison with the neurochemical effects of its N-desmethyl and N-ethyl analogs. *Eur J Pharmacol* 136: 81–88.

Schmidt, C. and Taylor, V. (1987) Depression of rat brain tryptophan hydroxylase activity following the acute administration of methylenedioxymethamphetamine. *Biochem Pharmacol* 36: 4095–4102.

Schmidt, C., Wu, L. and Lovenberg, W. (1986) Methylenedioxymethamphetamine: a potentially neurotoxic amphetamine analogue. *Eur J Pharmacol* 124: 175–178.

Scott, R., Hides, L., Allen, J. and Lubman, D. (2013) Subacute effects of ecstasy on mood: an exploration of associated risk factors. *J Psychopharmacol* 27: 53–61.

Seibert, J., Hysek, C., Penno, C., Schmid, Y., Kratschmar, D., Liechti, M. *et al.* (2014) Acute effects of 3,4-methylenedioxymethamphetamine and methylphenidate on circulating steroid levels in healthy subjects. *Neuroendocrinology* 100: 17–25.

Sessa, B. and Nutt, D. (2007) MDMA, politics and medical research: have we thrown the baby out with the bathwater? *J Psychopharmacol* 21: 787–791.

Spronk, D., Dumont, G., Verkes, R. and De Bruijn, E. (2014) The acute effects of MDMA and ethanol administration on electrophysiological correlates of performance monitoring in healthy volunteers. *Psychopharmacology* 231: 2877–2888.

Steele, T., Nichols, D. and Yim, G. (1987) Stereochemical effects of 3,4-methylenedioxymethamphetam ine (MDMA) and related amphetamine derivatives on inhibition of uptake of [3H]monoamines into synaptosomes from different regions of rat brain. *Biochem Pharmacol* 36: 2297–2303.

Taffe, M., Huitron-Resendiz, S., Schroeder, R., Parsons, L., Henriksen, S. and Gold, L. (2003) MDMA exposure alters cognitive and electrophysiological sensitivity to rapid tryptophan depletion in Rhesus monkeys. *Pharmacol Biochem Behav* 76: 141–152.

Vollenweider, F., Gamma, A., Liechti, M. and Huber, T. (1998) Psychological and cardiovascular effects and short-term sequelae of MDMA ('ecstasy') in MDMA-naive healthy volunteers. *Neuropsychopharmacology* 19: 241–251.

Wallinga, A., Grahlmann, C., Granneman, R., Koolhaas, J. and Buwalda, B. (2011) Gender Differences in hyperthermia and regional 5-HT and 5-HIAA Depletion in the brain following MDMA administration in rats. *Brain Res* 1398: 13–20.

Wardle, M. and De Wit, H. (2014) MDMA alters emotional processing and facilitates positive social interaction. *Psychopharmacology* 231: 4219–4229.

Yubero-Lahoz, S., Kuypers, K., Ramaekers, J., Langohr, K., Farre, Farre, M. and De La Torre, R. (2014) Changes in serotonin transporter (5-HTT) gene expression in peripheral blood cells after MDMA intake. *Psychopharmacology*. 20 December 2014. [Epub ahead of print]

Rachel Patel of Green Templeton College and Daniel Titheradge of St Hugh's College in the United Kingdom study the neurochemical properties of psychostimulants.

EXPLORING THE ISSUE

Can Ecstasy or Molly (3,4-methylenedioxy-methamphetamine, MDMA) Effectively Psychological Disorders?

Critical Thinking and Reflection

1. What are the symptoms of PTSD and what are the treatments used to manage them?
2. What are the pharmacological properties of MDMA? What does the drug do to the brain and to the body? What are the effects of MDMA on behavior and health?
3. What are the potential benefits of MDMA to help people with PTSD? How is the drug used in a clinical setting and how is the clinical use different from the use of MDMA, as ecstasy or molly, at parties?
4. Why is there resistance to the use of MDMA in the treatment of PTSD and the symptoms of other psychological disorders?

Is There Common Ground?

Psychedelic therapy involves the use of drugs such as LSD, psilocybin and MDMA to assist in psychotherapy. Supporters believe that these drugs' psychedelic, entactogenic and empathogenic properties facilitate therapy by expanding consciousness, minimizing bad thoughts, and making one more willing to explore one's own psyche. Early studies and clinical anecdotes suggested LSD as a treatment for alcoholism, psilocybin to minimize anxiety at the end of life, and MDMA for marriage therapy. The current issue critically evaluated the use of MDMA for PTSD and anxiety. Psychedelic therapy has not gained the acceptance and prominence enjoyed by traditional pharmacotherapy (e.g., Prozax, Zoloft, and Xanax) to help people with psychological disorders.

In the United States a major impairment to the thorough investigation of psychedelic therapy is the legal status of most of the drugs with the putatively-beneficial psychedelic, entactogenic and empathogenic properties. These, along with marijuana, are classified as Schedule I drugs, which means they have no accepted medical use and a high potential for abuse. The Schedule I status also limits available of funding, and drug, for clinical research to validate the claims of supporters and/or provide clear guidelines for clinical efficacy for therapists.

The United States Department of Veterans Affairs estimates the lifetime prevalence of PTSD among adult Americans to be 6.8%, and the current (past year) PTSD prevalence was estimated at 3.5%. PTSD prevalence may be two to three-fold greater in veterans of Operation Enduring Freedom and Operation Iraqi Freedom. Regardless if MDMA is sued in managing the symptoms of PTSD, the goals of therapy are to reduce symptom severity, to learn to live with existing symptoms, and to learn to cope with PTSD symptoms. Existing therapies can be beneficial for many with PTSD; however, the use of MDMA may produce a more-rapid decline in symptom severity and have better long-term success.

Additional Resources

Fadiman, J. (2011). *The Psychedelic Explorer's Guide: Safe, Therapeutic, and Sacred Journeys*. Park Street Press. The author recommends the use of psychedelics (e.g., LSD) for healing and self-discovery. The benefits and risks of psychedelic use are described.

Holland, J. (2001). *Ecstasy : The Complete Guide: A Comprehensive Look at the Risks and Benefits of MDMA*. Park Street Press. Experts in the study of MDMA describe its pharmacological properties, therapeutic potential and dangers.

McClelland, M. (2017). The psychedelic miracle: How some doctors are risking everything to unleash the healing power of MDMA, ayahuasca and other hallucinogens. *Rolling Stone*, March

9. The author describes the benefits of psychedelics and hallucinogens to help manage the symptoms of psychological disorders and aid therapy.

Sessa, B. (2017). Why psychiatry needs 3,4-methylenedioxymethamphetamine: A child psychiatrist's perspective. *Neurotherapeutics*, May 5. The author assessed the benefits and risks of MDMA use as a therapeutic agent, and concludes that MDMA's pharmacological profile translates well to its proposed agent to assist trauma-focused psychotherapy.

Vizeli, P. & Liechti, M.E. (2017). Safety pharmacology of acute MDMA administration in healthy subjects. *Journal of Psychopharmacology* 31(5):576–588. Pharmacologists from the University Hospital Basel and University of Basel used a double-blind, placebo-controlled study to examine the safety of MDMA in healthy subjects. No serious adverse events occurred, and MDMA produced predominantly acute positive subjective drug effects.

Internet References . . .

Erowid: Documenting the Complex Relationship Between Humans and Psychoactives

https://erowid.org/

Multidisciplinary Association for Psychedelic Studies

http://www.maps.org/

National Institutes of Health – National Institute of Drug Abuse – MDMA (Ecstasy/ Molly)

https://www.drugabuse.gov/publications/drugfacts/ mdma-ecstasymolly

National Institutes of Health – National Institute of Mental Health – Anxiety Disorders

https://www.nimh.nih.gov/health/topics/anxiety-disorders

National Institutes of Health – National Institute of Mental Health – Depression

https://www.nimh.nih.gov/health/topics/depression

Unit 3

UNIT

Drug Prevention and Treatment

*D*rugs are widely available. Some say they use drugs because they like it, or drug use takes away the stress and anxiety typically experienced during the day. But, when does drug use transition to drug abuse—when the user consumes the drug in amounts that harmful to themselves or others. When does drug use transition from a behavior that is common, and perhaps socially promoted, into a behavior that is a psychological disorder?

Different forms of drug addiction are classified as psychological disorders in the Diagnostic and Statistical Manual of Mental Disorders (DSM). The DSM provides the diagnostic criteria for psychiatric disorders, such as depression and schizophrenia. It also provides the criteria for diagnosing addictive behaviors. The current edition of the DSM describes substance use disorder. The issues in this unit focus on different perspectives that can be taken to prevent and manage addiction disorders.

Selected, Edited, and with Issue Framing Material by:
Dennis K. Miller, *University of Missouri*

ISSUE

Should Addiction to Drugs Be Labeled a Brain Disease?

YES: **Alan I. Leshner,** from "Addiction Is a Brain Disease," *The Addiction Recovery Guide* (2016)

No: **Steven Slate,** from "Addiction Is Not a Brain Disease, It Is a Choice," *The Clean Slate* (2016)

Learning Outcomes

After reading this issue, you will be able to:

- Discuss the causes of drug addiction.
- Discuss the argument that addiction is a disease and not a behavioral issue.
- Understand the various types of treatment for drug and alcohol addiction.

ISSUE SUMMARY

YES: Alan I. Leshner, director of the National Institute on Drug Abuse at the National Institutes of Health, believes that addiction to drugs and alcohol is not a behavioral condition but a treatable disease.

NO: Addiction theorist Steven Slate counters that addiction is a personal choice and cannot be considered a brain disease.

There are many different theories as to why some individuals become addicted to alcohol or other drugs. Historically, drug and alcohol dependency or addiction has been viewed as either a disease or a moral failing. In more recent years, other theories of addiction have been developed, including behavioral, genetic, sociocultural, and psychological theories. It appears that an individual's genetic makeup can play a major role in developing an addiction. For example, children with an addicted parent are four times more likely than children without an addicted parent to become addicts themselves. Furthermore, over 60 percent of individuals struggling with alcoholism have a family history of alcoholism though it may be a combination of heredity and learned behavior. Many individuals who are suffering from an underlying psychiatric condition, such as anxiety, depression, or mood illnesses, have a higher chance at becoming an addict and vice versa. An addiction can typically start when psychiatric disorders overwhelm individuals with feelings of sadness, anger, and confusion. Troubled with these feelings, individuals may self-medicate with drugs and/or alcohol which can lead to addiction. Also, an individual who lives, works, or studies in an environment prevalent with drug or alcohol usage is also more likely to become addicted to drugs or alcohol. Factors such as peer pressure, societal norms, and access to alcohol and drugs can all play a part in this. Finally, suffering from a traumatic event such as abuse or neglect during childhood, sexual abuse, or the loss of a loved one can strongly factor into an individual's use of alcohol and/or drugs. Overall, while genetic and environmental factors interact with critical developmental stages in a person's life to impact the vulnerability to addiction, adolescents experience a double challenge. Although taking drugs at any age can lead to addiction, the earlier that drug use begins, the more likely it is to progress to more serious abuse. And because adolescents' brains are still developing in the areas that govern decision-making, judgment, and self-control, they are especially prone to risk-taking behaviors, including experimenting with drugs and/or alcohol.

The view that drug addiction and alcoholism are moral failings maintains that abusing drugs is voluntary behavior that the user chooses to do. Users choose to over-indulge in such a way that they create suffering for them-selves and others. American history is marked by repeated and failed government efforts to control this abuse by eliminating drug and alcohol use with legal sanctions, such as the enactment of Prohibition in the late 1920s and the punishment of alcoholics and drug users via jail sen-tences and fines. However, there seem to be several contra-dictions to this behavioral model of addiction. Addiction may be a complex condition that is caused by multiple factors, including environment, biology, and others. It is not totally clear that addiction is voluntary behavior. And from a historical perspective, punishing alcoholics and drug addicts has been ineffective.

In the United States today, the primary theory for understanding the causes of addiction is the disease model rather than the moral model. Borrowing from the modern mental health movement, addiction as a disease has been promoted by mental health advocates who tried to change the public's perception of severe mental illness. Diseases like bipolar disorder and schizophrenia were defined as the result of brain abnormalities rather than environmen-tal factors or poor parenting. Likewise, addiction was not a moral weakness but a brain disorder that could be treated. In 1995, the National Institute of Drug Addiction (NIDA) supported the idea that drug addiction was a type of brain disorder. Following NIDA's support, the concept of addic-tion as a brain disease has become more widely accepted.

This model has been advocated by the medical and alcohol treatment communities as well as self-help groups such as Alcoholics Anonymous and Narcotics Anonymous. The disease model implies that addiction is not the result of voluntary behavior or lack of self-control; it is caused by biological factors which are treatable. While there are somewhat different interpretations of this theory, it gen-erally refers to addiction as an organic brain syndrome with biological and genetic origins rather than voluntary and behavioral origins. It appears that an addicted per-son's impaired ability to discontinue using drugs or alco-hol relates to deficits in the role of the prefrontal cortex, the part of the brain involved in executive function. The prefrontal cortex has several important purposes which include self-monitoring, delaying reward, and integrating whatever the intellect indicates is important with what the libido is relaying. The difficulty also has to do with how the brain, when deprived of the drugs to which it is accustomed, reacts to physical and emotional stress. The response is usually exaggerated negative emotion, and even despair. In this setting, the strong association of learned environmental cues (for instance, smelling alcohol beverages at a party or seeing the location where the drug dealer can be found) aggravates the craving for the substance. And the flood of intoxicating brain chemi-cals called neurotransmitters (chiefly dopamine) during drug use makes the brain relatively insensitive to "typi-cal" sources of pleasure such as a tasty meal or a beautiful sunset.

Alan Leshner believes that taking drugs causes changes in neurons in the central nervous system that compel the individual to use drugs. These neurological changes, which are not reversible, force addicts to con-tinue to take drugs. Steven Slate disagrees. He believes that most addicts are not innocent victims of chronic disease but individuals who are responsible for their choices and recovery.

YES ↵

Alan I. Leshner

Addiction Is a Brain Disease

A core concept evolving with scientific advances over the past decade is that drug addiction is a brain disease that develops over time as a result of the initially voluntary behavior of using drugs (drugs include alcohol).

The consequence is virtually uncontrollable compulsive drug craving, seeking, and use that interferes with, if not destroys, an individual's functioning in the family and in society. This medical condition demands formal treatment.

- We now know in great detail the brain mechanisms through which drugs acutely modify mood, memory, perception, and emotional states.
- Using drugs repeatedly over time changes brain structure and function in fundamental and long-lasting ways that can persist long after the individual stops using them.
- Addiction comes about through an array of neuroadaptive changes and the lying down and strengthening of new memory connections in various circuits in the brain.

The Highjacked Brain

We do not yet know all the relevant mechanisms, but the evidence suggests that those long-lasting brain changes are responsible for the distortions of cognitive and emotional functioning that characterize addicts, particularly including the compulsion to use drugs that is the essence of addiction.

It is as if drugs have highjacked the brain's natural motivational control circuits, resulting in drug use becoming the sole, or at least the top, motivational priority for the individual.

Thus, the majority of the biomedical community now considers addiction, in its essence, to be a brain disease.

This brain-based view of addiction has generated substantial controversy, particularly among people who seem able to think only in polarized ways.

Many people erroneously still believe that biological and behavioral explanations are alternative or competing ways to understand phenomena, when in fact they are complementary and integrative.

Modern science has taught that it is much too simplistic to set biology in opposition to behavior or to pit willpower against brain chemistry.

Addiction involves inseparable biological and behavioral components. It is the quintessential biobehavioral disorder.

Many people also erroneously still believe that drug addiction is simply a failure of will or of strength of character. Research contradicts that position.

Responsible for Our Recovery

However, the recognition that addiction is a brain disease does not mean that the addict is simply a hapless victim. Addiction begins with the voluntary behavior of using drugs, and addicts must participate in and take some significant responsibility for their recovery.

Thus, having this brain disease does not absolve the addict of responsibility for his or her behavior.

But it does explain why an addict cannot simply stop using drugs by sheer force of will alone.

The Essence of Addiction

The entire concept of addiction has suffered greatly from imprecision and misconception. In fact, if it were possible, it would be best to start all over with some new, more neutral term.

The confusion comes about in part because of a now archaic distinction between whether specific drugs are "physically" or "psychologically" addicting.

The distinction historically revolved around whether or not dramatic physical withdrawal symptoms occur when an individual stops taking a drug; what we in the field now call "physical dependence."

Leshner, Alan I. "Addiction Is a Brain Disease," *The Addiction Recovery Guide*, October 2016. Originally from SCIENCE 278: 45(1997).

However, 20 years of scientific research has taught that focusing on this physical versus psychological distinction is off the mark and a distraction from the real issues.

From both clinical and policy perspectives, it actually does not matter very much what physical withdrawal symptoms occur.

Physical dependence is not that important, because even the dramatic withdrawal symptoms of heroin and alcohol addiction can now be easily managed with appropriate medications.

Even more important, many of the most dangerous and addicting drugs, including methamphetamine and crack cocaine, do not produce very severe physical dependence symptoms upon withdrawal.

What really matters most is whether or not a drug causes what we now know to be the essence of addiction, namely:

The uncontrollable, compulsive drug craving, seeking, and use, even in the face of negative health and social consequences.

This is the crux of how the Institute of Medicine, the American Psychiatric Association, and the American Medical Association define addiction and how we all should use the term.

It is really only this compulsive quality of addiction that matters in the long run to the addict and to his or her family and that should matter to society as a whole.

Thus, the majority of the biomedical community now considers addiction, in its essence, to be a brain disease:

A condition caused by persistent changes in brain structure and function.

This results in compulsive craving that overwhelms all other motivations and is the root cause of the massive health and social problems associated with drug addiction.

The Definition of Addiction

In updating our national discourse on drug abuse, we should keep in mind this simple definition:

Addiction is a brain disease expressed in the form of compulsive behavior.

Both developing and recovering from it depend on biology, behavior, and social context.

It is also important to correct the common misimpression that drug use, abuse, and addiction are points on a single continuum along which one slides back and forth over time, moving from user to addict, then back to occasional user, then back to addict.

Clinical observation and more formal research studies support the view that, once addicted, the individual has moved into a different state of being.

It is as if a threshold has been crossed.

Very few people appear able to successfully return to occasional use after having been truly addicted.

The Altered Brain—A Chronic Illness

Unfortunately, we do not yet have a clear biological or behavioral marker of that transition from voluntary drug use to addiction.

However, a body of scientific evidence is rapidly developing that points to an array of cellular and molecular changes in specific brain circuits. Moreover, many of these brain changes are common to all chemical addictions, and some also are typical of other compulsive behaviors such as pathological overeating.

- Addiction should be understood as a chronic recurring illness.
- Although some addicts do gain full control over their drug use after a single treatment episode, many have relapses.

The complexity of this brain disease is not atypical, because virtually no brain diseases are simply biological in nature and expression. All, including stroke, Alzheimer's disease, schizophrenia, and clinical depression, include some behavioral and social aspects.

What may make addiction seem unique among brain diseases, however, is that it does begin with a clearly voluntary behavior—the initial decision to use drugs. Moreover, not everyone who ever uses drugs goes on to become addicted.

Individuals differ substantially in how easily and quickly they become addicted and in their preferences for particular substances.

Consistent with the biobehavioral nature of addiction, these individual differences result from a combination of environmental and biological, particularly genetic, factors.

In fact, estimates are that between 50 and 70 percent of the variability in susceptibility to becoming addicted can be accounted for by genetic factors. Although genetic characteristics may predispose individuals to be more or less susceptible to becoming addicted, genes do not doom one to become an addict.

Over time, the addict loses substantial control over his or her initially voluntary behavior, and it becomes compulsive. For many people, these behaviors are truly uncontrollable, just like the behavioral expression of any other brain disease.

Schizophrenics cannot control their hallucinations and delusions. Parkinson's patients cannot control their trembling. Clinically depressed patients cannot voluntarily control their moods.

Thus, once one is addicted, the characteristics of the illness—and the treatment approaches—are not that different from most other brain diseases. No mater how one develops an illness, once one has it, one is in the diseased state and needs treatment.

Environmental Cues

Addictive behaviors do have special characteristics related to the social contexts in which they originate.

- All of the environmental cues surrounding initial drug use and development of the addiction actually become "conditioned" to that drug use and are thus critical to the development and expression of addiction.

Environmental cues are paired in time with an individual's initial drug use experiences and, through classical conditioning, take on conditioned stimulus properties.

- When those cues are present at a later time, they elicit anticipation of a drug experience and thus generate tremendous drug craving.

Cue-induced craving is one of the most frequent causes of drug use relapses, even after long periods of abstinence, independently of whether drugs are available.

The salience of environmental or contextual cues helps explain why reentry to one's community can be so difficult for addicts leaving the controlled environments of treatment or correctional settings and why aftercare is so essential to successful recovery.

- The person who became addicted in the home environment is constantly exposed to the cues conditioned to his or her initial drug use, such as the neighborhood where he or she hung out, drug-using buddies, or the lamppost where he or she bought drugs.
- Simple exposure to those cues automatically triggers craving and can lead rapidly to relapses.

This is one reason why someone who apparently overcame drug cravings while in prison or residential treatment could quickly revert to drug use upon returning home.

In fact, one of the major goals of drug addiction treatment is to teach addicts how to deal with the cravings caused by inevitable exposure to these conditioned cues.

Implications

It is no wonder addicts cannot simply quit on their own.

They have an illness that requires biomedical treatment.

- People often assume that because addiction begins with a voluntary behavior and is expressed in the form of excess behavior, people should just be able to quit by force of will alone.
- However, it is essential to understand when dealing with addicts that we are dealing with individuals whose brains have been altered by drug use.

They need drug addiction treatment.

We know that, contrary to common belief, very few addicts actually do just stop on their own.

Observing that there are very few heroin addicts in their 50s or 60s, people frequently ask what happened to those who were heroin addicts 30 years ago, assuming that they must have quit on their own.

However, longitudinal studies find that only a very small fraction actually quit on their own. The rest have either been successfully treated, are currently in maintenance treatment, or (for about half) are dead.

Consider the example of smoking cigarettes: various studies have found that between 3 and 7 percent of people who try to quit on their own each year actually succeed.

Science has at last convinced the public that depression is not just a lot of sadness; that depressed individuals are in a different brain state and thus require treatment to get their symptoms under control. It is time to recognize that this is also the case for addicts.

The Role of Personal Responsibility

The role of personal responsibility is undiminished but clarified.

Does having a brain disease mean that people who are addicted no longer have any responsibility for their behavior or that they are simply victims of their own genetics and brain chemistry? Of course not.

Addiction begins with the voluntary behavior of drug use, and although genetic characteristics may predispose individuals to be more or less susceptible to becoming addicted, genes do not doom one to become an addict.

This is one major reason why efforts to prevent drug use are so vital to any comprehensive strategy to deal with the nation's drug problems. Initial drug use is a voluntary, and therefore preventable, behavior.

Moreover, as with any illness, behavior becomes a critical part of recovery. At a minimum, one must comply with the treatment regimen, which is harder than it sounds.

- Treatment compliance is the biggest cause of relapses for all chronic illnesses, including asthma, diabetes, hypertension, and addiction.
- Moreover, treatment compliance rates are no worse for addiction than for these other illnesses, ranging from 30 to 50 percent.

Thus, for drug addiction as well as for other chronic diseases, the individual's motivation and behavior are clearly important parts of success in treatment and recovery.

Alcohol/ Drug Treatment Programs

Maintaining this comprehensive biobehavioral understanding of addiction also speaks to what needs to be provided in drug treatment programs.

Again, we must be careful not to pit biology against behavior.

The National Institute on Drug Abuse's recently published Principles of Effective Drug Addiction Treatment provides a detailed discussion of how we must treat all aspects of the individual, not just the biological component or the behavioral component.

As with other brain diseases such as schizophrenia and depression, the data show that the best drug addiction treatment approaches attend to the entire individual, combining the use of medications, behavioral therapies, and attention to necessary social services and rehabilitation.

These might include such services as family therapy to enable the patient to return to successful family life, mental health services, education and vocational training, and housing services.

That does not mean, of course, that all individuals need all components of treatment and all rehabilitation services. Another principle of effective addiction treatment is that the array of services included in an individual's treatment plan must be matched to his or her particular set of needs. Moreover, since those needs will surely change over the course of recovery, the array of services provided will need to be continually reassessed and adjusted.

ALAN I. LESHNER is the director of the National Institute on Drug Abuse at the National Institutes of Health.

Steven Slate

 **NO**

Addiction Is Not a Brain Disease, It Is a Choice

They're screaming it from the rooftops: "addiction is a disease, and you can't stop it without medical treatment"! But why are they screaming it so loud, why are they browbeating us about it, why is it always mentioned with a qualifier? You don't hear people constantly referring to cancer as "the disease of cancer"—it's just "cancer," because it's obvious that cancer is a disease, it's been conclusively proven that the symptoms of cancer can't be directly stopped with mere choices—therefore no qualifier is needed. On the other hand, addiction to drugs and alcohol is not obviously a disease, and to call it such we must either overlook the major gaps in the disease argument, or we must completely redefine the term "disease." Here, we will analyze a few key points and show that what we call addiction doesn't pass muster as a real disease.

Real Diseases versus the Disease Concept or Theory of Drug Addiction

In a true disease, some part of the body is in a state of abnormal physiological functioning, and this causes the undesirable symptoms. In the case of cancer, it would be mutated cells which we point to as evidence of a physiological abnormality, in diabetes we can point to low insulin production or cells which fail to use insulin properly as the physiological abnormality which create the harmful symptoms. If a person has either of these diseases, they cannot directly choose to stop their symptoms or directly choose to stop the abnormal physiological functioning which creates the symptoms. They can only choose to stop the physiological abnormality indirectly, by the application of medical treatment, and in the case of diabetes, dietetic measures may also indirectly halt the symptoms as well (but such measures are not a cure so much as a lifestyle adjustment necessitated by permanent physiological malfunction).

In addiction, there is no such physiological malfunction. The best physical evidence put forward by the disease proponents falls totally flat on the measure of representing a physiological malfunction. This evidence is the much touted brain scan.[1] The organization responsible for putting forth these brain scans, the National Institute on Drug Abuse and Addiction (NIDA), defines addiction in this way:

> *Addiction is defined as a chronic relapsing brain disease that is characterized by compulsive drug seeking and use, despite harmful consequences. It is considered a brain disease because drugs change the brain—they change its structure and how it works. These brain changes can be long lasting, and can lead to the harmful behaviors seen in people who abuse drugs.*

The NIDA is stating outright that the reason addiction is considered a disease is because of the brain changes evidenced by the brain scans they show us, and that these changes cause the behavior known as addiction, which they characterize as "compulsive drug seeking and use." There are three major ways in which this case for the disease model falls apart:

- The changes in the brain which they show us are not abnormal at all.
- People change their behavior in spite of the fact that their brain has changed in response to repeated substance use.
- There is no evidence that the behavior of addicts is compulsive (compulsive meaning involuntary; point two addresses this, as well as some other research that will be presented).

This all applies equally to "alcoholism" as well. If you're looking for information on alcoholism, the same theories and logic discussed here are applicable; wherever you see the term addiction used on this site, it includes alcoholism.

Brain Changes In Addicts Are Not Abnormal, and Do Not Prove the Brain Disease Theory

On the first count, the changes in the brain evidenced by brain scans of heavy substance users ("addicts") do not represent a malfunctioning brain. They are quite normal, as research into neuroplasticity has shown us. Whenever we practice doing or thinking anything enough, the brain changes—different regions and neuronal pathways are grown or strengthened, and new connections are made; various areas of the brain become more or less active depending upon how much you use them, and this becomes the norm in your brain—but it changes again as you adjust how much you use those brain regions depending on what you choose to think and do. This is a process which continues throughout life, there is nothing abnormal about it.

. . .

So, when the NIDA's Nora Volkow and others show us changes in the brain of a substance user as compared to a nonsubstance user, *this difference is not as novel as they make it out to be.* They are showing us *routine* neuroplastic changes which every healthily functioning person's brain goes through naturally. The phenomenon of brain changes isn't isolated to "addicts" or anyone else with a so-called brain disease—nonaddicted and nondepressed and non-[insert brain disease of the week here] people experience neural adaptations too. One poignant example was found in the brains of London taxi drivers, as Begley and Jeffrey Schwartz pointed out in *The Mind and The Brain*.[3]

Is Being a Good Taxi Driver a Disease?

A specific area of the brain's hippocampus is associated with creating directional memories and a mental map of the environment. A team of researchers scanned the brains of London taxi drivers and compared their brains to non-taxi drivers. There was a very noticeable difference, not only between the drivers and nondrivers, but also between the more experienced and less experienced drivers.

. . .

So, the longer you drive a cab in London (i.e., the longer you exert the mental and physical effort to quickly find your way around one of the world's toughest to navigate cities), the more your brain physically changes. And the longer you use drugs, the more your brain changes.

And indeed, the longer and more intensely you apply yourself to any skill, thought, or activity—the more it will change your brain, and the more visible will be the differences between your brain and that of someone who hasn't been focused on that particular skill. So, if we follow the logic of the NIDA, then London's taxi drivers have a disease, which we'll call taxi-ism, that *forces them to drive taxis*. But the new diseases wouldn't stop there.

. . .

These brain change don't need to be brought on by exposure to chemicals. Thoughts alone, are enough to rewire the very circuits of the human brain responsible for reward and other positive emotions that substance use and other supposedly "addictive" behaviors ("process addictions" such as sex, gambling, and shopping, etc.) are connected with.

The Stolen Concept of Neuroplasticity in the Brain Disease Model of Addiction

Those who claim that addiction is a brain disease readily admit that the brain changes in evidence are arrived at through repeated choices to use substances and focus on using substances. In this way, they are saying the disease is a product of routine neuroplastic processes. Then, they go on to claim that such brain changes either can't be remedied or can only be remedied by outside means (medical treatment). When we break this down and look at it step by step, we see that the brain disease model rests on an argument similar to the "stolen concept." A stolen concept argument is one in which the argument denies a fact on which it simultaneously rests. For example, the philosophical assertion that "reality is unknowable" rests on, or presumes that the speaker could know a fact of reality, it presumes that one could know that reality is unknowable—which of course one couldn't, if reality truly was unknowable—so the statement "reality is unknowable" invalidates itself. Likewise, the brain disease proponents are essentially saying "neuroplastic processes create a state called addiction which cannot be changed by thoughts and choices"—this however is to some degree self-invalidating, because it depends on neuroplasticity while seeking to invalidate it. If neuroplasticity is involved and is a valid explanation for how to become addicted, then we can't act is if the same process doesn't exist when it's time to focus on getting unaddicted. That is, if the brain can be changed into the addicted state by thoughts and choices, then it can be further changed or changed back by thoughts and choices. Conditions which can be remedied by freely chosen thoughts and behaviors, don't fit into the general understanding of disease. Ultimately, if addiction is a disease, then it's a disease so fundamentally different than any other that it should probably have a completely different name that doesn't imply all the things contained in the term "disease"—such as the idea that the "will" of the afflicted is irrelevant to whether the condition continues.

People Change Their Addictive Behavior In Spite of the Fact That Their Brain Is Changed—and They Do So without Medication or Surgery

In the discussion above, we looked at some analogous cases of brain changes to see just how routine and normal (i.e., not a physiological malfunction) such changes are. Now we're going to look directly at the most popular neuroscientific research which purports to prove that these brain changes actually cause "uncontrolled" substance use ("addiction").

The most popular research is Nora Volkow's brain scans of "meth addicts" presented by the NIDA. The logic is simple. We're presented with the brain scan of a meth addict alongside the brain scan of a nonuser, and we're told that the decreased activity in the brain of the meth user (the *lack of red* in the "Drug Abuser" brain scan presented) is the cause of their "compulsive" methamphetamine use. Here's how the NIDA explains the significance of these images in their booklet—Drugs, Brains, and Behavior: The Science of Addiction:

> *Just as we turn down the volume on a radio that is too loud, the brain adjusts to the overwhelming surges in dopamine (and other neurotransmitters) by producing less dopamine or by reducing the number of receptors that can receive signals. As a result, dopamine's impact on the reward circuit of a drug abuser's brain can become abnormally low, and the ability to experience any pleasure is reduced. This is why the abuser eventually feels flat, lifeless, and depressed, and is unable to enjoy things that previously brought them pleasure. Now, they need to take drugs just to try and bring their dopamine function back up to normal.*

. . .

When these studies were done, nobody was directly treating the brain of methamphetamine addicts. They were not giving them medication for it (there is no equivalent of methadone for speed users), and they weren't sticking scalpels into the brains of these meth addicts, nor were they giving them shock treatment. So what did they do?

These methamphetamine addicts were court ordered into a treatment program (whose methodology wasn't disclosed in the research) which likely consisted of a general mixture of group and individual counseling with 12-step meeting attendance. I can't stress the significance of this enough: their brains were not medically treated. They talked to counselors. They faced a choice between jail and abstinence. *They CHOSE abstinence (for at least 14 months!)—even while their brains had been changed in a way that we're told robs them of the ability to choose to quit "even in the face of negative consequences."*[4]

Even with changed brains, people are capable of choosing to change their substance use habits. They choose to stop using drugs, and as the brain scans above demonstrate, their brain activity follows this choice. If the brain changes caused the substance using behavior, that is, if it was the other way around, then a true medical intervention should have been needed—the brain would've needed to have changed first via external force (medicine or surgery) before abstinence was initiated. They literally wouldn't have been able to stop for 14 months without a real physical/biological medical intervention. But they did . . .

Substance Use Is Not Compulsive, It Is a Choice

. . .

If the theory is that neural adaptations alone cause uncontrolled behavior, then this proposition can easily be shown to be false. I demonstrated above that in the midst of having fully "changed" or "addicted" brains, people do indeed stop using substances, so essentially, it is case closed. But the depths to which the brain disease theory of addiction can be negated go even further, because the basic theory of addiction as representing uncontrolled substance use has never been explained. Explanation of the mechanism by which substance use happens without the individual's consent is conspicuously missing—yet such explanation is a necessary part of such a theory, as Lindesmith writes (again in Addiction & Opiates):

> *. . . besides identifying the two types of phenomenon that are allegedly interrelated, there must be a description of the processes or events that link them. In other words, besides affirming that something causes*

something else, it is necessary to indicate how the cause operates to produce the alleged effect.

There doesn't seem to be any explanation or evidence that substance use is involuntary. In fact, the evidence, such as that presented above, shows the opposite. Nevertheless, when the case for the disease is presented, the idea that drug use is involuntary is taken for granted as true. No evidence is ever actually presented to support this premise, so there isn't much to be knocked down here, except to make the point I made above—is a piano player fundamentally incapable of resisting playing the piano? They may love to play the piano, and want to do it often, they may even be obsessive about it, but it would be hard to say that at the sight of a piano they are involuntarily driven by their brain to push aside whatever else they need to do in order to play that piano.

There is another approach to the second claim though. We can look at the people who have subjectively claimed that their substance use is involuntary and see if the offer of incentives results in changed behavior. Gene Heyman covered this in his landmark book, *Addiction: A Disorder of Choice*.[2] He recounts studies in which cocaine abusers were given traditional addiction counseling and also offered vouchers which they could trade in for modest rewards such as movie tickets or sports equipment—if they proved through urine tests that they were abstaining from drug use. In the early stages of the study, 70 percent of those in the voucher program remained abstinent, while only 20 percent stayed abstinent in the control group which didn't receive the incentive of the vouchers. This demonstrates that substance use is not in fact compulsive or involuntary, but that it is a matter of choice, because these "addicts" when presented with a clear and immediately rewarding alternative to substance use and incentive not to use, chose it. Furthermore, follow up studies showed that this led to long-term changes. A full year after the program, the voucher group had double the success rate of those who received only counseling (80 to 40 percent, respectively). This ties back in to our first point that what you practice, you become good at. The cocaine abusers in the voucher group practiced replacing substance use with other activities, such as using the sports equipment or movie passes they gained as a direct consequence of abstaining from drug use—thus they made it a habit to find other ways of amusing themselves, this probably led to brain changes, and the new habits became the norm.

Long story short, there is no evidence presented to prove that substance use is compulsive. The only thing ever offered is subjective reports from drug users themselves that they "can't stop," and proclamations from treatment professionals that the behavior is compulsive due to brain changes. But if the promise of a ticket to the movies is enough to double the success rate of conventional addiction counseling, then it's hard to say that substance users can't control themselves. The reality is that they can control themselves, but they just happen to see substance use as the best option for happiness available to them at the times when they're abusing substances. When they can see other options for happiness as more attractive (i.e., as promising a greater reward than substance use), attainable to them, and as taking an amount of effort they're willing to expend—then they will absolutely choose those options instead of substance use, and will not struggle to "stay sober," prevent relapse, practice self-control or self-regulation, or any other colloquialism for making a different choice. They will simply choose differently.

But wait . . . there's more! Contrary to the claims that alcoholics and drug addicts literally lose control of their substance use, a great number of experiments have found that they are really in full control of themselves. Priming dose experiments have found that alcoholics are not triggered into uncontrollable craving after taking a drink. Priming dose experiments of cocaine, crack, and methamphetamine users found that after being given a hit of their drug of choice (primed with a dose), they are capable of choosing a delayed reward rather than another hit of the drug.

Three Most Relevant Reasons Addiction Is Not a Disease

So to sum up, there are at least two significant reasons why the current brain disease theory of addiction is false.

- A disease involves physiological malfunction, the "proof" of brain changes shows no malfunction of the brain. These changes are indeed a normal part of how the brain works—not only in substance use, but in anything that we practice doing or thinking intensively. Brain changes occur as a matter of everyday life; the brain can be changed by the choice to think or behave differently; and the type of changes we're talking about are not permanent.
- The very evidence used to demonstrate that addicts' behavior is caused by brain changes also demonstrates that they change their behavior while their brain is changed, without a real medical intervention such as medication targeting the brain or surgical intervention in the brain—and

that their brain changes back to normal AFTER they VOLITIONALLY change their behavior for a prolonged period of time

- Drug use in "addicts" is not compulsive. If it was truly compulsive, then offering a drug user tickets to the movies would not make a difference in whether they use or not—because this is an offer of a choice. Research shows that the offer of this choice leads to cessation of substance abuse. Furthermore, to clarify the point, if you offered a cancer patient movie tickets as a reward for ceasing to have a tumor—it would make no difference, it would not change his probability of recovery.

Addiction is NOT a disease, and it matters. This has huge implications for anyone struggling with a substance use habit.

References

1. NIDA, Drugs Brains and Behavior: The Science of Addiction, sciofaddiction.pdf.

2. Gene Heyman, Addiction: A Disorder of Choice, Harvard University Press, 2009.

3. Sharon Begley and Jeffrey Schwartz, The Mind And The Brain, Harper Collins, 2002.

4. Links to the 2 methamphetamine abuser studies by Nora Volkow: http://www.jneurosci.org/cgi/content/full/21/23/9414

   http://ajp.psychiatryonline.org/cgi/reprint/158/3/377

. . .

STEVEN SLATE is an addiction theorist.

EXPLORING THE ISSUE

Should Addiction to Drugs Be Labeled a Brain Disease?

Critical Thinking and Reflection

1. What are the root causes of drug and alcohol addiction?
2. What are the benefits to labeling addiction a brain disease?
3. Why could it be harmful to label addiction a brain disease?
4. Describe the types of treatment for alcohol and drug addiction.

Is There Common Ground?

One of the most valuable aspects of labeling addiction a disease is that it removes alcohol and drugs from the moral realm. It proposed that addiction sufferers should be treated and helped, rather than scorned and punished. Though the moral model of addiction has by no means disappeared in the United States, today more resources are directed toward rehabilitation than punishment. Increasingly, it is being recognized and understood that fines, victim-blaming, and imprisonment do little to curb alcohol and drug addiction in society.

An article, "New insights into the genetics of *addiction*" (*Nature Reviews Genetics*, April, 2009), indicates that genetics contributes significantly to susceptibility to this disorder, but identification of vulnerable genes has lagged. In "It's Time for Addiction Science to Supersede Stigma" (*Science News*, 11/8/09), the author discusses advances made in the scientific community in studying *addictions* and says that people should regard drug addicts the same they regard other people with *brain diseases*. To do this, it should be recognized that *addictions* are a form of *brain disease*, and rather than blaming people for becoming addicted, energy should be spent on finding solutions.

Critics argue, however, that this belief either underemphasizes or ignores the impact of self-control, learned behaviors, and many other factors which lead to alcohol and drug abuse. Furthermore, most treatment programs in the United States are based on the concept of addiction as a brain disease, and most are considered to be generally ineffective when judged by their high relapse rates. Many researchers claim that advances in neuroscience is changing the way mental health issues such as addiction is understood and addressed as a brain disease. While calling addiction a brain disease and medical condition legitimizes it, many scientists do not completely support this model.

It appears that the causes of addiction are complex and that brain, mind, and behavioral specialists are rethinking the whole notion of addiction. With input from neuroscience, biology, pharmacology, psychology, and genetics, they're questioning assumptions and identifying some common characteristics among addicts which will, it is hoped, improve treatment outcomes and even prevent people from using drugs in the first place.

Additional Resources

Alavi, S., Ferdosi, M., Jannatifard, F., Eslami, M., Alaghemandan, H., & Setare, M. (2012). Behavioral addiction versus substance addiction: Correspondence of psychiatric and psychological views. *International Journal Of Preventive Medicine, 3*(4), 290–294.

Campbell, M. (2015). Ten ethical failings in addiction treatment. *Alcoholism & Drug Abuse Weekly, 27*(10), 5–6.

Clark, K.J. (2016). Addiction is a chronic brain disease. *American Journal of Managed Care,* 14.

Elam, M. (2015). How the brain disease paradigm remoralizes addictive behaviour. *Science as Culture, 24*(1), 46–64.

Internet References . . .

American Psychological Association (APA)

www.apa.org

National Institutes of Health: National Institute on Drug Abuse

http://www.drugabuse.gov/nidahome.html

Web of Addictions

http://www.well.com/user/woa

Selected, Edited, and with Issue Framing Material by:
Dennis K. Miller, *University of Missouri*

ISSUE

Is Alcoholism Hereditary?

YES: Markus Heilig, from "Triggering Addiction," *The Scientist* (2008)

NO: Rajita Sinha, from "How Does Stress Lead to Risk of Alcohol Relapse?" *Alcohol Research: Current Reviews* (2012)

Learning Outcomes

After reading this issue, you will be able to:

- Understand the prevalence of alcoholism in the United States and its symptoms.
- Describe the factors that contribute to alcohol use disorders, including alcoholism.
- Consider the interaction of genetics and the environment in psychological disorders, such as alcoholism.
- Explain how scientists examine the role of genetics in a behavior or psychological disorder.

ISSUE SUMMARY

YES: Markus Heilig, Clinical Director of the National Institute on Alcohol Abuse and Alcoholism, argues that molecular changes in the brain result in positive reinforcement from alcohol. Heilig notes that alcoholism has a behavioral component, but certain genes may be responsible in individuals who abuse alcohol despite its adverse consequences.

NO: Research by Rajita Sinha indicates that alcohol use disorders are associated with dysfunction in emotion and stress responses and that these dysfunctional responses contribute to the motivation to drink. Stress levels and mechanisms to manage stress are key factors for the desire to use alcohol and relapse to alcoholism.

Data from the National Institute on Alcohol Abuse and Alcoholism (NIAAA) indicate that 87 percent of adults (i.e., 18 years or older) drank alcohol at least once in their life, 71 percent reported that they drank in the last year, and 56 percent drank in the last month. Rates of alcohol use in the United States appear to go through cycles that tend to correlate with public interest in health and well-being. A shift in mores about the benefits or risks of alcohol accompanies a shift in alcohol consumption; however, a rebound in the opposite direction follows a few years later. Regardless of whether we are at peak or trough levels in the United States right now, alcohol has been and will continue to be part of our culture.

There are a number of factors that influence whether an individual will consume alcohol and how much alcohol they consume. In controlled laboratory studies with free access for humans and animals, high consumption is observed for several days followed by a period of lower consumption. Men generally consume more alcohol than women, although this gap is becoming narrow in young people and college populations. Practically, there may be no difference between men and women when we consider that women experience intoxication at lower alcohol concentrations in the body than men.

Data from the NIAAA also indicate that problem drinking is prevalent in the United States. Almost a quarter of adults reported that they engaged in binge drinking (i.e., a pattern of drinking that brings a person's blood alcohol concentration to 0.08 grams percent or above) in the past month. Almost 17 million adults and almost a million youth (i.e., age 12–17) have an alcohol use disorder (i.e., alcohol abuse and dependence disorders; symptoms including drinking more than initially intended, experiencing a strong need to drink, and developing tolerance and withdrawal symptoms) and 1.4 million people sought treatment for alcohol disorders in 2013.

Historically, alcohol was the first drug that psychologists, psychologists, and social reformers investigated as a disease. Researcher E. M. Jellinek, a prominent researcher in alcohol and addiction in the 1950s and 1960s, led investigations into alcoholism and its treatment. His work was closely associated with Alcoholics Anonymous (AA), and both Jellinek and AA believed that alcoholism is a biological or genetic disease. People are born with alcoholism. All begin using alcohol as a social drinker (e.g., only drink occasionally, do not feel the need to drink to have a good time, never feel the need to control their overall drinking behavior, and do not do things they later regret while drinking); however, some progress to drink more heavily. While there are many factors that can contribute to the transition from social to heavy drinker, the presence or absence of the genetic/biological factors is an important determinant.

There is clear research evidence that biological and genetic factors contribute to alcoholism. If a close relative (e.g., biological parent or sibling) has alcoholism, an individual has a fourfold increased risk of developing alcoholism in their lifetime. Twin studies indicate that drinking behavior patterns are more similar in monozygotic or identical twins than in dizygotic or fraternal twins.

Scientists who study the genetics of alcoholism often separate research participants into two categories—family history positive (FHP) and family history negative (FHN). Those who are FHP come from family in which there is a history of alcohol problems, while FHN individuals are from families without a history of alcohol problems. Overall, FHP people have a greater risk of developing an alcohol use disorder than FHN people. Pharmacological research indicates few overall differences in alcohol pharmacokinetics (e.g., metabolism and elimination from the body) or in reports of alcohol "liking" between these groups; however, there are differences in the effects of alcohol on brain activity and sensitivity to the psychological and motor-impairing effects of alcohol.

Although many scientists and psychologists believe that there is a genetic component of alcoholism for many people, genetic theories are still inconclusive. Researchers have not identified a single gene that carries a predisposition to alcohol abuse. Some argue that risk factors for alcoholism cannot be translated directly into genetic and biological terms and factors such as personality traits, values, individual needs, attitudes, family upbringing, peers, and other sociocultural influences in a person's life affect one's use or abuse of alcohol.

Studies of family members show (1) common causal factors that are shared among relatives and (2) risk factors that are unique to an individual family member's life experiences and environment. In addition to sharing genes, many family members share similar environments, customs, culture, diet, and patterns of behavior. The interaction of these factors may be the foundation for a pattern of alcoholism in the family or individual family member. Thus, the conclusion that the sole cause of alcoholism is genetic is viewed skeptically because there are too many other psychological and environmental factors that play a key role in the onset of alcoholism.

In this issue Markus Heilig argues in the YES selection that alcoholism has a genetic component and is not the result of family environment. He maintains that changes within the brain reinforce the overuse of alcohol that may lead to alcoholism. In the NO selection psychiatrist Rajit Sinha focuses on the role of stress and emotion regulation in compulsive drinking behavior. Dr. Sinha also maintains that the brain plays a critical role in alcoholism, but believes that circuits that regulate anxiety and depression are key to alcoholism and relapse to drinking.

YES ↵

Markus Heilig

Triggering Addiction

Alcohol abuse is the third leading preventable cause of death (defined as death due to lifestyle choice or modifiable behavior). In the United States alone it accounts for more than 75,000 deaths annually. To put it another way, if all cancers were miraculously cured tomorrow, those lives and the life years saved would be a drop in the bucket compared to what would be achieved by eliminating alcohol-related death and morbidity. In contrast to many other common conditions, alcohol abuse affects people whose life expectancy would otherwise be considerable, robbing them of an average 30 potential life years. The unmet medical needs are enormous.

And yet, as striking as these numbers are, they don't begin to capture the despair and sorrow of alcohol problems. I had been teaching students about the pharmacology of addictive drugs for several years before I met my first patient as a clinician. Knowing alcoholic patients, and understanding their day to day struggle has shaped my thinking about the problem and informed the questions I have asked in the laboratory.

Beyond the tragedy of this disease, there is also a fascination. What makes people set aside their most obvious needs and continue to abuse alcohol? Why do they do this despite knowing that it will kill them, harm them, or destroy the lives of those they love? This puzzle offers a window on what makes us humans tick, whether addicted or not.

Fermented beverages have been used since the Neolithic period, through ancient Egypt and China down to the present. Alcohol is the one drug that remains socially and legally acceptable in most of the Western world. I, along with more than half of the adult population, drink—personally I enjoy a good wine. Even though alcohol use disorders are among the most common serious medical conditions, they still only affect about 10% of those who use alcohol.

The disease is not just about drinking too much. Nor is it just about physical dependence characterized by an increased tolerance over time and severe withdrawal when use is stopped. Neither of these phenomena are necessary or sufficient to capture the disease.

At its core, alcoholism is a behavioral disorder. Cravings lead to a narrowed behavioral repertoire, so that seeking and consuming the drug crowds out other normal behaviors. Then there is the loss of control that results in someone planning on having one glass of wine, but ending up passed out on the couch. The combination of craving, loss of control and impaired judgment results in compulsive use, despite an intimate knowledge of the harmful effects. For most—but not all—who reach this state, a return to moderation seems difficult if not impossible.

Modern approaches to treating this disease have focused on the behaviors associated with alcoholism. They help patients develop a set of skills to recognize and avoid situations carrying a high risk of relapse. Such situations involve stressors, primarily of a social nature, and exposure to alcohol-associated cues, such as environments and people. Although treatments based on these principles are clearly documented to provide some benefit, two-thirds of patients still relapse within a one-year period. So, while good behavioral methods should be available to patients, it is also painfully clear that we need something beyond that.

Thankfully, we are finally learning something about the molecular basis of the behavior and compulsion of alcoholism.

In the early 1990s, Charles O'Brien at the University of Pennsylvania, and later Stephanie O'Malley at Yale University, made a breakthrough. They showed that the opioid receptor blocker, naltrexone, could help prevent relapse to heavy drinking in alcohol-dependent patients. The logic, which has gathered considerable support since, goes like this: When you drink, your brain releases endogenous opioid-like substances, called endorphins. These act on opioid receptors and give the sensation of pleasure or, in psychological lingo, "positive reinforcement" of the effects of alcohol. The enjoyment of alcohol has long been thought important in driving excessive drinking. Naltrexone blocks the opioid signaling chain, helping make drinking less pleasant.

There had been some controversy regarding the efficacy of naltrexone, and not every study had replicated its beneficial actions. But 15 years and some 30 controlled studies later, there could be no question: Once all the data were put into a meta-analysis, it was clear that naltrexone could provide a benefit. However, the magnitude of the effect was not very impressive, leading some to dismiss the value of naltrexone as a treatment.

I always looked at opioid-mediated stimulation by alcohol with some degree of skepticism. Remember your high school or college class? There were always two or three guys who danced on the table, and did crazy things when they drank alcohol. Look closer and you'll find that many of them have a family history of alcoholism, and got in trouble themselves down the line. But the rest of us were more likely to experience a welcome relief of tension, followed, at higher doses, by an irresistible desire to fall asleep on the couch. Among that majority, quite a few still developed alcohol use disorders. And even among the people who started out by getting the characteristic kick out of alcohol, 10 years into alcoholism there is little if any pleasure or stimulation left. Clearly, there had to be other mechanisms at play in the development and maintenance of alcoholism besides chasing the buzz.

Clinicians began to notice that naltrexone had certain limitations, and that these matched broad behavior categories. In some patients, the treatment turns their lives around. For the majority, however, you'd have to work hard to convince yourself there was any effect at all.

These days, whenever a basic researcher sees these kinds of individual differences, we think "genetics." In this case, there was a particular reason to do so. Ten years ago, Mary-Jeanne Kreek at the Rockefeller University found genetic variation at the locus encoding the μ-opioid receptor, or OPRM1—the target for naltrexone's therapeutic action. Among Caucasians, about 15% carry at least one copy of a variant that might change the function of the receptor to make carriers more susceptible to both alcoholism and naltrexone therapy.

While researchers still debate what the variant does on the molecular level, carriers of the variant allele consistently experience more of a subjective high in response to alcohol. Human laboratory studies in which the effects of alcohol intake can be directly assessed are limited in the amount of alcohol that can be given to subjects. However, a functionally equivalent variant of OPRM1 has been found in rhesus macaques. Studies in our own program at the National Institute on Alcohol Abuse and Alcoholism (NIAAA) spearheaded by Christina Barr showed that carriers of the rhesus ORPM1 allele variant were much more stimulated by high doses of alcohol, and that these carriers—but not other monkeys—voluntarily consumed alcohol to intoxication when given the opportunity. This work suggests that pleasure-mediated reward from alcohol plays a particularly important role in carriers of the OPRM1 variant. A recent NIAAA sponsored COMBINE trial led by Raymond Anton, confirmed what had been suggested a few years ago by David Oslin and Charles O'Brien at the University of Pennsylvania. It showed that only carriers of the variant receptor benefit from naltrexone treatment. And that minority benefits quite a bit: Twice as many in that group achieved a good clinical outcome when treated with naltrexone compared to placebo.

We had a gene that contributed to differences in alcohol responses, and a drug that could treat the disease pharmacologically. But we had only scratched the surface. What happens in the brains of alcoholics in whom this mechanism is not driving the process?

In the last five years or so, research in experimental animals has shown that the brain undergoes long-term changes as a result of repeated exposure to cycles of pronounced intoxication and withdrawal. Data are consistent between our own laboratory, and those of George Koob at the Scripps Research Institute in La Jolla, Calif., George Breese at the University of North Carolina, Chapel Hill, and Howard Becker at the Medical University of South Carolina in Charleston.

The brain pathology induced by a history of dependence has three key features. One, a history of dependence established through repeated cycles of excessive alcohol intake and withdrawal leads to a long lasting, perhaps life-long pattern of excessive alcohol intake. Two, there is an equally persistent increase in responses to fear and stress. Three, while stress doesn't affect voluntary alcohol intake in non-dependent animals, it does so potently in animals with a history of dependence.

These findings are closely in line with patient reports and clinical experience. Some of them have already been translated into human studies. For instance, exaggerated responsiveness of brain stress and fear systems in human alcoholics has been shown by Dan Hommer's group in our program.

This suggests that long-term neuro-adaptations occur in the alcohol-addicted brain which provide a very different motivation for relapse than the pleasure-seeking response of those who have that genetic susceptibility. In the absence of alcohol, the individual will now find himself in a negative emotional state, which in the short term can be relieved by renewed intake of alcohol. The big question is what underlying biology is driving this shift into what George Koob has labeled "the dark side of addiction."

Since stress and fear are at the core of this new model of alcoholism, we started to look for molecular targets within the neural circuitry of stress. Our best bet was corticotropin releasing hormone (CRH). Discovered in 1982 by Wylie Vale, CRH is now in every medical textbook as the top-level control signal for the hormonal stress response. Much less recognized was the fact that extensive CRH systems within the brain mediate behavioral stress responses that are in concert with, but distinct from the physiological stress effects. A key target for this extrahypothalamic CRH is the amygdala complex, and studies from many laboratories have shown that CRH acting on CRH1 receptors within this structure mediate many behavioral stress responses.

Our recent work has shown that a history of alcohol dependence leads to a persistent up-regulation of CRH1 receptor gene expression and binding within the amygdala. This is exactly the type of molecular plasticity we would expect to see in response to stress and stress-driven excessive alcohol intake. But of course the gene expression data are only correlative. The only way to demonstrate causality is by pharmacology: Only if a CRH1 antagonist rescues the behavioral phenotype of post-dependent animals, that is, makes them normal again, would causality be demonstrated. Working with colleagues at Eli Lilly, we were able to show just that. George Koob's group verified the finding using several other antagonists for the CRH1 receptor. All these molecules have the same signature: They don't do anything to non-dependent animals with low alcohol intake levels, but totally eliminate the excessive drinking that occurs in the post-dependent state.

Based on these observations, the CRH1 receptor appeared to be a very promising target for treatment of the "dark," relief-driven alcoholism. Human trials are now in the planning stages to test this prediction, but continue to face extensive obstacles with regard to the chemistry and toxicology. For instance, making molecules that will dissolve and enter the brain after having been taken as a pill, has turned out to be hard nut to crack.

While investigating the properties of CRH, we badly wanted to find some tool that would allow us to test these ideas in humans sooner. The answer came in the form of a category of compounds that had been collecting dust on many pharmaceutical companies' shelves for years. Substance P (SP), an 11 amino acid peptide discovered by Nobel Prize winner Ulf von Euler back in the 1930s, had for many years been implicated in pain and inflammation. In 1991 researchers at Pfizer developed a small molecule that blocked the main human SP receptor for the transmission of pain, called the neurokinin 1 receptor (NK1R). This was followed by the discovery of several other chemical series that successfully targeted this receptor. But to the disappointment of many, these turned out to be ineffective in treating any pain or inflammation-related clinical condition you can imagine.

Several research groups showed that SP is released in both rat and human amygdala upon exposure to stress, and mediates at least some behavioral effects of the stressor. In fact, several of the effects were identical to those induced by CRH, although its actions were not as general as those of CRH, and less pronounced. It was clear that these were converging systems that generated the same functional outcomes. Jokingly, we started calling SP "CRH light." We realized that an NK1R antagonist might allow us to assess some of our ideas and experimental approaches in humans.

What followed was a rare experience. By any measure we applied, the predictions held up. Mouse mutants that lacked the NK1R drank markedly lower amounts of alcohol, and didn't seem to obtain any reward from this drug. Moving into humans, we treated a group of recently detoxified alcoholics with an orally available, brain penetrating NK1R antagonist for three weeks. Treated subjects had fewer alcohol cravings, and reported markedly improved overall well-being when evaluated weekly by a blinded physician who followed a standard assessment questionnaire. During a challenge session, we mimicked a real-life situation with a high relapse risk: A social stressor, followed by exposure to handling and smelling a preferred alcoholic beverage. This procedure induces powerful craving in placebo-treated subjects, but those responses were markedly suppressed in patients given the NK1R blocker. In parallel with the suppressed cravings, we also found a marked suppression of the hormonal stress-response.

Surprisingly, we could see some of the most striking effects using functional magnetic resonance imaging (fMRI). By looking at the degree of oxygen use, fMRI can visualize activity of neurons in response to various stimuli. As expected based on prior work, placebo-treated alcoholics had exaggerated activation of brain circuits that process negative emotions when presented with unpleasant or scary pictures. This was particularly pronounced in the insula, a region of the brain that has been associated both with perception of aversive experience and with drug cravings. These negative responses were almost eliminated by the treatment. Conversely, placebo treated subjects had all but absent brain responses to pleasant pictures, which otherwise typically activate brain reward circuitry. Remarkably, when treated with the NK1R blocker, the patients could once again respond to pleasant stimuli.

That brain responses to aversive stimuli were dampened by an anti-stress treatment was according to our hypothesis. But the ability of the anti-stress treatment to restore reward responses was an interesting surprise. It is typically thought that stress and reward are mediated through distinct systems. Based on our findings, it would appear that there is cross-talk between the two.

NK1R antagonists are now heading into full-scale outpatient treatment trials. As promising as the early data appear, one should remember that drug development is a high stakes game. Even having reached this stage, only about 10–20% of candidates succeed. With very few exceptions, medical progress is incremental. There is no single achievement one could say has cured childhood cancer. Yet when the outcomes of 20 years ago are compared with those of today, survival has improved dramatically. The same will happen with alcoholism, and we are only in the early days of improving outcomes.

Once the new treatments are developed, a key challenge remains. Alcoholism is a chronic relapsing disease, not unlike asthma, diabetes or hypertension. None of these conditions may be possible to cure, but they can all be successfully managed. Our ability to do so will improve as the range of therapeutics expands, and knowledge about mechanisms allows us to tailor treatment to the specific characteristics of the individual patient. But for all of this to succeed, the naïve notion that alcoholism can be cured in a 28-day rehab session has to give way to a realization that our brains undergo complex and long-lasting changes in addiction.

Markus Heilig is the Chief of the section of Molecular Pathophysiology at the National Institute on Alcohol Abuse and Alcoholism. His laboratory performs the basic science that is aimed at discovering novel molecular targets for treatment of alcoholism. Dr Hellig has authored more than 200 peer reviewed journal articles, including papers that have appeared in *Science, PNAS, Lancet, Archives of General Psychiatry*, and other high impact journals.

Rajita Sinha

 **NO**

How Does Stress Lead to Risk of Alcohol Relapse?

It has long been known that stress increases the risk of alcohol relapse (Sinha 2001). Clinical observations, surveys, and epidemiological studies document an association between self-reports of stressors and subsequent return to drinking. Studies assessing alcohol relapse after treatment completion and discharge also indicate the contribution of highly stressful events independent of alcohol use history that increase the risk of subsequent relapse (Brown et al. 1990). Furthermore, negative mood and stress are associated with increased craving, and high levels of urges to use alcohol predict relapse (Cooney et al. 2007). However, the mechanisms by which stress exposure increases alcohol relapse risk have been elusive, until recently. The last two decades have seen a dramatic increase in preclinical and clinical research to understand psychobiological and neural evidence linking stress and alcohol consumption. Evidence suggests that the neural circuits involved in stress and emotions overlap substantially with the brain systems involved in drug reward. Chronic alcohol use can result in neuroadaptive changes in stress and reward pathways. Such changes may alter an alcohol-dependent person's response to stress, particularly with respect to stress and emotion regulation and motivation for alcohol, which in turn may increase the risk of relapse (Sinha 2001, 2005).

To put the stress and alcohol relapse linkage in the clinical context, the sidebar presents sample descriptions of an acute stressful life event and an acute alcohol-related situation that led to subsequent alcohol use in a person with alcohol dependence. The patient vignettes are descriptions provided by patients currently in treatment and refer to previous experiences and episodes of alcohol use and relapse.

Chronic Alcohol-Related Changes in Emotion, Stress, and Motivational Systems

Converging lines of evidence indicate that regular and chronic alcohol use is associated with changes in emotion, stress, and motivational pathways. These changes may in turn influence alcohol craving and relapse risk. Chronic alcohol use increases stress-related symptoms and is associated with increased anxiety and negative emotions; changes in sleep and appetite; aggressive behaviors; changes in attention, concentration, and memory; and desire/craving for alcohol (Sinha 2001, 2007, 2009). Stress-related symptoms are most prominent during early abstinence from chronic alcohol use, but some of these changes also have been documented during active use of specific drugs. Chronic alcohol abuse and acute alcohol withdrawal states are associated with heightened activity in the brain stress systems, such as increased secretion of the stress hormones corticotropin-releasing factor (CRF), norepinephrine, and cortisol in a number of the brain's stress and emotion centers, such as the hypothalamus, amygdala, hippocampus, and prefrontal regions (Koob and Kreek 2007). Chronic alcohol abuse also alters dopaminergic signaling in the ventral striatum (VS) and the ventral tegmental area (VTA). And such changes are associated with increased alcohol seeking (craving) and alcohol self-administration in laboratory animals (Cleck and Blendy 2008; Koob and Kreek 2007; Koob et al. 2004; Rasmussen et al. 2006). Further corroboration from human neuroimaging studies indicates that chronic alcohol abuse reduces dopamine receptors (i.e., D2 receptors) in striatal regions and dopamine transmission in the frontal lobe in alcoholics during acute withdrawal and protracted withdrawal (up to 3–4 months) (see Volkow 2004 for review). Functional imaging studies indicate increased VS activity in response to alcohol cues and altered brain response in the amygdala to emotional stimuli with chronic alcohol use (Gilman and Hommer 2008; Heinz et al. 2004, 2005; Martinez et al. 2007).

The biological stress response is most commonly detected in humans by activation of the hypothalamic–pituitary–adrenal (HPA) axis involving CRF-stimulated release of adrenocorticotropin (ACTH) from the anterior pituitary, which in turn stimulates the adrenal glands to release the stress hormone cortisol, which is involved in mobilizing and regulating the body's stress response.

Rajita Sinha, "How does stress lead to risk of alcohol relapse?", from *Alcohol Research: Current Reviews,* Volume 34, Issue Number 4 (2012).

The second pathway involved in the biological stress response is the autonomic nervous system, comprising the sympathetic and the parasympathetic components. The sympathetic component mobilizes arousal by increasing heart rate and blood pressure; the parasympathetic component enforces the "brakes" for sympathetic arousal and functions to decrease and regulate autonomic function. Alcohol use stimulates the HPA axis and initially stimulates the autonomic systems by provoking sympathetic arousal, followed by depressing such activation (Ehrenreich et al. 1997; Lee and Rivier 1997). Reductions in this alcohol-related HPA axis response (similar to tolerance) has been demonstrated with regular and chronic alcohol abuse in animals (Lee and Rivier 1997; Richardson et al. 2008; Zhou et al. 2000) and in humans (Adinoff et al. 1998, 2005; Wand and Dobs 1991).

Likewise, chronic alcohol abuse increases physiological arousal as measured by heart rate but also decreases heart rate variability, which serves as a measure of parasympathetic function (Ingjaldsson et al. 2003; Rechlin et al. 1996; Shively et al. 2007; Thayer and Sternberg 2006). These data represent alcohol-induced changes in peripheral stress pathways, which parallel basic science findings of alcohol-related adaptations in central stress systems, namely the extrahypothalamic CRF and the noradrenergic pathways that are indicative of hyperresponsive brain stress pathways noted in the previous paragraph (Cleck and Blendy 2008; Koob and Kreek 2007; Koob 2009; Rasmussen et al. 2006). These neurochemical changes indicate specific dysregulation in the neurochemical systems that play a role in emotion, stress, and motivation functions in alcoholics. Such changes raise the question of whether these measures contribute to the high levels of emotional distress, alcohol craving, and compulsive alcohol seeking that may lead to increased relapse susceptibility.

Effects of Stress on Alcohol Craving and Arousal

Drug craving or "wanting" for drug is a hallmark feature of addiction. It is an important component in maintaining addictive behaviors (Dackis and Gold 1985; O'Brien et al. 1998; Robinson and Berridge 1993, 2000; Tiffany 1990). Chronic alcohol use leads to changes in the brain reward and motivation pathways that can increase alcohol craving in the context of alcohol and alcohol-related stimuli, but also in the context of stress. In support of these ideas, a growing literature indicates that people with alcohol abuse show greater alcohol craving than social drinkers (Glautier et al. 1992; Greeley et al. 1993; Kaplan et al. 1985; Pomerleau et al. 1983; Willner et al. 1998). Furthermore, severity of alcohol use has been shown

to affect the magnitude of cue-related physiological arousal, compulsive alcohol seeking, and stress-related changes, including alcohol-related morbidity (Fox et al. 2005; Grusser et al. 2006, 2007; Rosenberg and Mazzola 2007; Sinha 2008; Yoon et al. 2006). These data are consistent with large population-based studies indicating that the risk of alcohol-related problems, addiction, and chronic diseases increases with greater weekly or daily alcohol and drug use (Dawson et al. 2005; Rehm et al. 2009; Room et al. 2005). Given these responses, the author's research examined whether increases in craving are associated with altered stress responses that occur with chronic alcohol use.

In the clinical context, alcoholic patients entering outpatient substance abuse treatment report high levels of stress and an inability to manage distress adaptively, thereby increasing the risk of succumbing to high levels of drug craving and relapse to drug use (Sinha 2007). Although patients often are successful in learning cognitive– behavioral strategies in treatment, relapse rates remain high (Brandon et al. 2007; Sinha 2011). These data suggest possible difficulties in applying and accessing cognitive–behavioral strategies in real-world relapse situations. Thus, to understand the biobehavioral mechanisms underlying the high stress and craving state during early recovery, the author began to study this phenomenon in the laboratory, using an ecologically relevant method that models such relapse risk. This research used two of the most common relapse situations—emotionally stressful situations and alcohol-/drug-related situations—in order to develop a comparable method of provoking stress and the drug-related craving state, and these are compared to a relaxing situation that serves as an experimental control condition to account for the nonspecific aspects of the experimental procedures (Sinha 2009). . . .

Patient Vignettes

These patient descriptions illustrate several points about stress and motivation for alcohol use that are relevant from a clinical perspective. The first vignette is an example of an interpersonal stress situation that is a typical precipitant of relapse. Although patients are less likely to divulge specific details of craving situations in a clinical context, the second vignette illustrates that alcohol cues and increased craving states also promote anxiety and stress-related arousal in people who are alcohol dependent. These clinical situations raise many questions about the role of stress in drug seeking and relapse susceptibility. One such question is whether stress and alcohol cues provoke similar drug craving states that may be targeted in treatment. Additional research questions are whether the response to stress and alcohol-related stimuli differs for alcohol-dependent and non–alcohol-dependent people and whether stress responses and managing stress is altered as a function of chronic alcohol use. These vignettes provide anecdotal evidence; research is needed to address the question of whether craving and stress-related arousal are predictive of relapse outcomes and whether stress causes relapse. Finally, if stress plays an important role in both stress- and cue-related relapse, research is needed to identify the most beneficial types of interventions and how clinicians might use the stress and craving responses to better address the treatment needs of alcohol-dependent individuals in early recovery. The main article addresses each of these questions to elucidate how stress increases the risk of alcohol relapse.

Stressful Situation

This situation was rated as a 10 on a 10-point scale of "0 = not at all stressful," to "10 = highly stressful—most you've felt recently" and was narrated by an alcohol-dependent male patient who had been in recovery for 5 weeks. The patient is describing a stressful event that previously led to a relapse episode and an alcohol-related context that led to alcohol use.

> "I remember it was about 4:00 pm in the afternoon when Kay woke me up. Her face was red—she looked really upset. She was holding the phone in her hand. She was screaming that I have to call home. I felt tight all over. My heart was pounding. I rolled out of bed. My heart was beating faster. She wants me to call my Dad and tell him about the accident. I did not want to call him yet. She kept following me around the apartment. I tensed up the muscles all over my body. She is badgering me to call. Wherever I go, she was behind me with the phone. I clenched my jaw. I don't want to face this now, I was thinking. Just call them now and get it over with, she kept saying. My heart was racing. Suddenly, she dialed the number and throws the phone at me while it is ringing. I am gritting my teeth. I put the phone to my ear. My dad answers the phone.
>
> I hear his voice. My stomach is in a knot. I start to have a normal conversation. My fists are clenched. I am thinking, 'How am I going to tell him about the car accident last night?' I feel jittery and panicky all over. I am pacing back and forth. Casually I say I had a car accident last night.

I feel hot all over. He starts screaming, 'That's it! Pack your bags! You're coming home!' There are butterflies in my stomach. I see Kay burst into tears. I am breathing faster, gasping for air. She is listening to everything he is saying. 'What the hell will I tell your mother? I told her you'd be safe. Now I put myself on the line' he is shouting. My head is pounding. Kay is crying, and I can't do anything about it. I feel stuck. My heart is pounding. My father says he can't talk anymore now and hangs up the phone. I was so mad, I wanted to smash something. I slam down the phone. I did not want to call him. I knew he would be upset. There is a sinking feeling in my chest. If I could fix it, make it all better, I would. I see Kay crying. I get choked up. I had promised her this would not happen. I feel so mad at myself I want to scream. Now I've betrayed her and my Dad."

Alcohol-Related Situation

"It was a bright and sunny summer morning in June. M was gone for the day, and I had the whole day off. I am out working in the yard. It was a warm day and I start to feel hot. I sit down for a break. I've done my chores. I've paid the bills and vacuumed out the pool. I breathe in deeply. My eyes glance around the yard. I've got all the yard work done as well. It looks nice. Now I have half a day left. My heart quickens. I am thinking, 'is there anything else left to do'. I can't think of anything else. I feel warm all over. I sit back and try to relax. Now I start feeling very hot. I feel very thirsty. It would be great to have a nice cold beer, I think. I tighten the muscles of my face and forehead. I've worked hard, I deserve one, you think. I feel a rush of excitement inside you. I walk inside and head toward the refrigerator. My heart is beating faster. I promised M I won't drink. My jaws are tight. The thoughts start racing through my head– "She doesn't need to know." "She won't be home for another four hours." "She won't be able to smell it on my breath by then." My hands feel clammy. I open the fridge and grab an ice cold can of beer. My mouth starts to water. Holding that cold can of beer starts to cool down my whole body. I feel a tingling sensation inside me. I start to think— I shouldn't be drinking this. My stomach is in a knot. I look down at it—it's right here in my hand, and I deserve it. I wet my lips. Before I know it, I have cracked it open. I see the condensation vapor fly into the air. I can almost taste it now. I am holding on to the can tightly. I raise the can to my lips. I let the beer flow into my mouth and down my throat. It is so cold that it makes my teeth ache. It goes down quickly. I feel a sense of being more alive. Now I have a taste for it. I can't wait to have another one."

Stress Dysregulation and Enhanced Drug Craving in Addicted Individuals

As discussed in the previous section, alcohol-dependent individuals in early recovery show increased stress and alcohol cue–induced craving responses. In a study comparing 4-week abstinent alcoholics with matched social drinkers (drinking less than 25 drinks per month), Sinha and colleagues (2009) found that the recovering alcoholics showed greater levels of basal heart rate and salivary cortisol levels compared with the control drinkers. Upon stress and alcohol cue exposure, they showed greater subjective distress, alcohol craving, and blood pressure responses but blunted stress-induced heart rate and cortisol responses compared with control subjects (Sinha et al. 2009). Furthermore, after exposure to stress imagery, alcoholic patients showed a persistent increase in alcohol craving, subjective distress, and blood pressure responses across multiple time points compared with social drinkers, suggesting an inability to regulate this high alcohol craving and emotional stress state. These data indicate greater allostatic load in abstinent alcoholics, which is accompanied by dysregulated stress responses and high levels of craving or compulsive seeking for the preferred drug.

Together, these data indicate altered stress responses in alcoholics, and these alterations also include an enhanced susceptibility to stress and cue-induced alcohol seeking, which is not seen in healthy nonaddicted individuals. In addition, there are basal alterations in peripheral markers of stress (i.e., stress hormones, such as ACTH and cortisol and in heart rate), indicative of stress-related dysregulation in the CRF–HPA axis and in autonomic responses as measured by basal salivary cortisol and heart rate responses. These high basal responses are associated with lower or blunted stress-related arousal (Sinha et al. 2009). It is important to note that these alterations cannot be accounted for by smoking status or lifetime history of anxiety or mood disorders and therefore seem to be related to history of chronic alcohol abuse. The persistence of emotional distress and alcohol craving induced by stress and alcohol cue exposure suggests a dysfunction in emotion regulatory mechanisms. As HPA axis responses and autonomic–parasympathetic responses contribute to regulating and normalizing stress responses and regaining homeostasis, dysfunction in these pathways

and their related central mechanisms may be involved in perpetuating alcohol craving and relapse susceptibility. . . .

Clinical Implications and Conclusion

The previous sections cite evidence from clinical, laboratory, and neuroimaging studies to examine whether stress increases the risk of relapse. Psychobiological and neuroimaging research points to alcohol-related changes in brain volume and function and in biological stress responses. These alterations were found to contribute to higher craving and increased alcohol relapse risk. For example, early abstinence from alcohol is associated with higher levels of anxiety when relaxed and when exposed to alcohol cues, greater emotional distress, and increased stress- and alcohol cue-induced craving. These states are accompanied by disruption in normal functioning of the peripheral stress pathways, including the HPA axis and the autonomic components, which are involved in mobilizing the body for action during stress but also in physiological regulation of the stress response. A lack of normal stress regulation during this early abstinence period leaves the recovering alcoholic highly vulnerable to high craving, anxiety, and risk of relapse, particularly under stressful conditions and when faced with alcohol-related stimuli in the environment. The findings discussed indicate that stress- and cue-induced alcohol craving increase the risk of subsequent relapse. High levels of stress- and cue-induced anxiety are associated with less follow-up in aftercare during the recovery period. Furthermore, disrupted functioning of the HPA axis, particularly in people who have hyperresponsive cortisol release from the adrenal cortex in response to the ACTH signal (cortisol-to-ACTH ratio as a measure of adrenal sensitivity) in the neutral relaxed state, increased the risk of alcohol relapse 2.5 times more than those with lower cortisol release from the adrenal cortex. Finally, changes in volume and function of the brain regions involved in impulse control and emotion regulation also are predictive of alcohol relapse outcomes. Each of these measures could be further developed as biomarkers of alcohol relapse risk (see Sinha 2011). If validated in future studies, they may be used clinically to identify people at high risk of relapse. In addition, the findings reviewed also indicate that stress-related pathophysiology is important in the alcohol relapse process. Thus, individuals who show chronic alcohol-related effects on neural, biological, and psychological aspects of stress and craving could benefit from treatments that target stress effects on craving and alcohol seeking. Several novel medications that target the stress pathways, such as agents that block CRF, as well as noradrenergic and GABAergic agents, are being tested to assess their efficacy in stress-related relapse (Breese et al. 2011; Sinha et al. 2011a). Development of such treatment strategies may be of tremendous help in normalizing stress responses and decreasing alcohol craving so as to improve relapse outcomes in alcoholism.

Acknowledgments

Preparation of this review was supported by grants R01–AA–13892, UL1–DE019856, and PL1–DA024859 from the National Institutes of Health. Dr. Sinha also is on the scientific advisory board for Embera NeuroTherapeutics.

Financial Disclosure

The author declares that she has no competing financial interests.

References

Adinoff, B.; Iranmanesh, A.; Veldhuis, J.; and Fisher, L. Disturbances of the stress response: The role of the HPA axis during alcohol withdrawal and abstinence. *Alcohol Health and Research World* 22(1): 67–72, 1998. PMID: 15706736

Adinoff, B.; Junghanns, K.; Kiefer, F.; and Krishnan-Sarin, S. Suppression of the HPA axis stress-response: Implications for relapse. *Alcoholism: Clinical and Experimental Research* 29(7):1351–1355, 2005. PMID: 16088999

Brandon, T.H.; Vidrine, J.I.; and Litvin, E.B. Relapse and relapse prevention. *Annual Review of Clinical Psychology* 3:257–284, 2007. PMID: 17716056

Breese, G.R.; Sinha, R.; and Heilig, M. Chronic alcohol neuroadaptation and stress contribute to susceptibility for alcohol craving and relapse. *Pharmacology & Therapeutics* 129(2):149–171, 2011. PMID: 20951730

Brown, S.A.; Vik, P.W.; McQuaid, J.R.; et al. Severity of psychosocial stress and outcome of alcoholism treatment. *Journal of Abnormal Psychology* 99(4): 344–348, 1990. PMID: 2266207

Carter, B.L., and Tiffany, S.T. Meta-analysis of cue-reactivity in addiction research. *Addiction* 94(3):327–340, 1999. PMID: 10605857

Chaplin, T.M.; Hong, K.; Bergquist, K.; and Sinha, R. Gender differences in response to emotional stress: An assessment across subjective, behavioral, and physiological domains and relations to alcohol craving. *Alcoholism: Clinical and Experimental Research* 32(7):1242–1250, 2008. PMID: 18482163

Cleck, J.N., and Blendy, J.A. Making a bad thing worse: Adverse effects of stress on drug addiction. *Journal of Clinical Investigation* 118(2):454–461, 2008. PMID: 18246196

Cooney, N.L.; Litt, M.D.; Cooney, J.L.; et al. Alcohol and tobacco cessation in alcohol-dependent smokers: Analysis of real-time reports. *Psychology of Addictive Behaviors* 21(3):277–286, 2007. PMID: 17874878

Dackis, C.A., and Gold, M.S. New concepts in cocaine addiction: The dopamine depletion hypothesis. *Neuroscience and Biobehavioral Reviews* 9(3):469–477, 1985. PMID: 2999657

Dawson, D.A.; Grant, B.F.; Stinson, F.S.; and Chou, P.S. Psychopathology associated with drinking and alcohol use disorders in the college and general adult populations. *Drug and Alcohol Dependence* 77(2):139–150, 2005. PMID: 15664715

Ehrenreich, H.; Schuck, J.; Stender, N.; et al. Endocrine and hemodynamic effects of stress versus systemic CRF in alcoholics during early and medium term abstinence. *Alcoholism: Clinical and Experimental Research* 21(7):1285–1293, 1997. PMID: 9347091

Fox, H.C.; Talih, M.; Malison, R.; et al. Frequency of recent cocaine and alcohol use affects drug craving and associated responses to stress and drug-related cues. *Psychoneuroendocrinology* 30(9):880–891, 2005. PMID: 15975729

Gilman, J.M., and Hommer, D.W. Modulation of brain response to emotional images by alcohol cues in alcohol-dependent patients. *Addiction Biology* 13(3–4): 423–434, 2008. PMID: 18507736

Glautier, S.; Drummond, D.C.; and Remington, B. Different drink cues elicit different physiological responses in non-dependent drinkers. Psychopharmacology (Berlin) 106(4):550–554, 1992. PMID: 1579627

Goeders, N.E. The HPA axis and cocaine reinforcement. *Psychoneuroendocrinology* 27(1-2):13–33, 2002. PMID: 11750768

Greeley, J.D.; Swift, W.; Prescott, J.; and Heather, N. Reactivity to alcohol-related cues in heavy and light drinkers. *Journal of Studies on Alcohol* 54(3):359–368, 1993. PMID: 8487545

Grusser, S.M.; Morsen, C.P.; and Flor, H. Alcohol craving in problem and occasional alcohol drinkers. *Alcohol and Alcoholism* 41:421–425, 2006. PMID: 15127179

Grusser, S.M.; Morsen, C.P.; Wolfling, K.; and Flor, H. The relationship of stress, coping, effect expectancies and craving. *European Addiction Research* 13(1):31–38, 2007. PMID: 17172777

Heinz, A.; Siessmeier, T.; Wrase, J.; et al. Correlation of alcohol craving with striatal dopamine synthesis capacity and D2/3 receptor availability: A combined [18F]DOPA and [18F]DMFP PET study in detoxified alcoholic patients. *American Journal of Psychiatry* 162(8):1515–1520, 2005. PMID: 16055774

Heinz, A.; Siessmeier, T.; Wrase, J.; et al. Correlation between dopamine D(2) receptors in the ventral striatum and central processing of alcohol cues and craving. *American Journal of Psychiatry* 161(10):1783–1789, 2004. PMID: 15465974

Ingjaldsson, J.T.; Laberg, J.C.; and Thayer, J.F. Reduced heart rate variability in chronic alcohol abuse: Relationship with negative mood, chronic thought suppression, and compulsive drinking. *Biological Psychiatry* 54(12):1427–1436, 2003. PMID: 14675808

Kaplan, R.F.; Cooney, N.L.; Baker, L.H.; et al. Reactivity to alcohol-related cues: Physiological and subjective responses in alcoholics and nonproblem drinkers. *Journal of Studies on Alcohol* 46(4):267–272, 1985. PMID: 4033125

Koob, G., and Kreek, M.J. Stress, dysregulation of drug reward pathways, and the transition to drug dependence. *American Journal of Psychiatry* 164(8):1149–1159, 2007. PMID: 17671276

Koob, G.F. Dynamics of neuronal circuits in addiction: Reward, antireward, and emotional memory. *Pharmacopsychiatry* 42(Suppl. 1): S32–S41, 2009. PMID: 19434554

Koob, G.F.; Ahmed, S.H.; Boutrel, B.; et al. Neurobiological mechanisms in the transition from drug use to drug dependence. *Neuroscience and Biobehavioral Reviews* 27(8):739–749, 2004. PMID: 15019424

Lee, S., and Rivier, C. An initial, three-day-long treatment with alcohol induces a long-lasting phenomenon of selective tolerance in the activity of the rat hypothalamic-pituitary-adrenal axis. *Journal of Neuroscience* 17(22):8856–8866, 1997. PMID: 9348353

Litt, M.D., and Cooney, N.L. Inducing craving for alcohol in the laboratory. *Alcohol Research & Health* 23(3):174–178, 1999. PMID: 10890812

Martinez, D.; Kim, J.H.; Krystal, J.; and Abi-Dargham, A. Imaging the neurochemistry of alcohol and substance abuse. *Neuroimaging Clinics of North America* 17(4):539–555, 2007. PMID: 17983969

O'Brien, C.P. Anticraving medications for relapse prevention: A possible new class of psychoactive medications. *American Journal of Psychiatry* 162(8):1423–1431, 2005. PMID: 16055763

O'Brien, C.P.; Childress, A.R.; Ehrman, R.; and Robbins, S.J. Conditioning factors in drug abuse: Can they explain compulsion? *Journal of Psychopharmacology* 12(1): 15–22, 1998. PMID: 9584964

Pfefferbaum, A.; Sullivan, E.V.; Rosenbloom, M.J.; et al. A controlled study of cortical gray matter and ventricular changes in alcoholic men over a 5-year interval. *Archives of General Psychiatry* 55(10): 905–912, 1998. PMID: 9783561

Pomerleau, O.F.; Fertig, J.; Baker, L.; and Cooney, N. Reactivity to alcohol cues in alcoholics and non-alcoholics: Implications for a stimulus control analysis of drinking. *Addictive Behaviors* 8(1):1–10, 1983. PMID: 6880920

Rasmussen, D.D.; Wilkinson, C.W.; and Raskind, M.A. Chronic daily ethanol and withdrawal: 6. Effects on rat sympathoadrenal activity during "abstinence". *Alcohol* 38(3):173-177, 2006. PMID: 16905443

Rechlin, T.; Orbes, I.; Weis, M.; and Kaschka, W.P. Autonomic cardiac abnormalities in alcohol-dependent patients admitted to a psychiatric department. *Clinical Autonomic Research* 6(2): 119–122, 1996. PMID: 8726098

Rehm, J.; Mathers, C.; and Popova, S.; et al. Global burden of disease and injury and economic cost attributable to alcohol use and alcohol-use disorders. *Lancet* 373(9682):2223–2233, 2009. PMID: 19560604

Richardson, H.N.; Lee, S.Y.; O'Dell, L.E.; et al. Alcohol self-administration acutely stimulates the hypothalamic-pituitary-adrenal axis, but alcohol dependence leads to a dampened neuroendocrine state. *European Journal of Neuroscience* 28(8): 1641–1653, 2008. PMID: 18979677

Robinson, T.E., and Berridge, K.C. The neural basis of drug craving: An incentive-sensitization theory of addiction. Brain Research. *Brain Research Reviews* 18(3):247– 291, 1993. PMID: 8401595

Robinson, T.E., and Berridge, K.C. The psychology and neurobiology of addiction: An incentive-sensitization view. *Addiction* 95(Suppl. 2):S91–S117, 2000. PMID: 11002906

Room, R.; Babor, T.; and Rehm, J. Alcohol and public health. *Lancet* 365(9458):519–530, 2005. PMID: 15705462

Rosenberg, H., and Mazzola, J. Relationships among self-report assessments of craving in binge-drinking university students. *Addictive Behaviors* 32(12):2811–2818, 2007. PMID: 17524566

Shively, C.A.; Mietus, J.E.; Grant, K.A.; et al. Effects of chronic moderate alcohol consumption and novel environment on heart rate variability in primates (Macaca fascicularis). *Psychopharmacology (Berlin)* 192(2): 183–191, 2007. PMID: 17297637

Sinha, R. How does stress increase risk of drug abuse and relapse? *Psychopharmacology (Berlin)* 158(4):343–359, 2001. PMID: 11797055

Sinha, R. The role of stress in addiction relapse. *Current Psychiatry Reports* 9(5):388–395, 2007. PMID: 17915078

Sinha, R. Chronic stress, drug use, and vulnerability to addiction. *Annals of the New York Academy of Sciences* 1141:105–130, 2008. PMID: 18991954

Sinha, R.; Lacadie, C.; Skudlarski, P.; et al. Neural activity associated with stress-induced cocaine craving: A functional magnetic resonance imaging study. *Psychopharmacology (Berlin)* 183(2): 171–180, 2005. PMID: 16163517

Sinha, R.; Fox, H.C.; Hong, K.A.; et al. Enhanced negative emotion and alcohol craving, and altered physiological responses following stress and cue exposure in alcohol dependent individuals. *Neuropsychopharmacology* 34(5):1198–1208, 2009. PMID: 18563062

Sinha, R.; Shaham, Y.; and Heilig, M. Translational and reverse translational research on the role of stress in drug craving and relapse. *Psychopharmacology (Berlin)* 218(1):69-82, 2011a. PMID: 21494792

Sinha, R. New findings on biological factors predicting addiction relapse vulnerability. *Current Psychiatry Reports* 12(5):398-405, 2011. PMID: 21792580

Sinha, R. Modeling stress and drug craving in the laboratory: Implications for addiction treatment development. *Addiction Biology* 14(1):84–98, 2009. PMID: 18945295

Thayer, J.F., and Sternberg, E. Beyond heart rate variability: Vagal regulation of allostatic systems. *Annals of the New York Academy of Sciences* 1088:361–372, 2006. PMID: 17192580

Tiffany, S.T. A cognitive model of drug urges and drug-use behavior: Role of automatic and nonautomatic processes. *Psychological Review* 97(2):147–168, 1990. PMID: 2186423

Volkow, N.D. Imaging the addicted brain: From molecules to behavior. *Journal of Nuclear Medicine* 45(11):13N–22N, 2004. PMID: 15584131

Walker, B.M.; Rasmussen, D.D.; Raskind, M.A.; and Koob, G.F. alpha1-noradrenergic receptor antagonism blocks dependence-induced increases in responding for ethanol. *Alcohol* 42(2):91–97, 2008. PMID: 18358987

Wand, G.S., and Dobs, A.S. Alterations in the hypothalamic-pituitary-adrenal axis in actively drinking alcoholics. *Journal of Clincal Endocrinology and Metabolism* 72(6):1290–1295, 1991. PMID: 2026749

Weiss, F. Neurobiology of craving, conditioned reward and relapse. *Current Opinion in Pharmacology* 5(1):9–19, 2005. PMID: 15661620

Willner, P.; Field, M.; Pitts, K.; and Reeve, G. Mood, cue and gender influences on motivation, craving, and liking for alcohol in recreational drinkers. *Behavioural Pharmacology* 9(7):631–642, 1998. PMID: 9862088

Yoon, G.; Kim, S.W.; Thuras, P. et al. Alcohol craving in outpatients with alcohol dependence: Rate and clinical correlates. *Journal of Studies on Alcohol* 67(5):770– 777, 2006. PMID: 16847547

Zhou, Y.; Franck, J.; Spangler, R. et al. Reduced hypothalamic POMC and anterior pituitary CRF1 receptor mRNA levels after acute, but not chronic, daily "binge" intragastric alcohol administration. *Alcoholism: Clinical and Experimental Research* 24(10):1575–1582, 2000.

RAJITA SINHA is Foundations Fund Professor of Psychiatry and Professor in the Child Study Center and of Neurobiology at Yale University. Dr. Sinha is internationally known for her pioneering research on the mechanisms linking stress and emotions to addictive behaviors and health outcomes. Her research has been supported by the National Institutes of Health.

EXPLORING THE ISSUE

Is Alcoholism Hereditary?

Critical Thinking and Reflection

1. To what degree is alcoholism a genetic disease? Is there an "alcoholism gene"?
2. How might someone use information that they have a genetic predisposition toward alcoholism (e.g., they have genes associated with higher rates of alcoholism)?
3. If there is a genetic contribution to alcoholism, how should that knowledge change our society's view of alcohol availability and use? For example, should we have more or fewer legal prohibitions against alcohol use?
4. How might genes influence human personality and motivation? What are the possible limits of genetics in these traits that are central to "who we are"?

Is There Common Ground?

Is there a significant, substantiated relationship between heredity and alcoholism? The National Institute on Alcohol Abuse and Alcoholism (NIAAA) notes that numerous studies demonstrate a high probability of biological vulnerability to alcohol addiction. The NIAAA claims that there are differences in the brains of alcoholics compared to others. Critics agree that alcoholism runs in families, but they argue that there are critical environmental and psychological risk factors for alcoholism that cannot be overlooked. In the final analysis, this issue comes down to which research one chooses to accept.

Some experts have expressed concern for certain people who feel that alcoholism is a family legacy. An individual who believes that he or she is destined to become an alcoholic because his or her mother, father, aunt uncle, or grandparent has suffered from alcoholism may become alcoholic to satisfy a self-fulfilling prophecy. Some psychologists believe this may have lamentable consequences for such individuals who feel that alcoholism is their destiny anyway. Although it is true that alcoholism tends to run in families, most children of alcoholics do not become alcoholics. A person whose parent or parents were alcoholic should be more wary of the possibility of becoming an alcoholic, but becoming an alcoholic is not a foregone conclusion for children of alcoholics.

Whether or not alcoholism is genetic or environmental has serious implications. For example, if a genetic predisposition to alcoholism was conclusively proven, then medical therapies could be designed to help those who had the hereditary risk. Second, if a person was diagnosed as having a genetic predisposition, then he or she could adopt behaviors that would help avoid problem drinking. That is, they would become aware of the hereditary factor and adjust their attitudes and actions accordingly. If alcoholism is environmental, then one's environment could be altered to influence drinking behavior.

Because of the lack of conclusive evidence identifying heredity as the primary cause for alcoholism, it may be wise to err on the side of caution with regard to consigning children of alcoholics to a fate of alcoholism. On the other hand, research that consistently finds higher rates of alcoholism and alcohol abuse among children of alcoholics cannot be dismissed. This link alone provides ample support for additional funding of research studies that may delineate the exact nature of and risk factors of alcoholism. Still, efforts against the perils of alcoholism via progressive alcohol prevention and education programs to meet the needs of children of alcoholics as well as the general public need to be strengthened.

Additional Resources

Krishnan, H. R. et al. (2014). The epigenetic landscape of alcoholism. *International Review of Neurobiology*. 115: 75–116.

This paper summarizes recent developments in epigenetic research that may play a role in alcoholism. The authors report that epigenetic mechanisms (i.e., environmental factors that turn genes "on" or "off" and affect how cells read genes) that regulate changes in gene expression observed in alcohol use disorders respond to alcohol exposure and to the presence of other pathologies, such as depression and anxiety.

Littlefield, A. K. et al. (2011). Does variance in drinking motives explain the genetic overlap between personality and alcohol use disorder symptoms? A twin study of young women. *Alcoholism: Clinical & Experimental Research*. 35(12): 2242–2250.

This is a research report on how the relationship between personality and alcohol use disorder can be explained by genetic factors.

Mac Killop, J. & Munafo, M. R. (2013). *Genetic Influences on Addiction: An Intermediate Phenotype Approach*. Cambridge, MA: The MIT Press.

The authors of this edited volume explain potential biological mechanisms for a genetic contribution to alcoholism and how the genetics might influence the development and maintenance of alcoholism.

Von Stieff, F. (2012). Brain in Balance: Understanding the Genetics and Neurochemistry Behind Addiction and Sobriety. CreateSpace Independent Publishing Platform.

Dr. Von Stieff explains how the nervous system influences personality and behavior, including the psychological factors that may contribute to alcohol use and alcoholism.

Zajdow, G. (2002). *AL-ANON NARRATIVES Women, Self-Stories, and Mutual Aid*. Santa Barbara, CA: Praeger.

Grazyna Zajdow presents narratives of women married to men with alcoholism. Dr. Zajdow details and explores the lives women who belong to Al-Anon, where they may share their experiences and offer their stories in a nonthreatening and supportive environment.

Internet References . . .

Al-Anon Family Support Groups

http://www.al-anon.alateen.org/

Alcohol Answers

http://www.alcoholanswers.org/

National Council on Alcoholism and Drug Dependence, Inc.—Family History and Genetics

https://ncadd.org/for-parents-overview/family-history -and-genetics/226-family-history-and-genetics

National Institutes of Health—National Institute on Alcohol Abuse and Alcoholism

http://www.niaaa.nih.gov/

University of Utah—Learn Genetics

http://learn.genetics.utah.edu/

Selected, Edited, and with Issue Framing Material by:
Dennis K. Miller, *University of Missouri*

ISSUE

Can One Become Addicted to the Internet and Social Media?

YES: Elias Aboujaoude, from "Problematic Internet Use: An Overview", *World Psychiatry* (2010)

NO: Antonius J. Van Rooij and Nicole Prause, from "A Critical Review of "Internet Addiction" Criteria with Suggestions for the Future," *Journal of Behavioral Addictions* (2014)

Learning Outcomes

After reading this issue, you will be able to:

- Define drug addiction and understand how clinicians and scientists view it.
- Understand problems in defining behavioral addictions.
- Describe the factors that might make explain the popularity of social media and recreational Internet use.
- Critically assess the validity of a diagnosis of Internet addiction.
- Compare the symptoms and causes of drug addiction to those of Internet addiction.

ISSUE SUMMARY

YES: Internet access provides opportunities to learn and connect to others; however, excessive Internet use can become almost compulsive with feelings of dysphoria when one is offline. Can someone be "addicted" to the Internet as they might be addicted to drugs? Elias Aboujaoude describes behavioral addictions and the clinical scales that are used to assess Internet addiction.

NO: Antonius J. Van Rooij and Nicole Prause critically review addiction models and the limited research on Internet addiction. Their assessment is that there is not yet sufficient evidence to support an Internet addiction disorder, similar to that observed with drugs.

"**I** even slept with my phone by my side. It was what I fell asleep watching, and it was the alarm that woke me up. It was never turned off. I'm certain I texted while driving, in dark movie theaters, and out with friends around restaurant tables. It got so bad that I grew uncomfortable with any 30-second span of hands-free idleness. I felt obligated to reply to every Facebook comment, text, tweet and game request," wrote freelance writer Jenna Woginrich in *The Guardian*. Facebook, Twitter, and WeChat are filled with stories like Woginrich's.

Can someone become addicted to the Internet, their smartphone or social media like someone can become addicted to nicotine, alcohol or cocaine?

The National Institute of Drug Abuse (NIDA) views *drug* addiction as a chronic, relapsing disease consisting of compulsive drug seeking and use, despite harmful consequences. NIDA considers addiction to be a disease of the brain because drugs change the brain's structure and how it works.

Drug addiction begins with initial experiences, most often as a teenager or young adult. Drugs make people feel good, producing experiences of euphoria, self-confidence, satisfaction and/or relaxation. When we feel bad—stressed, anxious, depressed, or nervous—drugs allow us to feel better. Drugs can help us do better in our work, at school, or on the sports field. Drugs are used out of curiosity, to fit in with our peers or to model what we see in popular culture.

Regardless of the reason why drugs are initially used, with repeated drug exposure behavior and the brain change for many people. What was once pleasurable is no long pleasurable. Drugs might be used not to feel "high," but to just feel "normal" again. Drug use might escalate where larger-and-larger doses are used more-and-more frequently. The user may compulsively seek and take the drug, despite negative consequences, such as problems at school, at home, or with the law.

As mentioned, NIDA considers the development of drug addiction to be a disease of the brain where neural circuits for learning and memory, stress management, and pleasure and reward adapt to the acute and chronic presence of the drug. Brain imaging studies can clearly show differences in neural pathways and regions between those who are addicted to a drug and those who are not addicted. The interaction of genes and the environment can play an important role in these neural adaptations. No one factor determines whether a person will become addicted to drugs; however, risk factors such as genetics, socioeconomic status, culture, and developmental stage can increase the chance that taking drugs will lead to abuse and addiction.

Many psychologists and psychiatrists believe *behavioral* addictions can develop as well. The current edition of the *Diagnostic and Statistical Manual of Mental Disorders* (DSM-5), the primary guidebook used by clinicians to diagnose psychiatric illnesses, includes Gambling Disorder. Some symptoms of Gambling Disorder are being preoccupied with gambling, needing to gamble with increased amounts of money, having unsuccessful attempts to cut back or stop gambling, gambling when feeling stressed, and feeling anxious when unable to gamble. (Note that these symptoms must be severe enough to produce a clinically significant impairment or distress. Gambling Disorder is not losing a few extra dollars at the gaming tables on a boys' or girls' weekend in Las Vegas.) The symptoms of Gambling Disorder are similar, but not identical, to those of Substance Use Disorder, the diagnosis for drug addiction in the DSM-5. Substance Use Disorder symptoms include being preoccupied with procuring and using drugs, increasing the amount of drug consumed, having unsuccessful attempts to cut back or stop drug use, and feeling bad when the drug cannot be used.

The DSM-5 does not include other behavioral addictions—food, physical exercise, shopping, sexual intercourse, or the Internet, and social media. Subsequent revisions of the Manual may include these, although their potential inclusion is controversial.

- How prevalent or common is a behavioral addiction? For example, where does normal craving for food, experienced by all animals, become pathological?
- What is the empirical evidence for the behavioral addiction? For example, although there has been research on exercise addiction, valid and reliable diagnostic criteria have not been accepted by scientists and clinicians.
- Is it truly an addiction or is it only justification for immoral behavior? For example, the term "sex addiction" has been used by some to justify sexual infidelity.

From a neural perspective can behavioral addictions develop? As noted, NIDA considers drug addiction to be a disease of the brain. Many biological models of drug addiction focus on the mesolimbic dopamine pathway, a set of neurons from the ventral tegmental area in the back of the brain to the nucleus accumbens (NAc) in the front. Most drugs of abuse (e.g., cocaine, heroin and nicotine) change the activity of these neurons. For example, a dose of cocaine that produces a psychological "high" induces a rapid and profound increase extracellular dopamine levels in the NAc. With repeated drug administration these neural circuits change and become sensitized to the drug. In some drug addiction models (e.g., Terry Robinson and Kent Berridge's incentive-sensitization model), it is this change in dopamine activity that underlies the development of drug craving.

Beyond drug addiction, the mesolimbic dopamine pathway plays an important role in learning about rewarding and reinforcing stimuli. Both stimuli are salient—that is they are easily noticed. Rewarding stimuli are ones that are perceived as positive, desirable, and to be approached. Reinforcing stimuli are those that increase the probability of a behavior associated with the stimuli. For example, when a hungry rat in an operant box (a.k.a. "Skinner box") presses a lever, it receives a sweet treat. The treat is a salient, rewarding, and reinforcing stimulus, and the probability that the rat will press the lever again increases. The probability of the behavior occurring again increases even more if another stimulus (e.g., a light or tone) predicts that the lever press yields the treat. The release of dopamine and activity of mesolimbic neurons are crucial in the development and expression of this learning. Early in training, dopamine levels increase when the treat is presented. Later, dopamine levels increase to the predictive stimulus. For some rats, there is a greater increase in dopamine activity to the stimulus that predicts the treat than to the treat itself.

How might Internet access affect the activity of the dopamine circuits related to salient, rewarding, and reinforcing stimuli? Our smartphones provide access to a variety of rewarding stimuli—funny YouTube videos, coins in Mario Kart, or social validation from friends to our Instagram photos. Our devices are designed to produce salient stimuli—the tone predicting a text from a friend or a popup message telling us a Facebook post is "liked'. The Internet provides reinforcing stimuli—repeatedly checking our bank for our paycheck deposit, monitoring our

favorite team's progress, or returning to Zelda to complete a level. Can the Internet, smartphones, and social media "hijack" our brain's pathways responsible for learning, memory and motivation in the same way that drugs of abuse do?

Both the YES and NO sections acknowledge that there are limitations in defining and diagnosing behavioral addictions, specifically "Internet addiction". In the YES section Dr. Elias Aboujaoude focuses on the available definitions and questionnaires for symptoms that may help scientists study this phenomenon and clinicians help people with the disorder. In the NO section Dr. Antonius J. Van Rooij and Dr. Nicole Prause acknowledge that Internet use may be problematic, but they challenge the current models that are used to support Internet addiction. Drs. Van Rooij and Prause suggest some areas for future research in this domain.

YES ⤶

Elias Aboujaoude

Problematic Internet Use: An Overview

The "global village", a metaphor used to describe how the Internet has shortened distances and facilitated the flow of information, has grown to over one billion users (1).

Statistics from across the world highlight its reach and penetrance: 90% of South Korean households connect to high-speed, inexpensive broadband (2); Londoners spend an average of 45 days a year online, more than they spend watching TV (3); and the rate of increase in the number of Internet users in Africa and the Middle East exceeded 1,300% between 2000 and 2009 (4).

For the majority of Internet users, the World Wide Web represents a tremendous wellspring of opportunity that enhances well-being. For others, however, it can lead to a state that appears to meet the DSM definition of a mental disorder, described as a "clinically significant behavioral or psychological syndrome...that is associated with present distress... or with a significantly increased risk of suffering death, pain, disability, or an important loss of freedom" (5).

Scientific understanding of that state has lagged behind media attention (6), in part because of inconsistency in defining the problem (7), disagreement about its very existence (8), and the variable research methodology used in studying it. Still, a body of data by scientists from the East and West (with the East increasingly leading the way) tells a cautionary tale about the Internet's potential to bring about psychological harm.

Diagnostic Definition

In 1996, the psychologist K. Young became the first to publish a detailed case report of problematic Internet use (9). Her "patient zero" was a non-technologically oriented 43-year-old homemaker with a "content home life and no prior addiction or psychiatric history", who, within three months of discovering chat rooms, was spending up to 60 hours per week online. She reported feeling excited in front of the computer, and depressed, anxious, and irritable when she would log off. She described having an addiction to the medium "like one would to alcohol". Within one year of purchasing her home computer, she was ignoring household chores, had quit social activities she used to enjoy, and had become estranged from her two teenage daughters and her husband of 17 years.

Based on this and other patients she interviewed, Young proposed the first set of diagnostic criteria for what she termed "Internet addiction". She modeled them on the DSM-IV definition for substance dependence because of similarities she observed with the states of tolerance (needing more of the substance to achieve the same effect) and withdrawal (psychological and physical discomfort upon reducing or stopping the substance) (9).

Others conceptualized problematic Internet use as a *behavioral* addiction not involving an intoxicant (10), and Young subsequently updated her definition, adapting the DSM-IV criteria for pathological gambling, an impulse control disorder often described as a behavioral addiction, into her Diagnostic Questionnaire (11) (Table 1). The questionnaire, which required at least five of the eight criteria be met for the Internet addiction diagnosis, has not received adequate psychometric testing.

Table 1

Young's Diagnostic Questionnaire for Internet addiction (11)

Diagnosis suggested by five or more "yes" answers to:

1. Do you feel preoccupied with the Internet (thin about previous online activity or anticipate next online session)?
2. Do you feel the need to use the Internet for increasing amounts of time in order to achieve satisfaction?
3. Have you repeatedly made unsuccessful efforts to control, cut back, or stop Internet use?
4. Do you feel restless, moody, depressed, or irritable when attempting to cut down or stop Internet use?
5. Do you stay online longer than originally intended?
6. Have you jeopardized or risked the loss of significant relationship, job, educational or career opportunity because of the Internet?
7. Have you lied to family members, therapist, or others to conceal the extent of involvement with the Internet?
8. Do you use the Internet as a way of escaping from problems or of relieving a dysphoric mood (e.g., feelings of helplessness, guilt, anxiety, depression)?

Shapira et al (12) proposed five years later a more inclusive diagnostic schema in the general style of the impulse control disorders. They argued that definitions based solely on substance dependence or pathological gambling were too narrow to capture the population of problematic Internet users and could lead to premature conclusions about the new disorder and the patients. They eschewed the "Internet addiction" label for lack of scientific proof for true addiction and favored the less controversial "problematic Internet use", defining it as: a) maladaptive preoccupation with Internet use, experienced as irresistible use for periods of time longer than intended; b) significant distress or impairment resulting from the behavior; and c) the absence of other Axis I pathology that might explain the behavior, such as mania or hypomania. To date, only two studies have attempted to develop diagnostic criteria empirically by testing them against the diagnosis made on the basis of a systematic psychiatric interview. Ko et al (13) tested a set of criteria in 468 Taiwanese high school students. Starting with 13 candidate criteria, they eliminated those with low diagnostic accuracy, and determined that a cutoff of six out of the nine remaining criteria had the best diagnostic accuracy while maintaining high specificity (97.1%) and acceptable sensitivity (87.5%). The criterion for functional impairment was listed separately as criterion B and was required for the diagnosis (Table 2). In a second study, Ko et al (14) confirmed the diagnostic accuracy of their criteria in an older

cohort of 216 Taiwanese college students. However, the relatively small size of both studies and the non-representative nature of the groups studied limit the applicability of the proposed criteria to the general population.

Several assessment scales have been proposed to screen for, and help diagnose, problematic Internet use. As a group, these instruments show no consensus on the underlying dimensions that constitute the condition (6,15). In addition to Young's Diagnostic Questionnaire, two are in relatively common use in research and/or clinical settings: Young's Internet Addiction Test (16) and the Chen Internet Addiction Scale (17).

Young's Internet Addiction Test (16) consists of 20 "how-often" questions, each rated on a scale of 1 to 5 (1 = rarely; 2 = occasionally; 3 = frequently; 4 = often; 5 = always.) A score of 80 or above is consistent with problematic use (Table 3). The psychometric properties of the instrument were studied in 86 subjects (18). Six factors were extracted from the questionnaire: salience, excessive use, neglect of work, anticipation, lack of control, and neglect of social life. These factors showed good concurrent validity and internal consistency. Salience explained most of the variance and was also found to be the most reliable as indicated by its Cronbach's alpha. However, the selection bias introduced by online recruitment and the small size of the study limit its value.

The Chen Internet Addiction Scale (17) is a self-report instrument composed of 26 items rated on a 4-point Likert scale (adapted in Table 4). It assesses five domains of Internet-related problems: compulsive use, withdrawal, tolerance, interpersonal and health consequences, and time management difficulties. Scores range from 26 to 104. In a study of 454 Taiwanese adolescents who completed the scale and received a structured diagnostic interview, a cutoff of 64 was shown to have high diagnostic accuracy and specificity (88% and 92.6%, respectively) (19). The internal reliability of the scale and subscales in the original study ranged from 0.79 to 0.93 (17).

Prevalence

Due to the lack of consensus on diagnostic criteria and the dearth of large epidemiological studies, the prevalence of problematic Internet use in the general population has not been established. Overall, prevalence surveys conducted in various countries fall into two main categories, online vs. offline studies, with the former typically yielding higher rates, most likely because of inherent selection bias (20).

Only two epidemiological studies exploring the prevalence of problematic Internet use in the general

Table 2

Ko et al's proposed diagnostic criteria for Internet addiction (13)

Six or more of:
1. Preoccupation with Internet activities
2. Recurrent failure to resist the impulse to use the Internet
3. Tolerance: a marked increase in Internet use needed to achieve satisfaction
4. Withdrawal, as manifested by either of the following: a) symptoms of dysphoric mood, anxiety, irritability, and boredom after several days without Internet activity; b) use of Internet to relieve or avoid withdrawal symptoms
5. Use of the Internet for a period of time longer than intended
6. Persistent desire and/or unsuccessful attempts to cut down or reduce Internet use
7. Excessive time spent on Internet activities
8. Excessive effort spent on activities necessary to obtain access to the Internet
9. Continued heavy Internet use despite knowledge of physical or psychological problem caused or exacerbated by Internet use

B. Functional impairment. One or more of:
1. Recurrent Internet use resulting in a failure to fulfill major obligations
2. Impairment in social relationships
3. Behavior violating school rules or laws due to Internet use

C. The Internet addictive behavior is not better accounted for by another disorder

---

Table 3

Young's Internet Addiction Test (16)

Answer the following questions on the Likert scale:
1 = rarely; 2 = occasionally; 3 = frequently; 4 = often; 5 = always
1. How often do you find that you stay on-line longer than you intended?
2. How often do you neglect household chores to spend more time on-line?
3. How often do you prefer the excitement of the Internet to intimacy with your partner?
4. How often do you form new relationships with fellow on-line users?
5. How often do others in your life complain to you about the amount of time you spend on-line?
6. How often do your grades or school work suffer because of the amount of time you spend on-line?
7. How often do you check your e-mail before something else that you need to do?
8. How often does your job performance or productivity suffer because of the Internet?
9. How often do you become defensive or secretive when anyone asks you what you do on-line?
10. How often do you block out disturbing thoughts about your life with soothing thoughts of the Internet?
11. How often do you find yourself anticipating when you will go on-line again?
12. How often do you fear that life without the Internet would be boring, empty, and joyless?
13. How often do you snap, yell, or act annoyed if someone bothers you while you are on-line?
14. How often do you lose sleep due to late-night log-ins?
15. How often do you feel preoccupied with the Internet when off-line, or fantasize about being on-line?
16. How often do you find yourself saying "just a few more minutes" when on-line?
17. How often do you try to cut down the amount of time you spend on-line and fail?
18. How often do you try to hide how long you've been on-line?
19. How often do you choose to spend more time on-line over going out with others?
20. How often do you feel depressed, moody, or nervous when you are off-line, which goes away once you are back on-line?

Scoring: 20-49 points, average on-line user; 50-79 points, occasional or frequent problems because of the Internet; 80-100 points, Internet usage is causing significant problems

population have been published. One was conducted in the US, the other in Norway (20,21).

The US study used random-digit telephone dialing (cellular phone numbers were not included) to interview 2,513 adults taken from all 50 states in a manner proportional to the population in each state (20). More than half of the people reached agreed to be interviewed. Participants' average age was 48, and 51% fell in the middle class socioeconomic stratum. 68.9% were regular Internet users. The authors' diagnostic definition, based on published criteria and on similarities with impulse control disorders, substance dependence and obsessive-compulsive disorder, required: a) Internet use that interferes in personal relationships; b) preoccupation with the Internet

when offline; c) unsuccessful attempts at quitting or cutting down; and d) staying online longer than intended. This definition yielded a point prevalence of 0.7%. Less stringent definitions yielded higher prevalence rates, and individual features consistent with problematic Internet use were endorsed by as many as 13.7% (respondents who found it hard to stay offline for days in a row).

In the second study, Bakken et al (21) mailed Young's Diagnostic Questionnaire to 10,000 inhabitants of Norway, randomly selected from a database of the entire population. 3,399 completed questionnaires were returned (a somewhat lower response rate than the US

Table 4

Chen Internet Addiction Scale (17, adapted)

Focusing on the last three months, rate the degree of which each statement matches your experience (1 = does not match my experience at all; 2 = probably does not match my experience; 3 = probably matches my experience; 4 = definitely matches my experience)
1. I was told more than once that I spend too much time online
2. I feel uneasy once I stop going online for a certain period of time
3. I find that I have been spending longer and longer periods of time online
4. I feel restless and irritable when the Internet is disconnected or unavailable
5. I feel energized online
6. I stay online for longer periods of time than intended
7. Although using the Internet has negatively affected my relationships, the amount of time I spend online has not decreased
8. More than once, I have slept less than four hours due to being online
9. I have increased substantially the amount of time I spend online
10. I feel distressed or down when I stop using the Internet for a certain period of time
11. I fail to control the impulse to log on
12. I find myself going online instead of spending time with friends
13. I get backaches or other physical discomfort from spending time surfing the net
14. Going online is the first thought I have when I wake up each morning
15. Going online has negatively affected my schoolwork or job performance
16. I feel like I am missing something if I don't go online for a certain period of time
17. My interactions with family members have decreased as a result of Internet use
18. My recreational activities have decreased as a result of Internet use
19. I fail to control the impulse to go back online after logging off for other work
20. My life would be joyless without the Internet
21. Surfing the Internet has negatively affected my physical health
22. I have tried to spend less time online but have been unsuccessful
23. I make it a habit to sleep less so that more time can be spent online
24. I need to spend an increasing amount of time online to achieve the same satisfaction as before
25. I fail to have meals on time because of using the Internet
26. I feel tired during the day because of the Internet late at night

study). Recipients of the mailed questionnaire also had the option of completing it online. Among respondents, 87% were Internet users. The prevalence of "addicted Internet use" (≥5 questions answered "yes") was calculated to be 1%, whereas the prevalence of "at risk" Internet use (3-4 questions answered "yes") was 5.2%. Multivariate analysis showed young age, male gender, higher educational achievement, and financial stress to be positively associated with "problematic Internet use" (defined by the authors to include both "Internet addicts" and "at risk" respondents).

Prevalence rates among adolescents have been researched more extensively, perhaps because the so-called "digital natives" grew up incorporating the Internet in many aspects of life and as a result are perceived to be at higher risk. However, even when online-based surveys are excluded, the results can vary widely and are difficult to compare, due to differences in Internet access, recruitment methodology, the exact age bracket studied, and the definitions utilized. Considering only relatively large and offline studies, research from China (22), South Korea (23,24), Greece (25), Norway (26), and Iran (27) has yielded prevalence estimates ranging between 2% and 11%.

. . .

Conclusions

For a medium that has so radically changed the way we conduct our lives, the Internet's effects on our psychological health remain understudied. Simply stating that similar fears were raised when the radio, movies and early video games were introduced is not sufficient: the immersive and interactive qualities of the virtual world, and its sheer penetrance, make it potentially more serious.

Also deserving of exploration are the more subtle psychological changes that occur in the virtual world, such as online disinhibition and increased risk-taking (28). Those changes are not necessarily evidence of "Internet addiction", and may not be pathological, but, as important features of the new virtual psychology, should also be studied.

As our field continues to debate whether their condition belongs in the next edition of the DSM (29), patients continue to present with symptoms born out of the digital age, and their symptoms are changing as the technology evolves from browsers, to "crackberries", to "smart phones" that combine texting, talking, video games, and browsing in one device that to many is like a new appendage. Even the "problematic Internet use" designation now seems outdated, which is why some have wisely opted

for "pathological use of electronic media", instead (29). Technology, like media outlets, remains far ahead of scientific investigation. Given the dramatic changes that our society is undergoing as a result of the Internet revolution, it behooves us to try to bridge the gap.

References

1. comScore Inc. www.comscore.com.
2. Fackler M. In Korea, a boot camp cure for Web obsession. New York Times, November 18, 2007. www.nytimes.com.
3. MailOnline. Internet tops TV as most popular pastime. www.dailymail.co.uk.
4. Internet World Stats. www.internetworld-stats.com.
5. American Psychiatric Association. Diagnostic and statistical manual of mental disorders, 4th ed., text revision. Washington: American Psychiatric Association, 2000.
6. Liu T, Potenza MN. Problematic Internet use: clinical aspects. In: Aboujaoude E, Koran LM (eds). Impulse control disorders. Cambridge: Cambridge University Press (in press).
7. Shaw M, Black DW. Internet addiction: definition, assessment, epidemiology and clinical management. CNS Drugs 2008;22:353–65.
8. Miller MC. Is "Internet addiction" a distinct mental disorder? Harvard Mental Health Letter 2007;24:8.
9. Young KS. Psychology of computer use: XL. Addictive use of the Internet: a case that breaks the stereotype. Psychol Rep 1996;79:899–902.
10. Griffiths MD. Internet addiction: an issue for clinical psychologists. Clinical Psychology Forum 1996;97:32–6.
11. Young KS. Internet addiction: the emergence of a new clinical disorder. Cyber Psychol Behav 1998;1:237–44.
12. Shapira NA, Lessig MC, Goldsmith TD et al. Problematic internet use: proposed classification and diagnostic criteria. Depress Anxiety 2003;17:207–16.
13. Ko CH, Yen JY, Chen CC et al. Proposed diagnostic criteria of Internet addiction for adolescents. J Nerv Ment Dis 2005;193:728–33.

14. Ko CH, Yen JY, Chen SH et al. Proposed diagnostic criteria and the screening and diagnosing tool of Internet addiction in college students. Compr Psychiatry 2009;50:378–84.

15. Beard KW. Internet addiction: a review of current assessment techniques and potential assessment questions. Cyberpsychol Behav 2005;8:7–14.

16. Young KS. Caught in the net: how to recognize the signs of internet addiction – and a winning strategy for recovery. New York: Wiley, 1998.

17. Chen SH, Weng LC, Su YJ et al. Development of Chinese Internet Addiction Scale and its psychometric study. Chin J Psychol 2003;45:279–94.

18. Widyanto L, McMurran M. The psychometric properties of the Internet Addiction Test. Cyberpsychol Behav 2004;7:443–50.

19. Ko CH, Yen JY, Yen CF et al. Screening for Internet addiction: an empirical study on cut-off points for the Chen Internet Addiction Scale. Kaohsiung J Med Sci 2005; 21:545–51.

20. Aboujaoude E, Koran LM, Gamel N et al. Potential markers for problematic internet use: a telephone survey of 2,513 adults. CNS Spectr 2006;11:750–5.

21. Bakken IJ, Wenzel HG, Götestam KG et al. Internet addiction among Norwegian adults: a stratified probability sample study. Scand J Psychol 2009;50:121–7.

22. Cao F, Su L. Internet addiction among Chinese adolescents: prevalence and psychological features. Child Care Health Dev 2007;33:275–81.

23. Kim K, Ryu E, Chon MY et al. Internet addiction in Korean adolescents and its relation to depression and suicidal ideation: a questionnaire survey. Int J Nurs Stud 2006;43:185–92.

24. Park SK, Kim JY, Cho CB. Prevalence of Internet addiction and correlations with family factors among South Korean adolescents. Adolescence 2008;43:895–909.

25. Siomos KE, Dafouli ED, Braimiotis DA et al. Internet addiction among Greek adolescent students. Cyberpsychol Behav 2008; 11:653–7.

26. Johansson A, Götestam KG. Internet addiction: characteristics of a questionnaire and prevalence in Norwegian youth (12-18 years). Scand J Psychol 2004;45:223–9.

27. Ghassemzadeh L, Shahraray M, Moradi A. Prevalence of internet addiction and comparison of internet addicts and non-addicts in Iranian high schools. Cyberpsychol Behav 2008;11:731–3.

28. Suler J. The online disinhibition effect. Cyberpsychol Behav 2004;7:321–6.

29. Pies R. Should DSM-V designate "Internet addiction" a mental disorder? Psychiatry 2009;6:31–7.

Dr. Elias Aboujaoude is a Clinical Professor, Psychiatry and Behavioral Sciences at Stanford. Dr. Aboujaoude is the author of *Virtually You: The Dangerous Powers of the e-Personality* and studies impulse control disorders, anxiety disorders, and problematic use of electronic media.

Antonius J. Van Rooij and Nicole Prause

A Critical Review of "Internet Addiction" Criteria with Suggestions for the Future

INTRODUCTION

In recent years, the term "addiction" has been expanded beyond substance dependence to include nonsubstance-related behaviors that cause problems and impairment. Proposed "process" or "behavioral" addictions have included such varied themes as shopping; exercise; gaming; and forms of Internet-enabled behavior such as online video gaming, socializing through social media, and various forms of sexual behavior (Grant, Potenza, Weinstein & Gorelick, 2010; Griffiths, 2005, 2012; Kuss & Griffiths, 2011; Sussman, Lisha & Griffiths, 2011; van Rooij, 2011). Considerable research to support these new addictions appears to follow a "me too" approach as investigators test for similarities with substance addictions and impulse control disorders that already appear in diagnostic manuals (Heyman, 2009). Moreover, there exists a general lack of agreement regarding how excessive behavior syndromes are defined and described (Mudry et al., 2011).

Addiction to a substance and addiction to a behavior may look similar in their effects on behavioral patterns, emotions, and physiology. For example, people might engage in theft to buy heroin (Jarvis & Parker, 1989) or to finance problem gambling behaviors (Crofts, 2003). Numerous similarities between gambling disorder (GD) and substance use disorders (SUDs) have been demonstrated (e.g., Potenza, 2006), with these leading to the inclusion of GD alongside substance use problems in the fifth edition of the Diagnostic and Statistical Manual of Mental Disorders (American Psychiatric Association, 2013). GD is the first such behavioral addiction included under the DSM heading of "Substance Use and Addictive Disorders" (Petry & O'Brien, 2013). However, clear differences also exist between SUDs and behavioral addictions. Perhaps the main difference is that substances provide, by definition, physiological input beyond what the body can produce by behavior alone. Consequently, SUDs are marked by several physically oriented criteria such as tolerance and withdrawal; these criteria are not generally present in behavioral addictions. Thus, serious debate exists regarding the similarity of criteria for behavioral addictions and SUDs.

Consequently, SUDs typically include several physical criteria, such as tolerance and withdrawal. There is debate on their applicability to behavioral addictions. Where some authors argue that behavioral addictions should and do display withdrawal and tolerance (Demetrovics et al., 2012; Griffiths, 2005; Petry et al., 2014) their implementation is often quite different from that of the tolerance and withdrawal associated with SUDs. Tolerance and withdrawal are critiqued in the current manuscript (see below).

Within the field of behavioral addictions, the subject of Internet addiction (IA) is of considerable interest. A primary driver of this interest is the recent inclusion of the more specific "Internet gaming disorder" in the DSM-5 appendix in order to stimulate research (American Psychiatric Association, 2013; Block, 2008; LaRose, Lin & Eastin, 2003; Petry & O'Brien, 2013). In this work, we will critically review the current approach to the measurement and identification of the excessive behavior syndrome sometimes referred to as Internet addiction (IA). Ultimately, we argue that it is probably more useful to characterize individual differences that interact with environmental factors and lead to high Internet use, rather than diagnose Internet addiction.

MODELS OF INTERNET ADDICTION

Three popular models of IA will be discussed: Griffiths components model (Griffiths, 2005); Young's Internet Addiction Test (IAT) (Widyanto, Griffiths & Brunsden, 2011; Young, 1998a, 1998b); and the more recent diagnostic criteria by Tao et al. (2010). We selected these models for study because they propose specific criteria for IA disorder and are widely cited. As an example of their impact, Young's IAT was recently used as the basis for a large ($N = 11,956$) European study of IA (Durkee et al., 2012). There are various other models and scales available, like the CIUS

(Meerkerk, van den Eijnden, Vermulst & Garretsen, 2009), the OCS (Davis, Flett & Besser, 2002), and the (gaming oriented) POGQ (Demetrovics et al., 2012). Our approach is not meant to provide an exhaustive review of all currently available conceptual models of IA, but to discuss and critique the most salient trends. Thus, our approach resembles an empirically grounded critique of popular trends, rather than an exhaustive review.

The first model, by Griffiths, also known as the "components model" (Brown, 1993; Griffiths, 1996, 2005), posits that all addictions consist of six distinct and common components (i.e., salience, mood modification, tolerance, withdrawal, conflict, and relapse). Griffiths further argues that addictions are excessive behaviors that share key elements of biopsychosocial processes (Griffiths, 2005), with his component criteria originating from the gambling field described previously by Brown (1993). Numerous scales have been developed to assess Griffith's criteria for many domains, such as work addiction and gaming addiction (Andreassen, Griffiths, Hetland & Pallesen, 2012; Lemmens, Valkenburg & Peter, 2009; Meerkerk et al., 2009; Terry, Szabo & Griffiths, 2004; van Rooij, Schoenmakers, van den Eijnden, Vermulst & van de Mheen, 2012). Using confirmatory factor analysis, the criteria were recently found to fit the large sample data collected with two popular Internet addiction scales (CIUS/AICA-S) quite well (Kuss, Shorter, van Rooij, Griffiths & Schoenmakers, 2013).

Secondly, the work by Young takes the established criteria for pathological gambling as a starting point and defines Internet addiction as a failure of personal impulse control that does not involve external substances (Young, 1998b). This failure is described by the following set of criteria: (1) a preoccupation with the Internet, (2) the need to use the Internet for increasing amounts of time, (3) unsuccessful efforts to stop using the Internet, (4) mood change when attempting to stop or cut down Internet usage, (5) staying online longer than intended, (6) jeopardizing of significant relationships or opportunities due to excessive Internet usage, (7) lying about Internet use, (8) using the Internet as an escape from problems or seeking to relieve bad mood states (Widyanto & McMurran, 2004). Young's criteria note that only personal (non-work related) Internet use should be evaluated, and that addiction is thought to be present when a client reports experiencing five or more of the above eight criteria. Like Griffith's model, these criteria and this cut-off score can be viewed as a direct translation of criteria for PG in the DSM-5 (American Psychiatric Association, 2013). Other than replacing gambling behaviors with Internet behaviors, the only notable difference is

that the DSM mentions a 12-month period, while Young mentions no time-period.

Young's conceptualization has been popularized through the expanded 20-item IAT proposed in the 1998 self-help book *Caught in the Net* (Young, 1998a). Widyanto and McMurran (2004) characterized the IAT psychometrically using factor analysis. Using a convenience sample (online recruitment, $N = 86$), they obtained six factors in their analysis for Young's IAT scale: (1) salience, (2) excessive Internet use, (3) neglecting work, (4) anticipation, (5) lack of control, and (6) neglecting social life. While Widyanto and McMurran concede that a limitation of Young's instrument is that its main source of validity is face validity, they ultimately conclude that the IAT is both reliable and worthwhile as a tool for assessing subjects' level of Internet addiction.

Thirdly, Tao et al. (2010) developed their diagnostic criteria for IA by considering the clinical characteristics of a large group of Chinese patients thought to have IA, as reported by psychiatrist evaluators. Using this approach, and excluding patients with bipolar disorder and/or psychotic disorders, Tao et al. (2010) proposed the following set of criteria: (a) *symptom criteria* (both must be present): preoccupation and withdrawal symptoms; (b) *one or more of these criteria*: (1) tolerance, (2) persistent desire and/or unsuccessful efforts to control use, (3) continued use despite problems, (4) loss of other interests, (5) use of the Internet to escape or relieve dysphoric mood; (c) *clinically significant impairment criterion*: functional impairments (reduced social, academic, working ability), including loss of a significant relationship, job, educational or career opportunities. The criteria also include a *course criterion* (d): Duration of IA must have lasted for an excess of three months, with at least six hours of Internet usage (non-business/non-academic) per day.

The three sets of discussed criteria for IA (Griffiths, 2005; Tao et al., 2010; Young, 2003) contain some commonalities (see Table 1). All sets of criteria describe feelings of a lack of control over Internet use; ensuing psychological, social, or professional conflict or problems (including "excessive use"); and mental preoccupation or salience. Other relevant features are mentioned inconsistently across the three models: mood management, tolerance, withdrawal, and craving/anticipation.

Another commonality in the models is researchers' tendency to address Internet activities as a singular entity. The Internet incorporates a variety of potential activities, as demonstrated by the high correlations between measures of IA and time spent on online activities such as online gaming and social network use (van Rooij, Schoenmakers,

Table 1

Comparison of three prominent sets of descriptive criteria for Internet addiction using items from assessment instruments

	Griffiths (2005)	Young (1998b)	Tao et al. (2010)
Salience/Preoccupation	"dominates their thinking (preoccupations and cognitive distortions), feelings (cravings) and behaviour"	–Feel preoccupied with the Internet when off-line or fantasize about being online?	"thinking about previous online activity"
(Negative) Mood management	"use … behaviours as a way of producing a reliable and consistent shift in their mood state as a coping strategy to … make themselves feel better"	–Do you block disturbing thoughts about your life with soothing thoughts of the Internet? –Fear that life without the Internet would be boring, empty and joyless?	"uses the internet to escape or relieve a dysphoric mood"
Tolerance	"increasing amounts of the particular activity are required to achieve the former effects"	–Find that you stay online longer than you intended?	"marked increase in internet use required to achieve satisfaction"
Withdrawal	"unpleasant feeling states and/or physical effects which occur when the particular activity is discontinued or suddenly reduced"	–Feel depressed, moody, or nervous when you are offline, which goes away once you are back online?	"manifested by a dysphoric mood, anxiety, irritability and boredom after several days without internet activity"
External consequences/Conflict	"conflicts between the addict and those around them (interpersonal conflict) or from within the individual themselves (intrapsychic conflict) which are concerned with the particular activity"	–Does your work suffer (e.g., postponing things, not meeting deadlines, etc.) because of the amount of time you spend online? –Does your job performance or productivity suffer because of the Internet? –Choose to spend more time online over going out with others? –Do you prefer excitement of the Internet to intimacy with your partner? –Neglect household chores to spend more time online? –Lose sleep due to late night log-ins? –Do you check your E-mail before something else that you need to do? Snap, yell, or act annoyed if someone bothers you while you are online? Do others in your life complain to you about the amount of time you spend online?	"loss of interests, previous hobbies, entertainment as a direct result of, and with the exception of, internet use" or "deception of actual costs/time of internet involvement to family members, therapist and others" "continued excessive use of internet despite knowledge of having a persistent or recurrent physical or psychological problems likely to have been caused or exacerbated by internet use"
Relapse/Control	"tendency for repeated reversions to earlier patterns of the particular activity to recur"	–Try to cut down the amount of time you spend online and fail? –Find yourself saying "Just a few more minutes" when online?	"persistent desire and/or unsuccessful attempts to control, cut back or discontinue internet use"
Craving/Anticipation		–Do you find yourself anticipating when you go online again?	"anticipation of the next online session" or "a strong desire for the internet"
Lying/Hiding use		–Do you become defensive or secretive when anyone asks you what you do online? –Try to hide how long you've been online?	

van den Eijnden & van de Mheen, 2010). In some ways, saying someone is addicted to the Internet is akin to arguing that somebody with a drinking problem is addicted to a liquor store. As such, IA is ambiguous in terminology or is even a misnomer (Starcevic, 2013). That said, most authors, including the authors of the models reviewed, continue the general use of IA as a descriptor of specific addictive behaviors associated with Internet use. This critique follows that same approach by reviewing Internet use broadly. As future work allows, such critiques might be better tailored to specific Internet behaviors, such as the use of sexual media online.

A CRITICAL REVIEW OF POPULAR CRITERIA

Existing critiques of addictive behaviors include IA (Widyanto & Griffiths, 2006), sex addiction (Ley, Prause & Finn, 2014; Moser, 2011), behavioral addictions in general (Potenza, 2006), and impulse control disorders (Dell'Osso, Altamura, Allen, Marazziti & Hollander, 2006). The current critique differs by examining each of the criteria already proposed for IA, rather than attempting to create a new catalog of IA symptoms as many previous publications have proposed new criteria (Chakraborty, Basu & Vijaya Kumar, 2010; Shaffer, Hall & Bilt, 2000; Wood, 2007). Also, here we build on experimental findings to suggest new criteria that would provide stronger evidence of pathology than do the existing proposed criteria. This approach is consistent with the recent recommendation to move away from clustered criteria in a research context (Insel, 2013).

We critique each of the criteria proposed for behavioral addiction individually by the example of IA criteria reviewed above (see Table 1). While the cited authors were not unanimous in referring to the Internet as "addictive", they are all proposing diagnostic criteria to identify—and thus name—a specific disease. Thus, at a minimum, all the models studied here share the assumption that the Internet can produce a qualitative shift to a diseased state in humans. While clearly a single criterion by itself would be sufficient to identify a disorder, a full analysis of all possible counts and combinations of criteria is beyond the scope of this work.

NEGATIVE CONSEQUENCES

Most, if not all, models of behavioral addictions seem to agree that negative outcomes are necessary criteria of a disease state. In the proposed category of sexual addiction,

this may include the loss of a primary intimate relationship due to infidelity (Schneider, Corley & Irons, 1998), while problem gambling has included time lost from work/school and arguments with cohabitants over gambling behaviors (Lesieur & Blume, 1987). Online video gaming addicts reported more marital difficulties (odds ratio = 4.61) and work difficulties (odds ratio = 4.42), saw fewer friends (odds ratio = 5.78), and missed more financial obligations (odds ratio = 6.05) than those who game online in a non-addictive manner (Achab et al., 2011).

The negative consequences criterion has strong face validity, as it is difficult to imagine someone voluntarily choosing to suffer negative consequences. Mental illness, such as substance addiction, is often inferred from behavioral tenacity in the face of these negative consequences. However, research on decision-making consistently demonstrates circumstances under which healthy people engage in non-optimal, and often ultimately detrimental, behaviors. For example, the Iowa Gambling task is a card-drawing game in which healthy players have been shown to have a preference for drawing from a deck that loses money (Lin, Chiu, Lee & Hsieh, 2007). Specifically, players without any pathology tend to choose one (of four) card decks (Deck B) that provide a series of small wins, but also large infrequent losses, that result in overall loss. In this example, reframing negative consequences as the result of non-optimal decision-making might well be the more parsimonious approach to interpreting the behavior.

LOSS OF CONTROL AND/OR RELAPSE

As with negative consequences, a (perceived) lack of control of activities on the Internet is said to accompany Internet addictions. Items assessing controllability typically ask about efforts to reduce use. Surprisingly, such questions accounted for only small (6%) proportions of variance (as opposed to 9% negative effects, and 35% salience) in a survey measure of Internet use problems (Widyanto, Griffiths, Brunsden & McMurran, 2007). Interestingly, a perceived lack of control does not consistently emerge as predictive of problems in self-report assessments used to investigate IA (Widyanto et al., 2011).

Laboratory studies have found more convincingly that those individuals with Internet use problems might have problems with self-regulation. Poor decision making relative to controls has been demonstrated in problematic Internet gamers relative to controls in a dice game (Pawlikowski & Brand, 2011) and in inhibition trials such as go/ no-go sequences (Littel et al., 2012). The poor control has been attributed to Internet addicts' relatively enhanced sensitivity to rewards and their insensitivity to punishments in general decision making tasks (Dong, Huang & Du, 2011). Another way of thinking about controllability is the ability to change one's own emotional state, now commonly known as affective regulation. For example, a number of studies have highlighted a relationship between decreased regulation abilities and the increased risk of proposed behavioral addictions. In a Turkish study 6% of the variability of Internet use problems was explained by self-reported emotion management skills (Oktan, 2011). Tokunaga and Rains (2010) noted that the ability to regulate affect predicted time using the Internet, whereas depression, loneliness, or social anxiety did not.

Controllability of the addictive behavior in IA and various other addiction models is often mentioned as a key diagnostic factor, possibly because it ascribes fault to a disease and not to the affected individual. However, there is no reason that behaviors cannot be both destructive to the individual and voluntary (for a review, see Heyman, 2009). If an inability to control Internet behaviors could be demonstrated convincingly (beyond self-reports), this would be important and consistent with a disease model. In addition to the perception of feeling out of control, though, it would be important to demonstrate that, even in the presence of valued alternative reinforcers, the addictive Internet behaviors could actually not be stopped. For example, a person might enjoy a strong sex drive, yet decline opportunities to behave sexually with an appropriate, desirable partner in favor of Internet use.

PREOCCUPATION

In the Internet addiction model, preoccupation generally refers to obsessive and continuous thoughts about Internet activities that contribute to the negative outcomes associated with problem use. Preoccupation is thought to arise as a part of the self-regulation failure accompanying problem Internet use, and is cited as a primary indicator of withdrawal (Caplan, 2010). At least one paper includes time spent in the activity as evidence of preoccupation (Shapira et al., 2003). Time spent in the activity is discussed in other sections in the current review (see below), so will not be discussed further in this context. General measures of the ability to control one's thoughts do exist in both self-report (Wells & Davies, 1994) and (controversially) laboratory task analogues (Davison, Vogel & Coffman, 1997). However, instruments more specific to Internet problems are generally used with questions such as "When not online, I wonder what is happening online" (Caplan, 2002).

Unlike other addiction criteria, preoccupation with the Internet is a weak indicator of pathology, an intense hobby might just as well lead to preoccupation (Hellman, Schoenmakers, Nordstrom & van Holst, 2013). Also, the tendency to assess "preoccupation" with novel questionnaires prevents accurate comparisons with other studies. Such comparisons are needed to determine whether thoughts about the Internet exceed thoughts typical of other non-pathological activities, such as hobbies; finally, reliance on self-reported risks over- and under-reported by clients (Beard & Wolf, 2001). While a number of improvements could be made in the assessment of preoccupation, it remains unclear how this would support a disease model of Internet use.

MOOD MANAGEMENT

In addition to the lack of control discussed in the context of affect self-regulation, engaging in behaviors to manage mood has been characterized as part of the disease model in behavioral addictions. Use of media has been characterized as motivated "to minimize aversion and maximize elation (p.159)" (Mastro, Eastin & Tamborini, 2002). One author (Zillman, 1988) refers to this as selective exposure, wherein a person selects online media to maintain excitatory homeostasis between over- and under-stimulation. Some support has been claimed for this model by those who are induced to boredom subsequently generating more Internet site hits during browsing (Mastro et al., 2002). In a nationally representative sample, 8.3% of adults reported using the Internet to alleviate negative mood or to escape life's problems (Aboujaoude, Koran, Gamel, Large & Serpe, 2006).

If online activity helps a person cope effectively with negative affect, it is unclear why such a strategy automatically becomes a criterion for addiction. In fact, the Internet has been equally lauded for introducing new avenues for social support to reduce negative affect (Lamberg, 2003) and to develop social competence (Saunders & Chester, 2008). Furthermore, greater use of the Internet for support has been associated with greater feelings of pride in young women facing cancer (Seçkin, 2011) and providing communication about sexual safety for isolated men who have sex with men (Rhodes, 2004), among other examples. It may be that there are more effective methods of coping with negative affect than engaging in online activities or that some Internet activities are more beneficial than others. Hence, Internet use as mood management has to be considered in context, as the Internet can be used as an effective coping tool.

TOLERANCE OR WITHDRAWAL

The concepts of tolerance (requiring more of the stimulus to get the same result) and withdrawal (experiencing negative consequences if you stop) have roots in the substance-based approach to addiction. While withdrawal is mentioned infrequently as occurring with cessation of problem gambling (Fisher, 1992), no biological change consistent with reported withdrawal experiences has been demonstrated in gambling or Internet use.

Tolerance is sometimes viewed as neither sufficient nor necessary to support a disease state, even within substance use disorders (Langenbucher et al., 2000). Authors writing about IA sometimes struggle with these two components. Besides Young's discussed IAT, conceptualizations such as the Compulsive Internet Use Scale (Meerkerk et al., 2009) and ICD-10 Gambling criteria do not include tolerance as a criterion. The validation study by Meerkerk (2007) found little evidence of tolerance, which has resulted in its removal from the CIUS instrument. Although both Tao and Griffiths (and the current phrasing of DSM-5's Internet gaming disorder) indicate this criterion of tolerance as a component for identification, it remains unclear how 'marked increase in Internet use to achieve satisfaction' would manifest physiologically with IA. Relying on patient reports of distress as evidence of withdrawal or tolerance appears to be weak support (Pies, 2009). In short, tolerance and withdrawal are neither (1) the most replicable aspects of substance use problems nor (2) identified clearly in problem Internet users. Thus, tolerance and withdrawal symptoms do not appear to support an addiction model of high Internet use.

CRAVING OR ANTICIPATION

Craving has been described as the "anticipation of pleasurable relief" and a purely subjective phenomenon (Marlatt, 1987, p. 42). Assessments of cravings, then, are almost exclusively based on self-reports, e.g., separating hedonic desire aspects of craving (Caselli, Soliani & Spada, 2012). Also, craving seems to be an experience central to feeling that one is addicted, since craving is often labeled and believed to be a real phenomenon by patients (Kozlowski & Wilkinson, 1987). This is problematic, because it is tautological to suggest that a problem behavior is due to "craving", and that craving is evidence that the behavior is problematic (Heyman, 2011). Also, research participants' understanding of the term "craving" has been shown to differ markedly from researchers' interpretations of the word (Kozlowski & Wilkinson, 1987). Despite this, many researchers have associated craving criteria with behavioral addictions (Armstrong, Phillips & Saling, 2000; Freeman, 2008; Han, Hwang & Renshaw, 2010; Stoeber, Harvey, Ward & Childs, 2011), including IA. For example, those at higher risk for IA have been reported to exhibit lower peripheral temperature and higher respiratory rate when surfing the Internet as compared to resting baseline (Lu, Wang & Huang, 2010). Such physiological indices are non-specific, so they cannot be interpreted as direct evidence of craving.

More recently, fMRI studies have reported that areas of the brain active during drug craving are also active when craving online video games (Ko et al., 2009), and that drug treatment of gaming addicts reduces activation of brain areas associated with craving (Han et al., 2010). Of course, brain areas are not process specific. These areas may simply reflect wanting or liking the substance or activity, or even internal conflict about the substance or activity portrayed. While liking Internet use is necessary early in use to parallel other addictions, it is not sufficient evidence of a diseased state. The reason why liking is not sufficient evidence is that addictive use is characterized by a shift away from liking to craving (Robinson & Berridge, 2000). Moving forward, changes in craving a behavior certainly might predict the increased likelihood of the occurrence of behaviors; however, at present, evidence in this area is limited to the predictive utility of behavioral intentions (Webb & Sheeran, 2006), and changes in craving have not been convincingly linked to changes in behavior. In summary, characterizing craving—or even "high" craving levels, if such an assessment could be made—appears to be insufficient evidence of a disease state.

TIME CUT-OFFS

Many behaviors could be described as harmful due to excessive involvement (i.e., procrastination, insufficient or excessive exercise, over-eating) without warranting a "disease" label. Behaviors might be usefully defined as problematic by their frequency, but how to quantify "too much" or "too frequent" is often a major point of contention (Weinstein & Lejoyeux, 2010). For example, excesses might be quantified as total orgasm outlet(s) per week for sexual behaviors (Kafka, 1991), hours spent in the gym for exercise (Lejoyeux, Avril, Richoux, Embouazza & Nivoli, 2008), or the amount of specifically forbidden foods consumed for eating problems (Tuomisto et al., 1999). In the case of IA, hours spent online is typically used as one indicator of problematic behaviors (Armstrong et al., 2000). Debate exists as to whether time spent on the activity is a good indicator of having a problem. For example, a nationally representative sample concluded that problem video gaming (online or offline) was not predicted well by the time spent on the activity alone (Gentile, 2009). Moreover, spending time on the Internet is not in and by itself a pathological or even a negative activity. Given this unresolved difficulty of establishing relevance and relevant behavioral cut-offs, time spent alone seems a weak candidate for establishing diseased behavior.

. . .

AN ALTERNATIVE PATH: AWAY FROM DISEASE, TOWARD BEHAVIORS

Internet behaviors have been described as "problematic", "excessive", "addiction", "dependence", "pathological", "impulsive", "compulsive", or "abnormal", or prefixed as "hyper-" to delineate some disease state. Notably absent are behaviorally specific, statistically descriptive terms, such as "high-frequency Internet use". Additionally, many interventions already exist to change the frequency of specific behaviors, and the frequency and intensity of the behavior is often a main problem in reported cases of addiction.

Taking video games as an example, the amount of time spent playing video games has been associated with obesity (Vandewater, Shim & Caplovitz, 2004). Thus, it might make sense to try to reduce the time spent playing video games in order to prevent snacking that can occur while playing games. Simple behavioral, token economy interventions have proven successful for reducing the hours of television viewed (Schmidt et al., 2012) and could be adapted to modify gaming and other Internet involvement. Some might object that such a focus on behavior fails to treat some underlying cause of the behavior, which could result in relapse. A more straightforward focus on behavior and dimensions underlying behavior change, rather than development of another addiction model, appears reasonable.

Furthermore, attributing Internet behaviors to a disease state can be harmful. A diagnosis can be comforting, providing a label to describe isolating experiences and validating the challenges involved in changing a behavior (Rubin, 2000). However, diagnoses also can make change more difficult. For example, the primary mechanism of change when using biofeedback to treat chronic pain is increased self-efficacy, not changes in actual muscle tension (Holroyd, 2002). Addiction model treatments that teach the patient they are not in control of their addiction might actually reduce their self-efficacy and make behavior change less likely. A pragmatic focus on behavioral modification has already generated positive feedback from

psychologists treating a small group of self-diagnosed IA patients (van Rooij, Zinn, Schoenmakers & Mheen, 2012).

This review did not address some potentially important aspects of Internet behaviors in a desire to limit the scope of the review. For example, Internet use can be characterized as varying on social involvement (e.g., Facebook versus solitaire), immediate financial risk (e.g., online poker with bitcoin versus blogs), or social acceptability (e.g., perusing sexual videos versus nature photography). It may be that specific Internet behaviors follow addictive patterns, whereas Internet behaviors in general do not. Also, the three models reviewed were an editorial choice to provide further insight into a few of the more popular models. An alternative approach would have been to conduct a systematic review of publications about Internet behaviors to quantify, in greater breadth, the extent to which the different symptoms actually are used.

In summary, many challenges exist to conceptualizing problem Internet behaviors as a disease. While progress is being made setting up large-scale, longitudinal studies, such as a recent Europe-wide (eleven countries, $N = 11,956$) investigation (Durkee et al., 2012), the otherwise impressive study continues to rely on an eight-item version of the Young Internet Addiction questionnaire. The failure to develop and use strongly theoretical measures limits the strength of these investigations. This questionnaire continues to float on face validity to classify users into a "pathological" group using an arbitrary cut-off score. We believe that this leaves ample room for improvement in the field. It also provides researchers with an opportunity for methodological improvement in the field by focusing on theoretical modeling, experimental results, and a dimensional approach.

REFERENCES

Aboujaoude, E., Koran, L. M., Gamel, N., Large, M. D. & Serpe, R. T. (2006). Potential markers for problematic internet use: A telephone survey of 2,513 adults. *CNS Spectrums, 11*(10), 750–755.

Achab, S., Nicolier, M., Mauny, F., Monnin, J., Trojak, B., Vandel, P., Sechter, D., Gorwood, P. & Haffen, E. (2011). Massively multiplayer online role-playing games: Comparing characteristics of addict vs non-addict online recruited gamers in a French adult population. *BMC Psychiatry, 11*, 144.

American Psychiatric Association. (2013). *Diagnostic and Statistical Manual of Mental Disorders, 5th Edition* (p. 991). Arlington, VA: American Psychiatric Association.

Andreassen, C. S., Griffiths, M. D., Hetland, J. & Pallesen, S. (2012). Development of a work addiction scale. *Scandinavian Journal of Psychology, 53*(3), 265–272.

Armstrong, L., Phillips, J. G. & Saling, L. L. (2000). Potential determinants of heavier internet usage. *International Journal of Human-Computer Studies, 53*(4), 537–550.

Beard, K. W. & Wolf, E. M. (2001). Modification in the proposed diagnostic criteria for Internet addiction. *Cyberpsychology, Behavior, and Social Networking, 4*(3), 377–383.

Block, J. J. (2008). Issues for DSM-V: Internet addiction. *American Journal of Psychiatry, 165*(3), 306–307.

Brown, R. I. F. (1993). Some contributions of the study of gambling to the study of other addictions. In W. R. Eadington & J. Cornelius (Eds.), *Gambling behavior and problem gambling* (pp. 241–272). Reno, NV: Institute for the Study of Gambling and Commercial Gaming, University of Nevada Press.

Caplan, S. E. (2002). Problematic Internet use and psychosocial well-being: Development of a theory-based cognitive–behavioral measurement instrument. *Computers in Human Behavior, 18*(5), 553–575.

Caplan, S. E. (2010). Theory and measurement of generalized problematic Internet use: A two-step approach. *Computers in Human Behavior, 26*(5), 1089–1097.

Caselli, G., Soliani, M. & Spada, M. M. (2012). The effect of desire thinking on craving: An experimental investigation. *Psychology of Addictive Behaviors*. doi:10.1037/a0027981

Chakraborty, K., Basu, D. & Vijaya Kumar, K. G. (2010). Internet addiction: Consensus, controversies, and the way ahead. *East Asian Archives of Psychiatry: Official Journal of the Hong Kong College of Psychiatrists = Dong Ya Jing Shen Ke Xue Zhi: Xianggang Jing Shen Ke Yi Xue Yuan Qi Kan, 20*(3), 123–132.

Crofts, P. (2003). Problem gambling and property offences: An analysis of court files. *International Gambling Studies, 3*(2), 183–197.

Davis, R. A. (2001). A cognitive-behavioral model of pathological Internet use. *Computers in Human Behavior, 17*(2), 187–195. Davis, R. A., Flett, G. L. & Besser, A. (2002). Validation of a new scale for measuring problematic internet use: Implications for pre-employment screening. *Cyberpsychology, Behavior, and Social Networking, 5*(4), 331–345.

Davison, G. C., Vogel, R. S. & Coffman, S. G. (1997). Think-aloud approaches to cognitive assessment and the articulated thoughts in simulated situations paradigm. *Journal of Consulting and Clinical Psychology, 65*(6), 950–958.

Dell'Osso, B., Altamura, A. C., Allen, A., Marazziti, D. & Hollander, E. (2006). Epidemiologic and clinical updates on impulse control disorders. *European Archives Psychiatry Clinical Neuroscience,* 464–475.

Demetrovics, Z., Urbán, R., Nagygyörgy, K., Farkas, J., Griffiths, M. D., Pápay, O., Kökönyei, G., Felvinczi, K. & Oláh, A. (2012). The development of the Problematic Online Gaming Questionnaire (POGQ). *PLoS ONE, 7*(5), e36417. doi:10.1371/journal.pone.0036417

Dong, G., Huang, J. & Du, X. (2011). Enhanced reward sensitivity and decreased loss sensitivity in Internet addicts: An fMRI study during a guessing task. *Journal of Psychiatric Research, 45*(11), 1525–1529.

Durkee, T., Kaess, M., Carli, V., Parzer, P., Wasserman, C., Floderus, B., Apter, A., Balazs, J., Barzilay, S., Bobes, J., Brunner, R., Corcoran, P., Cosman, D., Cotter, P., Despalins, R., Graber, N., Guillemin, F., Haring, C., Kahn, J. P., Mandelli, L., Marusic, D., Mészáros, G., Musa, G. J., Postuvan, V., Resch, F., Saiz, P. A., Sisask, M., Varnik, A., Sarchiapone, M., Hoven, C. W. & Wasserman, D. (2012). Prevalence of pathological internet use among adolescents in Europe: Demographic and social factors. *Addiction (Abingdon, England),* 1–17. doi:10.1111/j.1360-0443.2012.03946.x

Fisher, S. (1992). Measuring pathological gambling in children: The case of fruit machines in the U.K. *Journal of Gambling Studies, 8*(3), 263–285.

Freeman, C. B. (2008). Internet Gaming Addiction. *The Journal for Nurse Practitioners, 4*(1), 42–47.

Gentile, D. A. (2009). Pathological video-game use among youth ages 8 to 18: A national study. *Psychological Science, 20*(5), 594–602.

Grant, J. E., Potenza, M. N., Weinstein, A. & Gorelick, D. A. (2010). Introduction to behavioral addictions. *The American Journal of Drug and Alcohol Abuse, 36*(5), 233–241.

Griffiths, M. D. (1996). Behavioural addiction: An issue for everybody? *Journal of Workplace Learning: Employee Counselling Today, 8,* 19–25.

Griffiths, M. D. (2005). A "components" model of addiction within a biopsychosocial framework. *Journal of Substance Use, 10*(4), 191–197.

Griffiths, M. D. (2012). Internet sex addiction: A review of empirical research. *Addiction Research & Theory, 20*(2), 111–124.

Han, D. H., Hwang, J. W. & Renshaw, P. F. (2010). Bupropion sustained release treatment decreases craving for video games and cue-induced brain activity in patients with Internet video game addiction. *Experimental and Clinical Psychopharmacology, 18*(4), 297–304.

Hellman, M., Schoenmakers, T. M., Nordstrom, B. R. & van Holst, R. J. (2013). Is there such a thing as online video game addiction? A cross-disciplinary review. *Addiction Research & Theory, 21*(2), 102–112.

Heyman, G. M. (2009). *Addiction: A disorder of choice.* Cambridge, MA: Harvard University Press.

Heyman, G. M. (2011). Received wisdom regarding the roles of craving and dopamine in addiction: A response to Lewis's critique of addiction: A disorder of choice. *Perspectives on Psychological Science, 6*(2), 156–160.

Holroyd, K. A. (2002). Assessment and psychological management of recurrent headache disorders. *Journal of Consulting and Clinical Psychology, 70*(3), 656–677.

Insel, T. R. (2013, April 29). Director's blog: Transforming diagnosis [Web log comment]. *NIMH Blog.*

Jarvis, G. & Parker, H. (1989). Young heroin users and crime. How do the "New Users" finance their habits? *British Journal of Criminology, 29*(2), 175–185.

Kafka, M. P. (1991). Successful antidepressant treatment of nonparaphilic sexual addictions and paraphilias in men. *The Journal of Clinical Psychiatry, 52*(2), 60–65.

Ko, C.-H., Liu, G.-C., Hsiao, S., Yen, J.-Y., Yang, M.-J., Lin, W.-C., Yen, C.-F. & Chen, C.-S. (2009). Brain activities associated with gaming urge of online gaming addiction. *Journal of Psychiatric Research, 43*(7), 739–747.

Kozlowski, L. T. & Wilkinson, D. A. (1987). Use and misuse of the concept of craving by alcohol, tobacco, and drug researchers. *British Journal of Addiction, 82*(1), 31–45.

Kuss, D. J. & Griffiths, M. D. (2011). Online social networking and addiction – A review of the psychological literature. *International Journal of Environmental Research and Public Health, 8*(9), 3528–3552.

Kuss, D. J., Shorter, G. W., van Rooij, A. J., Griffiths, M. D. & Schoenmakers, T. M. (2013). Assessing Internet addiction using the Parsimonious Internet Addiction Components Model – A preliminary study. *International Journal of Mental Health and Addiction, 12*(3), 351–366.

Lamberg, L. (2003). Online empathy for mood disorders: Patients turn to internet support groups. *The Journal of the American Medical Association, 289*(23), 3073–3077.

Langenbucher, J., Martin, C. S., Labouvie, E., Sanjuan, P. M., Bavly, L. & Pollock, N. K. (2000). Toward the DSM-V: The Withdrawal-Gate Model versus the DSM-IV in the diagnosis of alcohol abuse and dependence. *Journal of Consulting and Clinical Psychology, 68*(5), 799–809.

LaRose, R., Lin, C. A. & Eastin, M. S. (2003). Unregulated Internet usage: Addiction, habit, or deficient self-regulation? *Media Psychology, 5*(3), 225–253.

Lejoyeux, M., Avril, M., Richoux, C., Embouazza, H. & Nivoli, F. (2008). Prevalence of exercise dependence and other behavioral addictions among clients of a Parisian fitness room. *Comprehensive Psychiatry, 49*(4), 353–358.

Lemmens, J. S., Valkenburg, P. M. & Peter, J. (2009). Development and validation of a game addiction scale for adolescents. *Media Psychology, 12*(1), 77–95.

Lesieur, H. & Blume, S. (1987). The South Oaks Gambling Screen (SOGS): A new instrument for the identification of pathological gamblers. *American Journal of Psychiatry, 144*(9), 1184–1188.

Ley, D., Prause, N. & Finn, P. (2014). The emperor has no clothes: A review of the "Pornography Addiction" Model. *Current Sexual Health Reports, 6*(2), 94–105.

Lin, C.-H., Chiu, Y.-C., Lee, P.-L. & Hsieh, J.-C. (2007). Is deck B a disadvantageous deck in the Iowa Gambling Task? *Behavioral and Brain Functions, 3*, 16.

Littel, M., van den Berg, I., Luijten, M., van Rooij, A. J., Keemink,

L. & Franken, I. H. A. (2012). Error processing and response inhibition in excessive computer game players: An event-related potential study. *Addiction Biology, 17*(5), 934–947.

Lu, D. W., Wang, J. W. & Huang, A. C. W. (2010). Differentiation of Internet addiction risk level based on autonomic nervous responses: The Internet-addiction hypothesis of autonomic activity. *Cyberpsychology, Behavior, and Social Networking, 13*(4), 371–378.

Marlatt, G. A. (1987). Craving notes. *Addiction, 82*(1), 42–44.

Mastro, D. E., Eastin, M. S. & Tamborini, R. (2002). Internet search behaviors and mood alterations: A selective exposure approach. *Media Psychology, 4*(2), 157–172.

Meerkerk, G.-J. (2007). *Owned by the internet. Explorative research into the causes and consequences of compulsive internet use [Doctoral thesis]. IVO Reeks 50* (p. 144). Rotterdam, The Netherlands: Erasmus University Rotterdam.

Meerkerk, G.-J., van den Eijnden, R. J. J. M., Vermulst, A. A. & Garretsen, H. F. L. (2009). The Compulsive Internet Use Scale (CIUS): Some psychometric properties. *Cyberpsychology, Behavior, and Social Networking, 12*(1), 1–6.

Moser, C. (2011). Hypersexual disorder: Just more muddled thinking. *Archives of Sexual Behavior, 40*(2), 227–229; author reply 231–232.

Mudry, T. E., Hodgins, D. C., El-Guebaly, N., Wild, T. C., Colman, I., Patten, S. B. & Schopflocher, D. (2011). Conceptualizing excessive behaviour syndromes: A systematic review. *Current Psychiatry Reviews, 7*(2), 138–151.

Oktan, V. (2011). The predictive relationship between emotion management skills and Internet Addiction. *Social Behavior and Personality: An International Journal, 39*(10), 1425–1430.

Pawlikowski, M. & Brand, M. (2011). Excessive Internet gaming and decision making: Do excessive World of Warcraft players have problems in decision making under risky conditions? *Psychiatry Research, 188*(3), 428–433.

Petry, N. M. & O'Brien, C. P. (2013). Internet gaming disorder and the DSM-5. *Addiction (Abingdon, England), 108*(7), 1186–1187.

Petry, N. M., Rehbein, F., Gentile, D. A., Lemmens, J. S., Rumpf, H.-J., Mößle, T., Bischof, G., Tao, R., Fung, D. S., Borges, G., Auriacombe, M., González Ibáñez, A. & O'Brien, C. P. (2014). An international consensus for assessing internet gaming disorder using the new DSM-5 approach. *Addiction, 109*(9), 1399–1406.

Pies, R. (2009). Should DSM-V designate "Internet addiction" a mental disorder? *Psychiatry, 6*(2), 31–37.

Potenza, M. N. (2006). Should addictive disorders include nonsubstance-related conditions? *Addiction (Abingdon, England), 101 Suppl*(s1), 142–151.

Rhodes, S. D. (2004). Hookups or health promotion? An exploratory study of a chat room-based HIV prevention intervention for men who have sex with men. *AIDS Education and Prevention, 16*(4), 315–327.

Robinson, T. E. & Berridge, K. C. (2000). The psychology and neurobiology of addiction: An incentive-sensitization view. *Addiction (Abingdon, England), 95 Suppl 2*(March), S91–117.

Robinson, T. E. & Berridge, K. C. (2001). Incentive-sensitization and addiction. *Addiction (Abingdon, England), 96*(1), 103–114.

Rubin, J. (2000). William James and the pathologizing of human experience. *Journal of Humanistic Psychology, 40*(2), 176–226.

Saunders, P. L. & Chester, A. (2008). Shyness and the internet: Social problem or panacea? *Computers in Human Behavior, 24*(6), 2649–2658.

Schmidt, M. E., Haines, J., O'Brien, A., McDonald, J., Price, S., Sherry, B. & Taveras, E. M. (2012). Systematic review of effective strategies for reducing screen time among young children. *Obesity (Silver Spring, Md.), 20*(7), 1338–1354.

Schneider, J. P., Corley, M. D. & Irons, R. K. (1998). Surviving disclosure of infidelity: Results of an international survey of 164 recovering sex addicts and partners. *Sexual Addiction & Compulsivity, 5*(3), 189–217.

Seçkin, G. (2011). I am proud and hopeful: Age-based comparisons in positive coping affect among women who use online peer-support. *Journal of Psychosocial Oncology, 29*(5), 573–591.

Shaffer, H. J., Hall, M. N. & Bilt, J. V. (2000). "Computer Addiction": A critical consideration. *American Journal of Orthopsychiatry, 70*(2), 162–168.

Shapira, N. A., Lessig, M. C., Goldsmith, T. D., Szabo, S. T., Lazoritz, M., Gold, M. S. & Stein, D. J. (2003). Problematic internet use: Proposed classification and diagnostic criteria. *Depression and Anxiety, 17*(4), 207–216.

Starcevic, V. (2013). Is Internet addiction a useful concept? *The Australian and New Zealand Journal of Psychiatry, 47*(1), 16–19.

Stoeber, J., Harvey, M., Ward, J. A. & Childs, J. H. (2011). Passion, craving, and affect in online gaming: Predicting how gamers feel when playing and when prevented from playing. *Personality and Individual Differences,* 6–10.

Sussman, S., Lisha, N. & Griffiths, M. D. (2011). Prevalence of the addictions: A problem of the majority or the minority? *Evaluation & the Health Professions, 34*(1), 3–56.

Tao, R., Huang, X., Wang, J., Zhang, H., Zhang, Y. & Li, M. (2010). Proposed diagnostic criteria for internet addiction. *Addiction, 105*(3), 556–564.

Terry, A., Szabo, A. & Griffiths, M. D. (2004). The exercise addiction inventory: A new brief screening tool. *Addiction Research and Theory, 12*(5), 489–499.

Tokunaga, R. S. & Rains, S. A. (2010). An evaluation of two characterizations of the relationships between problematic Internet use, time spent using the Internet, and psychosocial problems. *Human Communication Research, 36*(4), 512–545.

Tuomisto, T., Hetherington, M. M., Morris, M. F., Tuomisto, M. T., Turjanmaa, V. & Lappalainen, R. (1999). Psychological and physiological characteristics of sweet food "addiction". *The International Journal of Eating Disorders, 25*(2), 169–175.

van Rooij, A. J. (2011). *Online video game addiction. Exploring a new phenomenon [PhD Thesis]*. Rotterdam, The Netherlands: Erasmus University Rotterdam.

van Rooij, A. J., Schoenmakers, T. M., van den Eijnden, R. J. J. M. & van de Mheen, D. (2010). Compulsive internet use: The role of online gaming and other internet applications. *The Journal of Adolescent Health, 47*(1), 51–57.

van Rooij, A. J., Schoenmakers, T. M., van den Eijnden, R. J. J. M., Vermulst, A. A. & van de Mheen, D. (2012). Video game addiction test: Validity and psychometric characteristics. *Cyberpsychology, Behavior and Social Networking, 15*(9), 507–511.

van Rooij, A. J., Zinn, M. F., Schoenmakers, T. M. & van de Mheen, D. (2012). Treating internet addiction with cognitive-behavioral therapy: A thematic analysis of the experiences of therapists. *International Journal of Mental Health and Addiction, 10*(1), 69–82.

Vandewater, E. A., Shim, M. & Caplovitz, A. G. (2004). Linking obesity and activity level with children's television and video game use. *Journal of Adolescence, 27*(1), 71–85.

Webb, T. L. & Sheeran, P. (2006). Does changing behavioral intentions engender behavior change? A meta-analysis of the experimental evidence. *Psychological Bulletin, 132*(2), 249–268.

Weinstein, A. & Lejoyeux, M. (2010). Internet addiction or excessive internet use. *The American Journal of Drug and Alcohol Abuse, 36*(5), 277–283.

Wells, A. & Davies, M. N. O. (1994). The thought control questionnaire: A measure of individual differences in the control of unwanted thoughts. *Behaviour Research and Therapy, 32*(8), 871–878.

Widyanto, L. & Griffiths, M. (2006). "Internet Addiction": A critical review. *International Journal of Mental Health and Addiction, 4*(1), 31–51.

Widyanto, L., Griffiths, M. D. & Brunsden, V. (2011). A psychometric comparison of the Internet Addiction Test, the Internet-Related Problem Scale, and self-diagnosis. *Cyberpsychology, Behavior, and Social Networking, 14*(3), 141–149.

Widyanto, L., Griffiths, M. D., Brunsden, V. & McMurran, M. (2007). The psychometric properties of the Internet Related Problem Scale: A pilot study. *International Journal of Mental Health and Addiction, 6*(2), 205–213.

Widyanto, L. & McMurran, M. (2004). The psychometric properties of the Internet Addiction Test. *Cyberpsychology, Behavior, and Social Networking, 7*(4), 443–450.

Wood, R. T. A. (2007). Problems with the concept of Video Game "Addiction": Some case study examples. *International Journal of Mental Health and Addiction, 6*(2), 169–178.

Young, K. S. (1998a). *Caught in the net: How to recognize the signs of Internet addiction – And a winning strategy for recovery.* New York, NY: Wiley.

Young, K. S. (1998b). Internet Addiction: The emergence of a new clinical disorder. *Cyberpsychology, Behavior, and Social Networking, 1*(3), 237–244.

Young, K. S. (2003). A therapist's guide to assess and treat internet addiction. Retrieved September 09, 2014, from http://www.netaddiction.com/articles/practitioners.pdf

Zillman, D. (1988). Mood management through communication choices. *American Behavioral Scientist, 31*(3), 327–340.

DR. ANTONIUS J. VAN ROOIJ is currently affiliated with the iMinds MICT group at Ghent University and his research focuses on the use of videogames for health.

DR. NICOLE PRAUSE is a neuroscientist who studies human sexual behavior, addiction, and the physiology of sexual response. Dr. Pruse founded Liberos LLC, a sexual biotechnology company that strives to use sexual stimulation to improve general health.

EXPLORING THE ISSUE

Can One Become Addicted to the Internet and Social Media?

Critical Thinking and Reflection

1. How do psychologists and clinicians define drug addiction? Can one truly become addicted to the Internet, social media, or smartphone use?
2. Adolescence and young adulthood is a critical developmental period for the development of drug addiction. Should Internet use be controlled in young people to prevent Internet addiction?
3. What is healthy, normal use of social media and smartphones, and when does Internet use become problematic?
4. How might smartphone and app designers intentionally or unintentionally use the properties that make drugs addictive to increase the use of their products?
5. If someone is addicted to the Internet or their smartphone, how might that addiction be treated? Can we apply the approaches used to help people addicted to drugs, or are new treatment philosophies needed?

Is There Common Ground?

The world was shocked in 2009 by news stories from South Korea of a couple whose consuming habit of playing video games led them to neglect their three-month-old baby. While their baby lived in a messy room and starved to death, the parents were on the Internet gaming all-day and all-night and, ironically, caring for a virtual baby. In 2014 a South Korean man was arrested for leaving his two-year-old son unattended for two weeks while he played games at an Internet café. In both cases Internet addiction was claimed as justification, in part, for the neglect. This Issue began with comments from author Jenna Woginrich on her experiences with her smartphone—focusing on social media, text messages, news feeds and games at the expense of activities in the "real world." Can someone become addicted to the Internet, smartphones or social media in the same way someone might become addicted to drugs?

NIDA proposes that drug addiction is a biological disease that develops in response to access to a salient, rewarding and reinforcing stimulus (e.g., cocaine, heroin or nicotine). The initial decision to take a drug is voluntary, but with repeated use the ability to stop is seriously weakened. Self-control is impaired as a result of changes in neural circuits associated with basic learning and motivational processes.

The goal of this Issue was to consider similarities and differences between drugs and the Internet. We have immediate access to information via the Internet on our smartphones. Is this immediate access similar to the immediate rush of euphoria produced by pushing the plunger on a needle filled with cocaine? Woginrich noted that, "I grew uncomfortable with any 30-second span of hands-free idleness." Is this similar to the physical and psychological pain someone addicted to heroin experiences when they are unable to acquire the drug? The World Health Organization reports that one billion people use tobacco on a regular basis and two billion regularly drink alcohol. How is this regular drug use behavior different from the online activities of the close to two billion people active on Facebook or WeChat?

Additional Resources

Chih-Hung, K. et al (2005) Proposed diagnostic criteria of Internet addiction for adolescents. *The Journal of Nervous and Mental Disease.* 193(11): 728-733. The researchers from Kaohsiung Medical University developed nine diagnostic criteria for characteristic symptoms of Internet addiction in adolescents. The validity of the proposed criteria was confirmed by comparing Internet-using characteristics between those with and without addiction.

Clive, B.K. (2016) *Hooked: Overcoming Social Media Addiction.* CreateSpace Independent Publishing Platform. Bernard Kelvin Clive addresses the need to overcome our negative addiction to "'likes, tweets, shares and comments" and to become more productive while enjoying our lives.

Montag, C. et al (2016) An affective neuroscience framework for the molecular study of Internet addiction. *Frontiers in Psychology* 7: 1906. Researchers developed a theoretical framework for the molecular underpinnings of Internet and smartphone addiction.

Potenza, M. (2014) Non-substance addictive behaviors in the context of DSM-5 Addictive Behaviors 39(1): 1-2. Addiction researcher Marc Potenza describes the current status of behavior addictions in the Diagnostic and Statistical Manual of Mental Disorders (DSM–5).

Robinson, T.E. & Berridge, K.C. (2008) The incentive sensitization theory of addiction: some current issues. *Philosophical transactions of the Royal Society of London* 363(1507): 3137–3146. Terry Robinson and Kent Berridge propose that addiction results from drug-induced changes in activity in the mesolimbic dopamine pathway. This review paper includes comments on the translation of the model from laboratory animal studies to human clinical populations.

Woginrich, J. (2016) How I quit my smartphone addiction and really started living. *The Guardian*, February 11. The freelance writer (http://coldantlerfarm.blogspot.com/) describes how she gave up her smartphone and how the decision impacted her life.

Internet References . . .

Cosmopolitan—16 Signs You're Addicted to Social Media

http://www.cosmopolitan.com/uk/entertainment/a44429/signs-youre-addicted-to-social-media/

Diagnostic and Statistical Manual of Mental Disorders (DSM–5)

https://www.psychiatry.org/psychiatrists/practice/dsm

Net Addiction—The Center for Internet Addiction

http://netaddiction.com/

Psychology Today – What is Addiction?

https://www.psychologytoday.com/basics/addiction

Social Media Daily

http://www.socialmediatoday.com/

Society for the Study of Addiction

http://www.addictionjournal.org/

Selected, Edited, and with Issue Framing Material by:
Dennis K. Miller, *University of Missouri*

ISSUE

Is Drug Addiction a Problem of Youth?

YES: National Institute on Drug Abuse, from *Drugs, Brains, and Behavior: The Science of Addiction* (National Institute on Drug Abuse, 2014)

NO: Olivera Bogunovic, from "Substance Abuse in Aging and Elderly Adults," *Psychiatric Times* (2012)

Learning Outcomes

After reading this issue, you will be able to:

- Identify the risk factors that make young people (e.g., teenagers and the college-aged) susceptible to drug addiction and the unique impact of drug use while young.
- Identify the risk factors that make older people (e.g., those 60 years and older) susceptible to drug addiction and the unique impact of drugs on older individuals.
- Describe the health challenges in aging that modify risk for addiction.
- Contrast drug addiction challenges between the two populations and identify where they are similar and different.
- Explain how society and biochemistry contributes to addiction in these populations.

ISSUE SUMMARY

YES: The National Institute on Drug Abuse (NIDA) is charged with bringing the power of science to bear on drug abuse and addiction. In its publication *Drugs, Brains, and Behavior: The Science of Addiction*, NIDA provides an overview—based on the scientific literature—of the drug addiction problem. A strong focus of this research has been in preventing drug addiction in young people.

NO: Psychiatrist and author Olivera Bogunovic indicates that drug addiction is a formidable problem for older adults. In her article "Substance Abuse in Aging and Elderly Adults," she describes the unique challenges faced by older people.

Monitoring the Future is a long-term study of the behaviors, attitudes, and beliefs of American high school and college students and young adults. Since the mid-1970s the researchers at the University of Michigan surveyed approximately 50,000 young people and then followed up with these individuals several years later. Questions cover a variety of diverse issues, such as government and politics, gender roles, protection of the environment, and alcohol and other drug use.

The 2014 survey reported that 37.4 percent of 12th graders reported using alcohol within the past month,

a decline from 2009 when 43.5 percent of 12th graders reported that behavior. Similarly, cigarette smoking declined between 2009 and 2014, as 11.2 percent of 12th graders reported smoking daily in 2009 and 6.7 percent reported it in 2014. Regarding illicit drugs, Monitoring the Future reports that use of illicit substances overall has generally declined over the past 20 years. There was little change between 2009 and 2014 for 12th graders in reports of having used marijuana in the past month. The rate for this population was 21.2 percent in 2014. Interestingly, although rates of marijuana use have remained relatively stable over the past few years, there has been a shift in teens' attitude about its perceived risks. The majority of high school seniors do not think occasional marijuana smoking is harmful, as only 36.1 percent say that regular use puts the user at great personal risk.

Data from Monitoring the Future and other sources are important because our nation has made prevention and treatment of drug abuse and dependence an important priority. According to the Office of National Drug Control Policy (ONDCP) in the White House, "High-risk drinking, underage drinking, and drug use are-all-too common among our Nation's teens and young adults. It threatens the present well-being of millions of college students and our Nation's future capacity to maintain its leadership in a fiercely competitive global economy." The goal of the ONDCP is to decrease drinking and drug use by young people by 10 percent over the next five years, which should contribute to another goal of increasing the percentage of young people graduating from college.

Why is adolescence an important period to combat drug abuse and dependence? According to the National Institute of Drug Addiction (NIDA), it is related to the nervous system. The brain systems that govern emotion and reward-seeking are fully developed by this time. However, the circuits governing judgment and self-inhibition are still maturing. As a result, teenagers act on impulse, seek new sensations, and can be easily swayed by their peers. All of these may draw them to take risks such as trying drugs of abuse. In addition, critical neural circuits are still actively forming in adolescents' brains, which make them particularly susceptible to being modified by those substances in a lasting way. This makes the development of substance dependence and other, related, psychological disorders more likely.

A comprehensive approach to treating drug addiction should include prevention efforts. Prevention often receives less focus and emphasis than treatment or punishment of individuals who already experience addiction; however, there have been successful prevention efforts that have markedly decreased rates of drug use. For example, prevention has contributed to the decrease in rates of tobacco use in young people (e.g., data from Monitoring the Future).

Prevention efforts often focus on adolescents and young people. Family-based prevention programs focus on family relationships and parenting skills. The goal is to develop and enforce family policies on drug use and to educate young people about drugs in the home. School-based prevention programs are designed to intervene as early as preschool to address risk factors (e.g., poor social skills and academic struggles) for drug abuse. At the middle and high school levels programs focus on

developing strong antidrug attitudes and strengthening personal prohibitions against drug use, in addition to addressing risk factors (e.g., poor social competence, struggles in peer relationships, and lack of academic competence).

Research in prevention in the young has focused on family dynamics and the roles of popular media and advertising in developing attitudes about drug use. Behavioral psychologists seek to help young people develop resistance skills—strategies to avoid the pressure to use drugs. Other research has focused on "gateway" drugs. Gateway drugs include alcohol and marijuana, and are those that precede the use of harder drugs (e.g., cocaine, methamphetamine, and heroin). The rationale is that we can close the "gateway" to using hard drugs in adulthood by preventing people from experimenting with drugs in their youth.

These surveys, political and social positions, and prevention efforts have focused on young people. However, should we limit our consideration of drug abuse and dependence to teenagers and young adults? Is drug addiction also a problem of older adulthood?

According to the United States Census, the national nation will experience considerable growth in its older population between 2012 and 2050. In 2050, the population aged 65 and over is projected to be 83.7 million—almost double its population of 43.1 million in 2012. The growth of the older population will present social and political challenges. It will impact government programs such as Social Security and Medicare, as well as families, businesses, and health care providers.

When we consider aging and drugs, we tend to focus on the use and availability of medications to manage disease and disorder symptoms. Those aged 65 years and older account for more than one-third of total outpatient spending on prescription medications in the United States, despite being only 13 percent of the population. Older individuals are more likely to be prescribed long-term and multiple prescriptions, and are more likely to experience problems with drug interactions and adverse drug experiences (e.g., improper use of medications due to cognitive decline, increased use of over-the-counter medications or alternative therapies, and altered drug metabolism). But what about drug abuse and dependence?

According to the Substance Abuse and Mental Health Services Administration (SAMHSA), substance abuse, particularly of alcohol and prescription drugs, among adults 60 and older is one of the fastest growing health problems. Even as the number of older adults experiencing drug addiction increases, there has been little work on assessing the scope of the problem, identifying individuals suffering from addiction, evaluating diagnostic criteria for older populations, and treating the symptoms. As the population ages (e.g., data from the United States Census), it will be difficult to ignore the problems of drug addiction in older people. Furthermore, not only is this population increasing from demographic shifts (e.g., aging of the Baby Boomers), but substance abusers are also living longer than ever before. SAMHSA has referred to substance abuse among older adults as an "invisible epidemic."

This issue contrasts the research, prevention, and treatment efforts in younger and older people. In the YES selection, NIDA describes addiction in youth and the importance of addressing the problem in adolescence and young adulthood. In the NO selection, psychiatrist and author Olivera Bogunovic describes the unique problems facing older individuals.

YES ⬅

National Institute on Drug Abuse

Drugs, Brains, and Behavior: The Science of Addiction

What Is Drug Addiction?

Addiction is defined as a chronic, relapsing brain disease that is characterized by compulsive drug seeking and use, despite harmful consequences. It is considered a brain disease because drugs change the brain—they change its structure and how it works. These brain changes can be long-lasting, and can lead to the harmful behaviors seen in people who abuse drugs.

Addiction is a lot like other diseases, such as heart disease. Both disrupt the normal, healthy functioning of the underlying organ, have serious harmful consequences, and are preventable and treatable, but if left untreated, can last a lifetime. . . .

Is Continued Drug Abuse a Voluntary Behavior?

The initial decision to take drugs is typically voluntary. However, with continued use, a person's ability to exert self-control can become seriously impaired; this impairment in self-control is the hallmark of addiction. Brain imaging studies of people with addiction show physical changes in areas of the brain that are critical to judgment, decision making, learning and memory, and behavior control. Scientists believe that these changes alter the way the brain works and may help explain the compulsive and destructive behaviors of addiction.

Why Do Some People Become Addicted to Drugs, While Others Do Not?

As with any other disease, vulnerability to addiction differs from person to person, and no single factor determines whether a person will become addicted to drugs. In general, the more *risk factors* a person has, the greater the chance that taking drugs will lead to

abuse and addiction. *Protective factors*, on the other hand, reduce a person's risk of developing addiction. Risk and protective factors may be either environmental (such as conditions at home, at school, and in the neighborhood) or biological (for instance, a person's genes, their stage of development, and even their gender or ethnicity).

What Environmental Factors Increase the Risk of Addiction?

- **Home and Family.** The influence of the home environment, especially during childhood, is a very important factor. Parents or older family members who abuse alcohol or drugs, or who engage in criminal behavior, can increase children's risks of developing their own drug problems.
- **Peer and School.** Friends and acquaintances can have an increasingly strong influence during adolescence. Drug-using peers can sway even those without risk factors to try drugs for the first time. Academic failure or poor social skills can put a child at further risk for using or becoming addicted to drugs.

What Biological Factors Increase Risk of Addiction?

Scientists estimate that genetic factors account for between 40 and 60 percent of a person's vulnerability to addiction; this includes the effects of environmental factors on the function and expression of a person's genes. A person's stage of development and other medical conditions they may have are also factors. Adolescents and people with mental disorders are at greater risk of drug abuse and addiction than the general population.

From National Institute on Drug Abuse, July 2014.

What Other Factors Increase the Risk of Addiction?

Early Use. Although taking drugs at any age can lead to addiction, research shows that the earlier a person begins to use drugs, the more likely he or she is to develop serious problems. This may reflect the harmful effect that drugs can have on the developing brain; it also may result from a mix of early social and biological vulnerability factors, including unstable family relationships, exposure to physical or sexual abuse, genetic susceptibility, or mental illness. Still, the fact remains that early use is a strong indicator of problems ahead, including addiction. . . .

The Brain Continues to Develop into Adulthood and Undergoes Dramatic Changes During Adolescence

One of the brain areas still maturing during adolescence is the prefrontal cortex—the part of the brain that enables us to assess situations, make sound decisions, and keep our emotions and desires under control. The fact that this critical part of an adolescent's brain is still a work in progress puts them at increased risk for making poor decisions (such as trying drugs or continuing to take them). Also, introducing drugs during this period of development may cause brain changes that have profound and long-lasting consequences.

Why Is Adolescence a Critical Time for Preventing Drug Addiction?

As noted previously, early use of drugs increases a person's chances of developing addiction. Remember, drugs change brains—and this can lead to addiction and other serious problems. So, preventing early use of drugs or alcohol may go a long way in reducing these risks. If we can prevent young people from experimenting with drugs, we can prevent drug addiction.

Risk of drug abuse increases greatly during times of transition. For an adult, a divorce or loss of a job may lead to drug abuse; for a teenager, risky times include moving or changing schools. In early adolescence, when children advance from elementary through middle school, they face new and challenging social and academic situations. Often during this period, children are exposed to abusable substances such as cigarettes and alcohol for the first time.

When they enter high school, teens may encounter greater availability of drugs, drug use by older teens, and social activities where drugs are used.

At the same time, many behaviors that are a normal aspect of their development, such as the desire to try new things or take greater risks, may increase teen tendencies to experiment with drugs. Some teens may give in to the urging of drug-using friends to share the experience with them. Others may think that taking drugs (such as steroids) will improve their appearance or their athletic performance or that abusing substances such as alcohol or MDMA (ecstasy or "Molly") will ease their anxiety in social situations. A growing number of teens are abusing prescription ADHD stimulants such as Adderall® to help them study or lose weight. Teens' still-developing judgment and decision-making skills may limit their ability to accurately assess the risks of all of these forms of drug use.

Using abusable substances at this age can disrupt brain function in areas critical to motivation, memory, learning, judgment, and behavior control. So, it is not surprising that teens who use alcohol and other drugs often have family and social problems, poor academic performance, health-related problems (including mental health), and involvement with the juvenile justice system.

Can Research-Based Programs Prevent Drug Addiction in Youth?

Yes. The term "research-based" means that these programs have been rationally designed based on current scientific evidence, rigorously tested, and shown to produce positive results. Scientists have developed a broad range of programs that positively alter the balance between risk and protective factors for drug abuse in families, schools, and communities. Studies have shown that research-based programs, such as those described in NIDA's *Preventing Drug Use among Children and Adolescents: A Research-Based Guide for Parents, Educators, and Community Leaders*, can significantly reduce early use of tobacco, alcohol, and illicit drugs.

The mission of the **NATIONAL INSTITUTE ON DRUG ABUSE** is to lead the Nation in bringing the power of science to bear on drug abuse and addiction. It supports and conducts research across a broad range of disciplines and ensures the rapid and effective dissemination of the results of that research to significantly improve prevention and treatment.

Olivera Bogunovic

 **NO**

Substance Abuse in Aging and Elderly Adults

As we are faced with a growing population of older adults, a better understanding of the issues that they confront is crucial.

In 2009, the elderly constituted 12.9% of the US population. This translates to 39.6 million—a number that is growing.[1] Perhaps as a result of generational stereotyping or ageism, the topic of substance abuse and dependence is rarely associated with the elderly. Although there is a dearth of literature regarding patterns of illicit drug use and abuse in older adults, recent surveys indicate that abuse of illicit drugs by older adults is on the rise.[2] A 2009 study by the Substance Abuse and Mental Health Services Administration (SAMHSA) yielded some sobering conclusions regarding substance use in individuals aged 50 years or older.[2]

Consequences of Substance Abuse in the Aging and Elderly

Clinical research is beginning to elucidate the consequences of unrecognized substance abuse or dependence on an aging population. Complications that occur with increasing frequency with age, such as medical comorbidity, cognitive impairment, and frailty, contribute to the potential adverse interactions between substance misuse and an aging brain.

The 2009 SAMHSA's National Survey on Drug Use and Health revealed dramatic increases in illicit drug use in older adults, including nonmedical use of prescription drugs among women aged 60 to 64. Overall, alcohol was the most frequently reported primary substance of abuse for persons aged 50 or older. Opiates were the second most commonly reported primary substance of abuse, reported most frequently by individuals aged 50 to 59. These individuals also had the highest proportions of inpatient admissions for cocaine, marijuana, and stimulant abuse.[2]

One-quarter of the prescription drugs sold in the United States are used by the elderly, and the prevalence of abuse of these agents may be as high as 11%.[3] Commonly prescribed drugs with abuse potential include those for anxiety, pain, and insomnia, such as benzodiazepines, opiate analgesics, and skeletal muscle relaxants. A review of medical records of 100 elderly patients who were dependent on prescription drugs and were admitted to the Mayo Inpatient Addiction Program between 1974 and 1993 assessed the frequency of abuse by type of prescription drug. The most commonly abused were sedative/hypnotics (mostly benzodiazepines) and opioid analgesics.[4]

Aging induces physiological changes that increase susceptibility to the deleterious effects of alcohol and other illicit substances. Given these changes, the National Institute of Alcohol Abuse and Alcoholism recommends the following for men aged 65 or older: no more than 1 drink daily (ie, 12 oz of beer at 5% alcohol, or 5 oz of wine at 12% alcohol, or a 1.5-oz shot of hard liquor at 40% alcohol), a maximum of 2 drinks on any occasion, and even lower limits for women. These recommendations highlight how alcohol use in the elderly can potentially be problematic, even if it does not cause abuse or dependence. . . .

Early vs Late Onset

Older adult substance abusers can be categorized as early-onset or late-onset abusers. In early-onset abusers, substance abuse develops before age 65. In these individuals, the incidence of psychiatric and physical problems tends to be higher than that in their late-onset counterparts. It is estimated that early-onset substance abusers make up two-thirds of the geriatric alcoholic population.

In late-onset substance abusers, these behaviors are often thought to develop subsequent to stressful life situations that include losses that commonly occur with aging (eg, death of a partner, changes in living situation, retirement, social isolation). These individuals typically experience fewer physical and mental health problems than early-onset abusers.[5]

Comorbidities

Clinical presentations of substance abuse in the elderly may not be suspected because the presenting picture often does not correspond with stereotypes based on younger populations. Severe substance abuse with major social consequences is certainly seen in elderly patients, but antisocial behavior and lower socioeconomic status are less common and clinical manifestations are more variable. Given the higher prevalence of comorbid medical problems, elderly patients are at greater risk for medical consequences associated with substance abuse.

Common medical consequences include liver damage; immune system impairment; and cardiovascular, GI, and endocrinological problems.[6] Elderly patients often present to the emergency department with severe illness. Symptoms of alcohol withdrawal are missed and are easily attributed to a cause other than alcohol abuse. Alcohol withdrawal disorders include tremulous syndrome, hallucinations, seizures, and delirium tremens. Although there is no evidence that the disorders occur at different rates in the elderly, data from animal studies show increased severity of symptoms.

The prevalence of alcohol-related dementia in late life differs depending on the diagnostic criteria used and the population studied; however, there is general consensus that alcohol contributes to cognitive deficits.[7] Substances such as opioids and benzodiazepines also increase the risk of cognitive impairment that ranges from confusion to delirium to dementia.[8]

The coexistence of substance abuse and psychiatric illness has been established in several studies, although the exact relationship remains unclear. Prevalence is estimated to be between 21% and 66%. Approximately 25% of elderly patients have comorbid depression. Also common are cognitive disorders and anxiety disorders, both of which occur in 10% to 15 % of elderly patients.[9]

The treatment of co-occurring disorders in patients with mental illness presents unique challenges. The literature, although extensive for younger adults, is almost nonexistent for older adults. An integrated approach to treatment of co-occurring disorders in severe mental illness provides better outcomes.[10] Using a multidisciplinary team to treat co-occurring disorders enhances cohesiveness of care and reduces conflicts between treaters. Both disorders should be treated as "primary" using a combination of different modalities, such as effective outreach and case management, motivational techniques, psychotherapy, and psychopharmacology.

Diagnosis

In older patients, substance abuse problems are often misdiagnosed. Part of the challenge when working with the older population is to confront one's own biases and beliefs. Another challenge is denial of substance use by the elderly, which can make accurate diagnosis and treatment more difficult.[11] In addition to a clinical interview, several screening instruments can be used (eg, the CAGE questionnaire, the Alcohol Use Disorders Identification Test, and the Michigan Alcoholism Screening Test—Geriatric Version [MAST-G]).[12]

A comprehensive evaluation should include a thorough physical examination along with laboratory analysis and psychiatric, neurological, and social evaluation. An increased focus on successful identification and subsequent treatment is warranted because research indicates that elderly patients reduce substance use when encouraged by their physician.

Treatment

There is a general lack of evidence-based treatment approaches for substance abuse in the elderly. As a result, much of what is recommended is based on interventions that have been validated in younger populations. It is important to understand specific ways to engage the elderly patient. In general, the choice of treatment depends on the severity of the condition and the level of functional impairment and varies from hospitalization to outpatient care.

Psychotherapy

Psychoeducation about the risks of combining alcohol with medications and excessive alcohol use is important. A number of clinical trials have shown that approximately 10% to 30% of problem drinkers have been able to reduce their drinking after brief 1- to 3-session interventions.[13]

The need for detoxification and the potential for serious withdrawal symptoms should be carefully evaluated. Regardless of the treatment modality chosen, psychotherapy and other interventions need to be tailored for each patient. Groups of patients of similar ages are ideal because they increase patient comfort and adherence.

Psychotherapy is often recommended on either an outpatient or inpatient basis, depending on the severity of the problem. Recommendations for specific therapeutic modalities are extrapolated from studies on younger populations because of the lack of such research on older adults. Motivational interviewing has been validated as an effective method to ascertain an individual's willingness to change and to enhance motivation for change.[14] Cognitive-behavioral therapy is also widely used in the treatment of substance abuse.[13] In addition, initial studies of brief therapeutic interventions have shown promise in older adults.[15]

Psychopharmacology

The opiate antagonist naltrexone reduces cravings for alcohol and is intended to be prescribed as adjunctive treatment to psychosocial support to reduce the risk of alcohol relapse. A dosage of 50 mg/d was found to be safe in a 12-week, randomized, placebo-controlled trial in 44 older veterans with alcohol dependence. However, there were no differences in the number of patients who experienced relapse or who remained abstinent in the naltrexone and placebo groups.[16]

Generally, disulfiram should not be prescribed for the elderly because of the increased risk of delirium and other serious adverse effects.[17] Acamprosate is thought to exert its therapeutic effect by modulating the excitatory glutamate amino acid system in the brain. It may be safer and more effective for patients with liver dysfunction; however, it should be used cautiously in elderly patients with impaired renal function. A meta-analysis of studies of acamprosate in younger adults showed a 13% improvement in 12-month continuous abstinence rates.[18]

Finally, there are no known pharmacokinetic studies of buprenorphine/naloxone in older adults with opioid dependence. Sublingual buprenorphine/naloxone must be administered with caution in the elderly because of the increased risk of respiratory suppression and sedation. Lower dosages in the elderly are recommended.

Conclusion

Participation in Alcoholic Anonymous meetings is an important part of treatment. Meetings that have an age-matched cohort provide mutual support, allow for peer bonding, and foster the establishment of peer sobriety networks.

As we are faced with a growing population of older adults, a better understanding of the issues that they confront is crucial. Studies are needed to identify the best ways to integrate screening into general medical settings as well as to understand the neurobiology of substance use disorders in the older adult with medical and cognitive comorbidities and to determine which specific treatment interventions are safe and effective.

References

1. Administration on Aging. Profile of older Americans: 2009. http://www.aoa.gov/aoaroot/aging_statisstics/profile/2009/2.aspx. Accessed July 10, 2012.

2. Results from the 2009 National Survey on Drug Use and Health: Volume I. Summary of national findings. www.samhsa.gov/data/NSDUH/2k9NSDUH/2k9Results.htm. Accessed July 9, 2012.

3. Culberson JW, Ziska M. Prescription drug misuses/abuse in the elderly. *Geriatrics*. 2008;63:22-31.

4. Jinks MJ, Raschko RR. A profile of alcohol and prescription drug abuse in a high-risk community-based elderly population. *DICP*. 1990;24:971-975.

5. Brennan PL, Moos RH. Late-life drinking behavior: the influence of personal characteristics, life context, and treatment. *Alcohol Health Res World*. 1996;20:197-204.

6. Weathermon R, Crabb DW. Alcohol and medication interactions. *Alcohol Res Health*. 1999;23:40-54.

7. George LK, Landerman R, Blazer DG, Anthony DC. Cognitive impairment. In: Robins LN, Reiger DA, eds. *Psychiatric Disorders in America: The Epidemiologic Catchment Area Study*. New York: Free Press; 1991:291-327.

8. Rogers J, Wiese BS, Rabheru K. The older brain on drugs: substances that may cause cognitive impairment. *Geriatr Aging*. 2008;11:284-289.

9. Bartels SJ, Blow FC, Van Citters AD, Brockmann LM. Dual diagnosis among older adults: co-occurring substance abuse and psychiatric illness. *J Dual Diag*. 2006;2:9-30.

10. Kranzler HR, Rosenthal RN. Dual diagnosis: alcoholism and co-morbid psychiatric disorders. *Am J Addict*. 2003;12(suppl 1):S26-S40.

11. Pennington H, Butler R, Eagger S. The assessment of patients with alcohol disorders by an old age psychiatric service. *Aging Ment Health*. 2000;4:182-184.

12. Moore AA, Seeman T, Morgenstern H, et al. Are there differences between older persons who screen positive on the CAGE questionnaire

and the Short Michigan Alcoholism Screening Test-Geriatric Version? *J Am Geriatr Soc.* 2002;50:858-886.

13. Fleming MF, Manwell LB, Barry KL, et al. Brief physician advice for alcohol problems in older adults: a randomized community-based trial. *J Fam Pract*. 1999;48:378-384.

14. Miller WR, Rollnick S. *Motivational Interviewing: Preparing People for Change*. 2nd ed. New York: Guilford Press; 2002.

15. Bartels SJ, Coakley EH, Zubritsky C, et al; PRISM-E Investigators. Improving access to geriatric mental health services: a randomized trial comparing treatment engagement with integrated versus enhanced referral care for depression, anxiety, and at-risk alcohol use. *Am J Psychiatry*. 2004;161:1455-1462.

16. Oslin D, Liberto JG, O'Brien J, et al. Naltrexone as an adjunctive treatment for older patients with alcohol dependence. *Am J Geriatr Psychiatry*. 1997;5:324-332.

17. Dunne FJ. Misuse of alcohol or drugs by elderly people. *BMJ*. 1994;308:608-609.

18. Mann K, Lehert P, Morgan MY. The efficacy of acamprosate in the maintenance of abstinence in alcohol-dependent individuals: results of a meta-analysis. *Alcohol Clin Exp Res*. 2004;28:51-63.

Dr. Olivera Bogunovic is a psychiatrist and a cofounder of Hingham Wellness, a clinical team focused on treatment of co-occuring psychiatric and addictive disorders. She is particularly interested in understanding the relationship between psychiatric illness and addiction, and has devoted her career to addiction and geriatric psychiatry. Dr. Bogunovic is on the faculty at Harvard Medical School.

EXPLORING THE ISSUE

Is Drug Addiction a Problem of Youth?

Critical Thinking and Reflection

1. Generally drug prevention and treatment programs in the United States have not focused on older individuals. Why?
2. Why might younger people be more susceptible to drug addiction than older people? Why might older individuals be more susceptible than younger individuals?
3. How would you focus prevention efforts on older individuals? What aspects of social life, culture, medicine, and the law must be considered for this population?
4. Are our drug laws at the federal or local level appropriate to deter drug abuse by older people? What changes would you propose for legal deterrence?
5. What questions and concerns should a health practitioner keep in mind when working with older individuals regarding addiction? What should a family member (e.g., child or grandchild) consider?

Is There Common Ground?

Drug addiction is not uncommon among older people. The Substance Abuse and Mental Health Services Administration (SAMHSA) estimated that approximately 6 percent of individuals aged 50–59 used an illicit drug in the last month, numbers comparable to those in young people, as determined by Monitoring the Future. While drug addiction exists in older people, it's not something people (e.g., family members, caregivers, and physicians) typically think about. When they do think about it, they may not be comfortable talking with the individual about their addiction.

SAMHSA identified several factors that are barriers to identifying and treating older adults with drug addiction problems. One factor is ageism, the tendency to assign negative stereotypes to older people and to explain away their problems as "being old," rather than to specific medical or psychological problems. This may lead to an assumption that it's not "worth it" to manage addiction in an individual or it's not a "real problem." A second factor is a lack of awareness about the problem by the individual and/or his social circle. People might not recognize addiction as a problem for older people in general and older people might have different attitudes about drugs and alcohol from different mores and assumptions. A third factor is that clinicians, just as non-clinicians, might not recognize addiction in an older individual. As older individuals will likely have other health concern, addiction symptoms might be misdiagnosed as something else (e.g., heart disease or Alzheimer disease). Finally, comorbid complications from other disorders can influence the treatment of addiction disorders in older people. For example, treatment programs might be able to accommodate older individuals with health problems beyond addiction.

Younger and older people likely do differ in some aspects of addiction. For example, comparisons indicate difference in the motivations to use drugs: Older individuals are more likely to abuse alcohol and use prescription medications (e.g., sedatives and opiates) inappropriately than they are to abuse illicit substances (e.g., cocaine, methamphetamine, and heroin). Older people are less likely than younger people to seek a "high" or thrill. Older individuals are more likely to be motivated to abuse a drug to manage physical or psychological symptoms; hence their increased likelihood of abusing sleeping pills, anti-anxiety medications, and prescription pain medications.

Additional Resources

Atkinson, S. (2012). *Geriatric Pharmacology—The Principles of Practice & Clinical Recommendations.* Eau Claire WI: PESI HealthCare.

This book is a reference to help health practitioners understand how aging can influence drug responses, and the unique challenges of pharmacotherapy in an aging population.

Kalikow, K. T. (2011). *Kids on Meds: Up-to-Date Information About the Most Commonly Prescribed Psychiatric medicals.* New York: W.W. Norton & Company.

Child and adolescent Psychologist Kevin Kalikow reviews the medications used to treat psychological disorders in children.

Koechl, B. et al. (2012). Age-related aspects of addiction. *Gerontology*. 58(6): 540–544.

The authors summarize the problems related substance addiction in older populations. They note that there is a lack of evidence on effective treatments for these individuals.

Substance Abuse and Mental Health Services Administration (SAMHSA, 1998). *Substance Abuse Among Older Adults*, Rockville (MD): SAMSA.

This guide from SAMHSA, available online at http://www.ncbi.nlm.nih.gov/books/ NBK64422/, provides a thorough overview of the problems of substance abuse among older adults, with an emphasis on alcohol and prescription abuse in this population.

White, A. & Hingson, R. (2013). The burden of alcohol use: Excessive alcohol consumption and related consequences among college students. *Alcohol*. 35(2): 201–218.

This review paper analyzes and summarizes research on the multiple factors (e.g., genetics, Greek life, and high school drinking) that cause and mitigate the outcomes from excessive drinking among college students.

Internet References . . .

American Association of Retired Persons (now, strictly AARP)

http://www.aarp.org/

Centers for Disease Control—Healthy Aging

http://www.cdc.gov/aging/

Monitoring the Future

http://www.monitoringthefuture.org/

National Institutes of Health—National Institute on Aging

https://www.nia.nih.gov/

National Institutes of Health—National Institute on Drug Abuse: NIDA for Teens

http://teens.drugabuse.gov/

Office of National Drug Control Policy

https://www.whitehouse.gov/ondcp/

Substance Abuse and Mental Health Services Administration

http://www.samhsa.gov/

Selected, Edited, and with Issue Framing Material by:
Dennis K. Miller, *University of Missouri*

ISSUE

Is Advertising Responsible for Alcohol Use by Young People?

YES: **Timothy S. Naimi, et al.**, from "Amount of Televised Alcohol Advertising Exposure and the Quantity of Alcohol Consumed by Youth," *Journal of Studies on Alcohol and Drugs* (2016)

NO: **National Institute on Alcohol Abuse and Alcoholism**, from "Parenting to Prevent Childhood Alcohol Use," *National Institute on Alcohol Abuse and Alcoholism Research Report* (2017)

Learning Outcomes

After reading this issue, you will be able to:

- Explain how advertising can influence behavior and attitudes through observational learning and modeling.
- Identify the factors that contribute to young people using alcohol.
- Critically evaluate research on advertising and behavior.
- Consider how a complex public health issue—underage drinking—may have many intertwined causative factors.

ISSUE SUMMARY

YES: Alcohol advertisements stabilize alcohol use to cultural norms and associate it with fun and success. Companies spend on marketing because advertisements increase the likelihood of purchase of specific brands. Dr. Timothy S. Naimi and colleagues examined the relationship between the amount of exposure to alcohol advertising and alcohol consumption in underage youth. Their findings revealed that advertising has an effect on drinking behavior.

NO: The National Institute on Alcohol Abuse and Alcoholism (NIAAA) notes that parenting style has an important impact on a child's alcohol use and attitudes toward drinking.

The legal drinking age in the United States is 21 years old. However, according to the National Institute on Alcohol Abuse and Alcoholism (NIAAA) one-third of 15 year olds and over half of 18 year olds have had a drink. Among underage (18–21 years) college students, NIAAA estimate that almost 60 percent had a drink in the last month and eighty percent had in the last year. Importantly, two-thirds of those that drank binge drank. Not all college students drink—one in five students abstain from alcohol. But, early alcohol use is a significant public health concern.

Alcohol can have negative effects on health and well-being throughout the entire lifespan. However, the consequences can be more severe in the short- and long-term when alcohol is consumed by teenagers and young adults.

- Underage alcohol use is an important contributing factor in injuries and deaths, according to the Centers for Disease Control (CDC). For example, automobile crashes are a leading cause of death and injury in teenagers, and the CDC estimates that at least a quarter of these accidents involve alcohol. Teenagers that drink are more likely to be involved in fights that result in medical attention than those that abstain.

- Drinking can lead to poor decision making about sexual behavior, intended or unintended, according to the CDC. Teenagers who drink are less likely to use protection during sex, which can lead to unplanned pregnancy and sexually transmitted diseases. Moreover, youth who drink are more likely to carry out or be the victim of a physical or sexual assault than peers who do not drink.

- The National Institutes of Health note that critical periods of brain development occur through young adulthood and alcohol can potentially affect brain structure and function. Teen alcohol use may cause cognitive and learning problems throughout lifespan and these challenges are more profound the younger drinking commences.

- The CDC and NIAAA note that early alcohol use is associated with increased trouble with the law and lower rates of school completion. College students who drink are less likely to graduate or graduate on time than those who abstain.

- People who start drinking as a teenager are three to four times more likely to develop substance use disorder at some point in their lives than those that postpone drinking until later in life, according to NIAAA.

Despite the known risks associated with underage alcohol use, why do young people drink? In the NO section for this issue the NIAAA describes a number of factors that contribute to the behavior. These include parenting style, parent–childhood interactions, genetics, and modeling.

Modeling is a type of observational learning—a long-lasting change in behavior after exposure to performance of the behavior by another. For example, after witnessing her older sister being punished by her father for taking a cookie, the younger child does not take cookies without first asking permission. The younger child does not need to be punished by her father to learn to avoid taking cookies. A pioneer in this field was Albert Bandura. In the early 1960s Bandura and his colleagues conducted series of studies where preschool children watched film of an adult playing with an inflatable toy (a Bobo doll). For half of the children, the adult played with the toy gently, while the other half of the children watched the adult furiously

and viscously attack the toy. Later, when all were allowed to play with the toy, those that observed the adult aggressively play with the toy were twice as likely to behave aggressively than those that observed the adult play with the toy gently.

The work of Bandura and others demonstrates that humans can learn through observation. We can be taught complex skills through demonstration and we readily imitate the action of others. The imitation of others' behaviors is referred to as modeling. Modeling is more likely to occur when the model is somewhat similar to ourselves, but is more attractive and has a higher status. For example, many of us imitate, or model, our fashion or ways of speaking from what we observe in celebrities. Research on tobacco use in the 1990s and early 2000s demonstrated that adolescents whose favorite actors smoked in movies were more likely to smoke themselves. The more smoking behavior an adolescent observes in the media, the more likely they are to have positive (or nonnegative) views of tobacco use. Changes in behavior due to modeling may not occur after a single observation; rather years of exposure may have a cumulative impact on attitudes and behavior. Watching a popular hero smoke in one movie may not cause someone to start using tobacco. But, a lifetime of seeing smoking associated with being attractive and wealthy may glamorize cigarette use and increase the chance that someone takes up the habit. Indeed, the United States Surgeon General concluded in 2012 that exposure to onscreen smoking causes young people to start smoking. The Motion Picture Association of America (MPAA), which assigns movie ratings, provides a label for some movies that contain smoking, just as they label violence, foul language and sexual behavior in movies. Although not completely eliminated, the occurrence of tobacco use in movies has declined since 2012 in an effort by some movie studios to decrease tobacco use in young people.

In response to research on observational learning and smoking behavior—and other public health campaigns to improve overall health—tobacco advertising has been severely restricted and banned in the United States. In the early 1970s the Federal Communications Commission prohibited tobacco companies from advertising on television. Gone was the handsome and rugged Marlboro Man and the sexy and fit Virginia Slim-smoking woman from television. The Tobacco Master Settlement Agreement in the late 1990s banned outdoor, billboard, and public transportation advertising of cigarettes and prohibited advertising campaigns targeted at young people.

If watching others smoke in person or in the media influences tobacco use, how does watching others use alcohol influence drinking behavior? The United States government does not directly regulate alcohol advertising. Rather, the Federal Trade Commission (FTC) has encouraged the alcohol industry to establish and adopt its own guidelines with standards that reduce the extent to which alcohol targets teens and young people. For example, the Distilled Spirits Council (DSC) of the United States established a code of principles to market their products to adults of legal age in a responsible and appropriate manner. The DSC's code notes, "beverage alcohol advertising and marketing materials should portray beverage alcohol products and drinkers in a responsible manner." The DSC and other industry groups are encouraged by the FTC to advertise in media that will be viewed by adults, not children. An audience that is at least 70 percent adult is the acknowledged standard. However, the DSC's code also notes, "beverage alcohol products and drinkers may be portrayed as part of responsible personal and social experiences and activities, such as the depiction of persons in a social or romantic setting, persons who appear to be attractive or affluent, and persons who appear to be relaxing or

in an enjoyable setting." Television and magazine advertisements for vodka often include celebrities and models enjoying spirits in high-end, expensive, and glamorous night clubs. How might this approach influence modeling behavior by young people?

The FTC encourages the alcohol industry to be responsible in its advertising, but does alcohol advertising contribute to alcohol use by young people? The YES section is a research study on the relationship between the amount of television advertising observed and the quantity of alcohol consumed by young people. The authors conclude that there is a positive association between these variables. The NO section does not eliminate or negate the role of advertising in alcohol use by young people. Indeed, it notes that parents influence attitudes about alcohol and drinking behavior through modeling. The NO section does indicate other factors—parenting styles, parent–child interactions, and genetics as making important contributions. Is advertising responsible for alcohol use by adolescents and young people? If it does play a role, what is its relative contribution?

YES ↵

Timothy S. Naimi, et al.

Amount of Televised Alcohol Advertising Exposure and the Quantity of Alcohol Consumed by Youth

Alcohol consumption contributes to the three leading causes of death (motor vehicle crash fatalities, suicide, and homicide) among underage youth ages 12–20 years (Donovan, 2013). Alcohol advertising exposure has been positively associated with youth's alcohol consumption, and restrictions on alcohol marketing are recommended as preventive interventions by the Institute of Medicine and the World Health Organization (Bonnie & O'Connell, 2004; World Health Organization, 2010).

Alcohol companies, through self-regulatory guidelines, tacitly acknowledge the importance of alcohol marketing by restricting advertising on television programs where the audience is disproportionately composed of underage persons, and by limiting the content of such advertising so that it does not primarily appeal to underage youth (The Beer Institute, 2011; Distilled Spirits Council of the United States, 2011; The Wine Institute, 2012). Even so, the role that advertising plays in drinking behaviors is still an area of scientific controversy (Nelson, 2010).

An important limitation of previous studies is that they have examined the relationship between total advertising exposure and total consumption across all types of alcohol or for broad categories of alcohol (e.g., beer, wine, distilled spirits). This approach does not permit an examination of the more specific relationship between brand-specific exposure and brand-specific consumption. This is important because advertising is brand specific, some brands advertise more than others, and different brands advertise to different populations.

Our research team has addressed this limitation by combining data about brand-specific advertising exposure with data on brand-specific alcohol consumption. After accounting for a variety of factors, including overall adult market share, we found a strong positive relationship between brand-specific exposure to television advertising and the likelihood of youth consuming a particular brand, at both the individual level (Ross et al., 2014) and the population level (Ross et al., 2014, 2015).

This finding is consistent with the Heuristic Marketing Receptivity Model, which posits that marketing-specific cognitions and attitudes in four domains mediate the association between alcohol advertising and consumption: alcohol expectancies, perceptions of alcohol norms, identifying oneself as a drinker, and brand loyalty (McClure et al., 2013). This result might also be understood as a "mere exposure" effect, by which consumers develop a preference for certain products simply because of their greater familiarity, and is an effect that can occur outside conscious awareness (Bornstein, 1989; Zajonc, 2001).

Our earlier study corroborated other studies indicating that advertising exposure is associated with brand selection by underage drinkers, but the question remains whether advertising affects how much of those brands a person drinks (Anderson et al., 2009; Smith & Foxcroft, 2009). A previous study by our research team found that increased brand-specific advertising exposure was significantly associated with increased brand-specific consumption (Ross et al., 2015). However, even if advertising has an effect on the quantity of consumption of a particular brand, another important question is whether this might lead to decreased consumption of other brands (i.e., brand substitution) and therefore have no impact or a minimal impact on total consumption.

The present study was designed to address the relationship between aggregate brand-specific advertising and total brand-specific consumption, overall and among various demographic groups and at different levels of advertising exposure. We hypothesized that increased aggregated exposure to brand-specific advertising would be associated with increased total consumption of those same brands.

Method

Study population used to assess alcohol consumption among underage youth

The Alcohol Brand Research Among Underage Drinkers (ABRAND) survey was the source of data for alcohol consumption among underage youth (Siegel et al., 2013). The national sample comprised 1,032 persons ages 13–20 who reported drinking alcohol in the past 30 days. Those ages 18–20 years were recruited directly from the Knowledge-Panel® maintained by Knowledge Networks (GfK Custom Research, Palo Alto, CA), a pre-recruited panel of approximately 50,000 adults (including young adults ages 18–20) who agreed to be invited periodically to participate in Internet-based surveys. . . .

Boston University Medical Center's institutional review board approved the study protocol.

Measures of advertising exposure and other covariates

The primary exposure was aggregated brand-specific television advertising. The survey provided participants with a list of the 20 most popular nonsports television shows among underage youth (by total viewership) that contained alcohol advertising and asked them to identify which programs they had watched in the past 30 days. Under a license agreement with Nielsen (2015 © The Nielsen Company, New York, NY, data from 2011–2012 used under license, all rights reserved), we had access to audience data and brand-specific advertising data for each of those shows for the year before the ABRAND survey, which allowed us to calculate a past-year cumulative advertising exposure (adstock) measure for each survey respondent.

Advertising exposure is measured in gross rating points (GRPs), which are per capita advertising exposure measures calculated by dividing the advertising exposures seen by a demographic group by the population size of the demographic group and multiplying by 100. Adstock is the pastyear cumulative advertising exposure for each participant based on GRPs. Advertising effects are not just driven by the most recent advertising exposure, but rather are the result of cumulative advertising exposure over time (Broadbent, 1997; Wind & Sharp, 2009). Past advertising exposures are discounted by a decay rate with a specified half-life, which is typically 3 to 4 weeks for frequently purchased consumer goods (Broadbent, 1997).

. . .

The outcome measure was the survey participants' aggregated consumption of the 61 alcohol brands that advertised during the past year on one or more of the 20

television programs. . . . Participants indicated the number of days in the past 30 days that they had consumed a specific brand of alcohol and how many drinks, on average, they consumed on a typical drinking day. For each brand, the total number of brand-specific drinks consumed in the past 30 days was the product of the number of drinks times the number of drinking days.

Covariates included age, which was calculated from the participants' date of birth. We classified self-reported race/ethnicity into four categories: non-Hispanic White, Black/African American, Hispanic, and other. We divided household income—into four categories: under $15,000; $15,000–$39,999; $40,000–$99,999; and $100,000 or higher. We assessed smoking with the question, "During the past 30 days, on how many days did you smoke cigarettes?" The responses options were *0 days, 1 or 2 days, 3–5 days, 6–9 days, 10–19 days, 20–29 days, and all 30 days*. We dichotomized the data as "reported smoking" versus "no reported smoking." We assessed risk-taking propensity by asking about seatbelt use as follows: "How often do you wear a seatbelt when you are riding in or driving a car?" The response options were never, *rarely, sometimes, most of the time, always, I don't know*, which we dichotomized as "always" versus any other answer. To assess parental drinking we asked, "Do you have a parent, guardian, or other adult caretaker who now or previously lived in your household who drinks alcohol at least once a month?" The respondents answered yes or no.

We controlled for other media use by assessing average daily television viewing hours (a weighted average of self-reported weekday and weekend television viewing time) and Internet use (typical daily usage in hours). To control for the consumption of additional alcohol brands, we calculated each participant's consumption of alcohol brands that were not advertised on the 20 television programs, which we refer to here as "non-advertised" brands, although they might have been advertised on other programs or in other media. We also calculated the proportion of non-advertised brands consumed relative to all brands.

Brand-specific covariates included the (a) alcoholic beverage type (malts, including beer and flavored alcoholic beverages; spirits, including bourbon, cordials and liqueurs, cognac, rum, scotch, tequila, vodka, and whiskey; and wine); (b) the average brand price (above or below the median price of a U.S. standard drink); and (c) brand consumption prevalence among persons ages 13–20.

We acquired brand prices from the ABRAND project's Minimum Financial Outlay database (www.youthalcoholbrands.com/outlay.html), which reports the average price per ounce of ethanol for 951 alcohol brands in 2011 (DiLoreto et al., 2012). . . .

Figure 1

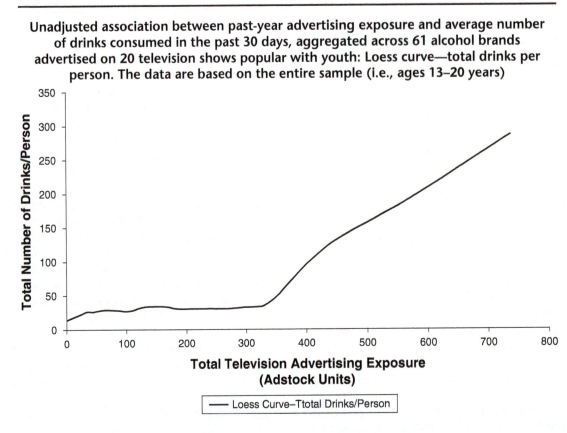

Unadjusted association between past-year advertising exposure and average number of drinks consumed in the past 30 days, aggregated across 61 alcohol brands advertised on 20 television shows popular with youth: Loess curve—total drinks per person. The data are based on the entire sample (i.e., ages 13–20 years)

We determined the prevalence of brand-level consumption among underage youth (to assess "popularity") by examining the ABRAND Brand Preference Database, which reports the proportion of persons ages 13–20 who had consumed each of several brands in the past 30 days. . . .

increased from 0 to 300 adstock units. For participants in the entire sample exposed to 300 or more adstock units of advertising, per-person consumption increased from 33 drinks to more than 200 drinks consumed during the past 30 days. . . .

Results

Among the sample of young drinkers, the median number of drinks consumed in the past 30 days was 5 drinks, with an interquartile range of 24 drinks. After weighting, the 61 brands advertised on those programs accounted for 46.9% of all alcohol consumption reported by the sample of underage drinkers.

Figure 1 shows the unadjusted association between past-year advertising exposure and the total number of drinks consumed in the past 30 days, aggregated across the 61 alcohol brands advertised on 20 television shows popular with youth. The average number of drinks consumed per underage youth during the past 30 days increased from 14 to 33 drinks per month as advertising exposure

Discussion

Among this national sample of underage youth, there was a significant positive relationship between their aggregated past-year exposure to advertising and the total quantity of alcohol consumed in the past 30 days, even after controlling for consumption of non-advertised brands. Although exposure to alcohol advertising is related to which brands underage youth drink (Ross et al., 2014), few studies have assessed whether the quantity of advertising exposure is positively associated with the total quantity of alcohol consumed by underage youth (Snyder et al., 2006).

We believe that this is the first study to examine this relationship using brand-specific advertising data and corresponding brand-specific consumption, which greatly increases the specificity of the exposure–consumption relationship and therefore makes it more plausible that advertising is in fact related to consumption. Furthermore, controlling for the consumption of non-advertised brands serves to address the question of whether advertising might affect the consumption of particular brands without affecting the overall amount of alcohol consumed. Our findings suggest that the increased consumption of advertised brands is not being cancelled out by the decreased consumption of other brands (brand substitution).

Although there was a temporal relationship between past-year advertising exposure (with a decay factor built in for the decreased effect of advertising over time) and current consumption, this study is largely cross-sectional in nature, so there is the possibility of reverse causation. Note, however, that there was a dose–response relationship: although the findings were significant among underage youth with less than 300 adstock units of advertising exposure, the exposure–consumption relationship was particularly strong among those with 300 or more adstock units of exposure. There were fewer youth with these higher levels of advertising exposure, but they consumed a disproportionately large amount of the alcohol consumed by the entire youth sample. Of note, youth who drink most heavily experience the majority of alcohol-related harms (Roberts et al., 2015).

Our finding of a stronger exposure–consumption relationship among participants with high levels of aggregate brand-specific advertising exposure differs from the traditional diminishing marginal product curve associated with advertising effects on brand selection and brand-specific consumption (Ross et al., 2015). Our results could be attributable to cross-brand advertising effects, where advertising for one alcohol brand is associated with increased consumption of other advertised brands (Hanssens et al., 2005; Vakratsas & Ambler, 1999). Alternatively, there may be differences in confounding factors or nonresponse biases among those with different levels of advertising exposure, or an artifact from measurement error amplification that arises from aggregating consumption and exposure measures across brands.

This study is subject to several caveats and limitations. Logistically, the study could not assess the participants' exposure to all television shows, and therefore the number of advertised brands we could examine was limited. Our strategy was to focus on the 20 most popular television shows among underage youth, and we found that the alcohol brands advertised on those programs during the past year accounted for nearly half of all alcohol consumed by the youth sample in the past 30 days.

Although we controlled for total television and Internet viewing hours, we could not fully account for the participant's exposure to other sources of alcohol advertising. However, controlling for the consumption of non-advertised brands and several other relevant covariates mitigated this potential limitation. In addition, we could only control for a limited number of other potential confounders that could be associated with both television viewing and alcohol consumption (e.g., psychological factors).

Finally, this study is subject to possible nonresponse bias. Because the sample of 18- to 20-year-olds drew from existing Knowledge Networks panelists, we compared 18- to 20-year-old respondents to nonrespondents based on demographic factors to help assess the nature of potential nonresponse bias, using a chi-square test to assess the significance of observed differences. The nonrespondents were slightly older ($p < .05$) but similar in gender ($p = .41$) and region of the country ($p = .11$). However, nonrespondents were more likely to be Black ($p < .0001$), be from lower income households ($p < .01$), and not have Internet access before being enrolled in the panel ($p < .0001$). This type of analysis was not possible for the 13- to 17-year-old nonrespondents, nor do we know how these factors associate with advertising exposure or alcohol consumption.

Conclusions

Our findings indicate that the amount of exposure to television alcohol advertising is associated with the quantity of alcohol consumed by underage youth, not just which brands they consume. In addition, there was a stronger association between advertising and consumption at higher levels of exposure. This study should prompt a reevaluation of the industry's self-regulatory framework (Federal Trade Commission, 2014) in order to reduce advertising exposure among underage youth, particularly at higher levels. Future research should examine exposure–consumption relationships longitudinally and in other media and should assess larger numbers of youth with higher levels of advertising exposure.

This research was supported by National Institute on Alcohol Abuse and Alcoholism Grant R01 AA020309-01. Access to Nielsen data was supported by Cooperative Agreement Number 5U58DP002027 from the Centers for Disease Control and Prevention. The funders had no role in the design or conduct of the study; the collection, management, analysis, or interpretation of the data; the preparation, review, or approval of the manuscript; or the decision to submit the manuscript for publication. The contents of this article are solely the responsibility of the authors and do not necessarily represent the official views of the National Institutes of Health or the Centers for Disease Control and Prevention.

References

Anderson, P., de Bruijn, A., Angus, K., Gordon, R., & Hastings, G. (2009). Impact of alcohol advertising and media exposure on adolescent alcohol use: A systematic review of longitudinal studies. *Alcohol and Alcoholism, 44,* 229–243. doi:10.1093/alcalc/agn115

The Beer Institute. (2011). *Advertising and marketing code.* Washington, DC: Author.

Bonnie, R. J., & O'Connell, P. M. E. (Eds.). (2004). *Reducing underage drinking: A collective responsibility.* Washington, DC: The National Academies Press.

Bornstein, R. F. (1989). Exposure and affect: Overview and meta-analysis of research, 1968-1987. *Psychological Bulletin, 106,* 265–289. doi:10.1037/0033-2909.106.2.265

Broadbent, S. (1997). *Accountable advertising: A handbook for managers and analysts.* Henley-on-Thames, England: Admap Publications.

DiLoreto, J. T., Siegel, M., Hinchey, D., Valerio, H., Kinzel, K., Lee, S., . . . DeJong, W. (2012). Assessment of the average price and ethanol content of alcoholic beverages by brand—United States, 2011. *Alcoholism: Clinical and Experimental Research, 36,* 1288–1297. doi:10.1111/j.1530-0277.2011.01721.x

Distilled Spirits Council of the United States. (2011). *Code of Responsible Practices for Beverage Alcohol Advertising and Marketing.* Washington, DC: Author. Retrieved from http://www.discus.org/assets/1/7/May_26_2011_DISCUS_Code_Word_Version1.pdf

Donovan, J. E. (2013). The burden of alcohol use: Focus on children and preadolescents. *Alcohol Research: Current Reviews, 35,* 186–192.

Federal Trade Commission. (2014). *Self-regulation in the alcohol industry: Report of the Federal Trade Commission.* Retrieved from https://www.ftc.gov/system/files/documents/reports/self-regulation-alcohol-industry-report-federal-trade-commission/140320alcoholreport.pdf

Hanssens, D. M., Leeflang, P. S. H., & Wittink, D. R. (2005). Market response models and marketing practice. *Applied Stochastic Models in Business and Industry, 21,* 423–434. doi:10.1002/asmb.584

McClure, A. C., Stoolmiller, M., Tanski, S. E., Engels, R. C. M. E., & Sargent, J. D. (2013). Alcohol marketing receptivity, marketing-specific cognitions, and underage binge drinking. *Alcoholism: Clinical and Experimental Research, 37, Supplement 1,* E404–E413. doi:10.1111/j.1530-0277.2012.01932.x

Nelson, J. P. (2010). What is learned from longitudinal studies of advertising and youth drinking and smoking? A critical assessment. *International Journal of Environmental Research and Public Health, 7,* 870–926. doi:10.3390/ijerph7030870

Roberts, S. P., Siegel, M. B., DeJong, W., Naimi, T. S., & Jernigan, D. H. (2015). Brand preferences of underage drinkers who report alcohol-related fights and injuries. *Substance Use & Misuse, 50,* 619–929. doi: 10.3109/10826084.2014.997392

Ross, C. S., Maple, E., Siegel, M., DeJong, W., Naimi, T. S., Ostroff, J., . . . Jernigan, D. H. (2014). The relationship between brand-specific alcohol advertising on television and brand-specific consumption among underage youth. *Alcoholism: Clinical and Experimental Research, 38,* 2234–2242. doi:10.1111/acer.12488

Ross, C. S., Maple, E., Siegel, M., DeJong, W., Naimi, T. S., Padon, A. A., . . . Jernigan, D. H. (2015). The relationship between population-level exposure to alcohol advertising on television and brand-specific consumption among underage youth in the US. *Alcohol and Alcoholism, 50,* 358–364. doi:10.1093/alcalc/agv016

Siegel, M., DeJong, W., Naimi, T. S., Fortunato, E. K., Albers, A. B., Heeren, T., . . . Jernigan, D. H. (2013). Brand-specific consumption of alcohol among underage youth in the United States. *Alcoholism: Clinical and Experimental Research, 37,* 1195–1203. doi:10.1111/acer.12084

Smith, L. A., & Foxcroft, D. R. (2009). The effect of alcohol advertising, marketing and portrayal on drinking behaviour in young people: Systematic review of prospective cohort studies. *BMC Public Health, 9,* 51. doi:10.1186/1471-2458-9-51

Snyder, L. B., Milici, F. F., Slater, M., Sun, H., & Strizhakova, Y. (2006). Effects of alcohol advertising exposure on drinking among youth. *Archives of Pediatrics & Adolescent Medicine, 160,* 18–24. doi:10.1001/archpedi.160.1.18

Wind, Y., & Sharp, B. (2009). Advertising empirical generalizations: Implications for research and action. *Journal of Advertising Research, 49,* 246–252. doi:10.2501/S0021849909090369

The Wine Institute. (2012). *Code of advertising standards.* Retrieved from http://www.wineinstitute. org/initiatives/issuesandpolicy/adcode/details

Vakratsas, D., & Ambler, T. (1999). How advertising works: What do we really know? *Journal of Marketing Research, 63,* 26–43. doi:10.2307/1251999

World Health Organization. (2010). *Global strategy to reduce harmful use of alcohol.* Geneva, Switzerland: Author.

Zajonc, R. B. (2001). Mere exposure: A gateway to the subliminal. *Current Directions in Psychological Science, 10,* 224–228. doi:10.1111/1467-8721.00154

Dr. Timothy S. Naimi, the corresponding and lead author for the YES section, is an Associate Professor at the Boston University Schools of Medicine and Public Health. Dr. Naimi's research is supported by the National Institute on Alcohol Abuse and Alcoholism (NIAAA) and he studies binge drinking, youth alcohol consumption, and the health effects of moderate drinking.

National Institute on Alcohol Abuse and Alcoholism  **NO**

Parenting to Prevent Childhood Alcohol Use

Drinking alcohol undoubtedly is a part of American culture, as are conversations between parents and children about its risks and potential benefits. However, information about alcohol can seem contradictory. Alcohol affects people differently at different stages of life—small amounts may have health benefits for certain adults, but for children and adolescents, alcohol can interfere with normal brain development. Alcohol's differing effects and parents' changing role in their children's lives as they mature and seek greater independence can make talking about alcohol a challenge. Parents may have trouble setting concrete family policies for alcohol use. And they may find it difficult to communicate with children and adolescents about alcohol-related issues.

Research shows, however, that teens and young adults do believe their parents should have a say in whether they drink alcohol. Parenting styles are important—teens raised with a combination of encouragement, warmth, and appropriate discipline are more likely to respect their parents' boundaries. Understanding parental influence on children through conscious and unconscious efforts, as well as when and how to talk with children about alcohol, can help parents have more influence than they might think on a child's alcohol use. Parents can play an important role in helping their children develop healthy attitudes toward drinking while minimizing its risk.

Alcohol Use by Young People

Adolescent alcohol use remains a pervasive problem. The percentage of teenagers who drink alcohol is slowly declining; however, numbers are still quite high. About 22.8 percent of adolescents report drinking by 8th grade, and about 46.3 percent report being drunk at least once by 12th grade.[1]

Parenting Style

Accumulating evidence suggests that alcohol use—and in particular binge drinking—may have negative effects on adolescent development and increase the risk for alcohol dependence later in life.[2,3] This underscores the need for parents to help delay or prevent the onset of drinking as long as possible. Parenting styles may influence whether their children follow their advice regarding alcohol use. Every parent is unique, but the ways in which each parent interacts with his or her children can be broadly categorized into four styles:

- Authoritarian parents typically exert high control and discipline with low warmth and responsiveness. For example, they respond to bad grades with punishment but let good grades go unnoticed.

- Permissive parents typically exert low control and discipline with high warmth and responsiveness. For example, they deem any grades at all acceptable and fail to correct behavior that may lead to bad grades.

- Neglectful parents exert low control and discipline as well as low warmth and responsiveness. For example, they show no interest at all in a child's school performance.

- Authoritative parents exert high control and discipline along with high warmth and responsiveness. For example, they offer praise for good grades and use thoughtful discipline and guidance to help improve low grades.[4]

Regardless of the developmental outcome examined—body image, academic success, or substance abuse—children raised by authoritative parents tend to fare better

National Institute on Alcohol Abuse and Alcoholism. "Parenting to Prevent Childhood Alcohol Use," *National Institute on Alcohol Abuse and Alcoholism Research Report*, 2017.

than their peers.[5] This is certainly true when it comes to the issue of underage drinking,[6] in part because children raised by such parents learn approaches to problem solving and emotional expression that help protect against the psychological dysfunction that often precedes alcohol misuse.[7] The combination of discipline and support by authoritative parents promotes healthy decision-making about alcohol and other potential threats to healthy development.[8]

Modeling

Some parents wonder whether allowing their children to drink in the home will help them develop an appropriate relationship with alcohol. According to most studies this does not appear to be the case. In a study of 6th, 7th, and 8th graders, researchers observed that students whose parents allowed them to drink at home and/or provided them with alcohol experienced the steepest escalation in drinking.[9] Other studies suggest that adolescents who are allowed to drink at home drink more heavily outside of the home.[10] In contrast, adolescents are less likely to drink heavily if they live in homes where parents have specific rules against drinking at a young age and also drink responsibly themselves.[11] However, not all studies suggest that parental provision of alcohol to teens leads to trouble. For instance, one study showed that drinking with a parent in the proper context (such as a sip of alcohol at an important family function) can be a protective factor against excessive drinking.[12] In other contexts, parental provision of alcohol serves as a direct risk factor for excessive drinking, as is the case when parents provide alcohol for parties attended or hosted by their adolescents. Collectively, the literature suggests that permissive attitudes toward adolescent drinking, particularly when combined with poor communication and unhealthy modeling, can lead teens into unhealthy relationships with alcohol.

Genetics

Regardless of what parents may teach their children about alcohol, some genetic factors are present from birth and cannot be changed. Genes appear to influence the development of drinking behaviors in several ways. Some people, particularly those of Asian ancestry, have a natural and unpleasant response to alcohol that helps prevent them from drinking too much. Other people have a naturally high tolerance to alcohol, meaning that to feel alcohol's effects, they must drink more than others. Some personality traits are genetic, and those, like impulsivity,

can put a person at risk for problem drinking. Psychiatric problems may be caused by genetic traits, and such problems can increase risk for alcohol abuse and dependence. Finally, having a parent with a drinking problem increases a child's risk for developing an alcohol problem of his or her own.[13]

Do Teens Listen?

Adolescents do listen to their parents when it comes to issues such as drinking and smoking, particularly if the messages are conveyed consistently and with authority.[5] Research suggests that only 19 percent of teens feel that parents should have a say in the music they listen to, and 26 percent believe their parents should influence what clothing they wear. However, the majority—around 80 percent—feel that parents should have a say in whether they drink alcohol. Those who do not think that parents have authority over these issues are four times more likely than other teens to drink alcohol and three times more likely to have plans to drink if they have not already started.[5]

Whether teens defer to parents on the issue of drinking is statistically linked to how parents parent. Specifically, authoritative parents—those who provide a healthy and consistent balance of discipline and support—are the most likely to have teenagers who respect the boundaries they have established around drinking and other behaviors; whereas adolescents exposed to permissive, authoritarian, or neglectful parenting are less influenced by what their parents say about drinking.[5]

Research suggests that, regardless of parenting styles, adolescents who are aware that their parents would be upset with them if they drank are less likely to do so, highlighting the importance of communication between parents and teens as a protective measure against underage alcohol use.[12]

What Can Parents Do?

Parents influence whether and when adolescents begin drinking as well as how their children drink. Family policies about adolescent drinking in the home and the way parents themselves drink are important. For instance, if you choose to drink, always model responsible alcohol consumption. But what else can parents do to help minimize the likelihood that their adolescent will choose to drink and that such drinking, if it does occur, will become problematic? Studies14 have shown that it is important to:

- Talk early and often, in developmentally appropriate ways, with children and teens about your concerns—and theirs—regarding alcohol. Adolescents who know their parents' opinions about youth drinking are more likely to fall in line with their expectations.

- Establish policies early on, and be consistent in setting expectations and enforcing rules. Adolescents do feel that parents should have a say in decisions about drinking, and they maintain this deference to parental authority as long as they perceive the message to be legitimate. Consistency is central to legitimacy.

- Work with other parents to monitor where kids are gathering and what they are doing. Being involved in the lives of adolescents is key to keeping them safe.

- Work in and with the community to promote dialogue about underage drinking and the creation and implementation of action steps to address it.

- Be aware of your State's laws about providing alcohol to your own children.

- Never provide alcohol to someone else's child.

Children and adolescents often feel competing urges to comply with and resist parental influences. During childhood, the balance usually tilts toward compliance, but during adolescence, the balance often shifts toward resistance as teens prepare for the autonomy of adulthood. With open, respectful communication and explanations of boundaries and expectations, parents can continue to influence their children's decisions well into adolescence and beyond. This is especially important in young people's decisions regarding whether and how to drink—decisions that can have lifelong consequences.

References

1. Johnston, L.D.; Miech, R.A.; O'Malley, P.M.; et al. *Monitoring the Future National Survey: Trends in Lifetime Prevalence of Use of Various Drugs in Grades 8, 10, and 12, 2016.* Ann Arbor, MI: Institute for Social Research, University of Michigan, 2016. Available at: http://www.monitoringthefuture.org/data/16data/16drtbl1.pdf. Accessed 12/13/16.

2. Grant, B.F., and Dawson, D.A. Age at onset of alcohol use and its association with DSM–IV alcohol abuse and dependence: Results from the National Longitudinal Alcohol Epidemiologic Survey. *Journal of Substance Abuse* 9:103–110, 1997.

3. Squeglia, L.M.; Jacobus, J.; and Tapert, S.F. The influence of substance use on adolescent brain development. *Clinical EEG and Neuroscience* 40(1):31–38, 2009.

4. Baumrind, D. Parental disciplinary patterns and social competence in children. *Youth and Society* 9:238–276, 1978.

5. Jackson, C. Perceived legitimacy of parental authority and tobacco and alcohol use during early adolescence. *Journal of Adolescent Health* 31(5):425–432, 2002.

6. Simons-Morton, B.; Haynie, D.L.; Crump, A.D.; et al. Peer and parent influences on smoking and drinking among early adolescents. *Health Education & Behavior* 28(1):95– 107, 2001.

7. Patock-Peckham, J.A., and Morgan-Lopez, A.A. College drinking behaviors: Mediational links between parenting styles, parental bonds, depression, and alcohol problems. *Psychology of Addictive Behaviors* 21(3):297–306, 2007.

8. Steinberg, L.; Lamborn, S.D.; Dornbusch, S.M.; and Darling, N. Impact of parenting practices on adolescent achievement: Authoritative parenting, school involvement, and encouragement to succeed. *Child Development* 63(5):1266–1281, 1992.

9. Komro, K.A.; Maldonado-Molina, M.M.; Tobler, A.L.; et al. Effects of home access and availability of alcohol on young adolescents' alcohol use. *Addiction* 102(10):1597–1608, 2007.

10. van der Vorst, H.; Engels, R.C.; and Burk, W.J. Do parents and best friends influence the normative increase in adolescents' alcohol use at home and outside the home? *Journal of Studies on Alcohol and Drugs* 71(1):105–114, 2010.

11. van der Vorst, H.; Engels, R.C.; Meeus, W.; and Dekovic, M. The impact of alcohol-specific rules, parental norms about early drinking and parental alcohol use on adolescents' drinking behavior. *Journal of Child Psychology and Psychiatry* 47(12):1299–1306, 2006.

12. Foley, K.L.; Altman, D.; Durant, R.H.; and Wolfson, M. Adults' approval and adolescents' alcohol use. *Journal of Adolescent Health* 35(4):e17–e26, 2004.

13. Schuckit, M.A. An overview of genetic influences in alcoholism. *Journal of Substance Abuse Treatment* 36(1):S5–S14, 2009.

14. U.S. Department of Health and Human Services. *The Surgeon General's Call to Action To Prevent and Reduce Underage Drinking: A Guide to Action for Families*. Washington, DC: Office of the Surgeon General, U.S. Department of Health and Human Services, 2007. Available at: http://www.camy. org/_docs/resources/fact-sheets/Call_To_Action. pdf. Accessed 1/20/17.

THE NATIONAL INSTITUTE ON ALCOHOL ABUSE AND ALCOHOLISM supports and conducts research on the impact of alcohol use on human health and well-being. It aims to reduce alcohol-related problems through research, collaborating with institutions engaged in public health, and by disseminating research findings to health practitioners.

EXPLORING THE ISSUE

Is Advertising Responsible for Alcohol Use by Young People?

Critical Thinking and Reflection

1. Does advertising influence alcohol use in young people? Is it more or less of a factor than other variables, such as interactions with parents or genetics?
2. How does alcohol advertising influence alcohol behaviors in people who are middle aged or older? How might alcohol advertising affect a younger person differently than an older person?
3. Should the government regulate alcohol advertising? Should it be banned completely or should there be government regulations on television, billboards or the Internet?
4. Based on what you have learned about the causes of alcohol use in young people, what types of advertisements or approaches might be most effective to increase use?
5. How can advertising be used to decrease alcohol use or minimize some of the negative impacts of alcohol (e.g., accidents, sexual-related problems and violence, and substance dependence).

Is There Common Ground?

Children learn through observational learning and modeling. A girl swings a baseball bat without being taught how to do it after watching a baseball game on television. A boy shows that he has learned the basic steps of cooking by doing so at a play kitchen. A college student styles her hair from fashions seen on social media. Advertisements with models who are attractive, have high status and are somewhat similar to ourselves can change attitudes and behavior. Will a bourbon television commercial with Leonardo DiCaprio, a vodka magazine layout with Sean Combs, or a flavored liqueur web advertisement with Kim Kardashian increase the chance that a young person will use alcohol?

Both the YES and the NO sections for this issue indicate there are many factors that can contribute to whether or not a young person will use alcohol—genetics, relationship with parent, and modeling. Obviously, no one factor is solely responsible. Could regulating or eliminating alcohol advertising change attitudes about drinking in adolescents and could it change problematic drinking behaviors in college students?

In the United States advertising is generally protected by the First Amendment to the Constitution; however, there are limitations. Advertisements often do not have the same protections against government intervention that newspaper editorials cherish. For example, the Federal Trade Commission (FTC) may remove advertisements from

television that are misleading and deceptive. Regarding alcohol products, the FTC makes recommendations, but defers enforcement to industry groups, such as the Distilled Spirits Council. Critics comment that trade groups do not do enough and have conflicting interests (i.e., selling more products to as large an audience as possible). If alcohol advertising increases alcohol use in young people, should we ask for and/or accept greater regulation and control by the government? What is the balance between free speech and public health?

Additional Resources

Bandura, A. & Huston A.C. (1961) Identification as a process of incidental learning. *Journal of Abnormal and Social Psychology* 63(2): 311–318. In the 1960s Albert Bandura conducted series of experiments, such as this one to investigate if social behaviors (e.g., aggression) can be acquired by observation and imitation.

Dillon, P. (2011). *Teenagers, Alcohol and Drugs: What Your Kids Really Want and Need to Know about Alcohol and Drugs*. Allen & Unwin. Paul Dillon provides advice to parents on how to talk with their children about alcohol and drug use.

Morgenstern, M. et al. (2014). Favourite alcohol advertisements and binge drinking among adolescents: a cross-cultural cohort study. *Addiction* 109(12): 2005–2015. Using a population of European adolescents, the researchers observed a relationship between alcohol marketing receptivity and adolescent binge drinking.

Pennock, P.E. (2009) *Advertising Sin and Sickness: The Politics of Alcohol and Tobacco Marketing.* Northern Illinois University Press. Pamela E. Pennock describes the history of debates on alcohol and tobacco advertising. What is the role of government and temperance movements in regulating commercial speech?

Internet References . . .

Centers for Disease Control – Alcohol and Public Health

https://www.cdc.gov/alcohol/

Distilled Spirits Council Code of Responsible Practices

http://www.discus.org/responsibility/code/

Federal Trade Commission – Standards for Alcohol Advertising

https://www.consumer.ftc.gov/articles/0391-alcohol-advertising

Motion Picture Association of America

http://www.mpaa.org/

National Institute on Alcohol Abuse and Alcoholism (NIAAA)

https://www.niaaa.nih.gov/

NIAAA—College Drinking: Changing the Culture

https://www.collegedrinkingprevention.gov/

Selected, Edited, and with Issue Framing Material by:
Dennis K. Miller, *University of Missouri*

ISSUE

Does Drug Abuse Treatment Work?

YES: **National Institute on Drug Abuse**, from *Principles of Drug Addiction Treatment: A Research-based Guide* (National Institute on Drug Abuse, 2009)

NO: **Sacha Z. Scoblic**, from "The Dogma of AA Has Taken Over," *The New Republic* (2013)

Learning Outcomes

After reading this issue, you will be able to:

- Identify and describe the different approaches used by clinicians to treat drug addiction.
- Identify the different factors and variables that contribute to the success and failure of a treatment program and how they are assessed.
- Consider the different metrics used to determine whether a treatment program is successful from a political perspective and from the perspective of the person with addiction.

ISSUE SUMMARY

YES: The National Institute on Drug Abuse report acknowledges that drug addiction is difficult to overcome but that treatment can be effective and works best when individuals are committed to remain in treatment for an extended time.

NO: Sacha Z. Scoblic, a Carter fellow for mental health journalism, argues that anti-addiction programs, such as Alcoholics Anonymous, can be ineffective and are misused. Popular programs might not adhere to the vast body of research on addiction treatment.

Drug addiction is a complex disease that has many causes and dimensions. Men and women, younger and older people, members of every ethnic, religious, racial, and socioeconomic group, and residents from all communities experience addiction. Many individuals with addiction also suffer from other psychological or medical conditions that contribute to the development or maintenance of drug use, or make it difficult to stop using drugs.

The United States has generally accepted that drug addiction should be considered under a moral or criminal justice model. This perspective assumes that those with addiction have a problem with drugs and are deficient in their character, morals, and self-control. As such, drug use and compulsive use are behaviors should be punished by incarceration or civil penalties. However, research has demonstrated that addiction treatment is far less expensive

and far more productive than incarceration. The annual financial costs of some effective drug addiction programs (e.g., methadone for narcotic addiction) can be one-sixth the costs of keeping someone in prison. Treatment programs can decrease the lost costs (e.g., drug crimes, theft, and criminal justice expenses) incurred when addiction is managed by incarceration. Also, treatment can improve the quality of life of individuals with addiction by decreasing social conflicts, improving job prospects, and reducing incidents of other criminal behaviors.

There are a variety of treatment programs that can be used. For some, the final goal is total abstinence, while others focus on achieving controlled use. Total abstinence is the goal of Alcoholics Anonymous (AA). A basic principle of AA is that someone with alcoholism is different from someone without alcoholism in their control of drinking behavior. The difference between these two groups of people, possibly based in biology or genetics, is what is responsible for the individual with alcoholism to drink. Therefore, the person with alcoholism should not drink and is not to blame for their drinking behavior. Guilt for alcoholism should not be experienced. It is important to note that AA does not remove responsibility from someone with alcoholism. The individual is responsible to managing the disease of alcoholism day-by-day.

The AA program uses a group support and "buddy" system: AA members help each other with their alcoholism and encourage sobriety. For many members, AA is not a short-term treatment, but a long-term commitment to the program and its goal of total abstinence. Some AA meetings are open to anyone who has an interest, while closed meetings are for people with alcoholism who have a desire to completely stop drinking. A member of AA works to follow the twelve steps of the program that should be followed successively through the recovery process. These steps include admitting an addiction to alcohol, recognizing that the individual has no power over alcohol, a belief in a power that can help someone overcome shortcomings, ongoing personal assessments, admission of wrong doing, and making amends to those that have been hurt by the individual. Other drug treatment programs (e.g., Narcotics Anonymous) are modeled off of the AA approach to treatment.

While open and closed AA meetings can be found in almost every community in the United States and worldwide, the overall success of the twelve-step approach is unclear. AA has not been subjected to the scientific evaluation performed for other treatments. There is no doubt that AA has been successful for many people, but it is not possible to assert that its twelve-step approach is the "best" or "most successful."

AA is considered a behavioral or psychosocial addiction treatment because it helps the person with addiction engage in the treatment process, modify their attitudes and behaviors related to drug abuse, and increase healthy life skills. It is also an outpatient treatment because the individual visits the meeting or clinic on a regular basis, while living at home and taking care of normal responsibilities (e.g., family and work). Other outpatient behavioral treatments include cognitive-behavioral therapy, where the individual learns to recognize, avoid, and manage against the situations and emotions that contribute to drug use. Multidimensional family therapy focuses on the interaction between home life and drug use and its goal is to address the impact of family function

on addiction. Contingency management programs seek to use positive reinforcement to decrease or eliminate drug use.

Medications are also used in combination with behavior/psychosocial treatments or independently to treat addiction. Some medications are used for detoxification, the initial stage of treating addiction where the unpleasant physiological and psychological withdrawal symptoms accompanying sudden cessation of drug use are minimized. An example would be a nicotine gum that is used to treat the unpleasant withdrawal from long-term tobacco use. Medications that are used for detoxification can also be used for maintenance, the long-term prevention of relapse to using the abused drugs. Some maintenance drugs are used under substitution for the abused drug. An example is methadone for narcotic addiction. For some, methadone has been successful at preventing relapse and craving for heroin over a period of months or years. In contrast, antagonist drug therapies focus on blocking the pleasurable or reinforcing effects of the abused drug. For example, the narcotic antagonist naltrexone can minimize or prevent the reinforcing experiences of heroin use in someone with narcotic addiction. Finally, punishment drug therapies produce an unpleasant psychological or physiological state when someone uses the abused drug. Disulfiram (Antabuse) induces headache and nausea when someone drinks alcohol, but not when they are abstinent.

There are a variety of treatments available to help someone with drug abuse or dependence. As discussed, treatment programs are more cost effective and have greater long-term success than incarceration to manage addiction. Many drug experts believe that more funding should go toward treatment than toward the criminal justice system. However, how effective are drug treatment programs? Is greater success than incarceration really success? Furthermore, which drug treatment programs are actually successful? In the YES selection, the National Institute on Drug Abuse report maintains that treatment can be effective. However, it is necessary for the individual to be committed and to remain in treatment for an extensive time. Drug treatment results in lesser drug use and lower health and social costs. In the NO selection, Sacha Z. Scoblic argues that anti-addiction programs, such as AA, are not as effective as promised and are misused. Furthermore, drug treatment programs might be developed based on the scientific research and evidence, but they might not adhere to the research and evidence in practice, making them ineffective.

YES ↵

National Institute on Drug Abuse

Principles of Drug Addiction Treatment: A Research-Based Guide

1. Why Do Drug-Addicted Persons Keep Using Drugs?

Nearly all addicted individuals believe at the outset that they can stop using drugs on their own, and most try to stop without treatment. Although some people are successful, many attempts result in failure to achieve long-term abstinence. Research has shown that long-term drug abuse results in changes in the brain that persist long after a person stops using drugs. These drug-induced changes in brain function can have many behavioral consequences, including an inability to exert control over the impulse to use drugs despite adverse consequences—the defining characteristic of addiction.

Long-term drug use results in significant changes in brain function that can persist long after the individual stops using drugs.

Understanding that addiction has such a fundamental biological component may help explain the difficulty of achieving and maintaining abstinence without treatment. Psychological stress from work, family problems, psychiatric illness, pain associated with medical problems, social cues (such as meeting individuals from one's drug-using past), or environmental cues (such as encountering streets, objects, or even smells associated with drug abuse) can trigger intense cravings without the individual even being consciously aware of the triggering event. Any one of these factors can hinder attainment of sustained abstinence and make relapse more likely. Nevertheless, research indicates that active participation in treatment is an essential component for good outcomes and can benefit even the most severely addicted individuals.

2. What Is Drug Addiction Treatment?

Drug treatment is intended to help addicted individuals stop compulsive drug seeking and use. Treatment can occur in a variety of settings, in many different forms, and for different lengths of time. Because drug addiction is typically a chronic disorder characterized by occasional relapses, a short-term, one-time treatment is usually not sufficient. For many, treatment is a long-term process that involves multiple interventions and regular monitoring.

There are a variety of evidence-based approaches to treating addiction. Drug treatment can include behavioral therapy (such as individual or group counseling, cognitive therapy, or contingency management), medications, or their combination. The specific type of treatment or combination of treatments will vary depending on the patient's individual needs and, often, on the types of drugs they use. The severity of addiction and previous efforts to stop using drugs can also influence a treatment approach. Finally, people who are addicted to drugs often suffer from other health (including other mental health), occupational, legal, familial, and social problems that should be addressed concurrently.

The best programs provide a combination of therapies and other services to meet an individual patient's needs. Specific needs may relate to age, race, culture, sexual orientation, gender, pregnancy, other drug use, comorbid conditions (e.g., depression, HIV), parenting, housing, and employment, as well as physical and sexual abuse history.

Drug addiction treatment can include medications, behavioral therapies, or their combination.

Treatment medications, such as methadone, buprenorphine, and naltrexone, are available for individuals addicted to opioids, while nicotine preparations (patches, gum, lozenges, and nasal spray) and the medications varenicline and bupropion are available for individuals addicted to tobacco. Disulfiram, acamprosate, naltrexone, and topiramate are medications used for treating alcohol dependence, which commonly co-occurs with other drug addictions. In fact, most people with severe addiction are polydrug users and require treatment for all substances abused. Even combined alcohol and tobacco use has proven amenable to concurrent treatment for both substances.

From *Principles of Drug Addiction Treatment: A Research-Based Guide*, April 2009, National Institute on Drug Abuse.

Psychoactive medications, such as antidepressants, antianxiety agents, mood stabilizers, and antipsychotic medications, may be critical for treatment success when patients have co-occurring mental disorders, such as depression, anxiety disorders (including post-traumatic stress disorder), bipolar disorder, or schizophrenia.

Behavioral therapies can help motivate people to participate in drug treatment; offer strategies for coping with drug cravings; teach ways to avoid drugs and prevent relapse; and help individuals deal with relapse if it occurs. Behavioral therapies can also help people improve communication, relationship, and parenting skills, as well as family dynamics.

Many treatment programs employ both individual and group therapies. Group therapy can provide social reinforcement and help enforce behavioral contingencies that promote abstinence and a non-drug-using lifestyle. Some of the more established behavioral treatments, such as contingency management and cognitive-behavioral therapy, are also being adapted for group settings to improve efficiency and cost-effectiveness. However, particularly in adolescents, there can also be a danger of iatrogenic, or inadvertent, effects of group treatment; thus, trained counselors should be aware and monitor for such effects.

Because they work on different aspects of addiction, combinations of behavioral therapies and medications (when available) generally appear to be more effective than either approach used alone.

Treatment for drug abuse and addiction is delivered in many different settings using a variety of behavioral and pharmacological approaches.

3. How Effective Is Drug Addiction Treatment?

In addition to stopping drug abuse, the goal of treatment is to return people to productive functioning in the family, workplace, and community. According to research that tracks individuals in treatment over extended periods, most people who get into and remain in treatment stop using drugs, decrease their criminal activity, and improve their occupational, social, and psychological functioning. For example, methadone treatment has been shown to increase participation in behavioral therapy and decrease both drug use and criminal behavior. However, individual treatment outcomes depend on the extent and nature of the patient's problems, the appropriateness of treatment and related services used to address those problems, and the quality of interaction between the patient and his or her treatment providers.

Relapse rates for addiction resemble those of other chronic diseases such as diabetes, hypertension, and asthma.

Like other chronic diseases, addiction can be managed successfully. Treatment enables people to counteract addiction's powerful disruptive effects on the brain and behavior and to regain control of their lives. The chronic nature of the disease means that relapsing to drug abuse is not only possible but also likely, with relapse rates similar to those for other well-characterized chronic medical illnesses—such as diabetes, hypertension, and asthma (see figure, "Comparison of Relapse Rates Between Drug Addiction and Other Chronic Illnesses")—that also have both physiological and behavioral components.

Unfortunately, when relapse occurs many deem treatment a failure. This is not the case: successful treatment for addiction typically requires continual evaluation and modification as appropriate, similar to the approach taken for other chronic diseases. For example, when a patient is receiving active treatment for hypertension and symptoms decrease, treatment is deemed successful, even though symptoms may recur when treatment is discontinued. For the addicted patient, lapses to drug abuse do not indicate failure—rather, they signify that treatment needs to be reinstated or adjusted, or that alternate treatment is needed.

4. Is Drug Addiction Treatment Worth Its Cost?

Substance abuse costs our Nation over one half-trillion dollars annually, and treatment can help reduce these costs. Drug addiction treatment has been shown to reduce associated health and social costs by far more than the cost of the treatment itself. Treatment is also much less expensive than its alternatives, such as incarcerating addicted persons. For example, the average cost for 1 full year of methadone maintenance treatment is approximately $4,700 per patient, whereas 1 full year of imprisonment costs approximately $24,000 per person.

Drug addiction treatment reduces drug use and its associated health and social costs.

According to several conservative estimates, every $1 invested in addiction treatment programs yields a return of between $4 and $7 in reduced drug-related crime, criminal justice costs, and theft. When savings related to health care

Figure

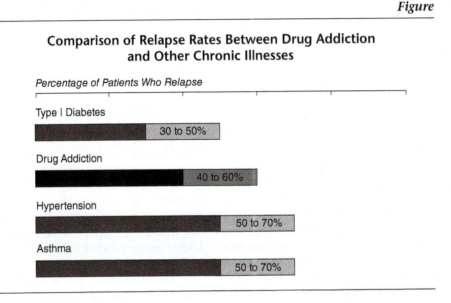

Comparison of Relapse Rates Between Drug Addiction
and Other Chronic Illnesses

Percentage of Patients Who Relapse

Type I Diabetes
30 to 50%

Drug Addiction
40 to 60%

Hypertension
50 to 70%

Asthma
50 to 70%

are included, total savings can exceed costs by a ratio of 12 to 1. Major savings to the individual and to society also stem from fewer interpersonal conflicts; greater workplace productivity; and fewer drug-related accidents, including overdoses and deaths.

5. How Long Does Drug Addiction Treatment Usually Last?

Individuals progress through drug addiction treatment at various rates, so there is no predetermined length of treatment. However, research has shown unequivocally that good outcomes are contingent on adequate treatment length. Generally, for residential or outpatient treatment, participation for less than 90 days is of limited effectiveness, and treatment lasting significantly longer is recommended for maintaining positive outcomes. For methadone maintenance, 12 months is considered the minimum, and some opioid-addicted individuals continue to benefit from methadone maintenance for many years.

Good outcomes are contingent on adequate treatment length.

Treatment dropout is one of the major problems encountered by treatment programs; therefore, motivational techniques that can keep patients engaged will also improve outcomes. By viewing addiction as a chronic disease and offering continuing care and monitoring,

programs can succeed, but this will often require multiple episodes of treatment and readily re-admitting patients that have relapsed.

6. What Helps People Stay in Treatment?

Because successful outcomes often depend on a person's staying in treatment long enough to reap its full benefits, strategies for keeping people in treatment are critical. Whether a patient stays in treatment depends on factors associated with both the individual and the program. Individual factors related to engagement and retention typically include motivation to change drug-using behavior; degree of support from family and friends; and, frequently, pressure from the criminal justice system, child protection services, employers, or the family. Within a treatment program, successful clinicians can establish a positive, therapeutic relationship with their patients. The clinician should ensure that a treatment plan is developed cooperatively with the person seeking treatment, that the plan is followed, and that treatment epectations are clearly understood. Medical, psychiatric, and social services should also be available.

Whether a patient stays in treatment depends on factors associated with both the individual and the program.

Because some problems (such as serious medical or mental illness or criminal involvement) increase the likelihood of patients dropping out of treatment, intensive interventions may be required to retain them. After a course of intensive treatment, the provider should ensure a transition to less intensive continuing care to support and monitor individuals in their ongoing recovery. . . .

Reducing this gap requires a multipronged approach. Strategies include increasing access to effective treatment, achieving insurance parity (now in its earliest phase of implementation), reducing stigma, and raising awareness among both patients and health care professionals of the value of addiction treatment. To assist physicians in identifying treatment need in their patients and making appropriate referrals, NIDA is encouraging widespread use of screening, brief intervention, and referral to treatment (SBIRT) tools for use in primary care settings. SBIRT—which has proven effective against tobacco and alcohol use—has the potential not only to catch people before serious drug problems develop but also to connect them with appropriate treatment providers.

7. How Can Families and Friends Make a Difference in the Life of Someone Needing Treatment?

Family and friends can play critical roles in motivating individuals with drug problems to enter and stay in treatment. Family therapy can also be important, especially for adolescents. Involvement of a family member or significant other in an individual's treatment program can strengthen and extend treatment benefits. . . .

The **NATIONAL INSTITUTE OF DRUG ABUSE** (NIDA) is charged with bringing the power of science to bear on drug abuse and addiction. In its publication "Drugs, Brains, and Behavior: The Science of Addiction," NIDA provides an overview—based on the scientific literature—of the drug addiction problem.

Sacha Z. Scoblic    **NO**

The Dogma of AA Has Taken Over

My favorite two sentences in the Alcoholics Anonymous literature are: "Alcoholics Anonymous does not demand that you believe anything. All of its twelve steps are but suggestions." When a drunk at the end of his tether, Bill Wilson, founded Alcoholics Anonymous in the late 1930s—a spiritual program based on meeting with other addicts—there was a fundamental humility to his ideology: It might work for some.

But that sentiment is often forgotten in the rooms of AA itself, where I spent a lot of time getting sober. There I found that what are suggestions to some are fundamentalist Scripture to others. In the rooms of AA, suggestions and traditions can sometimes feel more like ironclad laws, and when I inadvertently trespassed upon those laws, I was humiliated and rebuked. The predominantly AA-based culture of rehab in America has become one of imposition and tautology: If the program doesn't work for you, then you didn't work the program. If you succeed in staying sober, then you did a good job working the program; ergo, the program works.

In Anne M. Fletcher's excellent and exhaustive book (*Inside Rehab: The Surprising Truth About Addiction Treatment and How to Get Help That Works*, Viking), she finds that almost all rehabs adhere to this intransigent dogma. Some just have better views, higher thread counts, and more horses (you know, for equine therapy). There is no individualized treatment. You check in, detox, and then go to addiction-education lectures, group therapy, and AA twelve-step meetings. "I often found myself wondering, 'Where's the counseling?'" writes Fletcher. Patients attend these group gatherings for 28 to 90 days, and are then released back into the real world. Problem is, the real world is teeming with temptations, and most people relapse. So what do we do with them? More rehab! Because it isn't the rehab that has failed; it is you. Fletcher's multi-year-long dive into the realities of rehabs is deeply unsettling. "Once you've seen any substance abuse program, you have seen the great majority of them," Tom McClellan, co-founder of the Treatment Research Institute, tells Fletcher.

How did this come about? Addiction was stigmatized so fervently and for so long that for decades there was no body of science to advise desperate addicts. In that vacuum, McClellan says, the field "grew its own program." The twelve steps of AA became the template treatment for just about every compulsive behavior there is, from Narcotics Anonymous to Debtors Anonymous. Meanwhile, as AA grew, a movement was brewing in Minnesota: rehabilitation. In the 1950s, a recovering alcoholic, Austin Ripley, began a sanitarium for alcoholics based on AA principles out on a farm in Minnesota. (It became Hazelden, perhaps today's most well-known rehab.) Soon enough, this Minnesota model attracted more people from AA, and the prototype for modern-day rehab was born, guided by, as Fletcher writes, "the folk wisdom of recovering people, particularly through the perspectives of Alcoholics Anonymous and related twelve-step programs."

To be sure, that folk wisdom has benefitted millions, including myself. Striving for honesty, communing with people who don't judge, admitting when you're wrong, working on the content of your character, learning humility, being of service to others—these are deeply valuable principles, ones this alcoholic needed to find after years of boozy nonchalance. In fact, the steps could be beneficial to anyone.

But moral principles are not medical treatment. And using AA as the only rehabilitation treatment—rather than as an adjunct to treatment—defies the reality that there are many different effective treatment methods. Fletcher underscores this point with profiles of dozens of recovered addicts who quit in varied ways—through church, paid incentives for clean drug tests, psychiatry, cognitive behavioral therapy, medication, and even people who simply "matured out."

She also profiles dozens of addicts whose rehab experiences are unconscionable. Take Jessie, an alcoholic woman who was court-ordered to attend rehab or go to jail, after a drunk-driving conviction. Three days before finishing the rehab program, the police came for her. The rehab had kicked Jessie out, claiming she'd "failed to accept a higher power" (step two). Freedom of religion was apparently not a valid excuse. Other patients faced intense confrontations ("I heard clients characterized as dishonest, narcissistic, and selfish," writes Fletcher); were made to wear punitive signs around their necks if they broke the rules; or were forced to divulge painful secrets in a group setting. One woman who was deeply uncomfortable around men was pressured into discussing past sexual abuse in a co-ed program.

For some, sharing with a group might be valuable and—more important—validating, but for many, group therapy and meetings can be injurious and completely inappropriate. Regardless of the benefits or drawbacks, most experts agree that all addicts should have highly personalized attention from a therapist. After all, the sources of addiction are myriad: past trauma, self-medication, masking another mental illness, genetics, etc. The point is, each addict has very specific needs.

But, as Fletcher masterfully shows, rehab culture has created a deep schism between science and its twelve-step methods.[1] There is now a vast body of research on addiction treatment, including groundbreaking medications that can quell urges, safely fulfill an addict's need for dopamine, and often prevent relapse. And yet, Fletcher finds that some 80 percent of rehabs in the United States dispense no medication at all. In fact, many rehabs consider the use of opiate-replacement drugs and other medications—like naltrexone, Suboxone, and buprenorphine—as equivalent to drinking or using heroin, despite the overwhelming scientific evidence of their positive effects. In other words, you're not truly sober if you're "on" something. To that end, many rehabs kick addicts out for secretly using—that is, for being addicts.

By the end of Chapter 5, which is called "Rehab Isn't for Everyone: In Fact, It's Not for Most People," Fletcher begins to wonder if rehab is right for anyone. Mark Willenbring, a psychiatrist and the former head of the Division of Treatment and Recovery Research at the National Institute on Alcohol Abuse and Alcoholism, gives her a stark answer: "The idea of changing the life course for people with severe, recurrent forms of addiction through a time-limited intensive transformative rehab is a fatally flawed relic of ancient times. What other chronic disorder do we treat that way?"

Despite the evidence she amasses for the limitations of rehab, Fletcher does not condemn rehab and walk away, and this balanced approach is to her credit. A large portion of the book, in fact, reads like a Princeton Review Guide for Choosing Rehab: Fletcher highlights unique integrative facilities, offers nontraditional solutions, and lauds excellent traditional programs. She tells you specifically what to look for in a rehab and what to ask—like, what are you getting for the money, and do any of the staff at least have a bachelor's degree?[2]

Ultimately, Fletcher's book is less about the dismissal of rehab than the dismantling of the idea that there is one way to treat addiction. Rehab isn't wrong—it's just one way. She envisions a menu of options. Might heroin addicts need something different than alcoholics? Might women need something different than men? Might teens require special treatment? Fletcher addresses each of these issues and more—but the answer is always the same: Everyone needs truly individualized treatment.

This is an important argument to make. Ask someone in Alcoholics Anonymous if there are treatment options for addiction other than the twelve steps, and you're likely to hear: "Sure, you can end up in jail, be institutionalized, or die." But the science, Fletcher shows, tells a different story: The vast majority of people who get and remain sober, Fletcher shows, do so without AA. It's not that the traditional model is bad or wrong; it just isn't the only way. . . .

Notes

1 People with alcohol addiction get treatment consistent with scientific knowledge only about 10 percent of the time, according to Fletcher.

2 Some states don't require any degree for becoming a credentialed addiction counselor. Many require just a high school diploma, GED, or associate's degree, Fletcher reports.

Sacha Z. Scoblic is an author and contributing editor at *The New Republic*. She is the author of the book *Unwasted: My Lush Sobriety*, a memoir of her experiences with alcoholism. Ms. Scoblic was a contributor to *The New York Times*'s online series "Proof: Alcohol and American Life" and currently blogs about addiction at *TheFasterTimes.com*.

EXPLORING THE ISSUE

Does Drug Abuse Treatment Work?

Critical Thinking and Reflection

1. What should an individual and society expect from a drug treatment program that it considers successful? When should a treatment program be considered a failure?
2. What are the most important components of a successful drug addiction treatment program?
3. Is it feasible or realistic to expect total abstinence from an addiction treatment program?
4. What factors contribute to drug relapse and how can they be minimized in a treatment program?
5. How does the popular media (e.g., reports about famous people with addiction who experience relapse) influence society's views on addiction treatment?

Is There Common Ground?

Research on the efficacy of drug addiction treatment is inconclusive. Researchers and clinicians have not reached consensus on the best ways to measure if a treatment program is effective. It is controversial whether total abstinence or controlled use should be a program's goal. Determining the efficacy of a drug addiction treatment program is critical because the federal government and state and local governments debate how much should be allocated for drug treatment and what types of program should be funded. Experts in the addiction field argue that much of the money has not been wisely spent. It is essential to determine what makes an effective drug addiction treatment.

The National Institute of Drug Abuse (NIDA) in its guide "Drug Facts: Treatment Approaches for Drug Addiction" (available at http://www.drugabuse .gov/publications/drugfacts/treatment-approaches -drug-addiction) identified key principles that should be the basis for any effective program—behavioral/psychosocial or medicinal—for addiction.

- Addiction is a complex but treatable disease that affects brain function and behavior.
- No single treatment is appropriate for everyone.
- Treatment needs to be readily available.
- Effective treatment attends to multiple needs of the individual, not just his or her drug abuse.
- Remaining in treatment for an adequate period of time is critical.
- Counseling—individual and/or group—and other behavioral therapies are the most commonly used forms of drug abuse treatment.
- Medications are an important element of treatment for many patients, especially when combined with counseling and other behavioral therapies.

- An individual's treatment and services plan must be assessed continually and modified as necessary to ensure that it meets his or her changing needs.
- Many drug-addicted individuals also have other mental disorders.
- Medically assisted detoxification is only the first stage of addiction treatment and by itself does little to change long-term drug abuse.
- Treatment does not need to be voluntary to be effective.
- Drug use during treatment must be monitored continuously, as lapses during treatment do occur.
- Treatment programs should assess patients for the presence of HIV/AIDS, hepatitis B and C, tuberculosis, and other infectious diseases as well as provide targeted risk-reduction counseling to help patients modify or change behaviors that place them at risk of contracting or spreading infectious diseases.

Additional Resources

Daley, D. C. & Marlatt, G. A. (2006). *Overcoming Your Alcohol or Drug Problem: Effective Recovery Strategies Workbook*. New York: Oxford University Press.

This workbook provides the reader with practical information and skills to help them understand and change a drug or alcohol problem.

Johnson, B. A. (2010). We're addicted to rehab. It doesn't even work. *The Washington Post*. http:// www.washingtonpost.com/wp-dyn/content/ article/2010/08/06/AR2010080602660.html.

According to this article, "The therapies offered in most U.S. alcohol treatment centers are so divorced from state-of-the-art of medical knowledge that we might dismiss them as merely quaint—if it weren't for the fact that alcoholism is a deadly and devastating disease."

Scoblic, S. Z. (2011). *Unwasted: My Lush Sobriety*. New York: Citadel Press.

The author of the NO selection for this issue describes her life while drinking and while sober.

Smith, B. & Wilson, B. (2006). *The Big Book of Alcoholics Anonymous*. Seattle WA: CreateSpace Independent Publishing Platform.

This is the classic text written by the original founders of Alcoholics Anonymous. It is the originator of the seminal "twelve-step method" widely used to attempt to treat many addictions.

Smith, F. M. & Marshall, L. A. (2007). Barriers to effective drug addiction treatment for women involved in street-level prostitution: A qualitative investigation. *Criminal Behaviour and Mental Health*. 17:163–170.

Drug addiction treatments must be targeted to individual needs (e.g., gender, ethnicity, and socioeconomic status). This review article discusses the barriers for treatment for women who are prostitutes—an impoverished sense of self-worth, a lack of trust and consistency in treatment, and the absence of a comprehensive treatment package.

Internet References . . .

Alcoholics Anonymous

http://www.aa.org/

HBO: Addiction

http://www.hbo.com/addiction/

National Institutes of Health—National Institute on Alcohol Abuse and Alcoholism

http://www.niaaa.nih.gov/

National Institutes of Health—National Institute on Drug Abuse

http://www.drugabuse.gov/

Women for Sobriety

http://www.womenforsobriety.org/